PRAISE FOR

Lone V

"A standout in the true crime genre, Ms. Vollers's book is astute. . . . A cool, gripping investigation of the bomber's mind."

—*New York Times*

"Maryanne Vollers turns out another topnotch investigative work, tackling the enigma of Eric Rudolph. . . . Through incisive interviews . . . she zeroes in on the nature and nurture of homegrown terrorism."

—*Elle*

"The gripping story of one of America's most notorious domestic terrorists. . . . A disturbing and finely drawn portrait of a lone wolf, an unrepentant criminal who acted alone."

—*Los Angeles Times*

"A page-turning account. . . . Vollers captures the astonishing tale from all sides, including Rudolph himself."

—*Seattle Post-Intelligencer*

"Vollers's pacing and narrative instincts are masterful. Armed with a sea of reporting, she rises above the waterline with brief looks into law enforcement politics, right-wing ideological movements, and the science of bombs, then she dives back in to keep things moving. Her tone, dispassionate yet understanding, is exactly right."

—*San Francisco Chronicle*

"Captivating. . . . An engaging narrative, filled with vivid reportorial detail."

—*Chicago Tribune*

"The portrait that emerges . . . is humanizing, almost sympathetic. Vollers's account . . . opens up the many dimensions of the tale without disrupting its cinematic momentum." —*New York Times Book Review*

"There are plenty of surprises and conundrums in this breathtaking and deeply disturbing attempt to answer the question: Who is Eric Rudolph?"   —*Publishers Weekly* (starred review)

"A meticulous, compelling account."   —*People*

"Vollers is a smart, thorough reporter who . . . relies on facts rather than psychological profiling. . . . *Lone Wolf* is a fascinating narrative."
—*Portland Oregonian*

"The most fluid account of the fugitive's crime, flight, and capture. . . . Vollers baits you to the brink of liking Eric while not letting you forget completely about Rudolph."   —*Birmingham Weekly*

"A disturbing portrait of a lone and unrepentant criminal."
—*Baltimore Sun*

"Vollers fills in a lot of blank space about Rudolph, who he was as well as how and why he did what he did."   —*Denver Post*

"An insightful portrait of the homegrown terrorist."
—*Bloomberg.com*

© William Campbell

About the Author

MARYANNE VOLLERS's first book, *Ghosts of Mississippi*, was a finalist for the National Book Award. She coauthored (with Jerri Nielsen) the number one *New York Times* bestseller *Ice Bound* and collaborated with Senator Hillary Rodham Clinton on her memoir, *Living History*. A former editor at *Rolling Stone*, she has written for *Time*, *Esquire*, *GQ*, and the *New York Times Magazine*. The daughter of a New York City fire chief, Vollers lives in Montana with her husband.

LONE WOLF

OTHER BOOKS BY MARYANNE VOLLERS

Ghosts of Mississippi: The Murder of Medgar Evers, the Trials of Byron De La Beckwith, and the Haunting of the New South

Ice Bound: A Doctor's Incredible Battle for Survival at the South Pole (with Dr. Jerri Nielsen)

LONE WOLF

Eric Rudolph and the Legacy of
American Terror

MARYANNE VOLLERS

HARPER ⬤ PERENNIAL

NEW·YORK ● LONDON ● TORONTO ● SYDNEY

HARPER ● PERENNIAL

Grateful acknowledgment is made to Dorothy Smith for permission to reprint from "Run, Rudolph, Run!"

A hardcover edition of this book was published in 2006 by HarperCollins Publishers.

HarperCollins books may be purchased for educational, business, or sales promotional use. For information please write: Special Markets Department, HarperCollins Publishers, 10 East 53rd Street, New York, NY 10022.

FIRST HARPER PERENNIAL EDITION PUBLISHED 2007.

Designed by Renata Di Biase

Library of Congress Cataloging-in-Publication Data is available upon request.

ISBN: 978-0-06-059862-4
ISBN-10: 0-06-059862-X

ISBN: 978-0-06-059863-1 (pbk.)
ISBN-10: 0-06-059863-8 (pbk.)

07 08 09 10 11   ID/RRD   10 9 8 7 6 5 4 3 2 1

For Bill Campbell, and for all my family:
You keep my feet on the ground.

Liberty for the wolves means death to the lambs.

—ISAIAH BERLIN

Just who ends up being the good guy or the bad guy
depends on who gets to write the story.

—ERIC RUDOLPH

CONTENTS

TENNESSEE
MONROE COUNTY

GRAHAM COUNTY
Robbinsville

Snowbird Mountains   Topton   **6**

11   **9**   MACON COUNTY

Andrews   19 74   **1**

7 **8**

Marble

Valley River   **5**

• Unaka   Nantahala Lake

CHEROKEE COUNTY

19 74

10   **2**   Tusquitee Mountains

Murphy   CLAY COUNTY

4   Hayesville

64

Brasstown   N O R T H   C A R O L I N A

3

129

GEORGIA

1. Appletree campground (Task Force command center)
2. Fires Creek (Rudolph's winter camp)
3. Martins Creek (Rudolph's truck found)
4. Caney Creek Road, Murphy (Rudolph's trailer)
5. Bob Allison campground (Nordmann's truck found)
6. Partridge Creek Road, Topton (Rudolph's family home)
7. Andrews Murphy Airfield
8. Grain silos (Airport Road)
9. Long Branch Road, Topton (George Nordmann's house)
10. Rudolph's summer camp
11. Rudolph's dynamite caches discovered

0   5 miles

Appalachian Trail

LONE WOLF

LONE WOLF

In the end, the moon was just another enemy. It hadn't always been that way. When he started writing about his fugitive years the word he chose was "addicting": "There is something addicting about the full moon on an early summer or fall evening in the South …" Now the moonlight pinned him to the shadows, kept him off the roads and dirt tracks where the breeze would disperse his scent before the hounds could follow it. The damp grass and foliage would hold his trail for days. The years of hiding, he later said, had turned him into a nocturnal creature, sleeping in the day, prowling for food at night, always watchful.

Eric Rudolph kept his campsite orderly: hiking boots lined up like soldiers on the cardboard pallet beneath a double tarp; scavenged newspapers and magazines stacked up neatly beside them. A small ring of stones for a cooking fire, with two blackened pots upturned to drain. He had scattered overripe bananas, tomatoes, and onions to dry in the sun. He could store them, use them later when food was scarce. His life was consumed with planning: figuring out the movement of police patrols through town, knowing which days the grocery stores dumped their expired bread and vegetables. He traced a grid on notebook paper to make into a calendar and neatly crossed off each day as it passed. When the federal agents found the calendar at his camp, the last marked date was May 30, 2003.

It was a weekend night, not much of a moon, and Rudolph figured that the lone patrolman would be distracted by teenage drunks out looking for trouble. He pulled on his "rummaging" clothes: a black cotton T-shirt, dark slacks, old black tennis shoes. In the darkness his feet remembered the steep trail down the small mountain overlooking town. When he reached the bottom he watched for the glow of headlights approaching, and when it was safe he ran across the four-lane highway, following the bridge a short distance until it crossed the Valley River. One time a car had surprised him and he'd had to hang off the side of the bridge to keep from being seen. Tonight the trip went smoothly and he dropped down quietly into a field on the other side of the river. He followed another well-worn path through the grass and weeds to the alley behind a small shopping center. The patrol car usually passed this way every hour or so. He crouched in the darkness and waited.

It was late in the third shift on the first night of the long Memorial Day weekend, and Officer Jeff Postell was running through his routine business checks along Andrews Road in Murphy, North Carolina. At about 3:30 A.M., Postell cruised through the alley behind the Save-A-Lot grocery store and the Sears appliance retailer, past a cluster of old, one-story shops with their backs to the marshy bottomland of the Valley River. Then he turned his patrol car back into the deserted parking lot.

Postell was short and slight, a twenty-one-year-old rookie with less than a year on the Murphy police force. But as his colleagues had already noticed, Postell compensated for his size with hard work and enthusiasm. More seasoned police officers might slide through the bottom of the third shift, waiting for trouble to call itself in. Not Jeff Postell. He was flush with the optimism of inexperience, and he wanted to catch himself a burglar before he switched over to working days.

Murphy is the largest municipality in the mountainous western tip of North Carolina. The town has 2,500 people in a county with 25,000 scattered residents, a population that almost doubles in the summer months. Locals like to boast that the area is "two hours from anywhere": two hours' drive from Asheville to the east, Chattanooga to the west, Atlanta to the south. Due north is the Great Smoky Mountain National Park and the Appalachian heartland. Now that the textile factories and other light industries have packed up and moved to Mexico, Murphy's main industry is tourism. The visitors come for the clean air and wide mountain views, fishing and water sports. Four counties, Cherokee, Clay, Macon, and Swain, are set within the 500,000-acre Nantahala National Forest. If you don't count the transgressions of marijuana growers in the mountains or the crank syndicates that exploit the area as a regional distribution center, crime rates are pleasantly low. The most common police blotter items involve DUIs. Restaurants close early and the streets empty out after dark. People sleep soundly in the velvet warm nights of late spring, windows open to the breeze.

As soon as Postell was clear of the lot, he cut off his lights and swung the car around the corner and back into the alley, hoping to surprise any prowlers. It was then that he spotted the figure of a man crouched down and scurrying toward the supermarket loading dock. The rookie saw something long tucked under the subject's arm, like a rifle or a shotgun on a sling. The man heard him coming and darted behind a stack of milk crates. Postell turned on his "alley lights" while he radioed dispatch for backup. Then, using his open door for cover, he got out of the patrol car, drew his sidearm, and shouted, "Come out! Put your hands where I can see 'em!"

The man complied.

"Okay, drop to your knees. Now, down on the ground. Arms out. Cross your feet …"

The subject seemed so docile that Postell felt comfortable enough to approach and cuff him.

Cherokee County deputy Sean Matthews, known to all as Turtle, was walking out of Fatback's Citgo with a paper cup of coffee in his hand when he heard a commotion on his patrol car radio. As he climbed behind the wheel he could make out Jeff Postell's voice shouting, "Man with a gun!" It sounded pretty urgent. Jody Bandy, an officer with the Tennessee Valley Authority whose jurisdiction covered the federal lakes in the region, had stopped for coffee with Matthews and heard the call, too. He jumped into his own car, and both of them took off with their lights on and sirens blaring. By the time they arrived at the Save-A-Lot alley, a third backup had already arrived: Charles Kilby, an off-duty city policeman who had been finishing some paperwork at the station when the call came in.

As the four officers stood around the man lying facedown in the dirt, Postell started asking him the routine questions: What's your name? Where are you from and what are you doing here?

The man seemed calm and cooperative. Respectful. He said his name was Jerry Wilson, born December 19, 1964, but he had no identification on him. He was homeless, he said, just passing through from Ohio. He'd been living under a bridge, and he was hungry. He looked to be somewhere in his thirties, thin, average height, with short dark hair. He wore a dirty camouflage jacket, black tennis shoes, and dark pants tied at the ankles with string. A bulge underneath his jacket turned out to be a pair of binoculars. The object tucked under his arm was not a gun, but a long black Maglite slung on a piece of rope. Nearby they found an army rucksack, empty except for some plastic bags and string.

Postell called his dispatch to run an identity check, and the name and date of birth he gave came back "no match." That was odd. Most people had at least some sort of records in the system.

Jody Bandy asked "Mr. Wilson" if he had a social security number.

He'd lost his, he said, and added, "I don't believe in them."

Meanwhile Matthews was staring at the man on the ground. Matthews asked him to roll over, and the man turned his face away. Matthews asked him again, and this time he flipped himself over on his side. The deputy bent down and pointed his flashlight in the man's face. He had a few days' stubble on his cheeks, a noticeable scar on his chin, and searing blue eyes. Matthews's stomach started to churn. He was just about sure. And he might as well forget about the vacation he was planning to take, starting this morning.

He stood up and pulled his colleagues aside. "This looks like Eric Rudolph."

Postell shook his head, wondering at the possibility. Rudolph was one of the FBI's Ten Most Wanted. Postell had been in high school in 1998 when Rudolph's name first came up as a suspect in the fatal bombing of an abortion clinic in Birmingham, Alabama. He was also accused of a series of bombings in Georgia, including one at the 1996 Olympics in Atlanta where two people died. Postell had heard that Rudolph was some sort of survivalist with links to a racist militia group, and that he had been living alone in a trailer outside Murphy before he disappeared. When he was in high school, Postell used to work at the McDonald's in Andrews, serving morning coffee to the state and federal agents who arrived in droves to search the national forest for Rudolph. He'd even ridden around with some of them for a Boy Scout project. It was the biggest federal manhunt in history, but they never caught Rudolph. By now most people thought he was either dead or long gone. Postell thought this was a strange way for him to show up after five years. But Matthews had actually met Eric Rudolph years back. They'd both grown up in Macon County, just northwest of here. That put a certain weight behind his suspicions.

After some discussion about what to do with him, the officers agreed "Mr. Wilson" should be taken into custody under the safe-keeping statute, a state law designed to sweep vagrants and drunks off the streets for their own good. Then they could hold him for up to twenty-four hours. When Postell informed "Wilson" he was being taken to the county jail to be given a warm bed and a hot meal, the man showed no signs of alarm.

Matthews put the suspect in the back of Postell's cruiser and looked him in the eye. "You're not who you say you are," he told him, and the man said nothing, just smiled, as Matthews later recalled, "a big shit-eating grin."

Within three minutes they were at the county jail, a square brick building behind the courthouse. The jailhouse was half a century past its prime, and far too small for the county. The sheriff's offices, which were once housed in the building, had been pushed out to make room for more cells—enough to hold eighty prisoners in cramped quarters. The sheriff now occupied a cluster of white trailers on the other side of the parking lot. The city police station was on Peachtree Street, a block away.

As soon as they got "Mr. Wilson" settled in the booking room of the old jail, the cops looked around for a picture of the fugitive Eric Rudolph.

Nobody could find one. So Postell went on the Internet and printed out an FBI wanted poster. One of the images was clean-shaven, and sure enough, although in the old picture Rudolph looked much beefier than the subject at hand, he had the same attached earlobes, the same hairline, the same scar on his chin.

Jody Bandy from the TVA brought the poster into the booking room and held it up behind the man who sat placidly in his chair, saying nothing. Everyone gathered around. Matthews told him, "You look like someone I used to know."

He snickered.

Finally Bandy said, "Just tell us who you really are."

The man laughed softly, and Postell remembered it was "the coldest laugh I ever heard."

"I'm Eric Robert Rudolph," he said. "You got me."

Just like that.

He did not call himself "Eric Rudolph," the way his friends and family might have. No, this was Eric Robert Rudolph, a man familiar with his own legend.

Jeff Postell and Turtle Matthews looked at each other and decided it was time to wake up the sheriff and the chief of police.

Dispatch reached the sheriff, Keith Lovin, at home at 4 A.M. It had already been a long, difficult day that started with the execution of a major arrest warrant, and ended at the scene of a gruesome accident in a neighboring county. A state trooper had been killed in the wreck, and Lovin had gone to help with the scene. He'd known the dead man, having been a trooper himself before he ran for sheriff last year. Lovin had hit the pillow at 1 A.M., and three hours later was driving to the jail to have a look at someone who said he was Eric Rudolph.

Mark Thigpen, the Murphy police chief, met him there with a manila folder left by the FBI five years before: the protocol for identifying Eric Rudolph. They had to be sure this wasn't a hoax, or one of those characters with a compulsion to confess to famous crimes.

Lovin, a dark-haired man in his forties, sat down across from the prisoner and started asking questions. Thigpen, tall and sturdy, with a military flattop, stood out of sight behind an open door and checked the answers against the file. Lovin thought the man seemed fairly calm, considering his situation. Thoughtful, even.

"Where were you born?"

"Merritt Island, Florida."

"What's your driver's license number?"

He gave the right answer.

Sheriff Lovin notified the FBI regional office in Asheville that it looked as if they really had Rudolph. This set off a chain reaction of jingling cell phones and buzzing pagers from Washington to Atlanta to Birmingham and back as word spread through the community of agents, cops, and federal prosecutors who had been waiting for this moment for five long years. The news quickly leaked to CNN, and the network had the story on the air before the first federal agents arrived in Murphy. Satellite trucks and carloads of reporters soon followed. SWAT team snipers set up defensive positions on rooftops around the jail, gaining the attention of curious townspeople who had gathered to watch the commotion. The mayor and a former sheriff made themselves available for interviews in front of the blue marble courthouse.

Rudolph's arrest was welcome news in Washington, where the present administration was having a hard time tracking down the government's most infamous fugitives. Eighteen months after George W. Bush had declared a war on terror, U.S. forces were still chasing Osama bin Laden like a ghost dog through the Tora Bora mountains. Weeks after the U.S. invasion of Iraq, Saddam Hussein had yet to be extracted from his spider hole. Catching a domestic terrorist was a PR bonanza, and John Ashcroft, the attorney general, wasted no time releasing a triumphant statement. "Today, Eric Robert Rudolph, the most notorious American fugitive on the FBI's Most Wanted list, has been captured and will face American justice," he said. "This sends a clear message that we will never cease in our efforts to hunt down all terrorists, foreign or domestic, and stop them from harming the innocent."

Inside the old jailhouse the deputies fingerprinted Rudolph and took a mug shot before they let him clean up a bit. To a man, nobody who saw Rudolph that morning could believe he'd been living in the mountains for so long. He was scruffy and not too fragrant, but his hands were soft and his fingernails intact. His hair was trimmed and his teeth seemed sound. One jailer who saw him strip off his shirt in the washroom said his skin was clean and unscarred. Deer hunters returning home from a weekend in the woods looked worse than Rudolph. People were saying he should have been tanned like a leather strap if he'd spent years out in the wind and snow. But that was his story and he was sticking to it.

"This is the first time I've talked to anyone in five years," he told Matthews. Rudolph had a deep, sonorous voice that didn't quite fit with his skinny neck and gaunt, angular face. He asked for a cigarette, and one of the jailers gave him a Marlboro from a fresh pack. He said he was grateful to smoke something he didn't have to fish out of Taco Bell's outdoor ash can.

Turtle Matthews was assigned to sit with Rudolph. Since Matthews had the only connection to him, however tenuous, the sheriff thought the prisoner might open up with him. Matthews was told not to ask Rudolph any questions, but not to discourage him from talking, either. The jailers brought them some scrambled eggs and bacon, biscuits and gravy, juice and coffee—the first of two breakfasts for Rudolph, who wasn't lying when he said he was hungry. While they ate, Rudolph started to chat with Matthews. He asked about the outcome of a recent referendum in Murphy to allow beer and liquor to be sold by the drink in restaurants.

"It lost," said the deputy. Rudolph nodded. He said he followed the papers whenever he could find them. Then Rudolph looked Matthews in the eye.

"I knew you knew," he said.

"Then why did you lie to me tonight?"

"Well, it had happened before," he said, and proceeded to describe how he had been picked up by some cops back in 1999. He said a truck he had stolen to move his supplies ran out of gas outside Murphy. Two deputy sheriffs stopped to offer him a ride to the filling station. They even dropped him back at his stolen truck without a question asked. He thought he might get lucky again. Matthews got the impression, though, that Rudolph was just relieved the running was over. He said he was tired of eating out of Dumpsters. He told Matthews that he had never left the area, and that he had a camp just outside of town. Turtle could tell the bomb technicians not to worry; it wouldn't be booby-trapped. And they would find it neat and sanitary. "Cleanliness is next to godliness," he said.

As Matthews got up to report this information to the sheriff, Rudolph told him something else.

"No matter what you hear," he said, "tell them I'm not a monster."

Rudolph spent the next two days at the Cherokee County Jail. He was talking a blue streak to his local guards about the Old Testament and politics and how to live off acorns and salamanders; just about everything except his crimes. He seemed interested in his jailers' lives, and even inquired after their families. But he never asked anyone whether his own mother was still alive, or for any news about his sister and brothers. Finally, when it was obvious he wasn't going to confess to anything, the federal agents took custody of the prisoner. As he prepared to leave, Rudolph shook hands with the deputies and jail staff. He even signed wanted posters for them, like some kind of rock star. Rudolph inscribed one with a reference to Psalm 144, which begins: "Blessed be the Lord my strength, which teacheth my hands to war, and my fingers to fight." FBI agents confiscated every one of the posters—for handwriting samples, they said.

The camera crews who had been waiting outside the jail all weekend finally got what they wanted when Rudolph was moved from Murphy to a federal court in Asheville. It was a ritual "perp walk," the modern equivalent of a public stoning, where the accused is marched from the jailhouse door to a waiting vehicle. In the classic style, Rudolph was dressed in prison orange and fitted with a large bulletproof vest, shackled at wrist and ankle, and hustled along in a scrum of anxious-looking guards, quickly, but with enough time in the open for photographers to capture a few frames of his cool, watchful gaze. Timothy McVeigh, after his arrest for the Oklahoma City bombing, was photographed in this way, setting the gold standard for the terrorist perp walk. McVeigh looked menacing, scowling into the sun. He later said he was scanning the crowd for a gunman he was sure would appear, like Jack Ruby, and kill him on the spot.

Eric Robert Rudolph had a similar look on his face when he emerged from the Cherokee County Jail, flanked by Lovin and Thigpen. He turned his head to glare in the direction of the assembled media before he was hustled off in a convoy to a waiting helicopter, where he would be delivered to his enemies. He rode to the airport in silence, staring straight ahead. But as the chopper lifted off, Rudolph took one last look at the green river valley and the smooth-knuckled mountains of the Nantahala, folded like hands in prayer.

I arrived in Murphy a few weeks after Rudolph was captured. By then the media road show had moved on, leaving the local citizens in turn bemused and resentful. With far too much time on their hands, reporters and producers had started looking for some local color to fill in the twenty-four-hour news cycle. They wanted to know whether someone in this mountain community had helped Rudolph survive all these years on the run. This was not an unreasonable line of inquiry, since the FBI was looking for the same answers. In service of this story, however, a lot of old hillbilly clichés were dragged out of the dusty files on Appalachia. Significance was assigned to the gun racks and Confederate flags plastered on local pickup trucks, and the sign above the Peachtree Restaurant urging people to "Pray for Eric Rudolph." The Associated Press quoted more than a few local sympathizers who said they wouldn't have turned him in. Jeffery Gettleman of the *New York Times* wrote, rather elegantly, "If there is an antigovernment current here, coursing through the woods clear as a splashing brook or a pint of moonshine, it is nothing new." Television coverage gave the general impression that Murphy and the surrounding towns were nests of antigovernment zealots.

Murphy's mayor, Bill Hughes, was indignant. When I met him on a sunny Saturday afternoon at the city office building, the first thing he wanted me to understand was that Eric Robert Rudolph was not, as he put it, "a local product." Rudolph had been born in Florida. The family moved to western North Carolina when Eric was a teenager. Hardly anyone knew him.

Hughes sat at his big squared-off mayor's desk in front of a large American flag, sifting through a scrapbook of clippings, photographs, and letters "from all over the world" about the recent unpleasantness. The cameras and mikes disappeared after Rudolph was whisked away to Asheville, but the notoriety lingered. The mayor's bright blue eyes narrowed with resentment as he scanned a batch of newspaper articles. To his mind, many of them were inaccurate and downright offensive.

"The media blitz turned into a media circus, unfortunately," he said. "They portrayed us as ignorant illiterate hillbillies, painting us as the stereotype—distrustful of the federal government, totally ignorant of the outside world, close-knit, antigovernment. The things they said about us simply are not true."

What, then, was the truth about Murphy and the people of Cherokee County?

"I would say Murphy is just a typical small American town," said the mayor. "Our people are tolerant, they are law-abiding, they do respect authority."

I would spend many afternoons like this one in the next three years, dipping into the parallel and paradoxical narratives that run through the story of Eric Robert Rudolph. Like the perceptions of western North Carolina, the descriptions of Rudolph I encountered were so strangely divergent that I might have been hearing about twin brothers with the same faces and different personalities, one who committed the crimes and one who was captured and punished for them. Eric Rudolph was, by his own inclination, the most reclusive and enigmatic kind of outlaw. He left a faint trail to follow. And in doing so, Rudolph became less a real person than a touchstone for the expectations of others.

From the time he went into hiding after the Birmingham clinic bombing to the morning he was captured, Eric Rudolph had disappeared in more ways than the obvious one. In fact he had been slowly vanishing for years. He lived alone, paid cash for everything, lied about his whereabouts to his family and occasional girlfriends. When he was identified as the main suspect in the series of bombings, federal investigators profiled him as a "lone offender," or "lone wolf": a self-appointed avenger with no real alliances, no meaningful social ties. He tries to justify his actions by attaching them to a cause: saving babies, defending the white race, striking a blow against technology. The lone wolf believes history will judge him to be a hero. To psychologists, he is an inadequate male who converts his frustrations and longings into a campaign of murder.

The lawyers who were later chosen to defend Eric Rudolph prepared a very different picture of him. They describe him as a misguided but sensitive and engaging human being who isolated himself to protect his lonely mission. And this was not just a defense strategy; it was the honest impression of smart people who were not easily conned. They looked forward to visiting him in jail; some considered him a friend. And one of his attorneys, a Conservative Jew, came to love him like a son.

In many ways, political outlaws like Eric Rudolph are ciphers, blank screens upon which all interested parties can project their expectations and their agendas. And the more sensational their crimes, the more agendas emerge. To the radical anti-abortion movement, Rudolph became a source of inspiration; to the self-styled "patriots" of the militia movement, he was a government scapegoat; to watchdog groups and pro-choice advocates, he was a poster child for the dangers of the extremist right. Once he was charged with a capital offense, his cause was adopted by anti–death penalty advocates. He became a trophy as well for the federal agencies, investigators, lawyers, government bureaucrats, and members of the media, who fought for position to define him, hunt him, study him, defend him, and try him.

The government pursued Rudolph with such ferocity not just for the sake of his victims, although they were important, but for the audacity of his bombings. An attack on the Olympics while the games were being hosted on U.S. soil was more than just a bombing, it was domestic terrorism, a symbolic attack on America itself. The subsequent bombings in Atlanta and Birmingham, which appeared to be aimed at law enforcement personnel as well as the specific targets, amplified the government's response.

The sensational nature of the case affected, and sometimes distorted, every aspect of it. Rudolph's bombing campaign was what the federal agencies call a "major incident," a bland term for a Big Crime. Big Crimes are spectacles that draw public interest and law enforcement attention out of all proportion to the damage done to property or the number of casualties. Big Crimes are like plane crashes; more people are killed on the highways every day, but we are still transfixed by the special horror of the fuselage tumbling from the sky. Serial crimes are the most sensational of all because they are rare, frightening, and seemingly random, with a built-in dramatic hook: Where will he strike next?

The American public seemed both fascinated and repelled by Rudolph. As a society we tend to have at least two conflicting impulses when it comes to famous fugitives: The first is to ignore our legal presumption of innocence and assume they are guilty as soon as they are accused, to want them captured and executed without mercy. The other impulse is to romanticize them in some way, to separate them from the cowardice and brutality of their crimes and to fit them into the archetype of the outlaw hero. They become Robin Hood or Jesse James or Pretty Boy Floyd—guys who perform daring deeds, who outwit the authorities, who are forced by circumstance to ride on the other side of the law, and who always have some redeeming qualities to burnish their legends.

Rudolph seems aware that his story occupies the uneasy territory between the outlaw hero and the deranged killer, the Christian soldier and the despised terrorist. He is a prodigious reader of history, philosophy, and Russian literature, as well as current events. He followed his own publicity from wherever he was hiding, and while in jail obsessively watched news reports about his case. Rudolph held his silence for years before he finally tried to explain himself—first in brief court statements, then through a handful of broadsides published on the Army of God website, and, finally, in a series of written interviews with me.

I had my own agenda, of course. Eric Rudolph was a puzzle I needed to solve for the sake of a story I wanted to tell.

This book was never meant to be the biography of a serial bomber, or an academic study of terrorism. It is an extended act of journalism, a thin slice taken from a time in the life of our country in an attempt to illuminate a series of horrific events. The idea was not to mythologize Rudolph or his crimes, but to pick them up like rocks in a stream, to hold them up and see what's underneath. On its most elevated level the story is a journey into the darkest precincts of idealism, an exploration of how things can go terribly wrong in the name of doing good. But it is still a story, and in many ways an incomplete one. The challenge has been to take disparate and often contradictory facts and try to fit them into a sensible narrative. This is what prosecutors and writers have in common. So I began my study of Eric Robert Rudolph the way the investigators always begin: by looking at the crimes and at the evidence. And never forgetting the victims.

2

BY THEIR FRUITS

YOU SHALL KNOW THEM

A homemade bomb is more than a weapon; it is a statement. What it communicates is hatred, or revenge, or a desire for power, or any combination of these. It can also convey a great deal of information about its maker. How carefully the bomb is crafted; what it contains; how, where, and when it explodes: All these things are projections of the bomber's mind. The bomber may lie and dissemble, but his work never does. The bomb, in effect, is the bomber.

The bomb is where any investigation of a bombing begins. But if the device functions properly it is blown into hundreds of scorched and mangled fragments. There are only a handful of specialists in the United States with the knowledge and skill to identify and reassemble the pieces of an exploded bomb. Tom Mohnal, supervisory special agent for the FBI, is one of the most experienced forensic analysts in the country, and he was the first to inspect Eric Rudolph's handiwork.

The new crime lab at FBI National Academy in Quantico, Virginia, where Mohnal works, looks from a distance like a giant cruise ship anchored in a grassy field. Three sets of white smokestacks rise over a reflective facade the milky blue color of glacial ice. The architecture is solid and redolent of industry, the kind of building Margaret Bourke White might have once photographed. The lab was opened in 2003, replacing a cramped facility in the FBI headquarters in downtown Washington, D.C.

To get to the lab you have to pass through two military checkpoints on the Quantico Marine Base, about an hour's drive south of Washington, D.C. On a snowy Thursday afternoon the base seemed otherwise empty, reinforcing an eerie feeling that I had wandered onto the set of an *Outer Limits* episode during lunch hour. It got even stranger when the road narrowed and curved through a scruffy little town called "Hogan's Alley." I drove past a drugstore, a post office, a bank, a restaurant and motel. Everything seemed quite normal in Hogan's Alley except that it was completely deserted and all the windows were masked from the inside with sheets of brown paper. The marquee on the movie theater, the Biograph, announced the show times of *Manhattan Melodrama* starring Clark Gable and Myrna Loy—which happened to be the feature playing at the Biograph in Chicago in 1934 when a squad of G-men gunned down John Dillinger as he walked out of the movie. An insider's joke. The town was actually a training facility used by the FBI, the DEA, and visiting tactical teams to practice storming buildings, rescuing hostages, and capturing bad guys.

As I walked from the parking lot a muffled sound, like popping corn, bounced off the hard surfaces. It was gunfire from the nearby rifle range. The FBI lab has a small secured visitors' area where I waited for an escort to bring me up to visit Tom Mohnal in the lab's explosives unit. Mohnal turned out to be a friendly man with receding brown hair and wire-framed glasses, dressed in the bureau's regulation suit and tie, a holdover from the J. Edgar Hoover days. His job is to analyze bomb components and re-create the devices from their fractured remnants. The replicas are used to help investigators recognize components, to help bomb technicians identify and work with similar devices, and, sometimes, as courtroom exhibits.

Near the elevator bank on this floor is a wide hallway lined with cases and a large table where reproductions of some of the most famous bombs in recent history are displayed. Mohnal showed me how a few of them worked: There was a set of pipe bombs from the almost-forgotten "New York Subway Bomber" case in the mid-1990s. Police caught the bombers before they could attack New York's mass transit system. But a roomful of people in Brooklyn almost lost their lives when, during the raid, one of the plotters dove for the pipe bombs hidden under his bed and tried—unsuccessfully—to detonate them before he was shot.

Mohnal picked a book off the desk and opened it to show me its hollowed-out center. When Ted Kaczynski, the Unabomber, mailed a similar copy of *Ice Brothers* to Percy Wood, the president of United Airlines, the front flap was connected to an unusual "loop switch" that detonated a small pipe bomb in the man's hands. Wood survived with lacerations to his face, hands, and thigh. It was the fourth in a series of sixteen bombings that started in 1978 and did not end until Kaczynski was arrested in 1996 (with another bomb in his cabin, ready to go). The Unabomber was Mohnal's great white whale, and the case had consumed his professional life for almost the full length of the bombing campaign. Mohnal showed me more of Kaczynski's devices: There was the mock-up of an incendiary bomb hidden in a box that malfunctioned and failed to explode in Utah, along with models of a couple of booby-trapped package bombs that did explode, killing an advertising executive in New Jersey and a timber lobbyist in California. Even though Kaczynski's bombs had telltale signatures—the use of finely honed wooden components, the initials "FC" (for "Freedom Club," it was later learned) stamped into the devices and other tantalizing clues, none of the forensic evidence created a trail to the bomber. In fact, Kaczynski went out of his way to throw off investigators by planting in his bombs hairs that he had collected from the drain of a public restroom.

There were other, more recent bombs on display. At the end of the desk was a large Faded Glory hiking boot with an extremely thick sole—just like the one the convicted "shoe bomber," Richard Reid, had modified into an IED that he tried to blow up on a transatlantic flight. As a demonstrative aid, the lab techs had constructed a mock-up of the lower part of the shoe that was roughly the size of a baby's bassinet to show how Reid had molded a plastic explosive into the wafflelike sole. Luckily he was tackled by crew and passengers before he could successfully light the fuse. Another display showed the gaping hole the shoe bomb would have torn through the plane's fuselage.

Mohnal then gave me a quick tour of part of the lab devoted to detecting the chemical signatures of explosives, narcotics, and other substances of interest to law enforcement. Everything looked new and pristine. There were row after row of beeping, whirring machines: gas chromatographs, mass spectrometers, high-tech X-ray devices, and banks of computer screens. Many of the machines were robot-controlled, so results could be monitored from computers back in the chemists' offices. Other rooms held impressive-looking electron microscopes. I didn't even get near the ballistic, trace, and document evidence sections, which I imagine took up major floor space elsewhere in the lab.

Tom Mohnal clearly loved his lab and his work, and it seemed an inopportune time to bring up some of the scandals that have plagued the FBI in the past decade. Back in 1994 Frederic Whitehurst, an FBI chemist in the explosives section, turned whistle-blower and accused the lab of sloppy work, cross-contamination of samples, inaccurate results, and deliberate manipulation of evidence to favor the prosecution. Congressional hearings ensued. A report from the inspector general's office cleared the FBI of the most serious charges, but also chastised the lab supervisors for not adhering to standard practices. As a result of the investigation some changes were made in lab procedures. And in 1998 the world's most famous crime lab was accredited for the first time by the American Society of Crime Laboratory Directors.

Tom Mohnal led me into a cubicle where he opened a white laminate floor cabinet and hoisted out a green ALICE pack, a common cloth rucksack used by army infantry units. He slid out a model of the device Eric Rudolph had planted in Centennial Olympic Park. "This is the largest pipe bomb we've ever seen," said Mohnal, setting it on the counter with a certain awe.

Rudolph has insisted that the civilian casualties inflicted that night were a colossal mistake. He has said that he tried to clear the park of innocent people; he meant to kill only the police and federal agents he knew would respond to a threat. But the bomb that exploded in a park still crowded with people in the early morning hours of July 27, 1996, tells its own story.

The bomb that Tom Mohnal reconstructed based on bits and pieces found in the ground and on rooftops and in the flesh of its victims consisted of three metal pipes, each a foot long and two inches in diameter, each packed with a pound and a third of Accurate Arms No. 9 smokeless powder. The pipes were capped at each end; a hole was drilled into one side and electric matches inserted into the powder. An electric match is a dry flammable mixture of chemicals attached to a heating element, about the size of a regular match head. These devices are most commonly used by pyrotechnics experts to choreograph fireworks displays, setting off rockets in a timed pattern from a safe distance. When an electric current enters the match through one of two leg wires it activates a heater that ignites the chemicals, just like a kitchen match held to a stovetop coil. The matches were wired to a twelve-volt Eveready lantern battery through a Big Ben alarm clock, the almost comically old-fashioned relic that actually ticks as its hands circle the hours. The detonation mechanism was typical and quite basic; any twelve-year-old pyromaniac could download the instructions from the Internet if he knew where to look.

But there were other components that were not ordinary at all, and their configuration gave the bomb its special personality: The entire device was taped to an eighth-inch-thick steel plate before it was stuffed into the military backpack. The whole thing weighed about forty-five pounds, and the man who built it fashioned a handle out of a wooden dowel to lift the pack without compressing the components inside. To keep the steel plate from cutting into his skin when he carried it on his back, he made a special foam pad from two military-type sleeping mats laminated together. It would have taken hours to perform this task—one that, to the ordinary observer, was quite unnecessary. Heavier pads are available in camping stores. But technical overkill was a signature of this bomber. It was most apparent in the shrapnel he attached to the pipes. He chose 8d masonry nails, two-and-a-half-inch-long spikes that are cut from sheets of black metal and strong enough to penetrate concrete. The bomber arranged five pounds of these flat, wedge-shaped nails with meticulous care, head to toe, on strips of silver duct tape. Then he wrapped the pipes with the tape, precise as a surgeon dressing a wounded limb: four rows per pipe, forty-five nails per row.

The smokeless gunpowder that filled the pipes is what is known in the trade as a "low explosive," as opposed to a "high explosive" such as

TNT. The difference lies in the speed of detonation and way in which the substances explode. High explosives are chemical compounds in which oxygen and carbon-based fuel molecules are chemically bonded. When they are broken apart, usually by shock waves, the substance will detonate in a chemical reaction in which a solid (dynamite or C-4) or a liquid (nitroglycerin) instantly changes to gas, releasing a huge amount of energy. The shock wave created by dynamite, for instance, travels at 15,000 to 18,000 feet per second. The rate for low explosives, such as gunpowder, is about 3,300 feet per second. Instead of detonating, low explosives will deflagrate—another way of saying that they burn fast, changing low-volume solids into high-volume gases. This process only creates an explosion when the substance that is burning quickly is contained in something like a sealed pipe. Then it becomes deadly.

Crude pipe bombs are easy to make and common as ticks in law enforcement. The Bureau of Alcohol, Tobacco, Firearms and Explosives, or ATF, estimates that 90 percent of the bombs they investigate are pipe bombs containing powders. The numbers fluctuate from year to year, but the agency has investigated anywhere from 300 to 700 bombs and incendiary devices annually in the United States since 2000—a lot more than media coverage would suggest. Most of these bombs are small devices used to settle private scores, to extort money, or just as sick pranks. But sometimes bombers use them to intimidate and terrorize. Publicity is the point for these bombers, and the bigger the target, the more they have to gain.

In 1996 the most tempting target in the world was Atlanta, Georgia, host of the Centennial Olympic Games. Everybody remembered the 1972 Munich Olympics, in which Palestinian gunmen took the Israeli team hostage—an event that ended with eleven dead and a world permanently spooked by large sporting events. Only three years had passed since a band of Middle Eastern terrorists tried, for the first time and with limited success, to blow up the World Trade Center in New York. It had been just over a year since an antigovernment extremist named Timothy McVeigh had killed 168 people by exploding a homemade bomb outside the Oklahoma City federal building. There were concerns that an international spectacle was bound to attract miscellaneous crazies and true believers who were looking for a venue to air their grievances or publicize their causes. Because of the potential for trouble, as many as 30,000 local, state, and federal agents and private guards had been assigned to protect the games. Tactical units, bomb techs, rescue squads, and specialists of all sorts were standing by around the clock, ready to respond to any event. Among them were Tom Mohnal and a team from the FBI crime lab.

The Centennial Games, honoring 100 years of the modern Olympic movement, were billed as the biggest, most inclusive, most international, and most commercial games in history. All 197 of the invited countries sent athletes to compete before an estimated 3 million spectators. Atlanta used the games to renew its blighted downtown and to promote its modern image as a global city, the enlightened capital of the New South. A city, as the slogan boasted, "Too busy to hate."

On July 19, 1996, President Bill Clinton, Hillary, and Chelsea attended the lavish opening ceremonies along with 85,000 fans in the newly constructed Olympic Stadium. The former Olympian Muhammad Ali, shaking from Parkinson's disease, carried the Olympic flame the last few steps of the way to light the massive torch and open the games, the highlight of the spectacle for many in the crowd.

After the evening's events, many of the spectators headed to Centennial Olympic Park in the city center. The twenty-one-acre park offered restaurants, beer gardens, and free nightly concerts for Olympic revelers. Monuments erected by sponsors—the Swatch Pavilion, BudWorld, the AT&T/NBC sound tower—drew snarky comments from at least one Olympic official, who compared the park to a corporate flea market. But the greatest concern was not crass marketing; it was security.

Since Centennial Park was not an official Olympic venue, Atlanta's leaders didn't want to restrict access to it during the games. They wanted the city park to be as open and welcoming as possible, so, over the objections of some experts, security was kept as discreet as possible. A temporary fence was erected around the perimeter, with entrances watched by guards and remote video cameras. Suspicious-looking visitors could be stopped and searched for smuggled booze and weapons.

Yet in the early morning hours of July 27, a young man with a heavy military backpack managed to slip into the park unobserved. He sat down on a bench below the three-story sound and video tower erected by NBC-TV, the network sponsors of the Olympic events. Some raucous teenagers, who were swilling contraband beers nearby, described him as dark, medium build, with a goatee, wearing a sweatshirt and knit watch cap on the hot summer night. They didn't notice him leave. But after he was gone, one of them spotted the green cloth pack under the bench. He tugged at it, tipping it over, and, according to his statement, considered taking it with him as the group prepared to move the party to a bar. But it was too heavy to steal, so he left it behind.

On the music stage, an R&B band from Los Angeles called Jack Mack and the Heart Attack was putting on a free concert, churning through a set of original songs and standards like "Take Me to the River." It was well after midnight and the festive crowd was starting to get rowdy. There were still as many as 50,000 people in the park.

Richard Jewell, a thirty-three-year-old former sheriff's deputy from north Georgia, had hired on as a private security guard with AT&T during the Olympics. His nightly station was near an eastern entrance point, next to the AT&T/NBC sound tower. Jewell was a classic gung-ho cop, eager and proactive. He took his job seriously, and he wouldn't tolerate a bunch of drunks ruining everybody else's good times. When a group of teenagers started throwing beer cans and giving him lip, he recruited a security man with a badge—Tom Davis of the Georgia Bureau of Investigation—to back him up. When they returned to the bench the unruly kids were gone, but Jewell noticed that someone had left behind a backpack.

Davis started asking around if it belonged to anybody, but no one would claim it. Jewell took a closer look—it was just like a pack someone had left behind a week earlier. People were leaving stuff around all the time. But to be safe, Davis radioed for the bomb techs to check it out.

At the 911 center in Atlanta, the operator picked up the call at 12:58 A.M.

"Atlanta nine-one-one."

A deep, slightly nasal voice with a mild Southern accent said: "There is a bomb in Centennial Park. You have thirty minutes ..." Then the line went silent.

First the operator tried to call the Atlanta Police Department Command Center, but she got a busy signal. Three minutes went by. Finally she got a police dispatcher on the line.

"You know the address to Centennial Park?" the operator asked.

"Girl, don't ask me to lie to you," said the dispatcher with a chuckle.

"I tried to call ACC, but ain't nobody answering the phone. And I just got this man telling me about there's a bomb set to go off in thirty minutes in Centennial Park." But the operator couldn't get the system to recognize the name when she typed it in.

"Oh Lord, child," said the dispatcher, still not sounding very alarmed. "One minute, one minute ... Centennial Park. You put it in and it won't go in?"

"No, unless I'm spelling Centennial wrong ... How are we spelling Centennial?" asked the operator.

"C-E-N-T-E-N-N-I ... How do *you* spell Centennial?"

"I'm spelling it right. It ain't taking ..."

"Wait a minute. That's the regular Olympic Stadium, right?"

This went on for quite some time. Eventually the operator found a street address to enter into the system, which alerted Atlanta police units to the bomb threat. But, incredibly, there was no direct line of communication set up between the Atlanta Police Department and the command center at Centennial Olympic Park. They never got the warning.

Fallon Stubbs took a snapshot of her mother, Alice Hawthorne, posing in front of the huge, fan-shaped brass statue honoring the "spirit of the Olympics." Hawthorne, a small-business owner and community leader in Albany, Georgia, was celebrating her daughter's fourteenth birthday by treating her to a trip to Atlanta and the free concert in the park. Now it was after 1 A.M., and they were ready to call it a night.

Across a small courtyard from the statue, two bomb experts knelt in front of the bench below the sound tower and checked the exterior of the green backpack for obvious booby traps. It seemed routine; there had been dozens of bags and other lost items to examine in the past week.

Then one of them undid a strap and aimed his flashlight inside. He saw wires, part of a milky-colored plastic container, and the metal end cap of a pipe. The bomb guys carefully backed off and called the explosives disposal unit. Tom Davis and several other park personnel started herding people away from the site, as fast as they could without starting a stampede. Richard Jewell walked around to the entrance for the tower and started clearing the technicians out of there.

At 1:18 A.M. the hand on the Big Ben alarm clock clicked into contact with a metal screw that had been drilled into its face, completing the circuit. A surge of electrons traveled from the lantern battery through the metal clockworks and along the wires, igniting the electric matches and the gunpowder in the bomb. A moment later nearly a thousand white-hot pieces of pipe, clock, battery, and nails were sent hurtling through the air and into the crowd, each shot from the epicenter of the blast at more than 3,000 feet per second, faster than a thousand speeding bullets.

Several video cameras in the crowd recorded the event, and from a distance the sound of the bomb going off was like a heavy rifle shot—more an enormous crack than a boom. It was accompanied by a flash of light and a spray of shrapnel and burning debris, like a crude fireworks display, followed by a ballooning wave of white smoke and dust. Bystanders closest to the bomb were tossed and scattered like bowling pins. Fallon Stubbs saw her mother whirl around, like an ice-skater in a slow spin, before she dropped to the ground. Fallon was knocked flat by the shock wave as shrapnel tore into her leg and nearly slashed off one of her fingers. She got up and ran to her mother but a stranger urged her to lie down; she was bleeding, and the people who were helping her kept her from getting to her mother, who just lay there, quiet and still.

The ambulances kept coming and coming, paramedics walking over ground slick with blood from more than 110 people with injuries, many of them serious. A backpack buckle had lodged in one man's jaw. Other victims suffered gashes and broken limbs. A Turkish cameraman racing to record the scene had collapsed and died of a heart attack. As they loaded Fallon Stubbs on to a stretcher she kept repeating, "My mother, my mother," as if they couldn't understand who needed the help. The last time Fallon looked back there were so many paramedics and other people surrounding Alice Hawthorne that she couldn't see her anymore. Later, when she woke up in a hospital bed, her stepfather, John, and her whole family were standing all around her and they didn't have to say a thing. She knew.

Alice Hawthorne had died at the scene, killed by a piece of 8d masonry nail that penetrated her skull at the temple and tumbled through her brain.

Tom Mohnal was asleep in his motel room near Dobbins Air Reserve Base, just north of Atlanta, when his pager went off. He drove over to the command center at the base, gathered up his gear, and, within an hour, arrived at Centennial Park. The smoke had settled, but the scene was still hellish, illuminated by the pulsing colored lights of emergency vehicles. Scores of casualties and walking wounded were still waiting to be taken to area hospitals. First responders always have the right of way when there are injuries at a crime scene, but the evidence collection teams started working even before the last ambulances pulled away.

As soon as he saw the blast site Mohnal could tell it was a pipe bomb, and a huge one. There were recognizable chunks of ruptured pipe in the debris. He also noted a strange steel plate, ripped in three places and driven deep into the crater left by the blast. Evidence experts started to trowel samples of dirt from the crater into empty paint cans. Dozens of agents fanned out from the epicenter to pick up pieces of bomb components and nails. The scene was a mess because it had so recently been a construction site. Every sort of nail and screw and scrap used to build the park was mixed in with the torn-up sod and turned into "road trash," random debris that was not part of the bomb. The evidence was widely scattered. Several nails were later picked up on the roof of a twelve-story building. Because the bomb had been tipped over by the drunks, most of the shrapnel went straight up instead of toward the main crowd. If it had remained on its side, the bomb could have caused dozens, maybe hundreds more casualties.

It had already been decided in Washington that the FBI would take charge of any major incident at the Olympics. But Centennial Park was

not technically an Olympic venue, and when the bomb went off, the
ATF's National Response Team showed up to work the scene as well.
The smaller, more specialized ATF was charged with investigating all
major bombings and arson incidents on U.S. soil that were not classified
as terrorism. The NRT had more experience with bomb scenes than any
other agency's team, and they felt that they should lead the investigation. The FBI didn't see it that way. Bystanders in the park reported that
an argument—Tom Mohnal describes it as a "slight discussion"—broke
out between field commanders of the two federal agencies over who had
charge of the scene. It was the first skirmish in an interagency struggle
that would continue throughout the investigation.

The FBI prevailed, and Mohnal was placed in charge of evidence
collection and analysis, with ATF in a supporting role. Even though
the ATF had one of its three national crime labs just a few miles away
in suburban Atlanta, and offered its services to FBI technicians, it was
decided that all the bombing evidence would be flown to the FBI lab in
D.C. A jet was already being fueled up and standing by at Dobbins Air
Reserve Base for that purpose. "Their argument was 'our lab was a half
hour away.' But ours was an hour and a half by jet," Mohnal recalled.

By the time they were finished, the recovery team had collected 600
buckets of rubble to be sifted for evidence. The samples from the crater
that would identify the type of explosives used were immediately flown
to the lab for analysis. Tom Mohnal stayed in Atlanta until the crime
scene was completely processed, then flew up to D.C. with the rest of
the evidence.

Once at the lab, the debris was carefully poured onto clean brown
paper and methodically sorted into components for examination and
testing: nails, bomb fragments, tape, trace fabrics, organics, wire. Within
hours Mohnal had a good idea of what the bomb had looked like, even
what type of gunpowder was used in it. Out of some four pounds of
smokeless powder packed into the pipes, the evidence techs only tested
one tiny "unconsumed" grain of powder. But that was enough, said
Mohnal, to identify it as Accurate Arms No. 9 smokeless powder
and trace it to a batch manufactured in an Israeli plant prior to 1982;
once the powder was in the United States, it could have been sold and

bought almost anywhere. From the particular characteristics of the battery and the wires, the lab techs could narrow them down to a place and general time of manufacture, and which chain of stores sold them—but not who bought them. Most of the other components—even the electric matches—were also common items, difficult to trace to the purchaser. Except for the steel plate. That seemed unusual enough for further chemical analysis. And it was not only a good piece of forensic evidence, but it also revealed something about the bomber. The plate indicated that the device was probably designed to be an improvised Claymore mine, a type of bomb taught by the U.S. military in unconventional warfare training. The idea was to aim the blast in a certain direction by putting a backing on one side. Whether a thin steel plate could actually determine the direction of such a large bomb is a matter of debate, but the design was consistent with a Claymore. And that suggested a bomber with some military background.

Mohnal transmitted each piece of information back to Atlanta as it was confirmed. The case had been given a name—"CENTBOMB"—and a multiagency task force was already forming under the leadership of the FBI. The ATF ran the bomb through a database that compared it with 76,000 explosive devices previously recorded in the United States. There were no matches. Agents from the FBI, Georgia Bureau of Investigation, and ATF were assigned to trace the bomb components, in hopes they would lead them to the bomber. Other teams would interview witnesses and collect photographs and videotapes from spectators. But even as the different investigative teams were fanning out to follow the evidence, the FBI in Washington and Atlanta were already closing in on a suspect: the security guard Richard Jewell.

It had happened once before. During the 1984 Olympic Games in Los Angeles, a police officer discovered a small pipe bomb on a bus full of athletes. He saved the day by evacuating the bus and ripping some wires off the bomb to disarm it. It didn't take long for investigators to get him to confess that he had planted the device himself. They called him a hero-bomber. Lloyd Erwin, a forensic chemist and bomb analyst for the ATF in Atlanta who was famous for his encyclopedic knowledge of explosives, remembered the 1984 case well. Now Erwin was a member of the CENTBOMB Task Force, and he was stunned when he learned that the FBI was investigating Richard Jewell as a hero-bomber. The evidence just didn't fit the motive. Hero-bombers don't want to get hurt. The pipe bomb on the Los Angeles bus was no more powerful than a bundle of firecrackers; the bomb in Atlanta could easily have liquefied Richard Jewell. Other ATF agents were in agreement about this, and Erwin brought it up at a task force meeting.

"I told them it was a waste of time. Jewell wasn't the guy," said Erwin. "But it was four ATF agents versus a hundred FBIs. They wouldn't listen."

He is a living legend in the ATF; a balding, white-haired man with a trim mustache and deceptively avuncular face who has a seemingly preternatural sense of how to reconstruct bombs from the bits and pieces strewn around crime scenes. He attributes most of his talents to long experience and a knowledge rooted in the nonacademic world. He grew up in the mountains of northern Georgia, the son of a rural schoolteacher and a seamstress, and he spent his youth building everything from scratch, from toys to wagons. He knew his way around guns and dynamite, the poor man's bulldozer, before he knew his way around a lab.

Erwin joined the ATF back when it was still a department of the IRS and its agents, known as revenuers, still spent their time tracking down recalcitrant liquor importers, cigarette smugglers, and moonshiners. Lloyd knew all about moonshine. "All you had to do was follow a creek up in the mountains and you could find a still," he remembers. In 1964, when Erwin graduated from Western Carolina University with a chemistry degree, the Treasury Department recruited him. He would go along on the moonshine raids to collect evidence. That's how his agency developed an expertise with explosives. "Every revenuer had a trunk load of explosives in his car," says Erwin. "We used them to blow up the stills."

The lab equipment that Erwin uses to determine the chemical signatures of the explosives and other materials used in bombs had become more sophisticated over the years, the procedures more standardized. But to Erwin, his job is as much an art as a science, as intuitive as technical.

He says, for instance, that he can tell whether a bomb used low or high explosives before he takes any evidence samples.

"I can go to a bomb scene and tell you right away if it's dynamite," he told me. How did he know? "I get a headache." Nitroglycerin, the key ingredient in commercial dynamite, is a vasodilator—often taken in pill form by heart patients to prevent attacks. One side effect is a blazing headache. Erwin also says he can often tell what kind of explosive powders were used in pipe bombs just by looking at the debris.

"Black powder is shaped like gravel," says Erwin. "It's been pressed into a cake and broken up again." But particles of smokeless powder, a more potent explosive used to load high-powered rifle and pistol rounds, are more uniform in size and shaped like rods and disks. This is quite apparent under a microscope, but Lloyd Erwin says he can see the difference just by looking.

Tom Mohnal at the FBI rolls his eyes when he hears about Erwin's intuition. He believes in strict empirical analysis. The two men, in their rarefied profession, often find themselves working the same cases and disagreeing over lab procedures and investigative techniques. In a way, their relationship mirrors the long-standing rivalry between their agencies. It is a tension built into the system, and many would argue that it is often a positive thing.

Until very recently, and despite the considerable efforts of J. Edgar Hoover, Congress had always resisted granting total police power to one domestic agency. And so most federal law enforcement duties had traditionally been divided up between the Treasury and Justice departments: FBI under Justice; the U.S. Marshals, Secret Service, and IRS under Treasury. (The Homeland Security Act of 2002 transferred ATF to Justice, among other changes, and scrambled this balance in ways that are still being measured.)

The ATF has its modern roots in the Prohibition era of the 1920s and 1930s, when Elliot Ness and his Untouchables—hand-picked Treasury agents—busted up bootlegging rings, including Al Capone's syndicate. Toward the end of the 1960s several gun-control and explosives-control laws were adopted by Congress, and the Treasury Department was given the mandate to enforce them with the newly created Bureau of Alcohol,

Tobacco, and Firearms, soon to be known as the ATF. This creation exacerbated a long-term rivalry with the FBI, by then the 600-pound gorilla of federal law enforcement. The ATF is much smaller than the FBI; there are only about 2,000 ATF special agents in the United States, as opposed to about 12,000 FBI agents. The ATF has a history of recruiting from state and local law enforcement, so while many agents have college degrees, they are more likely to have street-cop backgrounds, while FBI agents are often recruited right out of college or law school. There is some truth to the old adage that the FBI is a white-collar agency and the ATF blue-collar.

The ATF worked in relative obscurity until the 1980s, when the National Rifle Association started pushing back against all firearms regulations and pressured Ronald Reagan to abolish the agency. But the ATF's worst days came after the botched raid of the Branch Davidian compound at Waco, Texas, in 1993, in which four ATF agents were killed by gunfire. The subsequent, disastrous storming of the compound on April 19, in which more than eighty people, many of them children, were incinerated, was actually an FBI operation. The debacle nearly destroyed the ATF, which Vice President Al Gore threatened but failed to disband as part of his sweeping government reform program. Some say what emerged from the ashes was a more efficient, focused ATF. But three years after Waco, the agency was still stinging from the experience.

The FBI was shaken as well. The Waco calamity had come on the heels of a deadly standoff in Ruby Ridge, Idaho, in which one federal agent died, and the wife and son of a white separatist named Randy Weaver had also been killed. Again, although another agency—in this case U.S. Marshals—started the raid, the FBI took over and made it worse by calling in snipers. In the fall of 1993 the recently elected president, Bill Clinton, replaced FBI director William Sessions with a youthful and eager former agent and U.S. prosecutor named Louis Freeh.

Freeh proved himself to be a hands-on director, often interjecting himself personally in major cases as they unfolded. His management technique involved sending loyal cadres from Washington to take charge of the investigations, which he directed from headquarters. The FBI has always had a more inductive approach to investigations, rooted in its counterespionage and counterterrorism missions to ferret out plots against the U.S. government. This philosophy harks back to the days of the Red Scare and the old agency adage about how to identify a Communist: "If it looks like a duck and quacks like a duck, then it's a duck." Sometimes you get the duck. And sometimes you get the wrong bird, like Richard Jewell.

It is still not entirely clear how the Richard Jewell incident went so wrong. Fallout from the fiasco affected the subsequent investigation of Eric Rudolph in both obvious and subtle ways.

Louis Freeh was particularly outraged by the Olympic Park bombing because it took place with the whole world watching, as he put it, "in the public eye, on a hallowed stage." He wanted it rolled up, and fast. Meanwhile the FBI Behavioral Science Unit was working up a profile of a potential bomber. Members of the unit, which was made famous in the movie *The Silence of the Lambs*, were reviewing television coverage of the bombing and saw Richard Jewell give an interview. Jewell described his role in discovering the bomb in polite, monotone sentences seasoned with cop-talk. When asked, he said he hoped to get another job in law enforcement, maybe with an agency in Atlanta. Something about Jewell's demeanor set off alarm bells with the profilers, who passed on to the Atlanta field division their speculation that Jewell might be a hero-bomber. At the same time, one of Jewell's former employers called the FBI to report that he thought Jewell was unstable. (Jewell later sued him.) Agents digging around in Jewell's background discovered that he'd had some employment problems in the past, and there had been a few complaints about his overzealousness as a campus policeman. Other bits of information fueled their suspicions. Among other things, Jewell, at age thirty-three, had no girlfriend and lived with his mother. (No one bothered to mention that he was staying with her temporarily while she recuperated from an operation.) Still, nothing connected him to the bombing. But that incomplete profile was apparently enough to make him a principal suspect, a fact that almost instantly leaked to the media.

Richard Jewell, the consummate cop, understood that everybody at the bomb scene should be interviewed as part of the investigation. And so he wasn't surprised when two FBI agents showed up at his mother's apartment. What he didn't expect was the presence of a dozen television crews camped outside. The guileless Jewell agreed to drive to the FBI Atlanta headquarters for his interview, as they suggested, to avoid the mob scene. Once there, the agents told him they wanted to tape the interview for a "training video" about how to interview first responders. He agreed. In fact, the taping was a ruse to allow the behavioral analysts to watch the interview. Although Freeh had signed off on the interview, when he found out that it was being taped in the FBI building, he ordered the agents to give Jewell a Miranda warning. They did, although they tried to pretend it was part of the training exercise. Finally Jewell got suspicious and talked to his lawyer. End of interview.

Next the FBI got a search warrant for Jewell's mother's home. Lloyd Erwin, on the task force, was assigned to help process the apartment. Jewell sat on the steps with his head in his hands while the agents turned the place inside out. It made the ATF man sick to his stomach to watch Jewell go through the ordeal. "I was ticked off on his behalf," said Erwin. "There was no call for what they did. They took his mama's plastic ware. They seized her videos." He paused, indignant. "They took *E. T.*!" They also took a roll of black electrical tape and a box of nails, even though none of the nails looked anything like the ones used in the bomb.

Agents investigated Richard Jewell for nearly three months but found no evidence connecting him to the bombing. Even then the FBI didn't apologize; all Jewell got was a letter from the U.S. attorney's office saying he was no longer a target of the investigation.

Lloyd Erwin had seen this kind of mistake before. So had Louis Freeh and several other key players in the CENTBOMB investigation. All of them had worked the Walter Leroy Moody case—known as VANPAC—and they had seen how a whole investigation can develop tunnel vision focusing on the wrong suspect.

Moody is a brilliant green-eyed psychopath who went on a bombing spree in the South in 1989. Right before Christmas, Moody sent booby-trapped packages containing pipe bombs through the mail, killing Robert Edward Robinson, an NAACP lawyer in Savannah, Georgia, and Robert Vance, a U.S. District judge in Birmingham, Alabama. To confuse investigators, Moody sent around letters claiming that the bombings were the responsibility of a group called "Americans for a Competent Federal Judicial System." One of those letters complained that civil rights rulings in the Eleventh Circuit—Judge Vance's court—had inspired black men to rape white women, among other things. Although Moody was a racist, his true motive was revenge against a court system he felt had treated him unfairly. Richard Thornburgh, the attorney general at the time, apparently fell for the ruse and became convinced the bombings were the work of a white supremacist group.

Lloyd Erwin, however, recognized a peculiar design in the VAN-PAC bombs: Instead of closing the pipe with threaded caps, this bomber placed a steel plate at each end, drilled holes in each plate, and ran a bolt between them through the pipe. He sealed in his gunpowder by tightening the bolt at each end and then welding them. Erwin remembered seeing that configuration only once before, in 1972, when a curious wife had been injured when she set off a pipe bomb in her husband's study. The husband was Moody, and after his wife's injury, he had spent three years in federal prison for explosives violations. He was now living in a small town in Georgia.

The ATF in Atlanta immediately started investigating Moody. But FBI headquarters in Washington discouraged its agents from following this lead because it did not conform to the white-racist theory. Meanwhile FBI investigators in Birmingham came up with another suspect, an eccentric, bigoted junk dealer from rural Alabama who had once sent angry letters to the Eleventh Circuit court using the same typewriter as the one used to write the VANPAC letters. Although the junk dealer claimed he had sold that typewriter to a young woman (it later turned out to be Moody's girlfriend), agents descended on Enterprise, Alabama, to raid his property in front of a throng of photographers and reporters. The humiliated junk dealer threatened to sue everyone, claiming his reputation was ruined.

The investigation stalled for months until the FBI director, William Sessions, appointed a special "inspector" from Washington to oversee and coordinate the VANPAC case. The attorney general's office, which decided it also needed to consolidate the efforts of five separate U.S. attorneys' offices, decided to send Louis Freeh to run the show. It was a wildly unpopular move, particularly in Birmingham, where Judge Vance was well-known and well-liked. Freeh, who was then a deputy U.S. attorney from the Southern District of New York, collected all the cases into one prosecution and tried it himself. Moody was convicted and given seven life sentences in federal court before going on to be tried for murder in Alabama state court. He was convicted and is now on death row.

During the investigation and trial, Freeh was impressed by three young FBI agents in Atlanta, John Behnke, Todd Letcher, and Tracey North. When he became FBI director, he brought first Behnke and then Letcher to headquarters to be his personal aides. When Freeh started reorganizing the CENTBOMB investigation he appointed Behnke and North as its administrative agents. Letcher was at his side in Washington, and in constant communication with his friends in Atlanta. It gave the director a back channel straight into the middle of the investigation, which was where he liked to be.

Without Richard Jewell, the task force investigators were down to interviewing the usual suspects: right-wing militia groups, previous bomb offenders, and cranks. Nothing checked out. By year's end they had run down every bomb component, sifted through every photo of the crowd, and couldn't come up with a viable lead. They would simply have to wait to see if someone who knew the bomber would give him up. Or wait until he struck again, and hope he made a mistake.

3

THE ARMY OF GOD

Just after 9 A.M. on January 16, 1997, ATF special agent Joe Kennedy was heading down I-85 on his way to the office in Atlanta when he heard a news report on the car radio: There had been an explosion at an abortion clinic in the suburb of Sandy Springs. Kennedy remembered that there was a clinic just off Roswell Road—he and Bill Briley from the Atlanta police bomb squad had given a bomb-threat class to the staff a few months before the Olympics. It had been part of an ATF outreach effort to prepare local groups that might be targeted by some of the extremists expected to be drawn to Atlanta that summer. Instead of continuing south to the ATF office, Kennedy took the beltway to the Sandy Springs exit and drove north, toward the suburbs.

There were only a few Fulton County police officers and a couple of fire trucks parked out front when Kennedy arrived at the scene. The Sandy Springs Professional Building was a white, three-story box with an arched Italianate facade, housing a mixed bag of medical facilities, law offices, and other small businesses. Kennedy could see that the device had been placed directly outside the Northside Family Planning Services office, shattering windows and causing some structural damage. The blast was in the rear of the building, so he pulled into the front parking lot. Kennedy, a young-looking thirty-three-year-old, put on his ATF windbreaker so the police didn't mistake him for some kind of rubbernecking kid trying to get into their crime scene. As soon as they saw the jacket, the cops and first responders came up to him, asking what to do next. One of the officers pointed out something unusual lying in the grass near the building, an eight-inch piece of metal that had been twisted and curled by the blast. Kennedy instructed a uniformed officer to make sure nobody moved this piece of evidence. Then, when Kennedy started helping the cops expand the secure perimeter around the scene, he noticed the chief of police and a Fulton County commissioner walking around the parking lot. A couple of sound trucks had pulled up with camera crews. Some FBI agents as well. Joe called in to his office, asking for every available agent to respond to Sandy Springs. And he needed someone high up, at least at the level of ASAC—assistant special agent in charge—to come out and handle the politicians and the media.

Soon everybody in the ATF office who could be spared was heading to the scene. About an hour had passed since the bomb had gone off and Kennedy was mainly concerned with preserving the evidence, and keeping the media and other unnecessary visitors out of the way. Joe was standing near his car, trying to work out a strategy with a police officer, when he saw a flash, and a sharp concussion boomed from the other side of the lot. Kennedy watched a plume of dirt shoot up into the air and a car lift up off the ground next to a Dumpster. At first he thought it was a car bomb. Everyone who wasn't already knocked over dropped belly-down on the pavement—including the police chief and the county commissioner—while soil and debris rained over them. Kennedy, an extremely methodical man, wasn't scared but he was irrationally angry that the noise and the commotion were interrupting his train of thought. He was thinking, "I'm trying to talk to this police officer about moving back that tape and would this *bomb* and everything just *stop* while I get this sorted out!"

It turned out that the bomb was not in the trunk of the car, but buried in the dirt beside the Dumpster. If the car hadn't blocked the shock wave and absorbed or deflected much of the shrapnel, Joe Kennedy and the other bystanders might have ended up with a lot worse than ringing ears and a face full of dirt. All told there were six injuries, including an ATF agent and an FBI agent with shrapnel wounds and one TV camera operator whose eardrums were ruptured by the sound of the blast.

Kennedy brushed himself off and shook his thoughts together. The bomber had clearly set a trap, placing a secondary device exactly where he knew law enforcement officers and first responders would gather. Kennedy found his supervisor, Steve Cordle, who was already at the scene. "Steve, let's call the NRT," Kennedy said.

"I'm already on it," said Cordle.

The FBI agents in the parking lot were also calling their bosses.

It was Jack Killorin's first day on the job as the new SAC of the ATF's Atlanta field division. He was carrying a paper cup of Starbucks coffee through the lobby when an agent came out to greet him at the elevator bank. "Mr. Killorin, welcome to Atlanta," she said. "There's just been an abortion clinic bombing." They went inside his new office and turned on the TV. A couple of local stations had sent live trucks to Sandy Springs and were soon broadcasting scenes of the second bombing. Killorin thought, "That one was for us." For a moment he had a vision of ending his first day visiting not with agents, but with their families. Then the word came back from the field that none of the injuries was critical. Just by luck.

Secondary devices like the one at Sandy Springs are pieces in a diabolical game of bait-and-switch: The first bomb lures police, fire, and ambulance workers to the site where a second device is timed to explode and kill them, too. This setup was quite common in IRA bombings in the United Kingdom, and is frequently used in Palestinian attacks in Israel. The U.S. military teaches the practice in counterinsurgency training. But the technique had rarely been employed on U.S. soil.

Killorin got on the phone with headquarters in Washington to bring them up to speed and to make sure he got the resources he needed for a major investigation. By noon he was able to break away and head to the scene. Killorin was a New Yorker, a Vietnam veteran, and like many ATF agents, he had started his career as a cop. But unlike your typical agent, his college degree was not in criminal justice but in English literature. After he joined the ATF in 1976, he worked the usual arson and bombing cases, along with some more exotic investigations, such as busting an American and South African gunrunning and rhino-horn smuggling syndicate. But Killorin often found himself rotating in and out of the agency's public affairs office because he had a way with people, and a way with words. It landed him in the middle of some of the ATF's most difficult operations. He was the agency's spokesman during Waco, and again for Oklahoma City. The experience gave him a certain long-range perspective, and a veteran's ability to sort through the bullshit to keep a case on track.

When Killorin arrived at Sandy Springs, a temporary command center had been set up in an office across the street. Woody Johnson, the FBI SAC in Atlanta, was already there. Johnson was the former commander of the FBI Hostage Rescue Team, and had maintained a stellar record until he got caught up in the Richard Jewell fiasco. Now he found himself in the middle of both an internal FBI and a congressional investigation As the top man on the ground, he had to take responsibility for the screwups, even the ones dictated from Washington.

Kent Alexander, the U.S. attorney in Atlanta, also visited the scene. He had already made some calls to the Justice Department in Washington, predicting the agencies would be battling each other to lead the investigation, and he offered to take over the case himself and then merge it with CENTBOMB. Everybody seemed ready for a classic turf battle.

As agents from both teams watched from the sidelines, Johnson strode up to Killorin and offered a handshake.

"Hi, I'm Woody Johnson and I understand we're fighting."

"Hi Woody, it's a pleasure to meet you. Let's make it a fair fight and tell me what it's about."

The two old pros smiled, each taking the other's measure. Killorin decided on the spot that Johnson was a man he could work with. SACs from both agencies have the authority to agree at the scene to form a task force and divide up the investigation themselves. If they can't agree, the dispute has to be settled in Washington, headquarters to headquarters, and sometimes goes all the way to the attorney general. And the last thing either of them wanted was Washington running the investigation.

The Salvation Army had come out and everybody ate salami sandwiches while they called their bosses and tried to figure out what was going on. Lloyd Erwin had been by with a couple of lab technicians to collect samples of explosive residues from the craters. With the lab so close, they already had results. This bomber used high explosives: nitro-glycerin dynamite, to be precise. And some pieces of shrapnel collected at the scene were cut nails, smaller than the ones used in the Centennial Park bomb, but similar enough to get everybody's attention.

It was getting late in the afternoon and the investigators were ready to close down the scene for the day. Johnson and Killorin put a meeting together in front of the key agents. Observing the rival agencies trying to take possession of a case can be like watching the face-off in a hockey game, where members of opposing teams slap at a dropped puck until one gains control and skates away. This time, to everyone's surprise, they skated off together. It simply required some negotiation.

Johnson reached into his pocket and showed Killorin a couple of nails. "We've got cut nails in this bomb, just like CENTBOMB," said Johnson. "So we think we should take over the investigation."

"Yeah but they're different sizes," said Killorin. "Four-penny nails, not nine-penny, so you can't say it's the same guy."

"It's still cut nails …"

"And your guy used smokeless powder. This guy used dynamite. Plus this one was a trap, with two devices. And we don't have a target link …"

It went on for a while, but in a good-natured way. The SACs finally agreed that there were enough significant differences in the bombings to keep the cases separate for the time being. They would use the NRT to finish processing the scene and send explosives evidence to the ATF lab in Atlanta. The FBI lab would process the evidence for items, like DNA, that were beyond its capacity. They would both deploy resources to the Sandy Springs task force. They would marry their lead management databases, Rapid Start and Ascme—Advanced Serial Case Management—and they would share information with the ongoing CENTBOMB Task Force.

The agents in attendance were told to work together and iron out their differences in the field or face "unpleasant consequences." Joe Kennedy was impressed with both bosses. They set the tone for the whole investigation.

Kennedy had been so busy and focused that he ignored his cell phone all morning and afternoon. When he finally checked in it was his wife calling—she had seen helicopter shots of the bombing on television, and saw his car parked near the crater. When she couldn't reach him she feared the worst. Now Joe had his own unpleasant consequences to face when he finally got home.

The new case was dubbed "TWINBOMB." At first there were ten or eleven agents, evenly divided among the FBI, ATF, and GBI, on each of three investigative teams. One focused on suspects, another on witnesses to the bombing, and a third on forensics. Joe Kennedy was made leader of the forensic team, charged with tracking down bomb components and other physical evidence. Most ATF agents get into the field because of their interest in firearms; Kennedy has always been a bomb guy. He is fascinated by everything mechanical and he loves figuring out how things work—particularly the explosive devices he encounters on the job. He is good with fine, detailed work, a talent that was honed when he worked his way through college as a watch mechanic in a Memphis, Tennessee, jewelry shop. There was supposed to be a specialist in bomb reconstruction working with the task force, but due to his unusual expertise—and his availability—Kennedy ended up with that job as well.

The TWINBOMB Task Force needed mock-ups of the Sandy Springs bombs as quickly as possible to see if anyone in local law enforcement had seen anything similar, and to show them what to look for if the bomber struck again. So Kennedy set up a bomb-making shop in the garage of the house he shared with his long-suffering young wife.

The TWINBOMB Task Force headquarters occupied a vacant floor below the ATF lab in an unremarkable mid-rise building in Atlanta's northern suburbs. It was part of an office park on the I-85 corridor that also discreetly housed several other federal agencies, including the IRS and the FBI. The ATF laboratory was humble by FBI standards, looking more like a chemistry lab at a small university than a big national facility. The equipment was a little older, but there were the same rows of computer screens and banks of humming, whirring, pulsating gas chromatographs, thermal energy analyzers, and other equipment designed to read the chemical signatures of various samples of explosives. Erwin already knew he was dealing with nitroglycerin dynamite because he had gotten a headache as soon as he arrived at Sandy Springs. The fancy equipment quickly confirmed this. Now he was trying to picture how the bomb was configured by examining where its components were blown by the blast, working with Joe Kennedy to piece it back together like a puzzle.

Every evening, task force members met to review the day's findings. The witness team reported that a patient at a methadone clinic in the Sandy Springs building had come forward to say he might have seen the bomber early that morning. When he arrived at 6 A.M. for his morning dose, a man wearing a track suit was hanging around by the Dumpster. He was carrying a backpack and a small shovel. The patient gave a description to an ATF sketch artist. One young couple had come to the substance abuse office for treatment, driving their newly acquired 1985 Nissan Pulsar. After the first bomb detonated, they moved the car around to the other side of the building. Theirs was the car that absorbed the brunt of the shrapnel from the second device, probably saving dozens of people, including agents. The car, of course, was totaled. A day or two later Jack Killorin was told that the owners were asking about their Nissan. They had put together $500 to buy it and it was their most valuable possession. Killorin decided to ask them if they would be willing to keep their ears open as they continued their treatment and report anything they might learn about the bombing. They agreed to register as informants, and he authorized giving them $500 as operating expenses. It seemed only fair.

Kennedy gave the forensic report. Within a short time he was able to report that both bombs were made of dynamite placed in metal ammunition cans, the kind that can be bought at any army surplus store. Erwin identified fragments of Baby Ben alarm clocks and D-cell batteries, which indicated a timed detonation. There were pieces of melted plastic containers, of unknown significance. He also noted that the "strange" piece of metal found on the grass wasn't part of the ammo cans and didn't seem to be part of a pipe. It appeared to have been cut with an oxy-acetylene torch. The difference between the two bombs was that the first device that exploded beneath the window of the clinic contained twenty-one half-pound sticks of dynamite and no shrapnel. The second device, the one placed to ambush police and first responders, was loaded with half as much dynamite but also contained four pounds of 4d flooring nails. The ammo can had been partially buried in the ground near the Dumpster, disguised, perhaps, with some plastic evergreen foliage. Most unusual: It appeared to have been wrapped around and around with more than a hundred feet of twisted iron wire, perhaps in a crude effort to keep someone from opening or tampering with it.

At the task force meeting, someone mentioned that it looked like safety wire that airplane mechanics used in their work. Kennedy called his brother, who worked as a mechanic for FedEx in Memphis. He recognized the twisted wire right away, telling him there was even a special set of pliers that mechanics used to create the double strands.

A week after the Sandy Springs bombing, Joe Kennedy caught the elevator with Lloyd Erwin in the lobby of the ATF lab building. On the way up, Erwin turned to him with a little twinkle in his eye.

"Remember that strange piece of metal I was telling you about?"

Kennedy nodded.

"It's a steel plate, and it's been cut with a torch."

"Whoa."

It was a signature of the Olympic Park bomber. It was too soon to tell what that meant, but Kennedy and Erwin were willing to bet the investigations would eventually be merged.

A little over a month later, on February 21, Joe Kennedy's supervisor called him at home just after 10:30 P.M. There had been another bombing, this time at a gay and lesbian nightclub in midtown Atlanta called the Otherside Lounge. There were injuries, but no fatalities.

Kennedy got there within an hour. The club was in a low-slung building with exterior wooden beams that gave it an Old English look. The scene was already taped off and the patrons and onlookers had been moved out of the area. A uniformed officer, aware of what happened at Sandy Springs, had looked around and found a second bomb hidden in some shrubbery above a stone retaining wall near the front entrance. This one was in a cheap nylon backpack. The Georgia Bureau of Investigation had brought out a bomb-handling robot to examine the bomb and try to render it safe. A majority of Kennedy's forensic group showed up to help secure the scene. The ATF National Response Team was on its way.

As the robot maneuvered into place, the forensic guys said a silent prayer that the bomb wouldn't explode. An intact device would provide a wealth of evidence to work with; it would be so much easier than sifting through burnt shards. The robot picked at the backpack for a good forty-five minutes, until, as Kennedy later told me, "They ended up attempting a technique that didn't work and the device functioned." Meaning the robot hit it with a blast of water and the bomb blew up. Kennedy remembers the bomb techs saying, "Okay, ready to shoot it, get ready." And the ATF guys, who were a little blasé after years of firing off explosives, just ducked down behind cars instead of getting behind a building. They were crouched down when—BOOM!—a humongous explosion shook the cars and rattled the windows for blocks. The ATF guys looked at each other, bemused. One said, "Wow. That was different."

The force of that blast sent one piece of metal almost a quarter of a mile through the air. It penetrated the roof of a vacant house and landed in the living room, where a real estate agent found it a couple of days later. It was a twisted chunk of steel, about the size of a CD and a quarter-inch thick: another steel plate. Although it was heftier than the eighth-inch plates found at Centennial Olympic Park and Sandy Springs, this new "directional plate" was enough to convince most of the agents on the task force that they were probably dealing with the same bomber.

If it was the same bomber, he was experimenting with different designs. The latest devices were also nitroglycerin dynamite, but packed in rectangular plastic cereal containers instead of ammo cans. He had used timers made from Baby Ben alarm clocks, but the batteries were different, and the shrapnel was ordinary wire nails instead of cut nails.

A forensic team was trying to track down the unusual cut nails, to see if they could match them to a specific batch and narrow down where the bomber got them. The FBI lab was examining the chemical composition of the plates to try to trace them to a steel manufacturer. Joe Kennedy was checking into any reports of stolen dynamite in the southeastern states. There was one particularly suspicious large theft of nitroglycerin dynamite from the Austin Powder Company in Asheville, North Carolina.

* * *

A few days after the Otherside bombing, the bomber introduced himself. Four news organizations in Atlanta—Reuters news service; NBC News; the local CBS affiliate, WSB-TV; and the *Atlanta Journal-Constitution* newspaper—all received envelopes printed in odd block letters from the same fictional return address: 170 Eighth Street, Atlanta, GA 30309. They were all postmarked on February 23 at the same North Metro postal station in Atlanta. Three of the four envelopes indicated that the contents contained a "NEWS TIP." Since these were the days before you might get a dose of anthrax along with your news tips, each of these letters was opened in the mailroom. All the letters were written on lined paper in felt-tipped pen with the same lettering and nearly identical messages, down to the misspellings, bad grammar, and weird punctuation. They read:

THE BOMBING'S IN SANDY SPRING'S AND MIDTOWN WERE CARRIED-OUT BY UNITS OF THE ARMY OF GOD.

YOU MAY CONFIM WITH THE F.B.I. THE SANDY SPRINGS DEVICE'S GELATIN-DYNAMITE-POWER SOURCE 6 VOLT D BATTERY BOX DURACELL BRAND, CLOCK TIMERS. THE MIDTOWN DEVICES ARE SIMILAR EXCEPT NO AMMO CANS, TUPPERWARE CONTAINERS INSTEAD. POWER SOURCE SINGLE 6 VOLT LANTERN BATTERIES DIFFERENT SHRAPNEL, REGULAR NAILS INSTEAD OF CUT NAILS.

THE ABORTION WAS THE TARGET OF THE FIRST DEVICE. THE MURDER OF 3.5 MILLION CHILDREN EVERY YEAR WILL NOT BE "TOLERATED." THOSE WHO PARTICIPATE IN ANYWAY IN THE MURDER OF CHILDREN MAY BE TARGETED FOR ATTACK. THE ATTACK THEREFORE SERVES AS A WARNING: ANYONE IN OR AROUND FACILITIES THAT MURDER CHILDREN BAY BECOME VICTIMS OF RETRIBUTION. THE NEXT FACILITY TARGETED MAY NOT BE EMPTY.

THE SECOND DEVICE WAS AIMED AT AGENT OF THE SO-CALLED FEDERAL GOVERNMENT I.E. A.T.F. F.B.I. MARSHALL'S E.T.C. WE DECLARE AND WILL WAGE <u>TOTAL WAR</u> ON THE UNGODLY COMMUNIST REGIME IN NEW YORK AND YOUR LEGASLATIVE— BUREAUCRATIC LACKEY'S IN WASHINGTON. IT IS YOU WHO ARE RESPOSIBLE AND PRESIDE OVER THE MURDER OF CHILDREN AND ISSUE THE POLUCY ON UNGODLY PREVERSION THAT'S DESTROYING OUR PEOPLE. WE ILL TARGET ALL FACILITIES AND PER-SONELL OF THE FEDERAL GOVERNMENT.

THE ATTACK IN MIDTOWN WAS AIMED AT THE SODOMITE BAR (THE OTHERSIDE). WE WILL TAR-GET SODOMITES, THERE ORGANIZATIONS, AND ALL THOSE WHO PUSH THERE AGENDA.

IN THE FUTURE WHERE INNOCENT PEOPLE MAY BECOME THE PRIMARY CASUALTIES, A WARNING PNONE CALL WILL BE PLACED TO ONE OF THE NEWS BUREAU'S OR 911. GENERALLY A 40 MINUTE WARNING WILL BE GIVEN. TO CONFIRM THE AUTHENTICITY OF THE WARNING A CODE WILL BE GIVEN WITH THE WARN AND STATEMENT.

THE CODE FOR OUR UNIT IS 4-1-9-9-3.

"DEATH TO THE NEW WORLD ORDER"

The FBI quickly confiscated the letters and extracted promises from the news organizations not to divulge the descriptions of the bombs or the code that identified the bomber. The letters, of course, provided a field day for every kind of evidence analyst in the federal government. But there seemed to be little useful information. The only fingerprints found belonged to employees who handled the letters. Atlanta's North Metro station processed mail from the whole of northern Georgia, so it was impossible to know where the letters were posted. The letter writer had accurately named the components in the Sandy Springs and Oth-erside bombs. Those details had never leaked to the public; only the investigators and the bomber himself would know them. But there was no mention of the Centennial Olympic Park blast. Was he deliberately misleading them? Or were there two separate bombers? It wasn't impossible: The Army of God had been exclusively associated with anti-abortion violence, which seemed to have nothing to do with the Olympics.

The identifying code, 4-1-9-9-3, seemed to be as significant as the antigovernment, antigay, anti-abortion rhetoric in the letters. April 19, 1993, was the day the compound at Waco burned to the ground. Two years later, to the day, Timothy McVeigh blew up the Murrah Federal Building in Oklahoma City. And "Death to the New World Order" was a rallying cry for a broad spectrum of antigovernment, anti-Semitic fanatics who believed that the United States was controlled by a Zionist Occupation Government bent on destroying the white race. That generic sign-off, in combination with the Waco code, was a powerful indication that the bomber's agenda was not just saving babies and making the world safe for homophobes.

The profilers at the Behavioral Science Unit had been edged out of the investigation since the mistake with Richard Jewell, so Park Elliott Dietz, a highly regarded forensic psychiatrist, was brought in to dissect the letters and work up an alternate profile of the bomber. Among his many observations, Dietz concluded that the writer had paranoid tendencies, and that he was likely acting on his own and not as part of a group. There were no "units" of the Army of God, just a lone wolf looking for validation. It's a truism of profiling: Bombers who write notes describing themselves as "we" and claiming to be part of an organization or cell almost never are. The Unabomber claimed to be a group called "FC." So did Roy Moody, with his "Americans for a Competent Federal Judicial System."

Jack Killorin didn't want to dismiss any possibilities, but so far the evidence pointed to a lone bomber. There was nothing in the bomber's delivery and technique that required a group. And the rhetoric in the letters didn't sound like a joint communiqué; it sounded like one guy with an ax to grind. The Waco code was the clincher. Killorin thought the bomber was most likely a guy who hated the government and wanted to lure federal agents into a trap, to strike at the organizations that protected the people he hated. The Olympics, abortion clinics, and gay bars: what better targets to attract the feds and get a shot at them.

He didn't buy the Army of God business, either. The Army of God wasn't really an army or even a militia; just a loose association of anti-abortion extremists who believed that violence was justified to save unborn babies. Killorin had been a public affairs spokesperson for the ATF in the mid-1980s when the agency was intensively tracking the alarming increase in bombings and arsons at women's reproductive health care centers, and he had seen individual bombers and arsonists use the term "Army of God" as a straw man in the past.

The first time anyone heard about the supposed Army was in 1982 when a fanatic named Don Benny Anderson and two accomplices, claiming to be members of the Army of God, kidnapped a doctor and his wife in Edwardsville, Illinois. After being convicted of the kidnapping and two clinic bombings in Virginia and Florida, Killorin said, Anderson admitted he had made up the group to scare the hell out of his enemies. The concept was catchy. In the mid-1980s an Army of God manual started circulating among militant anti-abortion types, with tips on how to burn and bomb clinics. Michael Bray, one of the most prolific clinic torchers in the D.C. area, signed his handiwork "A.O.G."

Although the Justice Department had convened a federal grand jury to investigate the Army of God "membership," the grand jury had disbanded in 1996 without coming up with enough evidence to launch a conspiracy prosecution. But the Army of God was still very much on the radar of the ATF and FBI, and there had been recent indications that fringe elements of the militant anti-abortion movement were merging with violent militia groups. The rhetoric of the bomber's letter and its identifying "code" suggested he might subscribe to just such a hybrid ideology, without actually belonging to a group.

In September 1997 the three investigations were finally merged into the Atlanta Bomb Task Force under an FBI inspector named Woody Enderson. There were still leads to follow, but within a few months it was clear that the witness and suspect investigations were going nowhere. The most productive activity took place in the teams of agents who were scrutinizing and indexing over 22,000 photographs and more than 2,000 videos—frame by frame—of the events surrounding the Olympic Park bombing. Enderson started telling his colleagues a little joke. "The good news is that we have 50,000 witnesses," he'd say. "And the bad news is that we have 50,000 witnesses."

In November the task force decided to hold a press conference to show the public mock-ups of the Atlanta bombs, along with photographs of their components. It was hoped that someone would recognize matching items sitting around a friend or relative's garage and turn him in. A $100,000 reward was offered for information leading to the bomber's arrest and conviction.

Joe Kennedy flew up to Washington, D.C., to answer the toll-free hotline after the press conference. There were very few calls, and nobody had anything useful to say.

4

WITNESS

The city of Birmingham, Alabama, lacks the magnolia-scented charm of older Southern cities. The place didn't even exist before the Civil War, and any lingering vapors in the air carry the smell of coal smoke and money. Birmingham was invented in 1871 by a group of real estate speculators who bet that two railroad lines intersecting in the rural Jones Valley of northern Alabama would spawn a new industrial mecca for the reconstructed South. After a few fits and starts, their gamble paid off. Birmingham sat beside or very near deposits of the three key ingredients needed to make pig iron: limestone, iron ore, and coal. The fledgling town was quickly transformed into an iron-making center to rival Pittsburgh.

The city fathers soon nicknamed Birmingham "The Magic City" to celebrate its booming prosperity. They commissioned an Italian sculptor to fashion an iron statue of Vulcan, the god of fire, to represent the city's iron industry at the 1904 St. Louis World's Fair. It was billed as the world's largest cast metal sculpture, standing fifty-six feet tall. Apparently art critics of the day didn't mind the statue's grotesque dimensions, with its cartoonish head and oversized arm holding aloft a freshly forged spear. Eventually Vulcan was returned to Birmingham and installed in his own little park on the top of Red Mountain, an iron-streaked ridge south of the city, looking over the soot-choked valley below.

In the early 1970s foreign competition, mismanagement, and tighter environmental regulations finally shut down the giant furnaces for good.

By then the Magic City had earned another nickname, "Bombingham," for the spate of civil rights era bombings that shook black neighborhoods with alarming regularity. The section northeast of downtown became known as "Dynamite Hill."

By 1998 the political upheaval had more or less passed into memory. A civil rights institute stood next to the Sixteenth Street Baptist Church where four young girls had been killed in a Ku Klux Klan bombing in 1963. The city once famous for images of marchers being blasted by fire hoses and torn at by police dogs now had a black police chief and a black mayor. Most of the white upper middle class had fled to the suburbs, as they had in most cities. But there were still jobs downtown, provided by a new health care service–based economy and a huge expansion of the University of Alabama at Birmingham.

The UAB campus stretches along the base of Red Mountain in an area of the city called "Southside." The main artery, University Avenue, runs east to west, crossed by numbered streets stretching north into the downtown business district and south into the residential neighborhoods that cling to the slope below Vulcan Park. In the winter of 1998, Tenth Avenue South was a real estate no-man's-land wedged between the UAB Hospital complex and the condo zone. It was scattered with parking lots, dormitories, quick-lunch restaurants, and small office buildings housing the businesses often found around big hospitals: chiropractors, physical therapists, family dental practices, and, at the corner of Tenth and Seventeenth Street, the New Woman All Women clinic, which, three days a week, provided abortions.

The clinic occupied a small painted brick building set a few yards back from the sidewalks. A wine red awning hung over the reinforced front door; otherwise the building seemed unadorned and vulnerable. In a time when other clinics that provided abortions were—as many still are—hidden behind heavy steel gates and thick privacy hedges, the New Woman stuck out from the steep hillside like a purple and white thumb. The lower parking lot was open to the street, and the two patches of lawn that flanked the front walkway were enclosed only by knee-high landscape fencing. There wasn't even a security camera, a fixture in most clinics since the rash of firebombings and shootings earlier that decade.

One security measure the clinic owners did take was hiring off-duty policemen to guard the building during business hours.

The guard who was there on the morning of January 28, 1998, Robert "Sande" Sanderson, was filling in for David Hale, who had been out on administrative leave from his police job. Like many Birmingham cops, they both moonlighted second and third jobs to make ends meet and put a little aside. The night before, Hale had called Sanderson to tell him he was cleared to go back to work and so Hale could take the clinic shift for him Thursday morning. But Sande asked if he could finish out the week for the extra pay. No problem, said Hale.

The off-duty job was convenient for Sanderson, who worked in the Southside precinct. There were some regular anti-abortion protesters who showed up to shout at the staff and the patients on days, like today, when abortions were performed. But there hadn't been much trouble here in years. There were occasional threats; one morning, a mysterious box of chocolates had shown up on the front step, and when the bomb squad X-rayed it, they found little plastic babies embedded in each piece of candy. But there hadn't been any overt violence or attempts to blockade the clinic since the Freedom of Access to Clinic Entrances (FACE) Act in 1994 made it a federal crime for protesters to get too close to the reproductive health care facilities, or to physically accost patients or staff. Sanderson's job, along with the other off-duty cops who worked the three abortion clinics in Birmingham, was to maintain a presence, make sure the doctors and nurses got inside safely, make sure everybody outside played by the rules.

Sanderson finished up his overnight tour at 7 A.M., and grabbed a coffee before heading over to the clinic. He was thirty-five years old, with nine years on the force, a pleasant, square-faced man with brown hair growing thin on top. Everybody knew him as an all-around good guy, the kind of cop who visited sick children in the hospital, did a lot of volunteer work. Because of his community service, in 1996 he was chosen as one of the runners carrying the Olympic torch through Birmingham on its way to the Centennial Games in Atlanta. Six months later, he was injured trying to catch a woman who jumped from the second floor of a burning apartment building. He was back on the job a few days later, while moonlighting weekends at a nightclub and days at the clinic.

When Sanderson parked his minivan in the staff lot next to the front entrance, a maroon SUV with out-of-town plates pulled into the lower parking lot off Tenth Avenue S. The SUV carried a mother, a father, and their teenage daughter. This was a difficult and awkward morning for them that had become even more difficult when they arrived an hour early and Minzor Chadwick, a regular protester, started bellowing at them to spare their baby. They had fled to another lot farther up Seventeenth Street, above the Domino's Pizza franchise and away from Chadwick, waiting for someone to show up at the clinic. No one in the car could remember seeing the other man waiting in that lot, probably standing behind one of the big oak trees, wearing a baseball cap and a field jacket and carrying a backpack.

The father got out of the SUV and walked over to talk to Officer Sanderson. Sande told him the clinic wouldn't open until 8 A.M., but that someone would be by soon to let him in. While they were talking a nurse named Emily Lyons pulled up in her BMW convertible and parked next to the maroon car. Like Sanderson, she wasn't supposed to be there that morning. But another nurse had just given birth and Emily was filling in for her, opening the clinic. Lyons was forty-one years old and had long auburn hair pulled back in a ponytail. She had a husband at home and two daughters living with her ex. Despite the cold morning air, she wore only pink scrubs and a blue sweatshirt as she headed up the walkway to pick up the morning newspaper. She remembers nothing of what happened that day, but the father recalled passing her on the steps as he returned to his car; she seemed to be pointing Sanderson toward a patch of odd greenery next to the entrance path. Sanderson walked up to the object, which looked to the witness like an upended planter. The policeman took out his ASP, a retractable nightstick, and leaned over for a better look.

Minzor Chadwick felt the blast before he heard it. A hot wave of air, like a sudden desert sandstorm, peppered him with grit and shards of concrete and just about knocked him off his feet. He ducked behind a parked car, thinking that somebody, one of the pro-abortionists, was trying to kill him. Because he was legally blind, he couldn't see much of what was happening around him. But when he picked himself up he could make out the crumpled body of Officer Sanderson slumped by the fence. He began to run.

Across Tenth Avenue, a nursing student was sitting in her parked car, waiting for her first morning classes to begin. She was watching the uniformed policeman as he bent over something along the clinic walkway. He seemed to be lifting up some plant, looking underneath it, when there was a flash of light and smoke and a loud crack and the policeman's body went sailing through the air. She jumped out of the car and ran toward the smoke and rubble.

The family in the SUV was also watching as the bomb exploded, pelting the area with dirt and shrapnel, tossing the policeman fifteen feet and dropping him in a heap right in front of them. The father backed up and tore out of there as fast as he could.

John Hicks, a student and a trained EMT, was walking near the UAB dorms when he saw the flash and felt the air rock him backward. He started to run up Tenth Avenue to see if there were victims he could help. As he passed a student parking lot, out of the corner of his eye he saw a long-haired man wearing a backpack walking across a small park away from the explosion. He thought it was odd that the man seemed uninterested in the mayhem behind him, but he quickly forgot about it as he reached the scene. A sickening, burnt smell hung in the cold morning air. There was a charred body on the ground, someone who seemed beyond help. Emily Lyons was lying on her back next to the door. Her sweatshirt had been blown over her head, so Hicks and another nurse who arrived at the scene cut it off her body and started to assess her injuries. Her face was burned and her eyes were damaged. Blood seeped from dozens of puncture wounds all over her. The skin and flesh had been blown off her shins, exposing her bones. There was a gaping hole in her abdomen. But she had a pulse and was breathing on her own. He shouted, "This one's alive!"

Several police officers arrived at the scene and tried to make him leave, but Hicks refused to move until an ambulance got there. A fire department rescue unit pulled up several minutes later. The EMTs took one look at Emily Lyons and radioed the emergency room at UAB hospital, only eight blocks away.

If there was anything lucky about this morning, it was that the head of every surgical specialty in the hospital was at a meeting near the emergency room when the bomb went off. By the time Lyons was wheeled in the door, the doctors were scrubbed and ready to dive in. They each took a section of her body and went to work. Even among all those skilled doctors, she was so critically injured that her prognosis was guarded at best.

The nurse who witnessed the bombing had found Sande Sanderson, although he was hard to recognize now. The force of the blast had blown him out of his shoes and torn off his uniform, leaving only his service belt around his waist. His skin was ripped by shrapnel and blackened by the heat of the explosion. His right arm had been blown off and a leg was almost amputated. The shock wave had ruptured his eyes and peeled back his face and scalp. A bomb fragment had torn away part of his skull, pushing out some brain matter. And yet, when the woman knelt next to him, his chest was still heaving, as if he was trying to draw breath. She picked up his hand and held it tight. Later she would tell the investigators she had been determined not to let him die alone. But eventually she, too, was evacuated from the area.

Bob Sorrell, a battalion chief with the Birmingham FD, arrived at the scene just as the rescue unit was pulling up. He immediately recognized the acrid smell of explosives and ordered the area cleared of all civilians and nonessential personnel who were flocking to the site to gape at the destruction. Just one month earlier the ATF had circulated a videotape to fire and police departments across the Southeast warning them to be wary of secondary devices at any bomb scene. The tape had featured, by way of example, the double bombings of the women's clinic in Sandy Springs, Georgia, and the Otherside Lounge in Atlanta.

While the medics loaded Lyons on to a gurney, Sorrell had to decide whether there were other viable candidates for rescue. He walked over to the victim lying by the fence. He couldn't tell the victim's race or sex. After a stint in the Marine Corps and more than twenty years on the job responding to everything from industrial accidents to car wrecks to knife fights, Sorrell still had never seen anything this bad. There were still some "sympathetic nervous responses," as Sorrell later put it, but he could tell the case was hopeless. News helicopters were starting to circle overhead, and he remembers placing a blanket over the body. It was what he would have wanted if he was the one lying there in the open.

Jermaine Hughes was taking his clothes out of the dryers on the first floor of the Rast Hall dormitory when he heard a sudden BOOM. He rushed to the window and saw a cloud of blue-white smoke coming from behind Domino's Pizza. His first thought was that the restaurant had blown up. Then he saw a white man walking deliberately away from the explosion, not even looking back to see what had happened. Everybody else in the area was either running toward the blast or staring in that direction. The man, he later told investigators, was about six-foot-one, 175 pounds, between the ages of thirty-two and forty-two, with long brown hair covered by a black baseball cap, wearing a thigh-length coat and dark pants, and carrying an empty black knapsack. As soon as he crossed the grassy park between Sixteenth and Seventeenth streets, he started walking faster, almost running. This made Hughes, an eighteen-year-old pre-med student at UAB, even more suspicious. "That guy ain't right," he thought, and decided to follow him.

When Hughes reached the parking lot in front of the dorm, the long-haired white guy was still in sight. Hughes checked his pocket and found his car keys, luckily still there from the night before. So he ran to his car and it started right up, also lucky, because the transmission had been leaking. Hughes drove around in the direction the suspicious man was heading, and sure enough, he spotted him on Sixteenth Street, walking south, up a steep hill. "I was thinking, this is good, this is good," Hughes remembered, and he followed for four blocks, hanging back so the man wouldn't notice him. But the man never looked back. Hughes drove a little closer as the man turned left into a small side street. He noticed the guy pulling something out of his jacket pocket, and at first he thought it was a gun, but then saw it was something "crinkled up" in his hand, like a plastic bag. Hughes watched from the street as the man ducked between two buildings in a small apartment complex. Hughes decided to drive around to the front of the building, and spotted the guy coming out onto the sidewalk. He looked different. He was no longer wearing the jacket, the cap was gone, and his hair was shorter, dark brown and flattened down. Now he was sporting large dark sunglasses and carrying a blue plastic shopping bag stuffed with something that didn't look too heavy.

The residential street was fairly empty, and Hughes was afraid he'd be spotted if he kept tailing the man. So he drove past him, pulled over at a stop sign, and pretended to have car trouble. He jumped out of the driver's seat and popped the hood, rummaging around like he was checking the engine while he watched the man walk toward him on the other side of the street. The man glanced in Hughes's direction but seemed not to register him: just another black kid with a broken-down car. Hughes got a look at him, but all he could remember about the face was those big black sunglasses "looming at me."

At this point, Hughes decided he needed to call 911, but he didn't have a cell phone. He flagged a young guy in a car and told him to call the cops, there was a bombing and that's probably the man who did it. But the guy shook his head—"Ah man, I'm late for class"—and drove away.

So Hughes got back in his car and followed some more, watched as the guy turned up Fifteenth Avenue S., a wooded residential street at the base of Red Mountain. He thought about knocking on a door to call for help, but he figured no one would open the door to a black guy with an old car—they'd think they were being robbed. He decided to risk stopping another car, just put on his brakes and jumped out with his hands up to show he wasn't armed, basically begging the woman to roll down her window. He tried to explain the situation but he couldn't seem to convince her to stop somewhere and call the cops for him, so he got back in his car. (As it turned out, she did stop to report the incident.) Now he had lost the man. He drove around looking for another ten, fifteen minutes, then gave up and decided to park somewhere and make the call himself.

* * *

On January 29 Doug Jones, a Clinton appointee as U.S. attorney for the Northern District of Alabama, had been in office only four months. That morning he had agreed to meet a reporter from the *Birmingham News* to give an interview about his first impressions of the job. He was driving to the meeting at the Original House of Pancakes, a landmark on Birmingham's Southside, when the deejay on his classic rock station ended the newsbreak by announcing "traffic problems with injuries" on Tenth Avenue S. Minutes later the deejay broke into the music program to say it was a bombing at an "abortion clinic." Jones was only minutes from the site. He called his office from his car phone and told his first assistant U.S. attorney, Bud Henry, that they needed to call the emergency hotline to the Justice Department in D.C., then get in touch with the ATF and the FBI. "I'm going to the scene," he said.

It was about 7:45 when he arrived. Seventeenth Street was already taped off with yellow crime scene ribbon, so Jones parked and ducked under it. He immediately ran into Lionel Wilson, a police officer he knew. Wilson seemed shaken.

"What have we got?"

"A police officer down. He's dead. And a nurse who probably won't make it."

Jones looked over toward the clinic and saw Sanderson's covered remains still crumpled by the iron fence. It was the most chilling thing he had ever seen. He instinctively started walking toward the body when an agent grabbed him by the shoulder and said, "We've got to move you back, there could be a secondary device." The fire department was still searching surrounding buildings and securing the Ronald McDonald House across the street. Protocol says that the fire department controls any incident until all victims are evacuated, then it becomes a crime scene. As the chief of operations, Bob Sorrell was still trying to keep the police and federal agents to a minimum, and he was the only one who knew the full extent of the damage.

When he was satisfied that there were no more victims, Sorrell started walking down Tenth Avenue, where fire trucks were parked, when a young man in a windbreaker with some kind of letters on it—the chief can't remember which kind—came rushing up and said, "Are you in charge?"

"Who wants to know?"

He pulled out a federal badge and started waving it. Sorrell said, "That's cute but who are you?"

"If you're in charge here I need you to talk to my boss." He handed him a cell phone, and Sorrell heard a husky female voice on the other end.

"I have just three questions," she said.

"Go ahead," said the chief.

"First, was it an explosion?"

"Yes."

"Was it an abortion clinic?"

"Yes."

"Were there injuries or fatalities, including a police officer?"

"Yes there were."

"Thank you, we'll take it from here," she said.

He was handing the phone back to the agent when he heard her voice again. Thinking she had another question, he held it to his ear and overheard her say, "Mr. President, did you understand that?"

"That was the attorney general," said the agent in the windbreaker. "You boys are about to be covered with feds."

Within hours of the blast, President Clinton issued a statement condemning the attack on the abortion clinic in Birmingham and the murder of an off-duty police officer. He announced that federal agents were already at the scene to help local authorities bring the bomber to justice.

Jermaine Hughes took Twentieth Street South, a four-lane highway that cut over Red Mountain along Vulcan Park, looking for a public telephone. He stopped at a McDonald's on the downward slope, and used the office phone to call 911.

At first it did not go well.

A tape of the call shows that Hughes was a bit flustered, trying to explain what had happened in a few sentences.

"Hello! This is really important. You know that explosion down-town?"

"Yes," said the operator.

"I seen a guy walking from that direction and he had a wig on … and I was like, 'what was that explosion?' You know I walked outside …"

"What kind of wig?" snapped the operator, sounding like an impatient shopkeeper with a difficult customer.

"And this guy … and he was …"

"Long wig, short wig?"

"He had a long wig but …"

"What color?"

"The wig was like brown color … But then he took … I was following him…."

"Was he white or black?" she demanded.

"He's … he's a white guy."

"What did he have on?"

"Say again?"

"What did he have on?"

"I … oh, God … I was following him and ah, first he had on flannel or something, I'm not exactly sure …"

It went on for a while, with the 911 operator and the witness talking past each other. At one point the woman scolded Hughes, "You can't even remember what he had on?"

"Ma'am! Ah …"

"You cannot remember a clothing description?"

"No … I don't remember clothes. I'm kinda exasperated right now …"

You could hear the frustration building in Hughes's voice. He lost the connection and called back, still trying to convince someone to believe him when suddenly he saw a man walking down Twentieth Street who looked familiar.

"I got him, I got him!"

"Where is he?" said the operator.

"I got him, I think this is him!"

"Is he on foot?"

"Yes, he's on foot ... He has black glasses on ... He's walking into the woods toward Vulcan ..."

Another customer at the restaurant, a lawyer named Jeff Tickal, looked up from his breakfast and saw the man, too. Tickal started calling out a description for Hughes to give the 911 operator. The man had changed his appearance again. Now he was wearing a green and black plaid shirt, jeans, and brown boots. The blue shopping bag was gone but the black backpack he was carrying now looked full. Hughes and Tickal watched the suspect turn off along a small trail and enter a wooded area.

"I can't see him now," Hughes told the operator. "I can't believe I'm standing here and there's not a cop here by now!"

"They're on the way. They'll be there in just a minute," she said, more respectful now. "Don't hang up!"

By now Tickal had decided to jump into his car and see if he could find the man when he came out of the woods. He was already gone when a patrol car pulled up to McDonald's and met Hughes. The two police officers crossed the road on foot to follow the suspect's trail, then drove up the hill to the Vulcan statue, where the suspect seemed to be heading. Hughes hopped into his car to join the search.

Meanwhile, Tickal drove along Valley Avenue, a divided residential roadway that ran perpendicular to Twentieth Street, along the base of the mountain. After a few blocks he decided he had driven as far as the man could have walked if he was heading that way. So he pulled into a side street to turn around—and there was the same guy, loading something into the camper shell of a gray Nissan pickup that was backed up to the woods. Tickal turned around as the truck pulled out and followed it to Valley Avenue. When it stopped, he wrote down the license plate number on his McDonald's coffee cup. It was a North Carolina tag: KND1117. Tickal followed the Nissan east on Valley Avenue, back to Twentieth Street South, where he spotted the police cruiser and stopped to report the truck. Meanwhile, Jermaine Hughes had the same idea as Tickal and was driving west on Valley Avenue and spotted Tickal's blue car right behind a gray truck. It made him glance at the driver of the truck; it looked like the same guy again. He pulled a U-turn on Valley and drove up alongside the Nissan and took a good look at the man in profile. Hughes was sure it was him. He dropped back again and wrote down the license plate number, KND1117. He tried to tail the truck but the Nissan quickly changed lanes and turned right. When Hughes tried to follow across traffic, the other drivers started honking and he was forced left, back toward McDonald's. ,

Both Hughes and Tickal separately reported the tag number to police. They spent the rest of the day repeating their stories to Birmingham detectives and FBI agents.

By midday the Alabama State Police and the Birmingham Police Department had issued a BOLO—be on the lookout—for the Nissan truck, along with a description of the driver. The vehicle was a 1989 pickup registered to Eric Robert Rudolph, a white male, age thirty-one, five feet, eleven inches tall, with brown hair and blue eyes, whose driver's license listed his residence as 30 Allen Avenue, Asheville, North Carolina. The vehicle had not been reported stolen.

The FBI office in Birmingham relayed a request for one of the resident agents in Asheville to ride over to that address and see if he could find Mr. Rudolph and have a talk with him.

5

A GREAT HAIL OUT OF HEAVEN

A sheville is the closest thing western North Carolina has to a real city. Tucked in the eastern furrows of the Great Smoky Mountains, with a population of 69,000, Asheville has become a trendy mountain boomtown whose upscale restaurants, coffee bars, and head shops have earned it the nickname "Berkeley East." But only a generation ago the place was a bucolic backwater, best known as the site of the colossal Biltmore estate, former playground of the Vanderbilt family, and the hometown depicted in Thomas Wolfe's *Look Homeward, Angel.*

In the late winter of 1998, Jim Russell was one of a handful of resident FBI agents in Asheville. His beat covered the whole western tip of the state, and he spent most of his time investigating violent crimes on the nearby Cherokee Indian reservation or on federal properties such as the Blue Ridge Parkway and the hundreds of thousands of acres of national forests in the region. It was an interesting, if remote, posting for Russell, a thirty-nine-year-old Chicago native with seven years with the bureau. Being a resident agent gave him the chance to wear a number of hats, and in addition to being an investigator, he was attached to the FBI SWAT team in Charlotte and was studying to become a certified bomb technician. All this extra training would be put to good use, starting on the afternoon of January 29 when Russell got the call from Birmingham to run down the owner of a suspicious vehicle.

The address on Eric Rudolph's driver's license turned out to be a sixty-four-unit apartment complex called Skyland Heights, and he did not live there. Russell asked the manager to check her records and found that a Patricia Rudolph had once been a tenant, and on her rental agreement she had left an emergency contact in the nearby town of Hendersonville. A man named Keith Rhodes answered the phone. Yes, he knew Eric Rudolph, he told Russell. His wife, Maura, was Eric's sister. And he wasn't surprised to hear that a federal agent was looking for him.

Rhodes agreed to meet for an interview in front of a bicycle shop in Asheville. What he told Russell that evening began a narrative whose core elements would come to define Eric Rudolph through his fugitive years and long after: His brother-in-law was a secretive loner, Rhodes told the FBI. He had never married and didn't seem to have any friends. Eric was unemployed, but had worked sporadically as a carpenter. He had a habit of dropping by the Rhodes house without warning once or twice a month, but nobody knew where Eric lived or how they might contact him. He had said he was staying in Tennessee in a place that had no phone, but Rhodes suspected he had moved back to the Topton area in far western North Carolina where the family once owned a house.

Eric Rudolph was born at home in the small coastal community of Merritt Island, Florida, on September 19, 1966, the fifth of six children. He had four brothers, Damian, Daniel, Joel, and Jamie, and one sister, Maura. His father, Robert Rudolph, had died of cancer in 1981; his mother, Patricia, and the younger children moved to North Carolina soon after his death. Bob Rudolph had been a carpenter and airline mechanic with TWA. Pat Rudolph was a former nun novitiate who had left the Catholic Church and gravitated to fundamentalist Christian and charismatic sects. She had recently returned to Florida to live in a mobile home park.

Eric was an ex-army paratrooper who was disappointed when he didn't make it into Special Forces. His life, said Rhodes, seemed to go sour after he'd left the army eight years ago. He was antigovernment, but his brother-in-law didn't remember him belonging to any group. He knew Eric owned some guns, but Keith had never observed him carrying one.

The last time Maura and Keith had seen Eric was the previous Saturday. He'd shown up unannounced, wanting to watch one of their sons play basketball, but he'd missed the game and left after about an hour.

Rhodes noticed Eric had a few days' growth of beard and smelled like he hadn't bathed for a while. He was driving a gray Nissan truck with a camper shell.

Russell made arrangements for a pair of agents to interview Maura the next day; others were dispatched through the Birmingham office to track down Rudolph's mother and his brothers, who were scattered across several different states. By then it was full dark and a contingent of federal and state agents had gathered in an Asheville motel room to come up with a strategy to find Rudolph. It was decided that Russell would drive to the Andrews area the next morning and start knocking on doors, trying to locate Rudolph or at least learn something about him.

By now the bureau had run an extensive background check on Rudolph. Outside of his current driver's license and an expired one from Tennessee, his vehicle registration, and an eight-year-old military record, Rudolph had left no paper trail. He owned no property, paid no taxes, never voted, had no bank accounts, and never used credit cards. He didn't have a criminal record, not even a speeding ticket. He was about as close to a phantom as a citizen of the United States can get.

Back in Birmingham the usual team of experts was combing through the crime scene, gathering forensic evidence. Since Lloyd Erwin and Joe Kennedy were both members of the ATF's regional response team, they were both called to the scene from Atlanta. When they pulled up in front of the New Woman clinic that afternoon, a 1,000-foot perimeter had already been taped off around the site. Officer Sanderson's body had been removed, but there was grisly evidence of the blast all around the site. Scraps of blue uniform dangled from the fence and were scattered in the dirt. Sanderson's gun had been blown into the parking lot, his shoulder patch was on the sidewalk, his brass name plate was later found embedded in a ceiling panel on the second floor of the clinic. Erwin immediately felt his head start to throb; this was probably another dynamite bomb, like the ones last year in Atlanta. This bomb, too, was packed with nails. Some were embedded in the metal door frame; others had shattered the front windows and sprayed the brick like bullets from a heavy-caliber machine gun.

First Erwin scooped up some soil samples from the crater to test for explosive residues. (A chemical analysis would quickly confirm that the charge was, indeed, nitroglycerin dynamite.) Then, starting at the crater and working out from there, a team of evidence techs picked up every bit of shrapnel and scorched remnant of the bomb, none of the pieces larger than a quarter. Even before the shards were brought back to the lab, Erwin was assembling the device in his head: There were bits of an alarm clock and an egg timer—he couldn't tell for sure, but it looked like a Sunbeam. Probably part of a safety switch. There were battery pieces. A metal lock. Flakes of plastic foliage. There were some perplexing fragments of green plastic imprinted with a square pattern. There were also scraps of wire on the ground and a few other bits and pieces that looked like parts of a radio receiver. He would keep quiet until he could test the samples and get a good look at everything back at his lab. But Lloyd Erwin already suspected this was the Atlanta bomber; he was simply escalating his attacks and his devices were becoming more sophisticated. This time he had used a command detonation system, most likely a model airplane controller, with a relatively short range. He would have been watching from a place nearby, and chosen the moment to set off his bomb.

This time there was no secondary device to trap the responders. A bomb-sniffing dog had indicated explosives in a hedge next to the clinic's front door, but no device was found there or anywhere around the clinic. Erwin speculated that the bomber had initially hidden the bomb in the hedge, then returned to bury it by the front walk when the coast was clear.

Since Joe Kennedy was the forensic team leader of the Atlanta Bomb Task Force and also a member of the regional NRT, he had extensive knowledge of all the bombing evidence, which would allow him to act as a bridge between the Atlanta and Birmingham investigations. Once the clinic scene had been processed, Kennedy met with the assistant U.S. attorneys from Birmingham to walk them through the site and explain the evidence collection process. He was showing them the crater, trying to describe how the bomb had been positioned in the ground, when he came up with an ingenious way to illustrate the blast pattern and the dispersal of shrapnel. He convinced the NRT leaders to assign agents to attach fluorescent pink strings from a crowbar driven into the dirt at the blast seat to each point of impact on the surface of the clinic. When they were done they had a stunning visual image of how much metal had flown through the air and, from inside the waiting area, an even starker reminder of the damage the bomber had intended. If the bomb had gone off a few minutes later, when patients would normally have been sitting behind the windows, the pregnant women, the receptionist, and everyone inside the waiting room would have been cut to ribbons.

Jim Cavanaugh, the special agent in charge of the ATF office in Birmingham, was in the middle of a conference in Charlottesville, Virginia, when his pager went off. He left the meeting and got on the next flight to Birmingham that morning, which transferred through Atlanta. While he was waiting at the gate he noticed a curly-haired woman talking on her cell phone. She was obviously upset, and he overheard her asking "How's the nurse?" Cavanaugh walked over to her and said, "Sounds like you're from Birmingham. Are you connected with the clinic?"

She said, "I'm Diane Derzis. And I own the clinic."

He introduced himself, and they sat together on the plane and talked about the case. Cavanaugh is a tall man with a soothing voice who favors wide ties and large eyeglasses. His New Jersey accent has been softened by years working in the South, first in Florida, then in Nashville, and later as SAC in Dallas, before he came to Birmingham. Anyone who has studied the Waco siege will remember Cavanaugh's voice in hours of taped phone conversations with David Koresh as he tried to talk the Branch Davidian leader into leaving the compound. He was the senior ATF agent on the ground during the failed operation, but also the lead hostage negotiator in the standoff, who helped arrange for dozens of women and children to escape before the tragic outcome.

Cavanaugh told Derzis that an off-duty officer had been killed in the bombing, although they couldn't confirm his identity yet. The nurse, Emily Lyons, had been gravely injured, and nobody knew if she would make it. Derzis found Cavanaugh to be reassuring and kind, qualities she had not often encountered in federal agents. And it was good to talk to somebody to keep herself from losing her mind with worry.

She told him her day had begun with a call from Michelle Farley, the administrator who ran the clinic, who said, "The sirens you hear are for us. They bombed the clinic." Derzis turned on CNN and saw the helicopter shots of the smoldering building while she called the airlines to get the next flight to Birmingham.

Derzis, who was in her early forties, now lived on a Virginia horse farm, but she had spent almost twenty years on the front lines of the abortion battle in Alabama. She was a law school graduate who served for eighteen years as executive director of Summit Medical Center in Birmingham, part of a national chain of abortion-providing clinics and a primary target for anti-abortion protesters. Derzis was an outspoken pro-choice advocate who wore fur coats and high heels and carried a .25 Beretta to work. She was constantly in the news, debating the antis on talk shows and providing colorful quotes to reporters. She was often harassed by the protesters, enough for her to install an $8,000 security system in her house. But the antis seemed to go for the more vulnerable targets. One night, someone crept up to the home of one of the clinic's counselors, a well-known animal lover, slit the screen door, and grabbed a pet cat. She found the decapitated body the next morning. That weekend, at a large rally, some protesters' signs read: "Where's the cat?"

Derzis told Jim Cavanaugh that she had been frustrated by the lack of support from Birmingham's former police chief and its politicians. "We just wanted them to enforce the law," she said. "But even when they arrested the protesters, they were back out in front of the clinic within hours."

In the early nineties, clinics in every state had to contend with Operation Rescue, an increasingly militant anti-abortion movement that resorted to blockades and invasions to shut down facilities. Then the shooting started. In March 1993 a protester named Michael Griffin murdered Dr. David Gunn outside a Florida clinic. Dr. Gunn had worked in clinics across the South, including the Summit clinic in Montgomery, Alabama, and it was a painful, personal loss for Derzis. In less publicized cases, several other doctors were shot and wounded by anti-abortion fanatics. And then in 1994, Dr. Bayard Brittan and his security escort were shotgunned to death by a beatific, Scripture-quoting assassin named Paul Hill. Diane Derzis decided she'd had enough of the daily stress of being the front woman in the Alabama pro-choice struggle. She left Summit in 1996 and returned to her hometown in the Blue Ridge Mountains. But a few months later the owner of the New Woman All Woman clinic, a controversial doctor named Bruce Lucero, called her with an offer to sell his business. To keep her hand in the fight, Derzis agreed to buy a majority share of the practice. She hired an able staff to run it for her.

The New Woman was a much more low-key operation than Summit or the Planned Parenthood clinic on the other end of Southside Birmingham and therefore less of a magnet for demonstrators. By 1998 the confrontations with anti-abortion protesters had calmed down to a ritualistic standoff. Still, some of the regulars seemed extreme enough to be violent, or to help someone else carry out a bombing. Diane Derzis gave Jim Cavanaugh a list of names. She was certain whoever did this wasn't acting alone.

Derzis and Cavanaugh parted ways at the Birmingham airport. She wanted to find her staff and make plans to reopen the clinic as soon as possible. But her first stop was University Hospital, where Emily Lyons's husband, Jeff, was still waiting for her to come out of surgery.

By the time Jim Cavanaugh arrived in Birmingham, a task force center had been set up on an empty floor at 2121 Eighth Street N, a downtown high-rise where the FBI maintained offices. The first order of business was a meeting with the heads of each law enforcement entity, since the bombing fell under a number of jurisdictions: Doug Jones, the U.S. attorney; Joe Lewis, the FBI's tall, affable African-American SAC for Birmingham; Mike Coppage, who had only recently been promoted to Birmingham police chief; and David Barber, the Jefferson County district attorney. Cavanaugh quickly realized that the typical bureaucratic tug of war had already started, with, as he later put it, "everybody trying to put the Burger King crown on their head." One of the first suggestions on the table was that the group have only one spokesman. Cavanaugh disagreed. He wanted a joint, unified command, and he gave a little speech.

"Look, the Birmingham police just lost an officer, I think the chief is gonna have to talk to the public and his department," he said. "The DA has a murder case, he needs to be able to speak. The FBI's gonna be interested in terrorism and they've got to talk about that. And the ATF has to investigate bombings, we have a duty to say what we have to say. We're all leaders. But the public needs to see a unified investigation. What we've got to do is have a cohesive message—we can't be talking with five separate voices." They agreed, and from then on it was handled as a combined, equal case. Whenever there was a public announcement, the five of them stood on the podium together. They were united by the desire to solve the crime, and by another common goal: All of them wanted this case kept in Birmingham.

Already the Atlanta U.S. attorney's office and the Atlanta Bomb Task Force, led by the FBI, were angling to take over the case. They had sent a team of lawyers and agents to Birmingham within hours of the bombing. Louis Freeh's lieutenants were circling around, looking for an opening. By now, it was a classic, predictable move, and Doug Jones was determined to head off the takeover before it happened. He knew that Freeh had edged the locals out of the Oklahoma City bombing case, and he had firsthand knowledge of the director's handling of the Leroy Moody case. Jones, as well as his criminal division head, Joe McLean, had both been AUSAs back in 1990 when Freeh came in as a special prosecutor and took the case out of their hands. The victim, Judge Vance, had been their friend, and the memory of being pushed aside by Freeh still smarted. Jones wasn't going to see it happen again.

Meanwhile, the newly formed Birmingham task force, named SANDBOMB, after Sande Sanderson, had to decide what to do about Eric Rudolph. His photograph fit the description provided by eyewitnesses, but the only solid link to Rudolph was the truck, and just because he owned it didn't mean that he had been the one driving it. Jones spent the rest of the day and night on the phone to Washington, conferring about a strategy for tracking down Rudolph.

By the next morning he and McLean had come up with a solution: They would issue a "material witness" warrant for Rudolph, a legal device often used in drug cases. This would allow any officer who saw Rudolph to arrest him and to hold him for questioning before a grand jury while they tried to determine if he had an alibi. But they would have to go public about it soon. The news media had heard about the BOLO for the North Carolina license plate number and had also traced it to Eric Rudolph. The story was about to break, and Jones wanted the government to get out ahead of it with a carefully worded statement. It would be important to emphasize that Rudolph was wanted only for questioning about what he saw, and that he was not at this time considered a suspect. Everybody remembered what had happened with Richard Jewell, and nobody wanted to repeat that fiasco.

Early on the morning of Friday, January 30, FBI agent Jim Russell drove from Asheville to Andrews, North Carolina, to meet with Tom Frye, a local agent with twenty years' experience with the North Carolina State Bureau of Investigation. Frye was a burly, taciturn man who was born and raised in the area and knew it well. But he'd never heard of Rudolph. He'd checked the usual places—utility and phone records for the region around Andrews and Topton—and had come up blank. Russell and Frye started asking around the local post offices to see if he'd ever received mail. The postmaster in Topton, a rural hamlet along the Nantahala River, couldn't help the agents with a current address, but he remembered Eric Rudolph and thought he might have a friend named Randy Cochran who still lived in Topton. Maybe he would know where Eric was living now.

It took a while to find Cochran's house, and when they knocked on his door just after 6 o'clock that night, Cochran didn't seem at all surprised to see them.

"I guess you're looking for Eric Rudolph," he said.

"What makes you think that?" said Frye.

"It's all over the news."

Russell and Frye gave each other a look.

Cochran invited the agents into his house and they all watched the tail end of the news reports about the press conference, and how Eric Rudolph was wanted as a material witness in the Birmingham clinic bombing. Nobody had thought to notify Russell or Frye that the task force was going public with Rudolph's name.

Cochran said he hadn't seen Eric for a while, but he'd heard Eric was living near Murphy, in the western part of Cherokee County. Frye had checked records only in Macon and eastern Cherokee counties, the areas closest to Rudolph's last known residence. So the SBI agent left the house to call Jack Thompson, the Cherokee County sheriff, and Thompson called someone in the utility company who drove to his office to check the records. Meanwhile, Cochran and Russell kept talking. Cochran was a mechanic who worked at a metal shop in Franklin, the Macon County seat. Randy said that he'd met Eric when they were students in middle school—Eric was a grade ahead of him. He hadn't talked to Eric for a couple of years, not since Eric had sold the family home in Topton. He wasn't close to Eric, he said. Nobody was. Eric had always been a loner, never played team sports. Cochran was closer to Eric's older brother, Joel. Cochran told the agents that Eric was an intelligent person, someone who read books and knew the Bible well. He was also a bigot. When he was in the army, Eric told Cochran, he couldn't stand saluting blacks or female officers. A woman's place, he'd said, was barefoot, pregnant, and at home. Rudolph hated Jews and thought the government was too powerful. He was also a survivalist and a seasoned outdoorsman who, four or five years earlier, had wandered off into the woods one snowy Christmas with only a poncho and sleeping bag and camped out for more than a week in Nantahala Gorge.

It didn't take long for Thompson to call Frye with a physical address for Rudolph, a trailer on Caney Creek Road in Murphy. It was just before 7 P.M. and the agents were at least a half hour's drive away. They told the sheriff not to do anything, just meet them at the old Ford dealership out on Highway 64. It was near Caney Creek Road, but not close enough to attract attention. John Felton, an ATF agent from Asheville, was waiting when they drove up. Russell and Felton, who were both members of their agency's SWAT teams, suited up with body armor and automatic rifles to sneak up on Rudolph's trailer. It was a cold, clear night, and the trailer was about an eighth of a mile off the road. Frye dropped them off at the foot of Caney Creek and waited while they low-crawled down the long driveway. When they got to Rudolph's trailer the lights were on inside, but the truck was gone. Felton covered Russell as the FBI agent circled through the woods behind the trailer to see if the truck was hidden there. Nothing. There was no movement inside. The storm door was closed but the front door was wide open and nobody was home.

Russell radioed Frye with the bad news. He stayed hidden in the woods until 10 o'clock the next morning on the off chance that Rudolph was just out on the town. Other agents kept up surveillance at the trailer for the next three days just in case Rudolph was clueless enough to show up back at his house.

In Murphy, agents tracked down the owner of the trailer, Jonathan Crisp. Crisp had rented out the property in November to a tenant who called himself "Bob Randolph," or maybe "Rudolph," he was never sure. "Bob"—whom Crisp identified as Rudolph from a picture the agents showed him—kept to himself and paid his $250 a month in cash. The agents also learned that from February to November 1997, Rudolph had rented a three-bedroom house on an acre of land from Susan Roper on Vengeance Creek Road, between Murphy and Andrews. Roper also thought Rudolph's name was Bob Randolph. He always paid on time, $500 a month in cash or money order. He said he didn't like banks, Roper later told a reporter from the *Birmingham News*. He'd told her, "No pets, no kids, no women, no problems," when he rented the place, and he kept to his word. But he was a bit different, she recalled. He never got a phone installed. And he lived in only one room, boarding up the basement windows and covering the rest of them with sheets. Still, he seemed nice. "I was comfortable around him," she told the reporter. "If I had a daughter thirty years old, I wouldn't mind if she dated him." Now she said she was locking her doors, afraid he might come back.

Meanwhile, Cal Stiles, owner of Cal's Mini Storage in Marble, North Carolina, called the FBI to volunteer that Eric Rudolph was renting a unit from him. Eric had told him he was storing household goods there, but maybe the agents wanted to check it out. Roy Neely, an ATF dog handler, brought his "explosives detection" canine, Garrett, over to Cal's and led him along the rows of metal roll-up doors. Garrett, a yellow Lab whose nose was trained to recognize the chemical agents used to make explosives, "alerted"—meaning he sat down—in front of unit

91, Rudolph's storage space. Garrett had found some sort of explosive residues on the door handle, and that was enough to apply for a search warrant. On Sunday night the agents got a warrant from a federal court in Asheville to search for illegally stored explosives. By Monday morning they felt they were good to go.

After checking for booby traps, the agents opened up the ten-by-ten-foot storage unit. Federal law enforcement is by design a team sport, and so once again an Evidence Response Team was put into action. It was led by an experienced FBI agent, Brian Roepe, who was assisted by evidence technicians and forensic chemists including Joe Kennedy and Lloyd Erwin; two of Erwin's bosses at the ATF crime lab in Maryland had flown down to supervise the job.

The team paid special attention to an old wooden toolbox filled with an assortment of rusty nails. Garrett alerted on it, and Erwin took some samples to test for explosive residues, including some spent bullet shells found underneath the box. Agents eventually returned with another warrant and sorted through a jumble of tools and rakes and other yard equipment, including a rusty brush mower. Much of it was junk. There were cardboard boxes of old sports equipment, spinning reels, old snorkeling gear left over from the family's Florida years. There was also an assortment of PVC and metal pipes, some with end caps, but none like the ones used in the bombings. There were a few banks of fluorescent "grow lights" and some potting soil and fertilizer, supporting some stories that investigators had been hearing around town—that Rudolph had once been a marijuana grower and dealer.

The cardboard boxes stacked along the walls of the unit contained the written record of Rudolph's life: his birth certificate, passport, military papers, an address book, and old textbooks—including the religious homeschooling materials he used to get his GED. One cardboard box had memorabilia from his army days: military clothing, some webbing, his helmet, a Confederate battle flag, and a full-sized American flag.

There were dozens of other books stashed in those boxes, most of them ordinary histories of the world's religions and philosophies. A couple of boxes held books about Germany, Hitler, and Nazism—much of it fairly mainstream, but there was fringe stuff as well, a minor pantheon of paranoia and racism, including *The International Jew* by Henry Ford. There were books and magazines denying the Holocaust (*Anne Frank's Diary: A Hoax*) and lauding American anti-Semites (*Besieged Patriot: Gerald L. K. Smith*) and racists (*The South Was Right*), and survivalist literature (*Guerrilla Capitalism* by Adam Cash and *Basement Nukes: The Consequences of Cheap Weapons of Mass Destruction*). And, presumably for those End Times after the conflagration, there was *The Wild Game Cookbook* and *Better Beer and Home Brew*. Tucked in with some old math texts was a copy of *All-American Monster: The Unauthorized Biography of Timothy McVeigh*. Rudolph also had a box of military manuals, most probably from his army days, some possibly bought at gun shows, including a pamphlet called "Guerilla Operations." He also collected several manuals listing the frequencies of local and federal radio signals, and how to monitor them on a scanner. Tucked in with his papers were some shooting targets, including one of a smirking, thick-lipped black guy sporting an Afro haircut. Even more interesting to the investigators were two books: *Shadowing and Surveillance: A Complete Guidebook* and another useful guide called *Methods of Disguise*.

On February 4 the agents gave up the stakeout of Rudolph's trailer on Caney Creek and executed another search warrant that gave them the right to look for any evidence of bombs, bomb-making texts or materials, or any household objects that could absorb explosive residues. Before they could start, a pair of bomb technicians dressed in one-piece white Tyvek suits and booties combed through the trailer looking for booby traps or live bombs. Finding nothing, they cleared the way for Ray Neely and Garrett to go to work. Neely also wore the protective Tyvek jumpsuit to avoid contaminating evidence; Garrett, as Rudolph's defense attorneys later pointed out in a unsuccessful attempt to suppress the evidence found in the trailer, did not. As soon as Garrett was brought into the residence he "alerted" on several items, including a pair of socks, a towel, a section of carpet, a videocassette, a cardboard box, a blanket, a bedsheet, rocking chair cushions, and a toolbox. When Garrett was finished Lloyd Erwin and his supervisors suited up and started to swab down areas and seize items for chemical analysis. Erwin sealed some of them in empty paint cans. Later that evening he would test the vapors in the cans on a portable EGIS machine to look for traces of explosives.

The EGIS is a higher-tech counterpart of the explosive-sniffing machines now used by Transportation Security Administration agents in American airports. The ATF chemists were particularly interested in finding molecules of EGDN, ethylene glycol dinitrate, an easily detectable component in nitroglycerin dynamite that is used to raise its freezing point. It had been identified in the samples Erwin took from the Birmingham bomb crater. They eventually found it on more than two dozen items, including all the ones Garrett had indicated.

The trailer had seen better days, but probably not since Jimmy Carter was president. Its outside panels were streaked with mildew and there was an overflowing bucket in the narrow hallway to catch leaks from the roof. The front door opened to a living room paneled with a dark wood laminate, carpeted with a thick wall-to-wall of indeterminate color. It was furnished with a plush velour sofa set and ruffled pink pillows—undoubtedly supplied by the landlord. A small eat-in kitchen was to the right; to the left the bathroom, two bedrooms, the laundry, and an added-on storage area.

In the kitchen, Rudolph kept a bachelor's refrigerator stocked with the basics: eggs, orange juice, a gallon of milk, bread, Dannon fat-free yogurt, a pound of ground beef, a box of taco shells. He seemed to have cleared out in the middle of a meal: There was an open container of Quaker Oats on the counter next to a saucepan of water on the stove. The kitchen was scrubbed and tidy. A clean dinner plate was drying on the rack next to the sink. There were some pieces of Rubbermaid Serv'n Saver plastic ware in the kitchen cabinets. A few canned goods and pots and pans were neatly arranged on the shelves above the counter, where Rudolph had also conveniently left a loaded Heckler & Koch 9mm automatic pistol.

In a spare bedroom used as a storage space, agents found a blue plastic Wal-Mart bag, just like the one Jermaine Hughes described in Birmingham. And in it was a receipt for several items that had been purchased at Wal-Mart for cash on Christmas Eve in 1997: a pair of gloves, some deadbolts, and a set of hose clamps. Lab technicians would later identify fragments of an identical metal clamp that had been embedded in Sande Sanderson's body by the force of the blast.

It looked as if Rudolph lived alone and spent most of his time in his bedroom at the farthest corner of the trailer, where a thirteen-inch TV-video unit was propped on an end table at the foot of a single bed. When the agents entered the room the TV was on and a rented videotape of *Kull the Conqueror* was ejected halfway from the slot. Rudolph didn't have satellite or cable hookup and there was no TV reception in the area. As the agents combed through the bedroom for evidence, the set hissed with static until one of them finally switched it off.

Eric Rudolph didn't want anyone looking in on him. The window by the bed was taped over with black plastic. A side door to the bedroom was also covered in plastic, and a rolled-up towel stuffed beneath it. There were drawers pulled out of the dresser and clothes strewn around the room, including a black and green plaid shirt jacket, much like the one described by witnesses on the day of the bombing. The agents also found a couple of baseball caps, black sunglasses, and a cheap brown hairpiece.

There were two small framed pictures on the windowsill in the bedroom. One was a peaceful landscape, the other a snapshot of Eric as a young adolescent, golden brown hair lit with sun, gazing happily at a falcon perched on his gloved hand. There were sixteen crisp hundred-dollar bills hidden in the frame. It was small enough to fit into a pocket, but he had left it behind.

A rifle case was open and empty in the middle of the bedroom, suggesting that Rudolph had taken at least one long gun with him. But he left behind a small arsenal in the trailer. In addition to the Heckler & Koch in the kitchen, there were three large knives and three more handguns stashed in the bedroom, including a SigSauer .45 and a .38 Police Special. There was a shotgun tucked under his blue jeans in a dresser drawer, and two hunting rifles, a .22 and a .30-06 propped up in a corner.

On his bedside table was an empty Mason jar of tea and a hardcover biography, *FDR: The New Deal Years*. There were other books on the dresser and stashed around the bedroom. Rudolph's current taste in reading materials was heavily weighted to history and philosophy: Will Durant's *The Age of Faith*, *The Story of Philosophy*, and *Rousseau and Revolution*. There were such classics as *Hamlet*, *The Iliad of Homer*, *The Canterbury Tales*, and Dostoyevsky's *Crime and Punishment*. And on a lighter note, Jeff Foxworthy's *You Might Be a Redneck If...*

What was missing was any pro-life literature whatsoever. Anti-abortion zealots often have a fetishistic attachment to the literature of the genre, with its bloody fetus pictures and polemic screeds. Rudolph had none. The only religious objects in the trailer were a stained-glass cross in the kitchen, a few reproductions of religious paintings, including one of Raphael's *Madonna with Child*—a standard for Catholic homes—and a black leather-bound Thompson Chain-Reference Bible on the dresser.

The Bible was a gold mine for investigators. Although it was initially seized to search for explosive residues (none was found), it also provided handwriting samples and, more important, insights into his thinking. Rudolph underlined passages and jotted notes in the margins to form his own narrative, a story of temptation, retribution, hatred of enemies, dominance over women, and the duty to strike out at those who don't obey God's laws. It could almost be read as a coded diary.

He drew stars next to certain sections that particularly interested him and cross-referenced them to others. He underlined Genesis 3:15: "And I will put enmity between thee and the woman and between thy seed and her seed ..." He gave it three stars and penned a reference to Revelation 12:17: "And the dragon was wroth with the woman and went to make war with the remnant of her seed, which keep the commandments of God and have testimony of Jesus Christ."

Alongside the story of Cain and Abel, Rudolph writes: *"Twin Birth two seed lines,"* which is a clear reference to the Identity Christian sect. Identity followers, who are not true Christians, believe the Bible is the history of the white race. In their version, Abel was fathered by Adam, but Cain was the result of fornication between Eve and Satan. Two separate lineages, or seed lines, descended from the offspring of Eve: True Israelites, who were white, came from Abel, while Cain spawned Jews and mud people, the nonwhite races. In this pseudotheology, which

Identity followers use to justify the most virulent forms of racism and anti-Semitism, the enemy is both satanic and nonhuman.

From there Rudolph delves deep into the oldest books, the primitive reptile brain of the Bible where all aberrant behavior is punishable by death, and love is accompanied by fear.

In Exodus 21:12 he underlines: "He that smiteth a man, so that he die, shall surely be put to death." And he stars the twenty-third and twenty-fourth verses: "And if any mischief follow then thou shalt give life for life, Eye for Eye, tooth for tooth ..." Rudolph notes *"eye for eye"* in the margin.

Another key note: Leviticus 18:22: "Thou shalt not lie with mankind, as with womankind: it is abomination." In the margin: *"Homosexuality is an abomination."*

He seems interested in all things in the Old Testament that warrant the death penalty, such as working on the Sabbath and being a witch. He underlined every line of the story of Phineas in Numbers 25. Phineas, a great favorite among Identity believers, was a grandson of Aaron who confronted a biblical example of race mixing. He chased down an Israelite man and Midianite woman who had entered the temple together, and drove a javelin through their bellies. This pleased the Lord, who turned his wrath away from the children of Israel. The story has inspired a self-selected, leaderless cult within Identity called the "Phineas Priesthood." Its members consider themselves vigilantes for Christ. In the margin next to the story of Phineas, Rudolph circled the reference *"death penalty."*

Rudolph also found harsh judgments in the New Testament. He underscored Romans 1:27–32: "And likewise also the men leaving the natural use of the woman burned in their lust one toward another, men with men working that which is unseemly ... Who knowing the judgment of God that they which commit such things are worthy of death ..." *"Homosexuality is (ungodly)."*

1 Corinthians 15:38: "... to every seed his own body." 39: "All flesh is not the same flesh: but there is one kind of flesh of men." *"Kind after kind."*

Hebrews 9:22: "And almost all things are by the law purged with blood and without shedding of blood is no remission." *"Sacrifice is all."*

Rudolph cherry-picked passages in the Bible to suit his vision. He noted Psalm 149:7: "To execute vengeance upon the heathen, and punishments upon the people," and wrote beside it: *"Christian soldiers requirement."*

Even in the most beautiful passage of all, he found an injunction to murder. In Ecclesiastes 3, in the passage that begins, "To every thing there is a season," Eric Rudolph circled the phrase, *"A time to kill."*

He marked up every page of Revelation, the most violent and hallucinatory book of the Bible, the one that drives certain believers to stockpile food and weapons for the coming apocalypse. Chapter 16:21, in particular, is underlined: "And there fell upon men a great hail out of heaven, every stone about the weight of a talent, and men blasphemed God because of the plague of the hail ..."

Beside it Rudolph wrote one word: *Bombs.*

THE INVISIBLE MAN

Two new letters arrived at the *Atlanta Journal-Constitution* and the Reuters news bureau on Monday morning, February 2. They were printed in the same block letters as the previous ones, with similar phrases, misspellings, and odd punctuation. They began:

> THE BOMBING IN BIRMINGHAM WAS CARRIED OUT BY THE ARMY OF GOD. LET THOSE WHO WORK IN THE MURDER MILL'S AROUND THE NATION BE WARNED ONCE MORE—YOU WILL BE TARGETED WITHOUT QUARTER—YOU ARE NOT IMMUNE FROM RETALIATION. YOUR COMMISAR'S IN WASHINGTON CAN'T PROTECT YOU!
>
> WITH THE DISTRIBUTION OF THE GENOCIDAL PILL RU-486 IT IS HOPED THE RESISTANCE WILL END. WE WILL TARGET ANYONE WHO MANUFAC-TURES, MARKET, SELLS AND DISTROBTES THE PILL.

There was no description of the bomb this time, but there was the same sign-off, "DEATH TO THE NEW WORLD ORDER," and once again, the Waco code: FBI NUMBER: 4-1-9-9-3.

The letters were postmarked in Birmingham on the afternoon of the bombing. The return address on them was a sick little joke: "A.O.G.,

17th ST S, BIRMINGHAM AL 35203," the address of the New Woman All Women clinic.

Once again the forensic scientists scoured the letters for clues but found nothing to link them conclusively to Eric Rudolph—no hair, no fibers or fingerprints. But the Atlanta Bomb Task Force saw this letter as an obvious link between the bombings and a reason to combine the investigations and put them under its control. And the U.S. attorney in Atlanta wanted to prosecute all the crimes together, claiming jurisdiction because Rudolph must have driven through a few miles of Georgia as he escaped to North Carolina after the bombing.

Doug Jones got a call from Janet Reno herself, who tried to make a case that the FBI in Atlanta had superior resources to coordinate such an enormous investigation.

"Wouldn't it be better to allow them to take charge?" the attorney general asked.

"Ms. Reno, I have incredible confidence in this task force," said Jones. He also had an ace in the hole. The Jefferson County district attorney was prepared to pull out of the multiagency task force and convene his own grand jury, which would lead to a state murder indictment for Rudolph—before the U.S. government had a chance to charge him. The last thing the Justice Department wanted was a local DA going off the reservation and trying the case first. To prevent that, Jones was allowed to keep his case separate but coordinate it with Atlanta.

A week and a day after Eric Rudolph went missing, a couple of men were out Saturday-night coon hunting in the fields south of Murphy when their headlights picked up a red taillight reflector deep in the woods. They followed a two-track farm road until it petered out in the overgrowth, and there they found a gray Nissan truck with a cream camper shell. The plate number: KND1117.

The hunters reported the truck to the sheriff's office, and county dispatch called C. J. Hyman of the ATF. Hyman was a supervisory special agent out of Charlotte, North Carolina, a good ol' boy in his early thirties with a humble, friendly manner and an Andy Griffith accent. He was also a crack investigator and a former member of the ATF's Special

Response Team, a super-SWAT unit established along the lines of the FBI's Hostage Rescue Team. Hyman and a small team of agents had set up a forward command post in an empty grocery store in Murphy and, after only a week in town, had already established a network of friends and contacts in the community. So C. J. learned the truck had been found about the same time the sheriff did. While two investigators interviewed the hunters, Hyman assembled a mixed team of about a dozen armed agents to check out the find.

At about 10:30 that evening, with a cold sleet pelting down, the hunters led Hyman's team up to the abandoned truck, which was only a couple of miles south of Rudolph's rented trailer. Hyman, with two other agents, crept up to the driver's side window and peeked inside. Frankly, he was expecting—and half hoping—to find Rudolph dead at the wheel. A suicide would have ended it all. But the truck was empty. Six unlucky agents got to guard the site for the rest of the night.

By Monday morning, with a search warrant in hand, bomb techs surrounded the truck and checked for booby traps by using ropes and hooks to pop the doors and engine hood. Then they had it towed out of the woods and taken on a flatbed wrecker to the National Guard Armory in Murphy to be searched and processed for evidence. News of the find had drawn the media back to Murphy; when C. J. Hyman counted twenty-two live trucks lined up on Martins Creek Road and dozens of reporters and camera operators recording every move, he knew he was in unfamiliar territory. He'd worked big cases before, but this was going to be something different.

The truck was the most direct link between Rudolph and the scene of the bombing, and it also was a good sign that Rudolph was still in the area. Garrett, the ATF bomb-sniffing dog, was called in to check the truck for signs of explosives. He alerted on the steering wheel and on a plastic grocery bag in the covered truck bed. The evidence technicians swabbed the surfaces of the truck, particularly where the dog had indicated explosive residues. They lifted Rudolph's fingerprints from the driver's seat belt buckle and from three paper receipts on the passenger-side floorboard. They inventoried dozens of items in the truck: There was a folded shovel under the driver's seat, and a tangle of antennae and electric wires in the truck bed. There were also personal items—envelopes containing photographs, a box of tapes, and a swastika medallion. A rosary dangled from the rearview mirror. In the glove compartment were personal papers, including Rudolph's rental contracts, sunglasses, two Trojan condoms, and a tape of music by Johann Sebastian Bach. One of the strangest finds was an audiocassette in the back of the truck. It was the recording of a man washing dishes, whistling, and singing to himself. Agents never positively identified the voice, but far as they could tell, it was simply Rudolph taping himself in his lonely trailer home.

Everything was cataloged and bagged as evidence. The items of most immediate concern to the investigators were the receipts on the floorboard.

From these clues and interviews with people around town, the agents put together a picture of Rudolph's life during the week of the bombing. Despite all his precautions, Rudolph had left investigators one reliable way to track his movements: his habitual movie rentals. The tape in Rudolph's video machine was quickly traced back to the Plaza Video rental store on Highway 64, where Rudolph was a regular customer. The manager remembered him as quiet, even withdrawn. The girls behind the counter noticed him, though, because he was so good-looking. Rudolph usually rented one or two movies at a time and returned them the next day, like clockwork.

A check of the rental records showed that on Sunday, January 25, the day after he visited the Rhodes family, Rudolph had checked out *The Game*, a Michael Douglas thriller. The sales clerk observed that Eric, whom she saw four or five times a week, was growing a beard. He returned the movie the next day and rented *Picture Perfect*, a light comedy starring Jennifer Aniston. He brought that video back the next day, Tuesday, but left without renting another. He showed up again at 5:31 P.M. on the afternoon of January 29, when he took out *City of Industry*, a crime drama starring Harvey Keitel. The ever-vigilant clerk noticed that Rudolph was now clean-shaven and his hair was damp, as if he'd just come out of the shower. As usual, Rudolph was alone and didn't talk to anyone when he was in the store.

At about 10 o'clock the next morning Rudolph showed up again to return his latest rental. Outside the store, he had a brief encounter with a local hiking guide he had never met before. The guide would later tell the FBI that he noticed Rudolph's well-kept Nissan truck because he was looking to buy one for his son. He mentioned to Rudolph that he liked his truck, and Rudolph replied that he liked it, too, then walked into the store, not too friendly. But while he was making his selection, Rudolph overheard the guide talking to a couple about the best places to hike in the area. He walked over and joined in the conversation, asking if the guide could recommend any good spots. The man suggested Turtle Town Falls in Tennessee, and some trails in the Nantahala forest. Rudolph nodded, but didn't say much of anything else. He rented a copy of *Kull the Conqueror*, a lame sequel to *Conan the Barbarian*, got back in his truck, and drove off.

A receipt in the truck indicated that Rudolph bought some groceries at the Ingle's store in Murphy at 2:40 P.M. The next time anybody saw him was at 5 P.M., when his neighbors on Caney Creek Road noticed his pickup pulling up to his trailer. Rudolph apparently put his latest video in the machine, and started making himself a bowl of oatmeal. Although he had no TV reception in the trailer and no phone, he did have a radio on which he listened to news and call-in talk shows.

The investigators did not know how Rudolph learned that he was being sought as a material witness, but they knew that within an hour of the news conference in Birmingham, he had started running: A receipt found in Rudolph's truck showed that at 6:56 P.M. he bought a Double Whopper with fries and a Coke ($4.65) at the Burger King on Highway 19, a ten-minute drive from his trailer. At 7:11 P.M. he paid cash for $109.06 worth of groceries from the BI-LO supermarket, just a few steps away from Burger King in the Valley River shopping center.

The items he bought that night seemed to indicate Rudolph's intentions: fourteen cans of oatmeal, eight containers of raisins, eight cans of tuna, eight cans of green beans, five cans of Planters peanuts, three jars of dry-roasted nuts, one pack of Ivory soap, three two-packs of D-cell batteries, and four four-packs of AA Duracell batteries.

The FBI later tallied up the calories in these supplies. Their nutrition experts concluded that, assuming he conserved his energy, Rudolph could survive for about six months in the mountains on these provisions alone.

By 9:15 P.M., when the first agents arrived at his home, Rudolph was already in the wind.

With Birmingham and Atlanta still engaged in a bureaucratic struggle over the investigation, there was a power vacuum on the ground in North Carolina during the earliest days of the search for Eric Rudolph. The Charlotte FBI and ATF offices were coordinating operations in Asheville and Murphy, running leads generated out of Birmingham. Woody Enderson kept his distance, sending only Charles Stone, a portly ASAC in the Georgia Bureau of Investigation, to observe the investigation and report back to the Atlanta Bomb Task Force. Meanwhile, back at Martins Creek where the truck was found, dozens of additional agents had been called in to knock on doors and search empty sheds and barns for the fugitive.

The manhunt was captured on tape by dozens of TV cameras, and to some Americans with fresh memories of Waco and Ruby Ridge, it was disturbing to see big, burly guys in full tactical gear toting assault rifles and stalking through pastures and farmyards. It was not, to put it mildly, the best public relations move for government agencies recently accused by the NRA of being "jack-booted thugs." The scene became even more chaotic when a team of bloodhounds arrived from Texas to try to pick up Rudolph's trail. The hounds led a convoy of agents all over Cherokee and Clay counties and even into northern Georgia, where the dogs were let out at every crossroad in hopes that they would pick up Rudolph's week-old scent. C. J. Hyman, who was monitoring the search from the forward command post in Murphy, was getting increasingly alarmed phone calls from agents who were out following the hounds to a series of dead ends. Finally, after the bloodhounds swarmed a convenience store, apparently attracted by the smell of warm hot dogs, they were pulled off the chase and sent back to Texas.

The local sheriffs, the region's most important elected officials, fell through the cracks in the earliest days of the investigation. In fact, the Macon County Sheriff's Department first learned that Rudolph was wanted as a material witness when a reporter called from the *Asheville Citizen-Times* newspaper. Jack Thompson in Cherokee County was soon grumbling that he could have captured Rudolph if he'd only been given a chance. If someone had told him why they were looking for Rudolph, Thompson could have had the trailer staked out well before the feds got there. The official reason for withholding the information would be that the feds didn't want to risk a dangerous confrontation and possible shootout, especially if Rudolph wasn't their man. The sheriffs believed otherwise. Fair or not, the perception was that the FBI was interested in the glory, and didn't want anyone else making the arrest. Ignoring the sheriffs would later be recognized as a tactical mistake.

By now details of the investigation were starting to leak to the media. Sheriff Thompson was openly talking to reporters about the trail of videotapes. Other "investigative sources" were chattering about everything from bomb parts to Rudolph's grocery lists. CNN seemed to have an inside track on many of the leads, and within days of the bombing, the network was running stories that supported the link between the Birmingham and Atlanta investigations, including reports that the same type of nails were used in the bombs in both cities. In North Carolina the media staked out investigators and followed them everywhere they went, from the video store to the machine and metal shop where Randy Cochran worked in a neighboring county. This led them to interview quite a few of the same people, who quickly grew tired of the attention. The agents had a special interest in the local Radio Shack, which was in the same shopping plaza as the video store, because the Atlanta and Birmingham bombs had all used wires manufactured for the chain.

A reporter for the *Birmingham News* interviewed the manager, Doug Hearl, who said Rudolph came in often to buy batteries and circuitry. "He was easygoing and soft-spoken," said Hearl. "He was gentle and clean cut, the kind of guy you'd want to take home to mama." He talked about computers with Hearl, but never politics. The only odd note was Rudolph's refusal to give his name and phone number to the cashier, an annoying request Radio Shack makes even of cash customers. According to one employee, Rudolph once slammed his hand on the door and said, "I don't have to take this," before he stormed out of the store.

There was a collective public biography emerging of Eric Rudolph as a loner with two distinct personalities, someone who could be as ordinary as the boy next door, but who also had an arrogant, secretive, dark side that made him seem capable of calculated murder. Teams of FBI and ATF agents were bringing back similar profiles from interviews with Eric's family and old acquaintances. They were looking for evidence of a motive and clues to where he might run, but few of Rudolph's siblings had been in close contact with him for years, and none seemed to know where he lived or what he was up to.

His eldest brother, Damian, was thirty-eight years old and worked for a large beverage distributor near Cincinnati. Like Maura, Damian was married, with children, and seemed to have made a normal, uneventful life for himself. Daniel, the second oldest, had married in May 1996, just before the Olympics, and he worked as a carpenter in coastal South Carolina. Joel was in his mid-thirties, divorced, and still looking for a place in the world. He sometimes taught martial arts, but now he was living with Maura and Keith, helping them with some carpentry as they added on to their house. Jamie, the youngest, was twenty-eight years old and working as a clerk in New York City while he pursued a career as a techno musician. To the surprise of the investigators, Jamie was living in an open gay relationship in Greenwich Village. Neither Jamie nor the other siblings remembered Eric specifically criticizing Jamie's lifestyle, although he sometimes made antigay remarks around them. And nobody recalled Eric having any strong opinions about abortion. Only Daniel remembered Eric talking about bombs or having the manuals to make them.

At first all the Rudolph siblings were willing to be interviewed by federal agents. But as the shock wore off and the media onslaught began, the family retreated behind drawn blinds, and most of them avoided contact with investigators as well as reporters. Any hope of talking to Patricia was destroyed on the first weekend of the investigation because of a colossal, though perhaps unavoidable, gaffe by FBI agents in Florida.

At the time, Pat Rudolph was living alone in a mobile home park in Bradenton, Florida. Two agents from the Tampa office were sent to knock on the door and interview her, but she was getting ready for bed and wouldn't let them in. The next day when they drove up to her trailer there was a truck with a camper shell and North Carolina plates parked in the driveway, so a SWAT team was called in to storm the trailer. Pat Rudolph said she sat in her living room while armed agents pulled out drawers and searched under her bed. That was her introduction to the FBI. As it turned out, the truck belonged to a friend of hers, and after that, she refused to have anything to do with any federal agents.

By now the Southern Poverty Law Center, a watchdog group that monitors racist and extremist organizations and sometimes takes them to court, had compiled its own dossier on Eric Rudolph, which it was sharing with the media. The SPLC has strong connections with law enforcement agencies, as well as an extensive network of its own sources, and is an invaluable resource for journalists and researchers. Newspapers from the *Asheville Citizen-Times* to the *Washington Post* repeated the center's contention that Rudolph had "a long history of involvement with right-wing leaders." The SPLC spokesman revealed that Rudolph had once lived in Schell City, Missouri, as part of Dan Gayman's "Church of Israel" Identity congregation. Although Gayman now denounced violence, he had once received money from a murderous paramilitary group called "The Order." And the SPLC, citing authoritative sources, asserted that Rudolph was also a "disciple" of the late Nord Davis Jr., usually identified as a "local militia leader" from Andrews, North Carolina. Davis was another Identity advocate who made money off an anti-Semitic, conspiracy-obsessed newsletter he sold to his followers. He lived with his family and a few members of his "preparedness" group, called the Northpoint Tactical Teams, on a large wooded compound outside of town.

Reporters also discovered that Rudolph had once lived next door to a Topton man named Thomas Branham, an eccentric, self-described "free man" who had been tried in federal court in the 1980s on charges of possessing a machine gun and illegal explosives. Although the conviction was thrown out on appeal, Branham was of great interest to the ATF and FBI because of his close relationship with the Rudolph family, particularly Eric. He'd also had ties to Nord Davis Jr. It appeared, on the surface, that there should be an obvious connection between Rudolph, Branham, and Davis and his group, since they lived in the same area and shared an association with the Christian Identity movement and a deep antipathy for the U.S. government. But like so many aspects of the developing case, things were not as simple as they seemed.

In Birmingham, forty-five detectives from every unit in the police department had teamed up with federal agents to comb the city for leads in the murder of a cop. They canvassed the neighborhood around the clinic, tracking down every possible witness to the bombing, including the family in the SUV that fled the scene after the blast. Until the father came forward with the story of his daughter's abortion, police had suspected his car might be involved in the bombing.

The investigators paid special attention to the coterie of anti-abortion activists who picketed the clinics, including some from neighboring counties and states who openly advocated the use of force to end legalized abortion. Despite the shadowy Army of God letter, nobody in the movement claimed responsibility for the bombing. But the most militant anti-abortion activists endorsed it as a tactic. "Everyone has the right to protect innocent persons," David Trosch, a Catholic priest from southern Alabama, told the *Birmingham News*. "When the government fails to do this, it is mandatory for others to do it. In effect, the government has made abortion clinics war zones." More moderate leaders, such as the Reverend Jim Pinto of Pastors for Life, condemned the bombing, which he called "an evil act."

Even though investigators hadn't been able to establish connections between Rudolph and any anti-abortion group, pro-choice advocates were quick to point out that this was beside the point. The extremists and even the mainstream anti-abortion groups, they said, created an atmosphere of hatred and intolerance that encouraged people like Michael Griffin, Paul Hill, and whoever was responsible for the Birmingham bombing to feel that they were doing the right thing, God's work, in murdering people outside clinics. For organizations that had been tracking crimes committed in the name of the Army of God, this latest bombing was more evidence that the conspiracy was real. "Clearly you've got a cell here somewhere," said Kathy Spillar of the Feminist Majority foundation, who noted other recent acts of vandalism and burglary against clinics in the region.

If the goal of the bomber was to shut down the clinic and turn public opinion against abortion, his plan had backfired, at least in the short term. Thousands of people attended the funeral of Sande Sanderson, who was mourned as a hero. Emily Lyons, the nurse who was injured in the clinic bombing, had emerged from intensive care and was now expected to live, although the blast had left her maimed and nearly blinded. She would soon become an outspoken advocate for reproductive rights and a living testimony against clinic violence. And the politicians of Birmingham, whom Diane Derzis had accused of being indifferent in enforcing laws that protected clinics, finally took notice of the problem. The Birmingham City Council publicly expressed sympathy for the victims of the bombing and called for more security around the city's clinics. Councilman Jimmy Blake noted that while he didn't personally condone abortion, it was still legal. Protesters, he said, "are criminals if they are engaged in threats, intimidation or violence. In this country we don't yield to terrorism by backing off."

After her visit from the FBI, Patricia Rudolph decided to take refuge with her son Daniel and his wife, Christine, at their house near Charleston, South Carolina. The task force set up "discreet surveillance" of that house, along with other places they suspected Rudolph might show up. Dan's phone number was among a dozen or more to which the task force was granted permission to attach a "trap and trace" system, meaning they could monitor the activity on the line, although they would need another warrant to listen in on the calls. They could see who was calling whom, and sometimes an unknown caller would get a visit from the FBI.

When the surveillance produced nothing, the investigators stepped up the pressure on some of Rudolph's more likely contacts. It was unnerving for the family members, particularly Daniel. The agents came back to talk to him several times, including at least one visit at his job site. It rattled him, and he cut off all contact with the FBI. Members of the media were calling at all hours to ask for interviews. Sound trucks camped out on his suburban street, and TV reporters used bullhorns to shout: "Mr. Rudolph! Mr. Rudolph! Will you please come out for the 6 o'clock news!"

James Bell, a Charleston attorney who made his services available to the family, called a news conference in a public park. Although, "after much thought and prayer," the family had decided not to give interviews, they wanted it known that they believed Eric was innocent. Bell reminded the reporters present that Eric Rudolph hadn't been convicted of any crime. The reason Rudolph was on the run, he suggested, was not that he was guilty, but that he was afraid of the government. Bell denied that Eric Rudolph was a fanatic with ties to militia groups. "He is deeply religious, but as far as I know there's no law against that," said Bell. He also called the government's evidence "shallow."

"If the only hard evidence they have against him is this tag number, that's a pretty good idea he may be connected as a witness or passerby, but it sure doesn't seem like enough evidence to make him the suspect," Bell said. "It may be we've got the makings of another Richard Jewell."

For weeks after Eric had been identified as a suspect, Dan and Christine Rudolph were virtual prisoners in their house in South Carolina. The marriage was showing signs of strain. Finally, one Sunday afternoon in early March, Dan Rudolph couldn't take any more.

In the video that was later recovered, Dan walks in front of a camera that he has set up on a tripod and switched on. The lighting is dim, but you can make out that the scene is a garage, and that Dan is wearing a suit jacket and tie. He is tall and thin, with a taut, handsome face and sandy brown hair. Dan removes his jacket and takes a seat. The only sound is a low mechanical thrumming in the background. He calmly rolls up his sleeve and ties off his upper left arm with a tourniquet. Dan stares into the camera, and, in a slow, deliberate voice, says, "This is for the FBI and the media."

Agents who have seen the video agree that the sound is even worse than the picture. Dan breathes deeply and rhythmically for a few moments. Then, all in one motion, he stands, walks partly out of the frame, and leans over a nearby table where he runs his arm over a circular saw. The sound changes to a grating whine as the blade severs his left hand just above the wrist. Dan gasps, grabs his arm, and wraps it in a towel, moaning as he struggles to stay conscious. Then he disappears from sight. A short time later you hear the sound of a truck starting up. The tape runs in silence for another half hour or so until noises can again be heard outside the garage. A policeman and a paramedic peer through a window and break the glass to get inside. You then see them pick up the severed hand and place it in a container of ice.

Luckily for Dan, he was able to drive himself to a medical center without passing out. And one of the doctors in nearby Charleston happened to be an expert in microsurgery. Apparently it was also helpful that Dan was a skilled and experienced carpenter. His wrist was sliced straight as a joist, and the surgeon was able to reattach the hand without complications.

When Eric Rudolph was not immediately rousted from the North Carolina hills, a crew from the popular television show *America's Most Wanted* arrived in Cherokee County to tape a special segment on the case. The program had enjoyed a symbiotic relationship with the FBI since it debuted in 1988. The bureau offered producers its cooperation in recreating notorious crimes; in turn the show provided the FBI with publicity for its crime-fighting programs, along with access to millions of viewers who are encouraged to phone in tips about suspicious neighbors and coworkers. Other law enforcement agencies have enjoyed similar arrangements, often with good results. Eighteen years after it started airing, *AMW* tips had led to the capture of nearly 900 fugitives.

The segment on Eric Robert Rudolph emphasized the urgency of catching him before he could bomb again. Yet even though the *AMW* staff was standing by the open phone lines after the show, only forty-five calls came in, and none led to his capture. There were, however, false sightings of Rudolph look-alikes from Denver to Canada. It seemed that the only place Rudolph wasn't spotted was in the North Carolina mountains, where the task force commanders were starting to realize they might be in for a long-term operation.

7

AN ARMY OF ONE

Topton, North Carolina, is a tiny community anchored by a filling station and a post office just off Highway 19/74 between Andrews and the Nantahala Gorge. Most of the houses are scattered along gravel roads that wind along the creek beds and up into the mountain hollows. Thomas Wayne Branham lives on just such a road in an unpainted, tin-roofed, cinder-block house surrounded by forest and patches of unkempt lawn. Old cars and assorted junk line the driveway and adorn the steep acres surrounding the main dwelling. The next house along the road is a simple, more conventionally appointed rancher, set on a wide, mown lawn in a cleared patch of forest—the house where Eric Rudolph and his family lived as Branham's neighbors for fifteen years.

Agents Jim Russell and Tom Frye had been warned by people who knew Branham not to try to knock on his door. He didn't take kindly to strangers, and he was known to own guns. So Frye called him and arranged a meeting at a public park in Andrews to ask him some questions about Rudolph.

Branham arrived with his own tape machine to record the interview. He told Russell and Frye that he didn't trust any government agents, not since he was framed on federal weapons charges back in 1984. He only got off that time, Branham said, because he had secretly taped the agents telling lies. After Russell and Frye assured Branham that nobody wanted to frame him, they only wanted information about Rudolph, he started talking. He hadn't spoken to Eric Rudolph since the family sold the house in 1996, he said. In fact, he'd had a falling-out with the Rudolph family years before that, although there had been a time they had been as close as his own kin.

The Rudolphs met Tom Branham in Fort Lauderdale in the late 1960s. Bob Rudolph was then working for TWA at Miami Airport, while he and his wife, Pat, volunteered as youth ministers in a Baptist church in Fort Lauderdale. Branham, a young member of the congregation who had drifted in from the Northwest, was essentially taken in by the Rudolphs as a member of the family. He repaid their friendship by building an addition to their house. The Rudolphs held prayer meetings at home, where Bob would play guitar and sing his own compositions for the group. According to other informants who knew the family, they were a Pentecostal offshoot of the Baptist congregation, and the meetings often ended with "outpourings of the spirit" when the believers would fall to the floor and speak in tongues. The youngest Rudolph children sometimes huddled in their bedrooms while the adults carried on in the living room.

In 1973 Tom Branham got the call from God to go "back to the land." He responded by purchasing a piece of property on Partridge Creek Road in Topton, North Carolina. It was perfect: abundant water, southern exposure, surrounded by Forest Service land, and extremely isolated. He lived in a tent while he fixed up an old barn on his property and staked out a building site. Bob Rudolph drove up alone to visit Tom and camped out with him for a couple of weeks while he looked for a place to build a retirement home. While Branham was building a house on his land, the whole Rudolph family came up to visit. The kids, especially Dan and Eric, were frequent visitors over the years, often staying with him for weeks at a time during the summer.

When Bob Rudolph was diagnosed with malignant melanoma in 1980, the family went into a tailspin. Neither Pat nor Bob trusted modern medicine, so Patricia started searching for alternative treatments for his cancer. To relieve the pressure on the family, Eric went to live with Tom Branham in Topton for several months while Bob's health declined. Pat mixed up wheatgrass juice to cleanse his system. He was given doses of potassium. Bob even traveled to a clinic in Tijuana, Mexico, for laetrile treatments. (Laetrile is a substance derived from poisonous apricot pits that is purported to be effective in treating advanced cancer. Since these claims have never been proved, the drug has been banned in the United States.)

When Charles Stone, the GBI investigator, learned about this, he shared his theory with the media that Bob's inability to get the laetrile in the United States was the trigger that turned the Rudolphs into government haters and Eric into a serial bomber. "We weren't antigovernment because we couldn't get laetrile, whatever those crazy people say," Pat told me. Eric later issued a statement saying, "When my father was diagnosed with cancer I was not even old enough to know what laetrile was let alone be aware of any controversy surrounding its use." To say that the laetrile ban triggered his actions, he wrote, was "laughable."

After the Tijuana treatment, Bob returned to Florida and quickly faded. To pay the mounting bills, Pat increased her hours working part-time in the X-ray department of a local hospital.

Soon after Bob's death in 1981, Pat moved with Jamie and Maura into a trailer near Homestead so that Maura could finish high school. Damian, Dan, and Joel were old enough to be on their own. Eric, who was fourteen, stayed with Branham. Maura married Keith Rhodes soon after graduation, and Pat bought a parcel of property that had come up for sale next to Branham's place on Partridge Creek Road. When they moved in, the family scattered Bob Rudolph's ashes at the base of a walnut tree in the front yard.

In a letter he later wrote to me, Eric fondly recalled his early years in North Carolina and his relationship with Branham: "I was enamored of his rustic lifestyle and the beauty of the Appalachians," he wrote.

It was a big contrast to the monotony of the South Florida suburbs. After moving to Homestead I went to Tom's for a few weeks during the summer break (79 or 80). Dan and Joel later moved up for extended stays. We like the rugged pioneer life of cutting wood, cooking on a cook stove and tending livestock.

When my father died we were able to convince my mother to purchase a piece of property next door to Tom's. The property was in the rough: there was the shell of a Jim Walters' home, an outhouse and little else. Over the next few years we made a little homestead from the ground up. My brother, Dan, and I did most of the work, while living in the shell.

Tom taught me rudimentary construction and mechanical skills, basic farming and wilderness survival techniques. He was notorious for finding an alternative method for doing things. This is the only real influence he has had on me or the other boys. He prided himself on being self-sufficient where others were dependent. Tom had a dozen ways of making a living: He did construction, hauled scrap metal, sold coupons, and supplemented his diet and fed his chickens on food found in the dumpsters of grocery stores. On one occasion we broke down on the side of the road half way to Asheville. For three days we did major engine work and slept under the truck at night. There was no such thing as AAA in his dictionary. This being able to deal with any situation in a novel unconventional way that most people are not capable of gives a sense of self reliance, independence and pride and this rubbed off on me. He worked for months building a truck that operated on wood for fuel.

Branham opened his home to others as well; for a while his brother and his two sons lived with him, and there always seemed to be a pack of teenage boys hanging around the house or out in the woods. Sometimes they shot targets with a .22. One of their friends remembered the Rudolph and Branham boys making homemade explosives and blowing them up in the forests, but the investigators couldn't confirm this.

Branham's politics had apparently evolved from Christian fundamentalism into a kind of apocalyptic ultraconservatism over the years. According to FBI interviews with the Rudolph children, Tom wanted to be prepared for the coming confrontation between the forces of good and evil. He stockpiled supplies, hoarded books, and combed flea markets for anything he might find useful in the coming conflagration.

His sideline collecting and trading grocery store coupons got him into trouble in the 1980s, when the Heinz food company sued him in civil court for allegedly trading forged coupons. In the course of the lawsuit, the ATF got involved and executed a search warrant on Branham's home in which they seized parts of a machine gun, blasting caps, dynamite, and bomb-making manuals. Branham was not home during the search, but Eric Rudolph came over to watch the proceedings. Rudolph, who was about eighteen at the time, accused the agents of acting like troops from the Soviet Union. He apparently became so upset that he was ordered out of Branham's house while the agents carted off boxes of evidence.

When Branham was later arrested on federal explosives and weapons charges, Pat Rudolph and her youngest sons visited the court in Bryson City and helped Tom post bail. He was convicted and sentenced in 1986, although the case was overturned by a federal judge. Branham spent some time in jail before the reversal, and during that period had a falling-out with Pat Rudolph, whom he felt had been insufficiently loyal to him. The Heinz lawsuit was also dismissed. According to court records, he had retained Nord Davis Jr., the Identity Christian pamphleteer, to represent him as "counsel of choice" in that case, although Davis was not a lawyer. Neither Branham nor Davis recognized any government authority beyond the level of county sheriff, something that apparently brought them together on a number of issues. They had each arrived in western North Carolina in the early 1970s, both of them refugees from the increasingly crowded and multicultural state of Florida.

Davis was a former IBM executive who had, sometime in the 1950s, made a sharp turn off the deep end. He was neither as militant nor as influential as some of his contemporaries in the radical right, such as Ed Fields and William Pierce, author of *The Turner Diaries*. But the dense and feverish pamphlets he produced reveal a virulent hatred of taxes, foreign aid, and Zionism, along with a fundamentalist reading of the U.S. Constitution. Like many of his followers, Davis denounced mainstream medicine—he died in 1997 of untreated prostate cancer—and promoted weird nutritional substances, such as "Blue Green Manna," which, he decreed, could be promoted as a possible cure for AIDS and other immune disorders if only the "unconstitutional" FDA would stop suppressing information about it.

Taking along the paid subscriber lists he had built while living in Massachusetts and Florida, Davis moved his operation to thirty bucolic acres just outside Andrews, North Carolina. Several dozen of Davis's admirers followed his lead, settling in the mountains nearby, where they started stockpiling supplies for the coming onslaught. Davis rarely spoke to members of the media, although when he did it was memorable. In 1995 he told a reporter from the *Greensboro News and Record*, "If you are an enemy of God, then I am obliged to kill you." A year later, he reprinted a negative article about him from the *Asheville Citizen-Times* along with a rebuttal denouncing and threatening the writer: "Let the record show that Northpoint Teams and some of our associates in western North Carolina have been compiling lists of those citizens who are, like [the reporter], involved in anti-patriotic activities tending to give aid and comfort to the secret enemies of the American Republic ... Whether I am around or not to see it come to pass, certain good mountain men will understand what needs to be done, and like a certain Invisible Empire of years ago, it will be carried out. Caveat. Nord Davis Jr."

The chambers of commerce of Murphy and Andrews are unlikely to include this fact in their tourist brochures, but several branches of the racist Identity and neo-Nazi movements in America have sprouted in the mountains of North Carolina. The region isn't the true American mecca for right-wing subversives—the Bitterroot Mountains and the Yaak Valley of my home state of Montana, along with pockets of northern Idaho and the Ozark Mountains, contend for that distinction—but western North Carolina is clearly an attractive place to set up a separatist compound. There is something here to soothe most varieties of paranoia: It is a relatively unpolluted, forested, isolated, and unindustrialized region with a minimal federal presence. The "Earth Changes" people, who obsessively prepare for the natural disasters foreshadowing the End Times, believe it to be one of the more geologically stable pieces of real estate in the United States. It is safer—a loaded term in the doomsday lexicon—than the soon-to-be-flooded coasts, volcano-plagued Rockies, and seething urban corridors. Another bonus: While western North Carolina is technically part of the South, it has almost no tradition of slavery, and subsequently very few African Americans.

In the 1930s, around the time Thomas Wolfe's *Look Homeward, Angel* was scandalizing Asheville society, the city became the sanctuary of a lesser-known fiction writer, a prominent American Nazi named William Dudley Pelley. After winning two O. Henry awards for short story writing, Pelley drifted into the occult, and eventually formed a Nazi group called the "Silver Shirts." Pelley openly touted the anti-Semitic hoax known as the "Protocols of the Elders of Zion," a supposed exposé of the international Jewish conspiracy. (Pelley was not alone in his promotion of the phony Protocols—American industrialist Henry Ford published them in his newspaper.)

After WWII, news of the Holocaust took the air out of the American Nazi movement for a decade or so. Pelley was jailed for subversion. But the racism that spawned the movement never died out. Like a virus, it went dormant for a while, mutated and slept and waited for another opportunity to emerge. That came with the social upheaval of the late fifties, when the U.S. Supreme Court essentially ended legal segregation of schools and other public facilities. Some saw this as evidence that the Jewish plot—under the guise of world Communism and, later, a vague amalgam called the "New World Order"—was regaining strength, taking over institutions.

Soon, another generation of American neo-Nazis sought sanctuary in western North Carolina. The most prominent of these was Ben Klassen, founder of the World Church of the Creator, author of *The White Man's Bible* and coiner of the term "RaHoWa"—short for Racial Holy War. Klassen, a former member of the Florida state legislature, moved his operation to Otto, North Carolina, a few dozen miles east of Murphy, in the early 1980s. Until his suicide in 1993, Klassen influenced a passel of racist lunatics, including his successor, Matthew Hale, currently in federal prison for conspiring to assassinate a federal judge, and his acolyte, Benjamin Smith, who went on a forty-hour shooting spree in the Midwest in 1999, killing two and wounding nine. Klassen's compound was eventually sold to the National Alliance leader and *Turner Dia-*

ries author, William Pierce (who quickly turned it over for a profit).

Other white supremacists lurking around the Smokies included James Bruggeman, an Identity preacher based in Asheville, and Kirk Lyons, a lawyer associated with the Klan and the Aryan Nations who lived on nearby Black Mountain. There were also assorted gun clubs and mini-militia groups in the surrounding mountains. A handful of so-called freemen, who refused to recognize the U.S. government or its court system, were briefly active in Macon County, where Davis, Branham, and the Rudolphs lived.

In the mid-1990s the militia movement and the most militant anti-abortion groups came to realize that they shared some common ground. New organizations, such as the U.S. Taxpayers Party, formed around the themes of owning guns, disowning government, and fighting to save "preborn" babies. Although abortion was not a focus for Nord Davis Jr., he was not above exploiting it as an issue. Tucked into his screeds denouncing the United Nations, the IRS, and the media was this nugget: "Understand, in all 'leftist' nations such as America today, the Right to life, protected by our constitution, no longer exists! Thus, from abortion to 'ethnic cleansing,' the right to life is denied—for the good of the State, of course." Such sentiments could only bolster his appeal in the Bible Belt communities of western North Carolina, where anti-abortion billboards were as common as Dairy Queen signs.

It would seem that with so many like-minded individuals in close proximity, Eric Rudolph would have made some political or operational allies to help carry out his bombing campaign. Or at least to talk about it with. But after hundreds of interviews and thousands of hours of digging, the task force investigators could not find any tangible links between Rudolph and Davis or any other group or individual. Rudolph often remarked that the Klan was a "bunch of buffoons." He was never seen attending meetings or political rallies. It appeared that, at least when it came to his politics, Rudolph was truly dependent on no one, and trusted nobody. It was a habit of solitude he developed early in his life.

When Patricia Rudolph moved with her younger sons from Florida to Topton in 1981, the only public schools in the area were a small elementary school, middle school, and high school clustered on a flat piece of ground in the nearby community of Nantahala. According to school records, Eric enrolled in Nantahala High as a ninth grader in the fall of 1981. His test scores indicated an average intelligence, although his math skills were poor. His vocabulary was very good, and he could use words with more that one meaning, but his comprehension skills were well below average. In other words, he had superior language abilities; he just couldn't interpret what he was reading in a conventional way. His grades improved from Cs, Ds, and Fs to Bs after the transfer to Nantahala, but he didn't last long in the new school.

Eric was remembered by his teachers as witty but stubborn and strange. He wore his hair short and dressed in a uniform of jeans, flannel shirts, and sneakers. He tried to fit in with the locals by chewing tobacco and driving around in pickups. But the Rudolphs were still considered outsiders, and Jamie, in particular, was teased for being a "city boy."

What made Eric stand out most in school was his peculiar view of history. He shocked his ninth grade history teacher, Angie Bateman, when he turned in an essay denying that the Holocaust took place. He produced a pamphlet from home as his source material. Another school official remembered Rudolph getting into arguments with other students over his political outlook. The only ones who stood up for him were the daughters of a fellow transplanted Floridian and eccentric named George Nordmann. According to his mother, one of them later developed a crush on Eric and used to follow him around like a puppy.

FBI agents interviewed an array of former classmates. Eric made his extremist views known even as an adolescent. One girl remembered him mouthing off about "queers," "dykes," and "niggers." But he had a calmer side as well. He loved the woods, and would always be off camping. He showed his friends survival techniques, edible plants, how to build fires and shelters in the mountains. One friend used to call him "Mr. Boy Scout."

Eric started dating a local girl when she was in the eighth grade and he was in the ninth. According to this girl, when he brought her home to meet his mother, Patricia Rudolph informed the girl that if she and Eric had a baby, Pat would deliver it at home. She'd had midwife training, Pat said, and there would be no need for doctors or hospitals, no rec-ord of the birth, and no need to give the child a social security number. Another topic of conversation at the Rudolph house was survival. Eric and Daniel had an ongoing discussion of building survival shelters and stockpiling food. Dan was an enormous influence on Eric, his girlfriend thought, and he may have terrified him. Once Eric's arm was bandaged from hand to elbow because of a bad burn. He wouldn't let anyone take him to a doctor, afraid Daniel would find out.

His girlfriend described him as shy to the point of paranoia. He didn't want his picture taken, saying it could be used against him. When his class graduated from middle school, he wouldn't sign anybody's yearbook because he didn't want his handwriting to be seen. He never told her where he was going when he was away. He said he could visit all his friends in the area without using the roads, just walking along the trails and ridges connecting the valleys. It was as if he was already preparing to disappear. As if he had been raised for it. Sometimes he would leave school on a Friday afternoon and spend the weekend alone in the woods, returning to school on Monday morning in the same, dirty clothes.

Eric was always shuttling back and forth to Florida, where his sister still lived, missing school. At the beginning of tenth grade, Eric dropped out of Nantahala High entirely. Pat had decided she could do a better job schooling her two youngest sons at home. Eric always was a voracious reader, anyway; his brother Dan even built him a wooden contraption so that he could read in bed while lying on his back. Eric and his girlfriend broke up after Eric dropped out of school, but they stayed friends for years, and he would often take her hiking or paddling in a canoe around Nantahala Lake. He would often come over to her house just to sit down to a quiet family dinner, and spend the night watching TV sitcoms. He just seemed to want something normal in his chaotic life, and her family provided that for him.

Pat continued her search for a spiritual path, while she pursued the life of a pioneer woman, keeping goats and chickens, growing her own vegetables, and making crafts to sell for cash. Otherwise she lived off social security benefits for herself and her dependent children.

When she had trouble finding the right curriculum for Eric and Jamie, Pat Rudolph decided to take the boys on a spiritual road trip. She said Tom Branham suggested that she could get the boys a good education at Dan Gayman's Church of Israel in Schell City, Missouri. At the time Gayman was one of the most prominent Identity preachers in the country. Shortly after Thanksgiving in 1984, the family of three pulled up at the Church of Israel compound in the rural Missouri flatlands.

When special agent James Cross traced the Rudolphs' trail to the Gayman property, on February 9, 1998, what he found was not quite what he'd pictured. He'd been told it would be isolated, which it was, but he expected it to be a "compound," which it wasn't. It was more like a farm, dotted with a few modest dwellings, a school, and a church, stuck out in the middle of nowhere. Schell City was a tiny community founded after the Civil War in the section of Missouri that was known as the "Burnt District." Union troops had torched every field, barn, and dwelling from here north to Kansas City in retaliation for the bloody cross-border massacres carried out by William Quantrill and his Confederate guerrillas, a band that included Frank James, the brother of Jesse. The freed slaves fled, never to return. More than a hundred years later, the ethnic composition of Vernon County was still almost 98 percent white. It had also been an enclave of Mormons who settled the region before they were driven farther west, to Utah. Dan Gayman's family belonged to a splinter Mormon group that returned to Missouri in the 1940s to set up a self-sufficient community in Schell City. Some Identity teachings, in fact, were distortions of the tenets of Mormonism, particularly the belief that there were lost tribes of Israel wandering around North America.

Cross had studied the Church of Israel and he wasn't expecting a warm welcome. Thomas Robb, a well-known Ku Klux Klan leader, had once been on the board of Gayman's church. And Gayman had a long history of association with some of the most violent white supremacist groups in the 1980s, including the Covenant, Sword and Arm of the Lord and the Order. Gayman, in fact, received a donation of $10,000 in proceeds from an armored car heist carried out by the Order. (Gayman said he had no idea where the money came from, was never indicted, and has publicly denounced racist violence.)

As an African American, Cross knew he would not be considered exactly human by Gayman and his followers—he would qualify as a "mud person," a being without a soul. This would be preferable, though, to being a Jew, otherwise known as the "spawn of Satan"—who ran the government, and therefore controlled the FBI. So Cross was somewhat surprised when he and another agent were greeted cordially by Dan Gayman and a handful of his followers, who then ushered the FBI men into a meeting in a small office building. Gayman was tall, slim, balding, and friendly. As the pastor hastily explained, just because someone might not think you were human didn't mean he meant you harm. You were just a different type of God's creation. Although Gayman wouldn't have used the word "God." It would have been "Yahweh." In fact, it turned out that Eric Rudolph's refusal to subscribe to this practice helped get his family kicked out of the congregation back in 1985.

According to Gayman, Patricia Rudolph arrived with Eric and Jamie in the late fall of 1984. The family seemed destitute, and Gayman installed them in a small trailer on the property. Pat taught art and worked on crafts with the community. Jamie attended school. But Eric, he recalled, didn't seem much interested in school or work.

By all accounts, Eric Rudolph chafed against Gayman's brand of Christian Identity. He complained that Gayman's outfit was too focused on religion, with not enough emphasis on survival training. Gayman, in turn, found Eric to be "undisciplined, belligerent, and not receptive to attempts to get him to improve his behavior." He was, said Gayman, "increasingly unable to get along with others at the church." The last straw came in April or May of 1985, when Eric was given the great honor of reading Scripture to the assembled congregation. To a stunned church full of Yahweh worshippers, Rudolph insisted on referring to the deity as "the Lord." This was blasphemy. Worse, he used "strange voices" for different parts in the Scripture, and generally "made a game of it." Gayman said that Patricia, as always, stood up for her son. He had no choice but to send the family packing, and they carried away all their belongings in the same car they had arrived in.

Gayman said he never saw or heard from any of them again.

Cross showed him pages from an address book that had been found in Rudolph's storage unit. The only names Gayman recognized were those of his own son, Timothy, and Timothy's wife, Sarah—from whom he had been estranged for years.

Cross went on to interview them as well. Tim and Sarah Gayman told a different story, both to the FBI and to a reporter from the Southern Poverty Law Center, which published the interview. Dan Gayman's son and daughter-in-law said that the Rudolphs became deeply entwined in Gayman's world. Eric found another father figure in Dan. In fact, they said that Gayman was grooming Eric to marry one of his daughters and eventually take over his ministry. They agreed that Rudolph never seemed to take to Gayman's teachings. But Gayman's plans for Eric really fell through when Eric fell in love with another follower, a pretty blond teenager named Joy. After he left the compound, Eric carried on a long-distance relationship with Joy for a while after the family went back to North Carolina. They had planned to marry, but his failure to conform to the group's doctrine came between them, and she broke off the engagement. Years later, Eric found out that Joy had married within the sect, and later committed suicide, killing herself and her two young children by flooding her car with carbon monoxide. Eric was distraught. He still kept a sweater she had knitted for him, one that could be seen in a wanted photo of Rudolph published by the FBI. (Cross told me that after Rudolph's campsites were discovered in the Nantahala, Joy's sweater was found carefully wrapped and hidden with his other prized possessions.)

When the Rudolphs returned to North Carolina they didn't move back to the house on Partridge Creek Road. Instead Pat rented a trailer in the town of Sylva, a half hour's drive east of Topton, where Eric and Jamie both lived with her while they enrolled in the nearby Western Carolina University. It wasn't Eric's first choice. In the summer of 1985 he applied for admission to Purdue University in Indiana, but Purdue required eight semesters of high school English, along with algebra, geometry, and biology—requirements he had not met. The admissions officer suggested he catch up on English, science, and math courses at a local college and then try to transfer. Eric spent two semesters at WCU, taking mostly history and art. Jamie studied music.

Patricia, perhaps seeking a new and less isolated life, threw herself into the local art scene and was elected president of the Jackson County Visual Arts Association. Eric and Jamie helped her renovate a gallery on Main Street. She had signed over the deed to her house and land in Topton to Eric and Daniel, reportedly so that she could qualify for government-subsidized housing. Daniel, who was still unmarried, lived in the house while the younger boys went to college.

Once again, Eric had trouble getting along with his fellow students and his professors, who described him as haughty and argumentative in class. He dropped out in the spring of 1987 with a new plan forming in his head: He would join the U.S. Army.

The FBI had pulled up Eric Rudolph's military record hours after his truck was identified in Birmingham. Within days agents had tracked down his former commanding officer and several of his army buddies. All of them told the story of a smart but immature young soldier who was mainly remembered for his arrogance and his fondness for smoking dope on the base.

Eric Rudolph was twenty years old, five-foot-ten and 140 pounds when he enlisted on August 4, 1987. His teachers and old friends might have been shocked to learn that the boy who detested authority and distrusted the government would sign up for the military. But Eric had told Tom Branham that he always wanted to be part of an elite military unit, like the Rangers or the Special Forces. Unfortunately, he would later learn, the army he joined was not the one he'd imagined.

Eric did well in basic training at Fort Benning, Georgia, and was posted to Company A, Second Battalion, 327th Infantry Regiment of the 101st Airborne, based in Fort Campbell, Kentucky. Rudolph earned his Air Assault badge the following February. Rudolph's commanding officer, Major Edward Frank Dorman, was a former Ranger who drilled his soldiers in search, escape, reconnaissance, and survival (SERE) tactics to prepare them to survive behind enemy lines. They were taught to evade capture, to live off the land, and to construct booby traps, including improvised shaped charges and Claymore mines. A favorite IED was an ammo can stuffed with half-sticks of dynamite and shrapnel such as nails and rocks. The soldiers were taught to ambush the enemy by setting a diversionary explosion that would concentrate them in the range of a second device, dug into the ground or set against a tree to direct the blast into the "kill zone."

Rudolph took advantage of a program to take an intensive history course at a nearby college—he got an A—and at first seemed to be adjusting to the military. But by the summer of 1988 something had changed. He was exhibiting what his superior officers described as "an attitude problem." He was counseled for behavior infractions such as sleeping on duty and "mocking authority."

He had a few friends who lived with Rudolph in the same barracks at Fort Campbell. They called him "Rudy" and described him as smart, funny, and highly opinionated. He knew his Bible backward and forward, but he wasn't a pious type. He chewed tobacco, drank beer, and smoked a lot of high-quality dope, golden buds that he told his friends he grew back in North Carolina from imported seeds. He spent most of his spare time reading in his bunk and getting high. To anyone who would listen, Rudolph railed about how the government had too much power and how he hated paying taxes. He resented the bureaucracy of the army and complained about being ordered around by blacks and women. He loved everything that was German; his bunkmates remembered him openly praising Adolf Hitler. He ranted about Jews controlling the banks and the media. The only way to shut him up was to stop questioning him. He was relentless. Not surprisingly, he had few friends at Fort Campbell, mostly other misfits and potheads.

Eric's posting was near enough to Nashville that he often visited his brother Joel and sister-in-law Debbie. In the summer of 1988 he started dating a blond high school student from Nashville named Claire For-rester. They spent every weekend together, either at the barracks or at her father's house. She later said she was attracted to him because he was "an older man" who seemed exciting and dangerous. He told her she had the right "Aryan traits," and he wanted to make Aryan babies together. This did not happen. But he was funny and smart and she went out with him for more than two years, despite what she called "his dark side" that emerged during those racist tirades. Claire often visited him back at his home in Topton, where they spent days hiking in the mountains, cutting trees in the forest for firewood, and tending his marijuana patches. He had planted them in clusters of five or six plants scattered in ditches along the power line cuts and under tall trees so they wouldn't be seen from the air. It was hard work hauling fertilizer and water in rucksacks up the mountainside, but Claire didn't mind.

Forrester told the FBI that Rudolph started obsessing about his dissatisfaction with the army that summer. He told his counselors that he wasn't learning anything and wanted out before his four-year obligation was up. So in November 1988 he deliberately failed a urinalysis test for marijuana. He was offered a general discharge from the service and he took it.

A few months later he wrote one of his buddies, by then stationed in Germany: "Surprise, surprise! I'm out of the Army since 25 January. No more slavery, no more nigger standing over me in the morning ..." He wrote about the great feeling of being free again, but also of the "sense of not knowing exactly what to do with one's self ..." To direct this new-found liberty, Rudolph had apparently come up with a plan that included recruiting a couple of his army buddies to move to North Carolina and help him expand his marijuana business. Rudolph suggested that this friend get himself sectioned out of the military ("the Sooner the Better!") so he could join Rudolph's little Hole-in-the-Wall Gang. Rudolph acknowledged the lifestyle would require hard work, but that shouldn't hold him back from the opportunities that awaited him. He signed the letter, which his ex-friend later turned over to federal investigators as evidence, "Your comrade, King of the Mountain, Eric R. Rudolph IIII."

Another letter followed a month later, with an increasingly pleading, cajoling tone. First, he jokingly apologized for the "faggish" stationery his mother had given him, then he demanded to know what was taking his buddy so long to drop out of the army. "Don't let the fuckers dissuade you!" he warned. He signed this letter with a friendly, jokey "Give your little fraulein a squeeze for me and have a Guten tag yourself. Der furher [sic], Adolph Rudolph."

Things became less friendly later that year when the man was out of the army and Rudolph called him at home from a pay phone. He still wanted him to move to North Carolina. When the buddy said no, Rudolph yelled at him, asking why he had bothered to write, then slammed down the phone. It was the last he heard of Eric Rudolph until a decade later, when he got a call from the FBI, asking about his old pal. Another of Rudolph's army friends told the investigators that he'd gotten the same treatment after he refused to move to North Carolina to join in the outlaw life.

Even without their help, Rudolph grew his marijuana business with a single-minded dedication. He studied *High Times* magazine for cultivation tips, and even made a trip to Amsterdam to bring back the perfect seeds for his sinsemilla crop. He bought a generator to power the lights for the hydroponic plants in his basement (the DEA watches for spikes in electric bills to identify growers). When the plants were harvested he stuffed gallon bags of dope into hidden compartments in his old yellow Subaru to transport his crop to sell in Nashville. Or he would sometimes dress in his old army uniform and take the bus, stashing the weed in his duffel bag.

As soon as Eric Rudolph was named as a material witness in the Birmingham bombing, a handful of "confidential sources" started calling in to police and FBI offices in Nashville. This is how the task force investigators got their first inkling that their suspected bomber had an intense and lucrative involvement in the marijuana trade. It was a surprise to the profilers, who expect bombers to be desperate loners with few social connections. Dealing is a highly social activity—although Rudolph apparently mainly dealt in bulk with a few select distributors. Bombers were also not expected to be drug users, since dope smoking and drinking diminish one's sense of self-control—and bombers are all about control. Then again, there was no evidence that Rudolph was a bomber during his marijuana-growing years.

Some information about this phase of Rudolph's life came from sources who had to be offered immunity from prosecution. But one informant who spoke freely was Deborah Rudolph, also known as Debbie Givens, Joel's ex-wife. Deborah, who divorced Joel in 1991 but remained close to him, provided details of the family's background and radical beliefs as well as Eric's marijuana business. Deborah, who has given lengthy interviews to CNN and the Southern Poverty Law Center, described Eric's relationship with Joel as a scene out of *Bill and Ted's Excellent Adventure*. Eric would spend weekends at their apartment in Nashville, sleeping all day and staying up all night, smoking dope, eating pizza, and watching Cheech and Chong movies. When they watched network television—which Eric called "the Electric Jew" or the "Jew Tube"—he would watch for Jewish names in the credits and scream at them.

When Eric wasn't with Joel and Debbie in Nashville he could be found hanging out with Claire, who lived at her father's house. "Dana," one of Claire's friends at the time, partied with the couple every weekend and described herself as "the third wheel in the relationship." She told investigators that she thought Rudolph was a domineering boyfriend, always ordering Claire around, saying, "Woman, go get me this or that." But Claire told her "Rudy" wasn't like that in private, and could be very affectionate. Dana told the investigators that Rudolph seemed like a normal, funny guy about 85 percent of the time. It was during that other 15 percent you wanted to avoid him. He told her he wanted to be a preacher, and one time actually stood on a milk crate to deliver one of his improvised sermons. Gays, he said, were "Satan's children" and ought to be killed. Dana was disturbed by the "Nazi" tirades, and she knew about his dope business, but she wasn't a snitch. For some reason, Dana told the investigators, Rudolph befriended her and chose to confide in her that he wanted to start making bombs. He even described what kinds he would make: pipe bombs with explosive powder and ammo cans stuffed with nails and screws. She tolerated the talk while they were drinking and getting stoned together. But eventually Rudolph's rhetoric started to scare her and she stopped hanging out with the couple.

Another of Rudolph's associates at the time described him as a "Jekyll and Hyde" personality. He was extremely secretive and paranoid. This associate even saw him wear a bulletproof vest to bed—he said he needed to be "ready," although he didn't elaborate about what he needed to be ready for. While this topic interested the agents who tracked him down, they paid even more attention to the man's hobby: building and flying model airplanes. Eric Rudolph developed a keen interest in this hobby, the agents learned. He was mainly curious about the remote radio device that the man used to control his airplanes. The man said he gave Rudolph some catalogs so he could research buying a system of his own.

Claire broke off her relationship with Rudolph in 1991. In the end, she was simply not willing to give up all her city comforts for the life of a pioneer wife. Rudolph took up with another woman in August of that year. They carried on a long-distance relationship for the next three years, seeing each other on weekends to camp on the edge of the woods, or go rafting and fishing. But once again, they drifted apart because she wasn't willing to move to the mountains, and Rudolph told her he could never live in a city.

Although Eric Rudolph had not accomplished his academic or military goals, and he had failed to recruit a cell of like-minded ex-soldiers to join him in North Carolina, he was still, by all accounts, a successful marijuana grower and distributor. He had all the right traits: mental and physical stamina, planning skills, and paranoia. He never sold locally, and he never got caught. At the height of his dope-growing days, some of his former associates estimated that he was grossing $70,000 a year, a figure that he and his family would later scoff at. If he was making that much money, he certainly wasn't living it up. His only extravagant purchase was apparently a $10,000 computer system and laser printer of the kind of quality that could replicate anything, including U.S. currency.

Daniel Rudolph had finally moved away from home in 1992. Hurricane Andrew badly damaged a house Maura and Keith Rhodes owned in Homestead, and he moved back to Florida to help them fix it. Two years later he met his future bride, Christine Pollard.

Tom Branham, who had by now married and started a family, told agents that during this time he noticed some suspicious activity around the Rudolph house. He began to worry about the strange vehicles with Tennessee plates pulling in at all hours. He also noticed that Rudolph had returned from the army a different person, more radical, bitter, and secretive. He told investigators that Rudolph had said he would retaliate against anyone who informed on him to police, which he took as an indirect threat. About this time, Branham thought someone had been breaking into his house when he was away—not stealing, but moving things around. He suspected Eric or his brother Dan was behind it, something they both denied. He said Eric had a mean streak, and even shot one of his own dogs, a pit bull, because it barked too much. Around the same time, Branham claimed, Eric shot his daughter's pet cat. When Branham confronted him, Rudolph said the cat was killing wild rabbits that he might need to hunt to survive someday. Rudolph was banned from visiting the Branhams after he brought a loaded pistol into his house while the children were there. When the family sold the house in the spring of 1996, Tom said he was relieved. He thought it was the last he'd have to hear about the Rudolphs.

Frank Sauer wanted to get away from the crowded highways and poor public schools of Florida. He was a plumber by trade and, like Pat Rudolph, originally from Philadelphia, so he and Pat hit it off when he came by to look at the house for sale on Partridge Creek Road. It was a nice place, six acres with a trout pond and a separate cottage with a weight room and Jacuzzi, perfect for his wife and two boys. But he was sold when he turned on the water, which came directly from a spring on the hill above the house. It was the sweetest water he had ever tasted, and it flowed at forty-eight feet per second. Even better, the hot water pipes went right through the woodstove. You could easily live up here without electricity if you needed to.

The Rudolphs, he quickly learned, had been dedicated survivalists. Eric Rudolph, in particular, was convinced the country would soon erupt in chaos and civil war. Frank Sauer thought Eric was a nice enough young man, despite his strong opinions. Eric was reserved at first, but very funny once you got him to open up. He did a wicked imitation of Senator Bob Dole, who was running for president at the time. Eric could mimic him right down to the pen he held in his withered hand. But the young man seemed to have no direction in his life. Sauer wondered why, for instance, at twenty-nine years old he was still living with his mother. But it wasn't his place to pry. Eric told him he planned to head out West after he sold the house. He never said why he was going.

When Sauer's wife and sons came up to look at the house they made a videotape of Eric giving them a tour of the rooms—including the underground room where, Sauer later learned, Eric cultivated his marijuana plants. During the tour of the garage, you can clearly see the drywall sander later found in a search of Rudolph's storage unit. But here, months before the Centennial Olympic Park bombing, its wooden handle is still attached.

Sauer spent a couple of days living with the Rudolphs while he negotiated a mortgage with the bank. He slept on a mattress on the floor of Eric's room, and during the days Eric drove him around the area, giving him tips about the locals. "Don't trust them," Rudolph said. "They can seem nice, but you'll always be an outsider to them."

Later, after the FBI was looking for Eric Rudolph, the Sauers noticed something unusual had been carved on one of the oak planks in Eric's old dresser. There was a Star of David circled and with a line drawn through it, next to the words "No Juden." On the other side someone had scratched the faint outline of a swastika.

In mid April 1996 the sale went through and the bank cut a check to Eric Rudolph, who had title to the house, for $65,000. He apparently split the money with Dan, Joel, and Patricia. In May, Dan and Christine were married in Atlanta. The whole Rudolph family gathered for the event, spending a weekend together at a Days Inn north of the city. Afterward, Eric stayed with Maura and Keith Rhodes in Hendersonville for a couple of weeks before taking off on a long trip. He told everyone he was driving to Montana, Colorado, and Idaho to look for property out West. He would even call family members from pay phones, telling them he was in Idaho. But federal investigators found no evidence that Rudolph had made the trip; they even traced some of his calls back to phone booths in North Carolina. And they were certain he was in Murphy on June 13, when he rented a trailer under the name Bob Randolph.

Frank Sauer also thought Eric had left the area, so he was surprised to run into him in the Wal-Mart in Murphy in late July 1996. "Aren't you living out West?" he asked Eric. No, said Rudolph, he was living up in Unaka, a tiny hamlet a dozen miles northeast of Murphy. Sauer didn't think much of the encounter until the FBI asked him about it almost two years later. A week after Sauer saw Rudolph coming out of the hardware section of Wal-Mart, the bomb that killed Alice Hawthorne and injured 110 others exploded in Centennial Olympic Park.

Eric Rudolph lived like a specter in and around Murphy for the next year and a half. He paid cash to rent places for a few months at a time, then moved on. He was rarely in touch with his family. After showing up at Maura and Keith's house in Hendersonville for Thanksgiving dinner in November 1996, he disappeared again for months. Eric resurfaced the following fall to take Patricia on a long road trip to New York. Along the way they explored as many Civil War battlefields in Virginia and Maryland as Pat could tolerate. They stopped to visit her brother in Cape May, New Jersey, then continued on to New York City, where they stayed with Jamie at the Village apartment he shared with his gay partner, Cameron. The four of them toured Manhattan and ate Thai food at a downtown restaurant. At Eric's suggestion, they rented a movie to watch that evening. Cameron found another place to sleep that night. Jamie would later recall the visit as pleasant and uneventful. Whenever politics came up, someone would simply change the subject.

After the trip, Eric and Keith Rhodes moved Pat into her rented trailer in Bradenton, Florida. And then Eric vanished again.

Bonnie Baird (not her real name) was visiting her new boyfriend in Atlanta when she got a call from a girlfriend in Andrews. "Turn on the TV," she said. "Eric Rudolph is wanted for bombing an abortion clinic in Birmingham." She said the FBI had been around looking for her and asking questions about Rudolph. Baird actually had to pause for a second to search for a face to go with the name. Then it clicked. "Eric *Rudolph* ... Oh my God!" In her time, Bonnie had known a few men who might be wanted by the FBI, but had never expected Eric to be one of them. Eric seemed so quiet, and, well, ordinary. Not that she knew much about him, even after a few dates. He was cute, but he was kind of boring. He would never talk about himself and he wouldn't give her a phone number.

She contacted the FBI, and they asked her to come in for an interview at the National Guard Armory building in Murphy. The agents were clearly hoping she was still in contact with Rudolph, or could at least tell them more about Rudolph's associates. They pressured her for months, and brought her to testify before a grand jury in Atlanta before they finally believed she was telling them the truth.

I sat down with Bonnie one rainy afternoon at a restaurant near Murphy. She is tall and sassy, with long polished nails and creamy skin, a full package of laughs and misfortune topped with a mane of yellow hair. She waits tables for a living, and she's good at it. Her customers enjoy her playful banter. Off work, she speaks with the soothing, tentative voice of a woman who's had some hard knocks. But her attitude is more positive now that she's got her life together, she said. She told me about a string of bad relationships in her past, some poor choices and rough characters. Eric Rudolph was one of the near misses.

Sometime in the early spring of 1997 Baird was browsing the aisles at Plaza Video when her daughter gave her a nudge. "That guy keeps looking at you," she whispered. Baird glanced over and saw a dark-haired man staring at her, not even being subtle. He looked familiar, so she walked up to him and said, "I know you." When he introduced himself she remembered: she'd met him at a dinner party at a mutual friend's house a few years back. Baird had been set up to meet his older brother, Joel. They never clicked, but she remembered this guy, Eric Rudolph. He'd seemed so distant at the party, like something was on his mind. But now he was looking at her with these piercing blue-green eyes, almost the color of turquoise, and she definitely had his attention. He was a few years younger, but she was in great shape back then, and there was a mutual attraction.

They started talking, and ended up making vague plans to go hiking together sometime. She wrote down her phone number for him and said, "You might get an answering machine, but just leave your number and I'll call you back."

"But I don't have a phone," he said. He told her he lived with an uncle on a farm in Tennessee, and that it would be a long-distance call for her, even if they had a phone. He'd try to reach her next time he was in town.

Two days later, he called from a pay phone.

He took her on a date at a fancy restaurant at a resort near the Georgia border, but it didn't go too well. Rudolph didn't want to talk about himself, and Bonnie found it kind of dull trying to keep the conversation going. All he said was that he had a job as a firefighter with the Forest Service, and that he sometimes had to take off without warning and be gone for long periods of time. He drove her home, kissed her good night, and that was it. The thing that impressed her most about the date was how clean he kept his truck.

Rudolph called her again and they rented a movie together that they watched with her teenage daughter. The next weekend, he showed up unannounced when her daughter was home alone, and he ended up driving the daughter out to join Bonnie and some friends for a cookout. They drank some beer and smoked some weed, and stretched out in the cool grass to look at the sky and talk. But they never had a chance to be alone together. It just never happened. Then he showed up again another Saturday afternoon that summer. She was in the bathroom, leaning over to blow-dry her hair, when she heard a vehicle pull up. She was expecting some friends to come by to play spades, so she thought they had arrived. But when she threw her hair back over her shoulders she saw Eric standing in the doorway, watching her. It gave her a start.

"What'cha doin'?" he said. When she told him some friends were coming over, he got a little prickly. "But I want you to do something with me," he said. The way he said it bothered her, as if he owned her or something. "Well, I've made plans," she said. "We can do something together another time." He didn't seem happy, but her friends pulled up before he could talk her out of it.

"We kind of all hung out in the kitchen for a few minutes," said Bonnie. "And when he saw I wasn't gonna budge, he said, 'I'm going to run to the store and get a pack of cigarettes.' And I go, 'okay.' And I thought he was gonna come right back." He never returned, and he never called again.

She bumped into him about six months later, around Christmastime. They were both in the grocery line at Ingles, and she saw he was buying some cigarettes. She was tempted to ask if he was just now getting those smokes, but she thought better of it. She said hello, and asked how it was going. He said a few words, but he was cold as could be. Bonnie just put him out of her mind.

A month later the FBI was all over her. Looking back, she wondered if he wasn't trying to protect her by keeping his distance. But maybe, she thought, he just wasn't a people person.

8

THE BONE THROWERS

On Valentine's Day, 1998, the U.S. attorney's office in Birmingham officially charged Eric Rudolph with the fatal clinic bombing. A federal warrant was issued for his arrest. At a news conference in Birmingham, Joe Lewis, the SAC of the Birmingham FBI office, announced a $100,000 reward for information leading to Rudolph's arrest and conviction, which, he added, could result in the death penalty. At the same conference, Jim Cavanaugh of the ATF tried to talk Rudolph in from the cold: "I'm concerned for everyone involved, including Eric," said Cavanaugh. "It would be a whole lot easier if Eric would call us and come in voluntarily ... We have found that Eric is an intelligent person, he's a veteran, and he knows what I'm saying is the best way to resolve this situation, for him to call us and come in ... For Eric this is the first step toward the future."

Reporters in attendance noted the peculiar phraseology of Cavanaugh's statement and his repeated use of Rudolph's first name. It was a sign that the profilers had arrived in Birmingham.

Cavanaugh, who used to run his own agency's profiling program, calls the agents in the FBI's Behavioral Analysis Unit "the bone throwers," a joking reference to an area of law enforcement that seems part art, part science, and part voodoo. In Cavanaugh's case, it's an affectionate term. He likes using profilers to "get ahead of the suspect, figure out what he's gonna do before he does it."

The Behavioral Analysis Unit, or BAU, is the new name for the old

Behavioral Science Unit, and it has been folded into the bureau's Critical Incident Response Group, based in Quantico, Virginia. What the unit has to offer to both federal and local law enforcement agencies is spelled out on the FBI website: "crime analysis, investigative suggestions, profiles of unknown offenders, threat analysis, interview strategies, major case management, search warrant assistances, prosecutive and trial strategies and expert testimony." Although some members of the unit have degrees or training in psychology, they are essentially cops with specialized skills in analyzing and predicting human behavior.

"Just like forensics, surveillance, and polygraph are tools—behavioral analysis is also a tool," said Tom Neer, a BAU agent who was sent to Birmingham to help with the investigation. Neer explained that behavioral analysts—he dislikes the term "profilers"—are best used by field commanders as operational consultants, although sometimes the commanders have to be "educated" to recognize their value. And after the disastrous use of profiling in the Richard Jewell incident, many agents were wary of the BAU. Although Neer and his partner, Ron Tunkel, were not responsible for the Jewell profile, it would still be a struggle for the unit to maintain a presence in the case. Lucky for Neer and Tunkel, Jim Cavanaugh was a sympathetic boss. He freed up an ATF agent to brief them and walk them through the crime scene as soon as they arrived in Birmingham.

Neer, who joined the FBI in 1984, is ginger-haired, tall, and angular. Tunkel, shorter and round-faced, is an ATF agent who, in the spirit of interagency cooperation, works with the BAU through a program called VICAP, the Violent Crime Apprehension Program. Both agents speak in hushed, funeral-director voices, as if they were accustomed to soothing people in extreme distress.

The blasted clinic hadn't yet reopened and the site was still cordoned off with yellow tape when the agents got there. They scrutinized the building from every angle, then climbed the hill to the small tree-lined parking lot across from the clinic. They stood next to the tall oak where Rudolph had likely stood when he detonated his bomb with a model airplane controller. They walked the route Rudolph was said to have taken through the Southside neighborhood, up through Vulcan Park, past the

McDonald's and to the place where he parked his truck. Then they drove
to other abortion clinics in town and tried to imagine why the bomber
had chosen New Woman All Women as his target. Once they saw the
others they knew: This bomber liked to watch. All the other clinics were
concealed behind fences and thick hedges. He might have been able
to damage those buildings and to kill people, but there was no vantage
point from which to observe his work. New Woman was out in the open
and provided a better view.

"This was someone who spent a lot of time and energy, had probably
surveilled this place many, many times, and probably enjoyed it," said
Tunkel. "That was part of the thrill. Just like with a serial killer or rapist,
sometimes it's the thrill of the hunt. The actual sex or murder is actually
anticlimactic."

Modern psychological profiling was first used by law enforcement to
catch a serial bomber who terrorized New York City during the 1940s
and 1950s. The "Mad Bomber" always followed up his attacks with oddly
worded letters, signed "FP," that cast blame on the "crooks" at Con Edison, the public power company. Desperate to solve the case, New York
detectives enlisted the help of Dr. James Brussel, a psychiatrist special-
izing in criminal behavior. Brussel studied the bombings and came to the
following conclusions: The Mad Bomber was a male (almost all bombers
are male), unmarried, who lived with a female relative somewhere in
Connecticut (based on where the letters were mailed). The bomber was
paranoid, a disease that usually develops in a man's thirties, so he would
be about fifty years old, a former employee of Con Edison who had a
grudge against the company. He was meticulous, polite, and very neat.
Based on the syntax of his letters, he was probably foreign born, most
likely a Slav. The coup de grace was the psychiatrist's final prediction for
the detectives: "One more thing," said Dr. Brussel. "When you catch
him—and I have no doubt you will—he'll be wearing a double-breasted
suit. And it will be buttoned."

After searching old Con Ed records for information on any dis-
gruntled former employees of Eastern European descent who lived in
Connecticut, detectives knocked on the door of George Metesky in Wa-

terbury. He admitted he was FP—which stood for "Fair Play." When he dressed to be taken to jail, Metesky chose a double-breasted suit, neatly buttoned.

When special agent Howard D. Teten began teaching crime-solving techniques at the FBI training academy in the late 1960s and early 1970s, he asked Dr. Brussel to tutor him in psychological profiling. Soon civilian police departments were requesting assistance from Teten's instructors to help solve unusual and serial crimes. By the mid-seventies a separate Behavioral Science Unit was formed at the academy. Two agents, John Douglas and Robert Ressler, and a psychiatric nurse, Ruth Burgess, embarked on a famous study of confessed assassins, serial killers, and rapists. They interviewed them in prison and came up with a set of behaviors associated with certain types of crime scene evidence that could be used to help identify the offenders. Douglas went on to write a series of books that glamorized the FBI profilers, something that, according to Tom Neer, has led to a number of misconceptions about the profession.

"We went through five or six name changes in the unit, from Behavioral Sciences to Behavioral Analysis and so on," said Neer. "But the most significant change was away from 'psychological profiling.' It's hard to be both a psychologist and an FBI agent. It takes two different skill sets. If you're a psychologist, chances are you're interested in diagnosis and treatment. If you're FBI, chances are you want to find bad people and put them in jail."

Even though the first case of psychological profiling involved a bomber, by the time Eric Rudolph was identified as the main suspect in the Birmingham bombing, there was still no scientific study available to help agents search for serial bombers or arsonists. All the information on them was anecdotal, or lumped in with other serial killers. Tunkel would later earn his Ph.D. with the first statistical survey of bombers. Although the sample was small—about fifty inmates jailed for various types of bombings and threats—according to the survey a bomber was, statistically, most likely to be a heterosexual, unmarried white male, thirty-one years old, above average intelligence, who was raised by both parents but whose father left the home before the offender was eighteen, who had at least a high school education, and was employed as a construction laborer. Just like Eric Rudolph. But statistics do not catch criminals. The two agents wanted to examine the life of the current prime suspect to see if his background and psychological traits were consistent with what was known about other bombers. But they were more interested in behavior patterns that could provide clues to Rudolph's motivations and to his future actions.

Tunkel and Neer spent two weeks in Birmingham studying the SANDBOMB case file, reviewing the forensics and the 302s, or interview reports, of Rudolph's family and associates. They read the Army of God letters and learned what they could about the targets. All the signs indicated that Rudolph was a cold, calculating serial bomber, not an unstable zealot spontaneously reacting with rage to a recent event.

"Somebody who's completely angry probably wouldn't take some of these steps in preparation," said Tunkel. The agents agreed that the bomber was probably not part of a group, as he claimed in the Army of God letters. But while that claim was a ruse, the passions expressed in the letters were deadly serious. The phrase, "The murder of 3.5 million children every year will not be tolerated," was the tip-off. "That language shows us his commitment to this," said Tunkel. "His devices suggested that as well, the sophistication and lethality of them. He's committed to killing and will kill again."

Neer and Tunkel prepared a preliminary report in Birmingham in which they noted that the bomber's patterns "suggest that more than ideological needs were being met by this act. Needs of which the offender may not even be aware. These needs are internal and speak of degrees of anger and pride that have been found in other offenders who use explosives for evil intent. Anti-government, anti-abortion, anti-homosexuality, anti-technology, etc., were simply convenient positions for them to take in order to meet deeper needs."

Tunkel and Neer faxed their findings back to Quantico for peer review, and ended up with a "product" designed to help the field agents do their jobs. "The investigative agents are looking in terms of prosecution how to get more evidence," said Neer. "We're thinking things like 'how do you interview him?' And now that he's a fugitive, what might we take from what we're learning to instruct the SAC about what to say when he or she does a press conference. It may be inconsequential to Eric Rudolph, but to those witnesses who've been reluctant to come forward, maybe we say something that reveals that we have some insight and understanding of Eric, and it may free up some people to come forward."

The BAU analysts stayed in Birmingham long enough to advise Jim Cavanaugh on the wording of his appeal for Eric Rudolph to turn himself in. Then they returned to Quantico and were assigned to other cases, at least for the time being.

Meanwhile, the forensic teams continued their methodical quest to tie the bombings in Birmingham and Atlanta to Rudolph. Lloyd Erwin, the ATF chemist, once again lived up to his reputation for thinking outside the box of traditional bomb analysis. On the first Sunday night of the manhunt, while other agents were sitting in motel rooms, waiting for the search warrant, Erwin and a few of his colleagues, including Joe Kennedy, decided to take a stroll through the Wal-Mart in Murphy. Erwin had figured that every family within a twenty-five-mile radius did its shopping there, since there were no other big stores in the area. Rudolph probably shopped there as well, and if he was the bomber, he may have picked up some components. Erwin and the other agents cruised from aisle to aisle, and when they reached the checkout counter their shopping carts contained just about everything except the dynamite and the detonator. They picked up black electrical tape, duct tape, and size D Energizer batteries in the electronics aisle. They found Rubbermaid Serv'n Saver plastic containers in the housewares department. When Erwin turned into hardware, a row of toolboxes on the bottom shelf caught his eye. There it was, the same green-colored plastic with the indented square pattern that he had picked up outside the clinic. The Popular Mechanics–brand toolbox was exactly the right size to contain the bomb. Nearby he found a small brass lock, just like one he'd noted in the debris. A few aisles down he solved another mystery that had been bothering him since he'd arrived at the blast scene. There had been hundreds of tiny scraps of soft, green and white plastic material scattered around the site and tattooed in the officer's flesh. They looked like bits of artificial foliage, the kind you would find in a fake planter. The clinic manager had told Erwin there were no artificial plants decorating the building, so he presumed they had to be part of the device. Sure enough, in the crafts aisle, Erwin found a selection of plastic greenery and variegated ivy that could have been used to camouflage the toolbox in the low shrubs outside the clinic.

Joe Kennedy of the ATF returned to comb through Rudolph's trailer and storage unit several more times. He found more than a dozen hose clamps in various parts of Rudolph's property. He was able to establish that none was the model listed on the Wal-Mart receipt, strengthening the theory that Rudolph had used the Wal-Mart clamp in his bomb. The evidence teams later expanded their search to his former residences, including the old family home on Partridge Creek Road. Kennedy vacuumed out closets and tested carpets for traces of EGDN but came up empty.

That spring Kennedy also embarked on an odyssey through the world of nail manufacturing as he tried to find ways to match the nails found in Rudolph's storage unit with ones recovered at the bomb scenes. He had been able to trace 4d flooring nails recovered from the Sandy Springs site to a manufacturer in Massachusetts called the Tremont Nail Company. Kennedy and an ATF colleague visited the factory and observed the way the nails were cut from sheets. They found that, like bullets passing through barrels, batches of nails are marked by the tools with which they are manufactured. Based on this study, the ATF team concluded that seven of the flooring nails found in Rudolph's storage unit probably came from the same batch as the ones used in the Sandy Springs bombing.

Tom Mohnal and the FBI forensic specialists attached to the Atlanta Bomb Task Force also flew down to have a look through Rudolph's property, searching for links to the Centennial Olympic Park bombing. Agents learned that Rudolph had purchased a large quantity of smokeless gunpowder, probably at a gun show in Tennessee, before the Atlanta Olympics. It was the same brand—Accurate Arms—that was used in Centennial Park. Government chemists had also isolated the specific alloys in the steel plates used in three of the Atlanta bombs. The steel had been manufactured by a company in Kentucky called Gallatin Steel in a batch made on February 18, 1996. Six coils of this product were distributed around western North Carolina in May 1996. One of the businesses that purchased a coil was the Franklin Machine Company, where Rudolph's friend Randy Cochran worked as a mechanic. When agents interviewed Cochran, he told them that Eric Rudolph had once visited him at the shop on a Saturday. Although he had never seen Rudolph take any steel, he knew that the shop gate was left unlocked on weekends.

One of the most compelling pieces of evidence against Rudolph was generated by a feat of old-fashioned police work by the FBI. The postmaster in Topton mentioned to agents that Rudolph used to buy a lot of postal money orders from him. The receipts had all been sent to a USPS warehouse in St. Louis. John Behnke, the case agent in Atlanta, was determined to find out what Rudolph had been buying with the money orders. So he sent a team of FBI agents to the warehouse to sort, by hand, through hundreds of thousands of fragile paper receipts of all the money orders issued in the country over a period of a year. They were looking for anything issued from Topton with Rudolph's name on it or with similar names that he often used as aliases. Since the warehouse was open during the day, the agents could only work at night. After a month of nights in St. Louis, one of the agents hit the jackpot: It was a money order for $14.97 sent to Loompanics Unlimited of Port Townsend, Washington, from Z. Randolp of Topton, North Carolina. The FBI contacted Loompanics, a now-defunct publisher of weapons manuals and sundry subversive handbooks, which matched the receipt to an order form for one of its titles: *Kitchen Improvised Fertilizer Explosives*. When the U.S. attorneys subpoenaed all other book orders placed by Z. Randolp, the company produced another receipt for a thin paperback titled *Ragnar's Homemade Detonators*. The crimped aluminum tube depicted on the jacket illustration was a match for the improvised detonator used in the Birmingham bombing. And Z. Randolp's handwriting was a match for Eric Robert Rudolph.

9

NANTAHALA

Eric Rudolph was not the only serial bomber making news in 1998. One week before the Birmingham clinic attack, Theodore Kaczynski appeared in federal court in Sacramento, California, to plead guilty to murder. Kaczynski was the classic "lone offender," a distrustful, solo operator on a self-imposed mission. Through careful planning and luck he managed to elude the FBI and ATF for eighteen years. He might never have been caught, except that his ego got the better of him, and in 1995 he made the mistake of trying to explain himself to the world. He posted letters demanding that a major newspaper or magazine publish a 35,000-word essay on the evils of technology, which was quickly dubbed "The Unabomber Manifesto." If they complied, he promised, he would stop his bombing campaign. After the *Washington Post* and the *New York Times*—at the urging of the FBI—reluctantly printed the essay, Kaczynski's brother, David, recognized Ted's distinctive writing style and turned him in. In April 1996 federal agents arrested Kaczynski just outside his cramped, dark cabin in rural Montana. He barely put up a struggle. Later, evidence techs discovered a functional package bomb, batteries included, stashed under his bed. Despite his promise, the Unabomber was ready to mail it to his next victim. On the eve of his trial Kaczynski pleaded guilty to avoid risking the death penalty. He was sentenced to life without parole. The former Berkeley math professor would later claim that his defense team had tricked him into the plea deal. Accepting it was the only way, he said, that he could prevent his lawyers from labeling him mentally ill—in his words a "sickie"—in court.

For Terry Turchie, leader of the FBI's UNABOM Task Force, the sudden plea bargain was a stunning anticlimax to an exhausting investigation. Turchie had spent four years obsessively preparing a case for trial. After the deal was announced, it took a while for the adrenaline to drain out of his system. When Kaczynski was finally shipped to the maximum security federal penitentiary in Florence, Colorado, Turchie returned to the Bay Area. He planned to start a new job as assistant special agent in charge of counterintelligence in the San Francisco field office and to finally spend some quality time with his wife, Joy, and their two young teenagers.

Turchie is tall and fit, with a receding hairline and an open, friendly face. He prefers hiking to hanging out in bars, cooks Italian food for his family, and loves Disney movies. According to his friends, he keeps pictures of Mickey Mouse in his office. They will also tell you that he has a steel-trap mind, a great sense of humor, and, as an agent, a finely tuned sense of how to operate within ethical boundaries in the bureau. He was the kind of boss who made people want to work with him.

Since joining the FBI in 1971, Turchie had risen steadily through the ranks without seeming to play politics, something that mystified his fellow agents. "Maybe it's because I was born in Berkeley," he told me. "But here's the deal—I'm very unconventional for our institution."

In February 1998, only two days after he started his new job, the San Francisco special agent in charge called Turchie into his office and told him the FBI director wanted him to go to Atlanta to spend some time on the Olympic Park bombing case.

"In what capacity?" asked Turchie.

"They just want you to talk about some of the things we learned in UNABOM."

Turchie envisioned a week or two down South, sharing the lessons he'd gathered from organizing the huge, multijurisdictional UNABOM investigation and bringing it to trial. It was one of the few times that Turchie, a chess player of an investigator, failed to see the next move coming.

When he arrived in Atlanta, the task force was already convinced they had enough evidence to make Eric Rudolph the primary suspect in the Atlanta bombings. And the pressure was greater than ever to combine the investigation with Birmingham. Turchie was still getting acquainted with the Atlanta team when Louis Freeh unilaterally announced that he was reorganizing the structure of the Rudolph investigation, increasing the number of agents assigned to the case and putting the whole thing under a new commander: Terry Turchie, former head of the UNABOM Task Force.

The ATF leadership, along with Doug Jones and the rest of the SANDBOMB Task Force in Birmingham, went ballistic at the news. Jones called Eric Holder, Janet Reno's deputy at the Justice Department, and asked the attorney general's office to intervene. The plan was put on hold until mid-March, when they arrived at a compromise: The SAND-BOMB Task Force would remain a separate entity—and convene a separate federal grand jury—although it would share information and resources under the umbrella of a new "Southeast Bomb Task Force." Woody Enderson would remain in his spot in Atlanta as coordinator of the investigations, while Terry Turchie was sent to western North Carolina to lead the fugitive hunt for Eric Rudolph. And he would be teamed with Don Bell, an ASAC from the ATF office in Charlotte, to make sure the ATF was represented in the new arrangement.

Turchie and Bell met for the first time later that month in Birmingham during their initial conference with the SANDBOMB Task Force. It went about as might be expected, with Doug Jones and the Birmingham contingent determined to mark their own hard-won territory. As soon as the agents left the meeting, Turchie turned to Bell and said, "Now comes the easy part." They both laughed. Don Bell was prepared to have to fight for his turf with this hotshot from the FBI, but he could tell right away that Turchie was different. He was an engaging guy and refreshingly free of attitude. They hit it off from the start. Turchie told him, "Don't worry. We're in charge and we'll work this out together." And while the agents didn't always agree, Bell felt that Turchie was true to his word: Turchie never held back information and always included Bell in the decision-making process.

It started the very next day in Murphy, when Turchie and Bell went office hunting for larger quarters. The first place they looked at was an empty funeral parlor—unoccupied except for the stacks of caskets stored in the basement. "Jeez, I hope those are empty," Bell remarked. They agreed that renting a funeral parlor might send the wrong message to the community, and soon settled on a duplex in nearby Andrews to use as a command center.

Then they started reorganizing the manhunt. The first decision they made was to keep their key people on duty for longer rotations. It was something Turchie had learned from UNABOM. After an initial surge of energy, things settle into a routine. Then people start coming and going, so that you have different staff every week. As soon as agents get up to speed, they're gone, destroying the continuity of a prolonged investigation. After some cajoling, all the agencies signed on to ninety-day assignments, starting April 1. Many task force members ended up renewing their tours several times, some staying on for a year or more.

Turchie was also determined to make friends with the locals instead of intimidating them. First he wanted to ramp down the paramilitary presence in the community. So he and Don Bell made some rules: Avoid wearing the raid jackets and black SWAT uniforms in town. Go for a casual look with jeans and flannel shirts. Try not to walk into restaurants with guns strapped on your legs. It was a part of a strategy, called "Circle the Forest," that Turchie and Bell had come up with to win the hearts and minds of the locals. They divided the agents into mixed investigative teams—ATF, FBI, U.S. Forest Service. Then they tacked a map of the Nantahala forest to a wall in their command post and drew a big circle around all the green areas on the map, including the towns of Murphy, Andrews, and Topton, then parceled them into beats for those teams to cover. They were told to go house to house in their beat and talk to as many people as they could.

"The idea was not just to blend into the community, but to go out and make friends with it," said Turchie.

Another of his objectives was to quickly find out whether there were any groups within the community that would harbor Rudolph or help him escape. Turchie kept hearing about this militia-type group in the mountains around Andrews and Topton, the remnants of Nord Davis's Northpoint Tactical Teams. He assigned agents to take a hard look. But they found no evidence that Rudolph was a member of the group or that Davis was linked to any of his activities. And once that was established, Turchie wanted his agents to avoid viewing these people as the enemy.

"Obviously we wanted to follow up if there would be an indication of somebody helping him. But we had to balance it against the fact that, yeah, a lot of people up there distrust the federal government," said Turchie. "It doesn't mean that all of those people are part of the big conspiracy to kill policemen and bomb the Olympics."

With heavily armed tracking teams still out in the woods, and agents knocking on doors, the last thing Turchie wanted was a misunderstanding that might lead to a tragedy. "The kind of us-against-them mentality that brought us scenes like the one in Ruby Ridge, Idaho," he said. "The whole bottom line was to put a face with the federal government. Here's who we are. We're not ten feet tall and mean and nasty. But we need your help. And if you look out while you're having your morning coffee into the back yard, and you see Eric Rudolph in your berry patch please call us. Because if he comes down from those mountains we really want to just arrest him and get him out of here."

Turchie also wanted to ease some of the tensions with local law enforcement by enlisting them as allies. The task force called a meeting at the courthouse in Murphy, inviting all the sheriffs, police, and representatives of other agencies like the U.S. Forest Service and Tennessee Valley Association police. Charles Stone, the GBI agent from Atlanta, gave a talk about the investigation and showed the audience some mock-ups of the bombs. Turchie and Bell invited all the agencies, if they could spare the personnel, to join the task force. In the end, Turchie estimated that more than twenty-five federal, state, and local entities took part in the fugitive task force in some capacity. And once he got the lay of the land, and learned about the history of the people who lived there, Terry Turchie knew he was going to need whatever help he could get.

When it comes to hide and seek, the mountains of North Carolina have always favored the hiders. This is mainly a function of the region's complex ecological personality. The Appalachian range was created by a collision of tectonic plates 480 million years ago; the resulting peaks once stood taller than the Himalayas. The mountains have been worn down like old teeth by eons of erosion so that now, from a distance, they seem benevolent and serene. The damp forests breathe out a soothing blue haze that softens the ridgelines. But beneath the oaks and hickories and the second canopy of dogwoods and mountain laurel lies a topography shot through with water-cut ravines and treacherous crags. The Cherokee named the region Nantahala, meaning "Land of the Noonday Sun," because the vertical gorges and deep creek bottoms lie in shadow most of the day. This kind of landscape favors the fugitives, outlaws, smugglers, moonshiners, and marijuana growers who have hidden among its caves and branches for as long as the mountains have endured human habitation.

When the first white settlers showed up in southern Appalachia in the seventeenth century, most of the region was Cherokee country. Back then the tribe's territory stretched from the Ohio River south through what is now Kentucky; Tennessee; northern Alabama and Georgia; and western Virginia, North Carolina, and South Carolina. The settlers were mainly Scots-Irish immigrants from Ulster who first homesteaded in Pennsylvania, then slowly drifted down the spine of the Appalachians in search of fresh frontiers. Some came to escape retribution after the Whiskey Rebellion in 1794. In that first uprising of the new republic, farmers in western Pennsylvania refused to pay a tax on spirits that was imposed to retire the government's war debt. They were quickly routed by a federal militia of tax collectors—the first ATF agents. Some of the insurgent whiskey makers packed up their stills and headed into the Appalachian frontier to get away from the meddlesome central government.

Realizing they had no chance resisting the new American regime, most of the Cherokee chose to assimilate rather than fight. Eventually 16,000 Indians were forcibly removed to the treeless plains of Oklahoma. A third of them would die on the 800-mile journey, known as the "Trail of Tears." But a handful of clans—some 1,000 Cherokee in all—refused to resettle. Some who held U.S. citizenship and owned private land were allowed to stay; others hid in the Snowbird Mountains of western North Carolina, undetected, for years.

Like most of his clan, a Cherokee farmer named Tsali tried to keep out of sight while he scraped a living out of the mountain hollows. But when a party of infantry troops tried to remove him to Oklahoma, Tsali fought back. Two soldiers were killed and Tsali's family escaped into the forest. Hundreds of U.S. troops were sent in to hunt them down, but they couldn't find a trace of the runaways. Eventually Cherokee collaborators joined the chase and tracked Tsali deep into the forest, where they killed him. It was generally agreed that without the local trackers, Tsali would never have been found.

When the Civil War broke out two dozen years later, the southern Appalachians became a refuge for bushwhackers and draft dodgers from both warring armies. A local highwayman and unionist named Goldman Bryson evaded capture in the Nantahala forest for five years. A unit of Cherokee Confederates shot him down outside Murphy, then galloped through the streets of town brandishing Bryson's bloody uniform.

The Indians who evaded removal were eventually given a reservation of their own. By the end of the twentieth century, the Eastern Band of Cherokee had 10,000 enrolled members and an 80,000-square-foot Harrah's casino poised at the southeast entrance to the Great Smoky Mountain National Park. Tourists can visit the Oconoluftee Indian Village to experience the illusion of traditional Cherokee life, and then drive north through the park or west and south to the Nantahala National Forest to soak up the illusion of wilderness.

The truth is, there is virtually no wilderness left in the Appalachians, even in the "designated roadless areas" that enrage the local logging operators. Most of the forest is second- and third-growth timber that had been clear-cut back in the nineteenth century to fuel the nation's appetite for railroad ties and building materials. The U.S. government eventually reclaimed the forests and let the trees grow back. Now sections of the Nantahala and the Pisgah forests resemble the precolonial landscape, but true wilderness is a rare commodity here, existing only in scattered pockets deep in the mountains. The 3 million acres of national forest outside the Great Smoky Mountain park are spider-veined with trails and logging roads. The forests are used hard by nature-hungry, sports-minded, refuge-seeking pilgrims from Raleigh, Atlanta, and Miami who want to build second homes, hike the Appalachian Trail, fish, run the rivers, ride mountain bikes or ATVs, or just look at the scenery. In fact, so many outsiders have moved into the area that the natives of Murphy and Andrews call the summer cabins and log palaces in the forest "Florida houses."

But despite civilization pressing in from every side, it is still easy to get lost in these mountains. There are caves and hollows and old mine shafts, sheltered ledges and sudden ravines that enforce seclusion for those who want it, and for some who don't. It seems as if every tourist season at least one child will wander off from the picnic pull-off and disappear into the laurel. Sometimes hikers get disoriented and lose their way.

Anyone who goes off the trail might run into the region's famous wild hogs, feral descendants of several imported boars that escaped from a gentleman's estate in the early twentieth century. They had been brought in from Europe to serve as amusing hunting prey. Now they've gone forth and multiplied into a bristling menace, tearing up native plants and barreling down the hollows with gnashing tusks to menace any intruder, two-legged or otherwise. At least that's what a visitor will hear from the locals, by way of a friendly warning to be careful in the woods. They'll also happily mention the nettles and poison oak as thick as a man's forearm. And the poisonous snakes. At the time of the Rudolph manhunt, the Andrews police chief told some reporters that there were rattlers back there big enough to puke up a deer.

The native people of southern Appalachia can be as tough as their mountains. You can feel it in the names they gave to their roads and settlements, some of them sounding like reprimands from the Bible—Vengeance Creek, Lord's Way Lane—and others reflecting frontier realities: Deep Gap, Wild Wolf Run, Hanging Dog, Shooting Creek. While paved roads, tourism, and satellite TV have helped modernize a once-isolated population, there are still families up in the hollows who cling to the old ways. You won't find roadhouse bars in this part of the country, but there are plenty of churches. Judging from the signs out front, the congregations pray to a harsh God. One church on Highway 19/74 between Andrews and Nantahala warns: "Are You Going to Heaven or Hell?" It is painted with flames for emphasis. Freelance evangelists have nailed hand-lettered plaques on trees along the highway that simply say: "Repent."

Satellite television and paved roads have opened Appalachia to outsiders and their ideas. But tradition clings like kudzu here. Social reformers, missionaries, and anthropologists who have tried to infiltrate Appalachian communities have been greeted with varying degrees of courtesy, suspicion, and disdain. The arrival of dozens of federal agents was generally viewed as yet another wave of invaders with dubious intentions.

"People were unsure why we were really up there," said Danny Sindall, an FBI agent from Atlanta. "They couldn't believe we were looking for just one guy. They thought we were meddling in their affairs. It took us a while to get their confidence.

"Actually, it took close to two years."

Danny Sindall arrived in North Carolina days after Rudolph was identified as a suspect. Sindall is what the bureau used to call a "brick agent," a street-level investigator, the workhorse of every criminal case. He is compact and wiry and sports a sandy mustache, which distinguishes him in a number of news photos of the Rudolph manhunt. Danny was usually seen out in front of his patrol, wearing camouflage pants and carrying an M-16. His love of the outdoors, along with his special weapons skills and SWAT training, made him a natural for the fugitive hunt. But after the initial few weeks of searching for Rudolph in the mountains, task force members like Sindall and Jim Eckel, another FBI agent from Atlanta, went back to working leads.

One of Eckel's contacts was a hermit named Richard Baxter, who lived in a rough shack near Unaka, a dozen miles north of Murphy, just past Hanging Dog and near the Tennessee line. Baxter, another back-to-the land Florida transplant, had befriended the Rudolph family when they first moved to North Carolina in the seventies. He had taught Pat Rudolph to paint watercolors, and he took an interest in Eric, who often came to visit. The white-haired octogenarian also subscribed to a lot of the same conspiracy theories as the Rudolphs. People who knew him said that Baxter was like a grandfather to Eric, someone who would listen to him talk about anything at all for hours on end without stopping him or passing judgment. He was also nearly deaf. The agents learned that Baxter was one of the last people to see Eric Rudolph before he went on the run. Rudolph had cut some wood from Baxter's lot, and brought a pizza to share with him for dinner.

The old man lived alone with a half-blind chow watchdog. Whenever Jim Eckel came to visit, he'd have to pound on the front door to get Baxter's attention, and the old chow would sneak up behind the agent and nail him. "That dog hated me," Eckel remembered. "He knew my smell, and he'd wait." As much as Baxter liked Eric Rudolph, he was willing to allow the FBI to watch his property in case Eric came by to ask for help. As far as the agents could tell, he never did.

ATF agent Paula Almond, on loan from the Charleston, South Carolina, field office, was later assigned to stop by Baxter's place once a week to check on him. Eckel had warned her about the chow dog, so Almond and her FBI partner would turn on the car siren to roust Baxter from his cabin.

Almond had other regular contacts in the community, as well. One of her investigative techniques was to hang out in the bleachers at community events at the Nantahala School, just meeting people and talking. She sat through games of donkey basketball and learned the joys of cow bingo. She traded recipes with an elderly woman named Effie, who tended a huge garden on a mountainside behind Topton. Effie assured Paula that if she caught Rudolph stealing her vegetables, she'd shoot him on sight and drag his body down to the road before she called the law.

The task force supervisors were also expected to get involved in community outreach. C. J. Hyman, the ATF SWAT specialist, was assigned to address the women's garden club in Andrews. Bill Lewis, Hyman's FBI counterpart, laughed when he heard about the speech. His job that week, he said, was to brief Chief Postell about task force operations. Later, when the supervisors met again at the command post, Lewis was unusually quiet.

"How was Chief Postell?" asked Hyman.

"He was fifteen," said Lewis. It turned out that the "chief" was the young Jeff Postell, then a Police Explorer hoping to arrange some ride-alongs for his Scout troop. (Years later, after Postell captured their man, the agents would all claim credit for encouraging the kid to go into law enforcement.)

While Terry Turchie's strategy to catch Rudolph was to "circle the forest," Woody Enderson's preference was to "tighten the noose." Enderson felt that the best thing to do was to make it so hot for Rudolph that nobody in the community would help him, even if they did sympathize with his views. For some reason—perhaps because Louis Freeh was, at the time, enthusiastically directing an investigation of President Clinton's sex life—the FBI chief decided it was not a good time to ask the attorney general for a favor. So it was Woody Enderson who approached Janet Reno's office with a request to increase the reward for Rudolph to $1 million. She agreed.

On May 5, 1998, Reno and Freeh stood together at a news conference in Washington, D.C., to announce the ten-fold increase in the reward money. And to amplify the publicity splash, Freeh announced that Eric Robert Rudolph had just been added to the bureau's Ten Most Wanted fugitives list. Like an actor who wins an Oscar, or a scientist with a Nobel prize, Rudolph now had a guaranteed opening line for his obituary.

Pat Curry, commander of the homicide unit for the Birmingham Police Department, had been hunting men for twenty-five years. He knew from experience that the best way to find a fugitive is to start with his mother. "That's the way policemen do their jobs," said Curry. "You go find the mother and you say, 'Hey look, little Johnny's in trouble and Johnny needs to come in. Because we don't want Johnny getting hurt. And if Johnny gets run up on by some hot-blooded young rookie cop, Johnny might get hurt. And we don't need that.' That's the way you always approach 'em. And it works. Because the mothers always have a strong say in what their sons do, no matter how old they are."

And so Curry was getting frustrated because, in the months since the FBI raided her trailer, nobody had tried again to interview Patricia Rudolph. Like dozens of his fellow officers, Curry had been working around the clock with the federal task force to find the killer of Sande

Sanderson. Curry, who has since retired from the BPD and now works as a coroner's investigator, is a well-read man with a colorful way with words. As an outsider observing the SANDBOMB investigation from within, he watched the huge federal bureaucracies at work with a mixed sense of amusement and irritation.

"It was a monumental effort," said Curry. "Anything we needed in terms of materials, we got. They sure had deep pockets. If the FBI runs out of money, they just print some more." The problem, as Curry saw it, was getting FBI headquarters to allow nonagents to conduct any interviews.

"It was like pulling out eyeteeth to get Washington to allow us to go talk to Rudolph's mother," said Curry. "The FBI didn't so much try to prevent the meeting, but they lawyer everything to death."

Charles Stone, the Georgia agent on the Southeast Bomb Task Force, finally got permission to set up an interview. Since Pat Rudolph had refused to meet with any federal agents, he chose the Birmingham homicide cop to be his partner. "I figured I was window dressing," said Curry, "but I went along for the ride."

Stone and Curry flew down to Tampa and met Pat Rudolph in a restaurant. Stone's plan was to try to win her over with his good ol' boy charm. They expected her attorney to be present for the interview, but they were surprised to also see her eldest son, Daniel, sitting at the table. Everybody said hello, and Stone tried to make some small talk to break the ice. Curry couldn't help sneaking looks at Dan's reattached hand. He had it in a brace, and as they chatted he kept stretching and manipulating it with his good hand. Curry thought the whole meeting was kind of spooky. And mostly a waste of time: They didn't uncover anything they didn't already know about Rudolph. They did learn something about his mother, though.

"She was very matter-of-fact," Curry recalled. "She told us, 'I raise my children to think for themselves. And if my son wants to come in, that's up to him.'" She said she wasn't going to get involved and try to contact him, no matter what her personal feelings were.

"It kind of floored me," said Curry. "I'd never heard such a thing from a mother in my entire career."

10

NORDMANN'S APOCALYPSE

In the spring of 1998 Eric Rudolph, or someone who looked like him, was spotted on the beach in Mexico. He was also seen in Ireland, Vietnam, and driving around Denver. The FBI investigated every Rudolph sighting and came up with nothing. This was because Rudolph was camped on a hillside a few miles from his childhood home in Topton. He spent his days watching through binoculars as an old family friend went about his daily routine, tending chickens and commuting to his shop in Andrews. It was early July, six months after his disappearance, and Rudolph had run out of food and supplies. George Nordmann, he figured, was the one person in western North Carolina he could count on not to shoot him or turn him in for the million-dollar reward. As everyone knew, Nordmann was a man with few earthly concerns, the least of which was money.

When I met Nordmann after Rudolph's capture he was seventy-six years old and in the process of retiring as owner and proprietor of the Better Way health food store on Main Street in Andrews. He could still be found there most weekdays, puttering around amid a dimly lit tangle of old fans, scales, metal chairs; dusty shelves of vitamins, herbal remedies, and supplements like wheatgrass pills and guar gum; and an ominous display rack of something called "Colon Clenz." Nordmann, a soft-spoken, thin man with thick glasses who usually dressed in a stained old army jacket, seemed unaware of the disorder around him. His eight surviving children, whom he raised more or less by himself, had all left home, and his concerns now focused on his faith—a hard-line traditional Catholicism—and the conspiracy scenarios he monitored every night on Internet sites and fringe talk-radio shows. He waited on the occasional customer from behind a counter awash in scribbled notes, photographs, and religious objects.

Sometimes Nordmann sat by the front window next to a decrepit cassette deck, listening as he made copies of inspirational lecture tapes by stern-voiced priests and other radical Catholics. One of Nordmann's favorites was Hutton Gibson, Mel's father, who preaches a primitive form of Catholicism that calls for a return to the Latin Mass, meatless Fridays, and other orthodox practices swept away in the reforms of Vatican II. Rome has condemned these views as near-heresy. Gibson is best known in the wider world for blurting anti-Semitic remarks just as his famous son's movie, *The Passion of the Christ*, was set for release. Nordmann, who may be a bit more extreme than Gibson, was once secretly videotaped by a *60 Minutes* TV producer expounding on his own conviction that the extermination of Jews was a hoax. He told me, while I openly took notes of our conversation, that the "Illuminati"—code word for the New World Order, the international Jewish cabal, and a number of other conspiracist fantasies—"control everything from the dark side." He believed that Pope John Paul II was an impostor, a sort of religious Manchurian Candidate planted in the Vatican by satanic Freemasons who want to undermine the true church.

George Nordmann lives in a terrifying world, but he says he is not afraid. He has faith that when the prophecies of Fatima and Garabandal have come to pass, and the visions of something called "the night of the screams" are revealed, he will have done what he could in this life to ward off the doom that awaits this planet. When I told him that I was raised a Catholic he advised me to "pray like hell."

Sometime during our discussion, a young couple, new in town, walked into the Better Way looking for some goldenseal to fight off the wife's cold. George greeted them warmly and spent fifteen minutes suggesting different vitamins and walking them through the benefits of ingesting colloidal silver (a heavy metal suspension said to have antibiotic proper-

ties, but which can also, in high doses, turn your skin blue) and quizzing
them on their knowledge of the true causes of disease. Did they know
why everyone was getting upper respiratory problems these days? Somebody was dropping bricks of flu-infested ice from airplanes, that's why.
The government, or the New World Order, or somebody was seeding the
country with disease bombs.

The couple nodded politely as they backed out of the store.

"Okay, then," he said, squinting myopically and waving good-bye.
"Come back again sometime!"

Then he turned to me.

"Now what was it we were talking about?"

We were talking about how George Nordmann had ended up at the
center of a massive manhunt for Eric Rudolph in the summer of 1998.
Nordmann described himself as a "Florida cracker," born and raised
among the fruit orchards south and west of Daytona Beach. He gave
up the farming life to study engineering, and took a job in the Pacific
Northwest. It was there that he first heard about a political pamphleteer
named Nord Davis Jr. In 1974 Nordmann moved his by-now very large
family to the mountains outside Andrews to be near Davis. His wife
soon left him.

Nordmann worked for a while as a shop teacher at the Nantahala
School, and later opened his health products business. He counted Tom
Branham as a friend, and kept a card advertising Branham's sawmill operation up on the bulletin board in his store. George allowed that he
knew Patricia Rudolph, too—as a customer—and claimed that he had
a casual acquaintance with her son, Eric. The most time he spent with
the boy, he said, was back in the late 1980s, when Eric was about to go
into the army.

"He was worried about all the vaccines he was going to have to get,"
Nordmann remembered. Patricia Rudolph hadn't allowed any of her
children to be vaccinated. "He came into the store and wanted to know
how he could avoid problems from the shots." Nordmann told him to
take massive doses of vitamin C and hope for the best. He said they also
got to talking about religion and politics, and particularly a book called
Imperium, by Ulich Varange, the pen name for an American Nazi named

Francis Parker Yockey. It was a rare book that Eric greatly admired, and he knew George had a copy. They also talked about the Ten Commandments and the nature of right and wrong.

Nordmann said that sometime in the past—he didn't remember when—he had invited Rudolph to attend a traditional Latin service with him at a Catholic chapel in Benton, a small town just over the Tennessee line. Nordmann claimed that he only saw Rudolph there once. Despite their mutual interests, Nordmann told me that he didn't really like Eric Rudolph. He said he was "headstrong" and "militant," a know-it-all who wouldn't listen to good advice. They couldn't be friends, he said, because Eric would "never let anyone get too close."

Nordmann's house lies on a steep piece of land off a paved road on the far side of Nantahala Lake, ten miles east of Andrews. The high mountain reservoir was one of the last TVA projects to dam the wild rivers of Appalachia, bringing flood control and electric power to the region over the objection of many irate and displaced natives. The water that covers old homesteads is now ringed with a scattering of summer homes, boat docks, and businesses catering to recreational fishers. The surrounding mountains are a mixture of national forest land and private in-holdings, populated by old families on their original parcels and newcomers, like the Nordmanns and the Rudolphs, who were attracted by the area's isolation and rustic charm.

Nordmann's house is a cobbled-together collection of cabin parts, passive-solar greenhouse panels, and galvanized tin. The steep drive is lined with an assortment of old cars and trucks, some of them operational, most not. There's a small orchard above the house, a shed and a chicken coop out back.

Sometime in late May 1998 George noticed that his hens were suddenly laying fewer eggs. Then his watchdog, a collie-chow mix named Bobo, disappeared. He later found its decomposed body in the woods. Nordmann isn't the most observant man, but he felt something was awry. Things were out of place in his house. He would come home from work to find a pan on the stove that he rarely used. Then some of his mineral and protein supplements went missing, including packets of Emer'gen-C, a vitamin powder that makes a tart, fizzy drink. Another day he found a hundred-dollar bill mysteriously sitting on the counter. Two of his grown daughters often stopped by the house during the week to clean and check up on him, but when he asked, both denied they'd taken or moved anything. Just to be safe, he changed the lock on his door. But he left the key outside where anyone could find it.

In the early evening of July 7, Nordmann was pulling into his driveway when he saw a man standing beneath a shade tree uphill from the house. He was wearing long pants, gloves, and a green fatigue jacket zipped up to his chin. His face was hidden behind a full brown beard, and a cap was pulled over his hair, but Nordmann recognized him. It was Eric Rudolph.

"What are you doing here?" was all Nordmann could think to say. Then he tried to shoo him like a pesky house cat. "You'd better get out of here!"

Rudolph smiled and said, "Why? I know there's no law around here. I've been watching you for a month."

Now the missing eggs and the strange events in his house made sense. Nordmann was more awestruck than resentful.

"George, I need you to get some things for me," Rudolph said.

"No, I don't want anything to do with you."

But Eric was undeterred and they ended up moving behind the shed, out of sight of the road, and talking for half an hour. Rudolph had always been well-groomed in the past, and he joked about his beard and the long hair he'd tied into a ponytail. "I look like a hippie," he said. He also tugged at his belt, showing how much weight had fallen off his waist. He'd been living on 500 calories a day, he told George.

Rudolph seemed to know all about the charges against him. He wanted Nordmann to understand that he was an innocent man, a fall guy, that the witness in Birmingham was lying and he was being framed by the feds. He wasn't ever going to give himself up, he said, and he needed supplies to survive for another year. He wanted George to collect them for him. "I can pay you," he said, patting his pocket. At first Nordmann agreed to go along with the plan. He fetched a pencil and paper from the house, and Rudolph—still wearing green gloves—wrote out a list of supplies he needed, mostly high-energy foods, protein and fats that were missing from his diet. He also wanted double-A batteries, because his radio was running low, and a camouflage tarp that he told George he could find at Wal-Mart. He added another request that was sure to appeal to a devout Catholic: Eric asked for a rosary.

And one other thing: He needed to borrow George's car.

Nordmann took the note and said he'd pray about it and let him know. He gave his visitor a paper sack of food—some corned beef, sardines, apples and oranges, a sixteen-ounce jar of coconut butter, and a loaf of homemade bread. Rudolph thanked him and said he would come back in two nights for the rest of the supplies. Nordmann left him standing in the lengthening shadows and walked back into his house, hoping God would tell him what to do next.

Kenny Cope, who was a Macon County deputy sheriff in 1998, lives just down the hill from Nordmann. He comes from an old Nantahala family, born and raised in the same place as his parents and their parents. He knows everybody in these mountains and he knows their business, too, because that's part of his job. Cope remembered when the Rudolph family moved up from Florida. Kenny was five or six years older than Eric, but he remembered him, too. You could tell he wasn't from this area, and maybe he was kind of strange, looking back. But he didn't stand out much. Basically the whole family kept to themselves.

Eric never really got Cope's attention until he came back home from the army and Kenny heard rumors that he was growing dope in the national forest. Kenny tried following his truck, even staked it out by the roadside while Rudolph disappeared for days in the Nantahala. Sometimes that truck would be parked on Old River Road for weeks at a time. But try as he might, he never could catch him. Danny Sindall later remarked that their relationship was just like the Road Runner and Wile E. Coyote: Cope would chase Rudolph to the edge of the cliff and then lose him in thin air. The cops, looking deep in the mountains, could never find the plants. As Cope later found out, this was because Eric planted his marijuana close to the road and along the power line cuts. And since Rudolph sold his dope in bulk in Nashville, he avoided the snitches and the general chain of gossip that defeated most criminals in Macon and Cherokee counties.

"Nobody here can keep a secret," Kenny Cope told me one Sunday afternoon as we sat on a picnic bench in a small park by the Nantahala River. It was the same reason Cope never believed any native was hiding Rudolph when he was on the run. "If it had been local people who was helping him, they would have turned him in—maybe not for the money, but by accident," said Cope. "They would have told somebody, their aunt or uncle or best friend, and it would have started from there." He chuckled. "But George Nordmann, he wasn't from here."

Cope is a tall man with a growth of beard, a ball cap, and a big truck. He looks rough but seems to find some humor in most things. He speaks softly, and from time to time I had to strain to hear him because groups of whitewater rafters were whooping and hollering as they shot through the boulders in a nearby set of rapids. Cope played with a folding knife, jabbing at the wooden planks as we talked. He still works narcotics cases for the regional drug task force, and this was one of his few afternoons off. He told me he always knew Rudolph was hiding in these mountains, and it was a matter of time before a local cop caught him.

When Cope was a deputy sheriff he was pretty much the only law enforcement officer in the area, and people would come to him directly with their problems. But he was surprised to find Nordmann on his front porch on a Saturday morning. Nordmann had never been to his house before. The first thing he said was, "Kenny, I might be in big trouble."

"What do you mean, you might be in trouble?"

"Someone stole my truck."

Cope was familiar with Nordmann's trucks—people in the country know each other's vehicles as well as they know each other's faces, and Kenny joked with him that he couldn't have lost much. "You've got to have some money somewhere, George, because you sure didn't spend it on your rig."

"No, you don't understand," he said. "Someone took my truck, and I know who it is."

"Well, why does that make you in trouble, George?"

"Because it was Eric Rudolph."

At first Cope thought Nordmann was crazy, or he had gotten into one of his herbal remedies. But he quickly realized that the man was genuinely terrified, so he sat him down and asked him to tell his story. It took a while to make sense of what Nordmann was saying, but when he handed Cope Rudolph's shopping list, the deputy recognized the handwriting straight away, from the samples the task force had passed around. George said that he knew Rudolph had been watching him all week, and that he had been too afraid to tell. He'd been spending the nights sleeping in his shop, and when he finally returned home on Friday morning, his old blue 1977 Datsun pickup was missing from the driveway. Inside the house, some food and supplies had been taken and there were five fresh hundred-dollar bills on the kitchen table, along with a note from Eric. Nordmann destroyed that note, but he remembered it said something like "Sorry you were afraid to help me. The feds and dogs will never find me." It also said that Nordmann would get a call to tell him where to find his car.

"But it can't get very far, Kenny," said Nordmann. "The lights don't work and the radiator on the truck overheats. It won't make it more than six or eight miles."

"Okay, stop right there," said Cope.

Cope made two calls—one to Sheriff Homer Holbrook and the other to Danny Sindall. Sindall called Terry Turchie, who was just about to leave for a trip to California. Turchie drove right over and sat on Kenny Cope's porch as he listened to Nordmann repeat his story. Then he asked George if they could all go over to his house and have a look around. Nordmann agreed. When they arrived Nordmann showed them the $500. While Nordmann started to take inventory of what Rudolph had removed from the house, Turchie made his own set of phone calls—to FBI headquarters, to Woody Enderson. It looked as if they would need to expand the manhunt, and fast. Then he called in Joel Moss to continue interviewing Nordmann.

Moss had been one of Turchie's supervisory agents and top lieutenants on the UNABOM Task Force. Moss was shorter than Turchie, with a boyish face and reserved manner. One of their colleagues described the relationship as Moss playing Mr. Spock to Turchie's Captain Kirk.

Moss had stayed behind in Sacramento to close down the UNABOM office, then joined Turchie in North Carolina in May. Now he was one of three supervisory special agents, with the amorphous role of "Special Projects Supervisor." Those projects included electronic surveillance and night flights, community outreach, and media management. Again, Joel was Turchie's most trusted agent, and Turchie wanted him to handle this crucial interview.

So Joel took over the questioning. At first Nordmann insisted that Eric Rudolph stole everything from him, and that all he gave him was the bag of food that first evening. But as George became more relaxed around the agents, a different story emerged, and he admitted he had actually bought some of the things on Eric's list. In fact Nordmann's encounter with Rudolph was much more extensive and his knowledge of the Rudolph family was much deeper than he first admitted. Over the following days and months, Joel Moss would interview Nordmann more than a dozen times, and each time he yielded more information.

Moss wanted to know everything Rudolph had said to Nordmann during the time that they spent together that first evening. Nordmann recalled that Rudolph admitted he had been stealing eggs and eating cherries from the orchard and that he had been sneaking into the house for quite some time. He had even watched survivalist videotapes on George's TV while George was at work. The first hundred-dollar bill he had left, he said, was a "test" to see if George would call the sheriff on him. When no feds showed up and no bloodhounds were launched, Eric decided to approach him for help.

He told Nordmann that he wanted him to buy the supplies he needed and then drop them by the side of the road for him to pick up later. George immediately balked at the suggestion. So Eric offered to take his car to make the drop-off. He could tie George up, or even handcuff him at his house to make it look like a robbery. Nordmann didn't like that idea, either. But he didn't dismiss it outright.

Rudolph seemed extremely interested in where the federal agents in Andrews had their command center, and he drew a basic map of the town for Nordmann to mark the spot. Rudolph boasted that he had a great hiding place, far away from Topton, where the search parties and dogs could never find him. And he seemed to go out of his way to mention some conversations he'd once had with his old friend, Randy Cochran. He told George that he knew Randy would cooperate with the feds if they pressured him, so he deliberately gave Randy false information about where he might hide in the woods.

Rudolph handed him a wish list of supplies and said he would be back in two nights to pick them up. Nordmann spent the next two days thinking and praying on it. He admitted that he did go shopping for some, but not all the items on the list. Then he drove home as usual on Thursday evening, July 9. He stuffed the goods in three layers of garbage bags, which he set out in plain sight on his kitchen table. He also left Rudolph a note to the effect that this was all the help he would give him; take it and never come back. He added, "God says no about the car." Then he drove back to Andrews and spent the night in his health food store.

The next morning Nordmann closed up shop before noon and drove back to his house to see what had happened. He noticed right away that the blue truck was missing from its spot along the driveway. The bag was gone from the kitchen. In its place were Eric's note and the hundred-dollar bills. George noticed other things had been taken from his basement storeroom, where he kept extra stock for the health food store.

Nordmann was asked to itemize everything that Rudolph took with him, either bought or stolen. It included gallon containers of raisins and bulgur wheat; a bucket of black beans; packages of pinto beans, black-eyed peas, and lentils; cans of creamed corn, beets, peas, and pork and beans; ten jars of coconut butter; three or four jars of tallow; assorted vegetables; and a five-gallon bucket of honey. There were a few large packages of cayenne pepper (which Rudolph perhaps thought he could use to throw the dogs off his trail). There were about ten packets of batteries, two Bic lighters, a blue spiral notebook, a bottle of peroxide and a bottle of rubbing alcohol, three books of matches, several large bottles of Now-brand vitamin and mineral tablets, and a hardbound book of New Testament sermons.

Members of the task force were divided over how to handle Nordmann. Don Bell wanted to pressure him to take a polygraph. Turchie argued against the test. He instinctively felt that Nordmann was telling the truth. He knew George believed the NRA's "jack-booted-thug" image of federal agents and probably couldn't decide whether he was more afraid of Rudolph or of the FBI. He had to make a devil's bargain with one or the other, and Turchie didn't want to punish him for making the right choice. Even though Nordmann had taken his time coming forward and at first had withheld information, the fact was that he cooperated in the end, even though cooperating might get him in trouble for aiding a fugitive. Threatening Nordmann would only confirm what he and a lot of his neighbors already thought about the feds. Turchie reasoned, Why should anyone else come forward with information if they were going to be treated like suspects?

Part of George's story was corroborated when a bunch of local kids on a four-wheeler, who had been watching the evidence response team buzzing around Nordmann's house from a nearby ridge, ran over a small campsite. They reported it to the agents, who found an empty Emer'gen-C packet and a buried plastic wrapper with Rudolph's fingerprint on it. Two other campsites were discovered around the Nordmann property, with remnants of cooked onions and broken eggshells—suggesting that Rudolph had been staking out Nordmann's house and pilfering from the chickens, just as George reported.

So Nordmann was handled gently. (A year later, after the San Francisco agents had left the task force, Nordmann was finally asked to take a lie detector test. He passed.)

On July 13, a U.S. Forest Service ranger named George Lynch found George Nordmann's Datsun parked behind some laurel just off a turnout near the Bob Allison campground, deep in the Nantahala forest. There was a note inside the windshield that said "Truck broke down. Trouble. Please contact George Nordmann at Better Way Health Food Store, Andrews, North Carolina." Lab analysis later confirmed it was Eric Rudolph's handwriting. Tests also indicated trace residues of dynamite on the steering wheel.

Nordmann said he had filled the truck with gas right before it was stolen. Based on how much was left in the tank, the agents figured that it had been driven less than fifty miles. There was no sign of the food or supplies. The only thing Eric didn't take with him was George Nordmann's rosary.

Two days after the truck was discovered, the task force announced that Rudolph had been sighted near Topton, and they released a new sketch of the fugitive, based on Nordmann's description. The media returned to western North Carolina in full force. For television news—particularly in what is known in the news business as "the silly summer season"—an active manhunt was a bigger ratings jackpot than a slow-motion car chase. A line of sound trucks, like Conestoga wagons, quickly circled the no-longer sleepy town of Andrews.

Eric Rudolph's reappearance also prompted a muscular response from the FBI. Within hours of the discovery of Nordmann's truck, semis loaded with agents and equipment were rolling south from the Critical Incident Response Group headquarters in Virginia. Overnight, a federal tent city was erected at the Appletree campground, a popular spot along the Nantahala River that was about midway between Nordmann's house and the Bob Allison location. Once again the dogs were called in, although not the Texas bunch that had sniffed and stumbled through northern Georgia. This time it was Duke Blackburn's bloodhounds from the Georgia Department of Corrections, a pack with an excellent record of tracking down escaped prisoners. Rudolph, the movie buff, might have thought he was in a scene from *Cool Hand Luke*.

Kenny Cope joined the tracking party since he knew the terrain and he knew Rudolph. They were hoping to pick up Rudolph's scent on Tuni Gap Road and follow it back to his hideout. "We got behind Eric's tracks at the truck, and we stayed on it, and stayed on it," said Cope. "We were finding footprints, his footprints. He went right back up the road to Tusquitee Gap. We stayed on it until the track went from walking to running, that's how close we got to him."

Once again, Rudolph had too much of a head start, and seemed to vanish in the forest.

The Nordmann sighting confirmed what the task force leadership had believed all along: Rudolph had never left the neighborhood, and he didn't have a network of supporters helping him survive. If he'd had other options, he wouldn't have been hungry and desperate enough to approach Nordmann. Jim Cavanaugh, who tracked the manhunt from the ATF offices in Birmingham, speculated that it would be a long time, if ever, before Rudolph trusted anyone again. He had finally rallied the courage to come out of hiding to ask for assistance, and suddenly there were helicopters hovering overhead day and night and his most familiar haunts were overrun with dogs and armed patrols.

The task force quickly swelled to more than 200 agents and support staff, with up to 80 men deployed in the mountains every day. In an unprecedented move, Turchie decided to appoint ATF agent C. J. Hyman to supervise the search teams. Hyman already had knowledge of the case, and he was an experienced SWAT leader. But it took some diplomacy for Turchie to convince bureau headquarters that every commander didn't have to be an FBI agent. SWAT leaders Danny Sindall and Jim Eckel joined the daily patrols, providing security for the Forest Service trackers on their teams. It quickly became routine. The patrols would meet up in a field near the Appletree command center at 5:30 in the soft morning air before the heat and humidity built up in the woods. Turchie and his team would brief them on the day's operations and Hyman would send them off. They would scour the trails for any sign of Rudolph—a dropped wrapper, a cigarette butt—and then head out cross country, following the tiny creeks back up the ridges to their sources. That's where Danny Sindall and Jim Eckel thought they would find Rudolph's hideout. It had to be on the high ground, for tactical advantage, but not too high, or he would lose his cover. There had to be a source of clean water—that was important or he'd get sick from giardia or other parasites that lived upstream. There were a lot of places like that, though. Fresh springs percolated out of almost every mountainside in the lush Nantahala, and the foliage was so dense in the summer, you couldn't see more than a few feet off the trails.

One day Sindall and his crew thought they'd hit pay dirt: a shelter made of planks covered in plastic sheeting, with a bunk bed inside and some canned food. But the evidence teams couldn't find fingerprints or

any other sign that Rudolph had used the place. It was probably an illegal hunter's camp. Sindall almost tripped over the hooch before he saw
it, the woods were so thick.

Among other "special operations," Joel Moss coordinated sorties in
which federal agents and specialists from the North Carolina Bureau
of Investigation planted special motion detectors and hidden cameras
along trails and in other places Rudolph might frequent. Agents set out
"bait" bags of food and other tempting items to see if he would take
them, or at least touch them and leave fingerprints. He never did. They
knew that Rudolph liked to eat trout, and there were a number of private trout hatcheries where the fish were so thick in the open tanks that
anyone could reach in and grab a meal. So the technicians set up remote
cameras to capture the images of any trout poachers. Moss said they
spent a lot of time looking at pictures of bears and raccoons gorging on
stolen rainbows and brook trout.

Joe Kennedy was called up from Atlanta to assist in the searches.
He helped set up a mobile crime lab at Appletree camp and at the National Guard Armory to speed the processing of evidence. Lloyd Erwin
came from Atlanta, too, to help sift through "trail trash" gathered by the
search teams for forensic clues. None of it panned out. Erwin, who grew
up just south of the North Carolina border, was amazed at how much
trash was being collected in the Nantahala forest during this search, and
he was tempted to start a rumor that Rudolph had been spotted across
the border, just so the government would clean up the Georgia section
of the Appalachian Trail.

The trail was like a highway that ran straight through Rudolph's
"comfort zone" in the Tusquitee and Snowbird mountains. The investigators knew Rudolph had frequently hiked the Appalachian Trail
with his friends, so they kept a close watch on it during the fugitive
hunt. They figured Rudolph would be traveling at night so they started
night reconnaissance flights equipped with FLIR (or forward looking
infrared) sensors. They cruised over the dark mountains looking for the
thermal image of Rudolph or his campfire. The main problem with the
system, Don Bell recalled, was that there were an awful lot of campers
out in the forest in the summer months. Worse, the infrared screens lit

up like Christmas trees with the body heat of every bear, deer, raccoon, and possum in the mountains.

Undercover agents posing as hikers walked the Appalachian Trail by day and camped at night, hoping Rudolph would approach them for food or help. SWAT teams equipped with special night vision gear staked out the trail, waiting to ambush Rudolph if he made a move. Bell recalled one night when an ATF agent radioed his unit, urgently whispering that he saw something walking down the trail. The next thing they heard was a shout and what sounded like a struggle. The agents came running to assist their teammate and quickly figured out what had happened. The figure moving on the trail was a huge black bear. When the agent jumped out to confront it, both man and bear were so startled to see each other that each fell backward off different sides of the narrow ridge. The agent tumbled down thirty feet of laurel and briars. Luckily when he landed his dignity was more injured than anything else. The bear, they say, didn't stop running until it was in the next county.

Because the patrols were so physically demanding, SWAT teams from around the country were rotated in every two weeks to keep the troops fresh. The units were all fit and ready, but most of them were from urban environments like Chicago and New York City and not accustomed to climbing mountains in the Southern heat. It was plainly miraculous that nobody got seriously hurt out in the field. There were a few sprained ankles, bumps, and bruises. Danny Sindall stepped on one of those famous rattlers, but it failed to bite him. Yellow jackets that nested in underground hives were the most worrisome trail hazard. One misplaced boot and the whole patrol would be swarmed by angry, stinging hornets. A National Guard helicopter was always standing by to medevac injured searchers, but it was rarely needed. ATF agent Paula Almond, who was also a trained medic, set up an informal clinic at base camp to treat stings, blisters, and minor cuts.

The Appletree command post was guarded by Georgia prison guards and catered by the Georgia Department of Corrections. They provided bag lunches for the task force staff and the patrols as they drifted back to camp. The commanders would meet around 6 P.M. for another briefing to chart the day's findings and plan the next day's operations. They would break at 7 or 8 for dinner. It was a fifteen-minute drive to Andrews, where most of the agents had rented rooms. Joel Moss figured that at the height of the manhunt, the government was spending roughly $16,000 a day on rent, food, hotels, gas. Nobody in town complained about that.

Turchie was happy to have Moss working with him again. After years of tracking the Unabomber, the two men thought alike and communicated in the comfortable shorthand of old friends. Whenever they could break away for a few hours, they hiked the trails they knew Rudolph had used. At night they drove together through the Nantahala with the maps out and their minds open. They would stop at turnouts high in the mountains and look out over the moonlit ridges. It was so quiet at night. They could hear the footfall of deer in the underbrush. They could easily hear a car coming from miles away and see its headlights lancing along the blackened tracks. They wondered: What did he see? Where would he be most at ease?

The more they talked, the more they were convinced that Rudolph was still out there. It came back to a lesson they had learned from UNABOM: An offender like this has a need to feel comfortable in his surroundings—and that need will determine his behavior. When Turchie took over the UNABOM case, he was intrigued by two bombings in which Kaczynski had returned to the scene of a previous crime. He had placed a device at Corey Hall at U.C. Berkeley in 1981 and then another in 1985. Why was he so secure in Corey Hall that he would come back again? Turchie and Moss visited the building at least twenty times. They walked around the classrooms, learned the layout, and saw the risks the bomber had taken: He could easily have been detected or trapped if he didn't know his way around. They refocused their investigation on past and present denizens of the Berkeley campus. Later, when Kaczynski was identified as the Unabomber, they learned he had once taught in the math building, a couple of hundred yards away from Corey Hall. After these and the other bombings, he retreated back to the safety of his Montana cabin to plan his next strike.

Although it was unclear how familiar Rudolph was with his bombing targets, the agents were confident that Rudolph, like Kaczynski, always preferred to return to a place of familiarity and comfort. During their evening drives around the Nantahala, Turchie and Moss tried to imagine Rudolph's comfort zone, visiting the spots where he took his old girlfriends to hike, where he played hide-and-seek war games with his brothers. They figured that if they went back again and again, they might come across something they had missed before. Someplace they had overlooked.

The Critical Incident Response Group that set up the small village of white tents and generators and radio antennae at Appletree camp was much more than a logistical support unit. CIRG was formed within the FBI in the aftermath of the Ruby Ridge and Waco tragedies to bring the bureau's tactical, behavioral, and technical specialists under one command. The idea was to mount a unified, coordinated response to major incidents, and to avoid the miscommunications that had led to grief in the past. And so, along with the drivers and computer techs, the elite commandos and snipers of the Hostage Rescue Team, or HRT, pitched up at Appletree. (Their daily stroll between their tents and the communal showers was dubbed by the women in camp as "the Walk of the Gods.") And along with the HRT came the BAU, and the two agents assigned to the Rudolph case, Tom Neer and Ron Tunkel.

"On major FBI cases the assumption is that whoever did this may someday decide to take a hostage," said Neer. "So CIRG will launch the Hostage Rescue Team. But we are the primary behavioral component. We like to think of ourselves as actually having the capacity to dive in deeper."

The analysts went into information-gathering mode for several days, traveling back and forth between the tent city near the banks of the Nantahala and the Valley View motel in Andrews. There was no cell phone coverage in the mountains, and no e-mail connection. So to contact Quantico they were obliged to borrow the motel fax and printer. Two weeks later they had a written report ready for the task force.

Their main concern was to come up with a plan of action should one of the SWAT teams actually find Rudolph. Or what if a group of campers or hikers saw him on the trail? What should they say or not say? Should they turn and run, or say, I'm on your side, can I help you?

It seemed to the analysts that the public had better knowledge of what to do if they were charged by a black bear than if they ran into Rudolph. They were also concerned that the GBI agent, Charles Stone, had been designated as lead negotiator should Rudolph take a hostage or barricade himself in somewhere. They thought Stone was the wrong choice, not just because they doubted his personal style would appeal to a fit, military perfectionist like Rudolph, but because he didn't seem to believe he could bring Rudolph in peacefully.

"Stone told us, 'I think he's going to die in a firefight.' We thought, 'What a horrible, pessimistic attitude for a primary negotiator.'"

The two behavioral analysts were also concerned about the psychological pressure the task force was putting on Rudolph in the woods. "On scene commanders sometimes get crazy ideas," said Neer. "Like at Waco, someone came up with the crazy idea, 'Let's play this loud music of rabbits being slaughtered.' There was a time in the hills of North Carolina when somebody came up with the great idea to fly a C-130 transport plane at treetop level over the area where they thought Eric was hiding. We could understand why that might scare the average person. But to a guy who has been on the loose for a long time and maybe has some paranoia already going on in his mind, that might just exacerbate it. So now you're going to be negotiating with a guy whose paranoia you've just increased? I mean is that really gonna make him say okay, I surrender? Or is it gonna harden his resolve to resist? Basically we're right back at Waco."

Neer suggested as gently as possible that the task force drop the C-130 idea. (Terry Turchie had immediately rejected it.) Other assessments were put into writing.

"Surrender cannot be ruled out as an option for [Rudolph] but at this time it appears unlikely," they wrote.

He is clearly in his comfort zone, he has rehearsed this part of his script. We know from his days in the military that during an exercise when he was presented with an option to surrender he declined. We did not have any information as to whether his fantasies of evading authorities ever included what to do when confronted. He does like running and hiding. He has had considerable time to discover and fortify hiding places, however if he feels he can no longer evade authorities in his comfort zone because they are closing in on him, he will probably opt to steal a car, as he did recently at Nordmann's house or to seek the assistance of a trusted friend. Thereby, suicide does not appear likely at this time. First, he knows we have not found him; second, there is nothing we have heard or read suggesting he has ever contemplated suicide; third there is no history of suicide in his family; fourth, depression is often associated with suicide. Judging from his last contact with Nordmann in which he requested food, Rudolph appeared fresh and alert. Also he announced with pride that no one would ever find him, that his base camp was many miles away. This suggested his satisfaction with this continuing game of hide and seek, and also suggested elements of future planning, generally not associated with one preparing to commit suicide. Suicide by cop, however, is a distinct possibility for individuals such as Rudolph who have expressed antipathy for law enforcement and are inclined toward passive-aggressive behavior.

The SWAT teams wanted to know the probability that Rudolph would take a long-distance shot at them while they were on patrol. Neer and Tunkel thought this was possible but not likely, since, being a bomber, he tended to avoid direct confrontation. But Rudolph was such a classic voyeur that they should always consider the possibility that they were being watched. "Rudolph's need to observe police activities underscores the need for continued vigilance in the vicinity of both command posts. We would suggest the deployment of covert forward observer teams on the ridge to the west of the camp, to observe the mountain to the east of the camp," the report suggested. It added, "He may have, and when he is apprehended, he will probably take great pride in saying he could have shot us."

As prescient as these observations turned out to be, the ones that got the most attention—and derision—from the tactical commanders and supervisors were the craftier proposals. Their suggestion that biodegradable leaflets urging Rudolph to surrender be dropped over the forest

did not go over well. Neither did a rewrite of the press releases referring to Rudolph as a "survivalist," which they said only made him seem
like more of a hero to himself and anyone in the region who might be
inclined to sympathize with him. They also noted that the latest sketch
artist's depiction of Rudolph showing him with a beard and long hair
made him look handsome and beatific, almost Christ-like. Perhaps, they
wrote, the drawing could be reissued showing the fugitive as leaner and
slightly more malevolent.

The last suggestion drew hoots of laughter from the macho command
circle, particularly Stone, who found the idea just too fey for words. But
I was later told by several women in the towns surrounding the search
zone that they were fascinated by the drawing of Rudolph. One middle-
aged customer at a soda fountain in Hayesville confessed that the wanted
poster gave her erotic dreams about Rudolph for months. So perhaps the
profilers were on to something after all.

Terry Turchie was not a fan of the FBI's Behavioral Analysis Unit.
When he took over the UNABOM case in 1994 he had pleaded with
the unit to come up with an updated profile of the bomber, and to initiate
a study of lone offenders to help him with the investigation. According
to agents who worked with Turchie, the BAU resisted all his suggestions. He considered them useless. He preferred to work with his own
circle of consultants, including Park Dietz, the forensic psychiatrist, and
Kathleen Puckett, a San Francisco–based FBI agent with a background
in clinical psychology. Turchie and Enderson, who had a similar disre-
gard for the unit, listened as politely as they could to Tunkel and Neer's
presentation. But within days the behavioral analysts were pulled off the
case and sent back to Quantico.

For the rest of the summer the heavy choppers flew contours over the
Nantahala forest, shaking birds and squirrels out of the trees and broadcasting to Eric Rudolph, in a language they figured he could understand,
that the federal government was still king of the mountain.

11

JACK TALES

As the weeks wore on and the vast army could not pry Rudolph from his refuge, more than a few locals started to find some humor in the situation, not to mention an economic opportunity. A few entrepreneurs printed up commemorative T-shirts and bumper stickers with clever sayings such as "Run, Rudolph, Run!" and "Eric Rudolph: Hide and Seek Champion 1998." The souvenirs were purchased mainly by members of the news media and the few tourists who were willing to risk getting caught in crossfire while enjoying the wonders of nature. The Lake's End Grill on the shores of Nantahala Lake posted a large sign announcing "Eric Rudolph Eats Here," although most of its customers were federal agents and the occasional bounty hunter. A folklore was growing around the elusive Rudolph, and at least two ballads had been composed to celebrate his getaway.

One of these, also called "Run, Rudolph, Run," was written and recorded by Dorothy Smith, a grandmother and a fixture in the local folk scene. It's a catchy number, which she performs in a serviceable nasal twang accompanied by her own flat-top guitar and a group of backup musicians.

Dorothy Smith grew up in Unaka, near where Richard Baxter, Eric Rudolph's friend, built his shack. Smith told me the name Unaka means "white man" in the Cherokee language. Her great-grandfather once bought 100 acres in the area, paying ten cents an acre, although the family land was divided up and most of it sold off long ago. Her father told her that outlaws used to hide out around there, since it was so far off the main road and deep in Indian country. When I first spoke to her she was working the night shift at a clothing factory near Andrews; later she started taking classes at the local community college. Her musical career was pretty much on hold. The Rudolph ballad got her some attention, but she couldn't persuade radio stations outside Cherokee County to play it, so she gave up. She admitted that some of the lyrics might have been controversial:

> ... He could not justify
> knowing all the things they done.
> So to stop that baby-killin' factory
> he made a homemade bomb ...
> You gotta run, Rudolph, run,
> or the FBI's gonna shoot you with his gun.
> A modern-day Billy the Kid,
> boy, you better run just like he did ...

When she wrote the song, Dorothy Smith didn't think Eric Rudolph was guilty of all the bombings he'd been accused of doing. Even after they caught him she was still not sure. "It's like Billy the Kid," she said. "They added a lot of things to his name that he didn't do. I guess that's the same with Rudolph. That's why I put it in the song.

"Plus, it rhymed."

Dorothy Smith knows something instinctively that David Brose has devoted a lifetime to studying: Eric Rudolph's story belongs in the ballad tradition, the secular liturgy of the Appalachian Mountains. Brose is the official folklorist at the John C. Campbell Folk School in Brasstown, North Carolina, which opened in 1925 with the mission to preserve and promote Appalachian culture. Brose is a musician and balladeer himself, though his roots are in the Midwest, not the mountains. His sartorial choices—trim black beard, wire-rimmed glasses, peacoats, and black Lenin caps—tend to set him apart from his neighbors. But he feels at home and accepted in this community, which he insists is far more diverse than most would expect. The locals have proved tolerant and friendly. Basically everyone finds a way to get along.

Brose has also noted a tradition of rebellion against central authority among his mountain neighbors that dates back to the Scots-Irish settlers. Legends of outlaws and fugitives are woven into their folk traditions.

"Some of the most characteristic tales in the mountains are lumped together as 'Jack Tales'; stories like 'Jack the Giant Killer' and 'Jack in the Beanstalk' being two of the most familiar," Brose told me one afternoon in his office at the edge of the rolling, green Folk School campus. "Mountain people still cling to Jack Tales because they celebrate a character who is greater than life. Jack is usually an everyday farm boy who, for whatever reason, goes out into the larger world and has adventures, takes action, and fights people bigger than himself and wins." It's a classic hero's tale, with a local twist.

"He's also kind of an idiot," Brose said. "You don't know whether he's outrageously brave or a fool."

Along with Jack Tales, there are outlaw, or "bad men," songs in the Appalachian repertoire such as "Sam Bass" and "The Ballad of Jesse James." The legend that grew around Rudolph fits the folk tradition, according to Brose. "Here's this rugged individualist who leaves the community, does super-human things, takes the bull by the balls, takes the law into his own hands." While the vast majority of people might not condone his actions, Rudolph makes for an interesting story simply because of the odds stacked against him, said Brose. "Anyone who kicks sand in the face of the establishment—people tend to cheer them on."

There are other figures like Rudolph in recent American folklore: "D. B. Cooper," an anonymous extortionist who hijacked a jet in 1971 and parachuted into the night with $200,000 in his satchel, never to be heard from again, fits the mold, if only for the daring of his crime and the mystery of his fate. Patty Hearst, the kidnapped heiress who joined her captors to become a bank-robbing revolutionary, is another. When David Brose was the folklorist for the state of Colorado in the 1980s, the outlaw of the day was a fugitive named Claude Dallas.

Dallas was a young man from Ohio who went out West in the late

1960s to live the life of a nineteenth-century cowboy. He rode with herds of cattle from Oregon down to the Mexican border, and even got his picture in *National Geographic* magazine with a bunch of other hands who symbolized, to the photographer William Albert Allard, the last of a dying American breed. When he wasn't being a buckaroo, Dallas lived a marginal existence in the Owyhee desert of Nevada and southern Idaho, often camping alone on public land, shooting his own meat, and trapping bobcats for their pelts. In the late 1970s, while Eric Rudolph's family and their friends were preparing for the End Times on the East Coast, Dallas was stockpiling weapons, gas masks, and ammunition in anticipation of a war between the government and its own citizens. That day came for Dallas in 1981, when two state game wardens confronted him in his camp and tried to arrest him for poaching. He shot them both dead and took off for the wilderness.

As with Rudolph, a massive manhunt ensued, and Dallas evaded the law for fifteen months. The sheriffs finally captured him in a shootout near his old haunts. At his trial in Boise, a group of female supporters calling themselves the "Dallas Cowgirls" gathered outside the courthouse every day. To the outrage and astonishment of the prosecutors and the victims' families, the jury rejected the murder charges and found him guilty of manslaughter. He got thirty years with a chance of early parole. Only months into his sentence, he escaped from Idaho State Prison and disappeared again. Ian Tyson, a famous Canadian folksinger and recording artist, noted the birth of a new outlaw legend and cowrote a song about it called the "Ballad of Claude Dallas." David Brose, who was studying Basque folksongs at the time, was appalled when several locals told him they were rooting for Dallas, that the wardens got what they deserved for interfering with a man's livelihood. Dallas was eventually recaptured and served twenty-two years in prison. There was a TV movie made about Dallas, but not many people remember him anymore. He has lived quietly since his release in 2005.

In the folk process, "bad men" like Dallas represent the dark side of the heroic ideal that runs through American culture. As with any sort of celebrity, it's hard to predict who will become a legend and who will not, although there do seem to be some ground rules. Killing innocent children disqualifies you. I have yet to see any songs about Timothy McVeigh. The villains who pass over into legend also have to have some redeeming traits to make them palatable to their audiences. Billy the Kid was said to be a victim of circumstance. Jesse James loved his family. Pretty Boy Floyd robbed banks during the Depression, when banks were the enemies of the common man. According to his legend, when Pretty Boy was on the run, poor farmers took him in and offered him meals; the bandit would often leave hundred-dollar bills under his plate. It was interesting to note that Eric Rudolph left five crisp hundreds on George Nordmann's kitchen table in exchange for the food and supplies he took. He was extremely concerned that no one think he was a thief. As Bob Dylan wrote the year Rudolph was born: "To live outside the law you must be honest."

Woody Enderson, head of the Southeast Bomb Task Force, was exasperated by Rudolph's growing mystique. "He may have been a hero in the minds of some people," he said. "But no one knew him."

Felecia Sanderson, the widow of the policeman killed in Birmingham, was so concerned about some of the things she was hearing out of North Carolina that she pulled herself out of her grief to appear on a new segment of *America's Most Wanted*. She wanted to remind people that Eric Rudolph was not a folk hero; he was wanted for murdering her husband. As she had done before, she visited the task force headquarters in Andrews to thank everybody who was working so hard on the manhunt.

For a while there were rumors that Patricia Rudolph planned to plead for her son to give himself up during a news conference in Andrews. It never happened. But there were others out there who were willing to offer their help. Like a projection of Terry Turchie's worst nightmare, Randy Weaver himself arrived in the Nantahala that August, riding shotgun for one of the most flamboyant and publicity-hungry right-wing extremists in the country: the ex–Green Beret, MIA hunter Colonel James "Bo" Gritz.

Bo Gritz says he was invited by the task force to join the search for Rudolph; the FBI says Gritz invited himself. In either case, the appearance of the bombastic war hero along with fifty or more wannabe rescuers provided a bizarre and illuminating sideshow to the Rudolph manhunt.

This much is known: In June 1998, Charles Stone, the GBI agent, had a conversation about the Rudolph case with Gritz at a "Preparedness Expo," a trade show for survivalist products and "Christian Patriot" paraphernalia being held in Atlanta. A couple of months later, Gritz (rhymes with "fights") was piloting his own Cessna across the country with Weaver in the copilot seat, heading for the Nantahala forest.

Like many ultra-right-wing celebrities in the 1990s, Gritz had his own talk-radio show, *Freedom Call*, which he broadcast on shortwave from his aerie in northern Idaho to an audience of lost and angry souls scattered around the county. Several weeks after he met Charles Stone in Atlanta, Gritz said he got a call from the GBI agent to ask for his help in bringing in Rudolph. Stone identified himself, said Gritz, as the "chief negotiator" on the task force. Stone told him he had intelligence that Rudolph admired Gritz, and might be listening to his radio show from his hideout in the mountains. It was not specified what kind of help Stone wanted. But Gritz, sensing a return to the limelight, said he would think about it.

Gritz was an interesting, if somewhat demented, choice. Of all the self-styled Patriot leaders, Colonel Gritz was as close as it came to a genuine American legend, a leader of the warrior elite Eric Rudolph had unsuccessfully tried to join. Gritz served several tours as a Special Forces commander in Vietnam, leading covert missions deep into Cambodia and earning sixty-two citations for valor. Gritz retired in 1979 but clung to an obsessive belief that Americans listed as "missing in action" were still being held in secret prison camps in the Laotian jungle. Gritz enlisted the Texas billionaire, H. Ross Perot, to help finance several unsuccessful and extralegal sorties into Laos in an effort to locate the ghost prisoners. He became famous for these exploits—the character Rambo was rumored to be based in part on Gritz, a claim he is happy to endorse. At the same time he gained a reputation as a blowhard and a charlatan who exploited the hopes of MIA families to feed his grandiose ego.

The decorated war hero soured on his government during his MIA rescue period. Gritz accused the federal government of hampering his missions and covering up the truth about the secret camps and worse. Gritz gravitated to the burgeoning Christian Patriot movement, a motley collection of tax protesters, Midwestern populists, doomsday prophets, New World Order bashers, Identity believers, and Second Amendment fundamentalists with a unifying hatred for the federal government, Jewish bankers, and the United Nations. Gritz's sense of mission was so great that he ran for vice-president on the Populist Party ticket in 1988. His running mate was the baby-faced Nazi and Ku Klux Klan leader, David Duke. Gritz, who insists he is not a racist, withdrew after a few days' stumping with the execrable Duke. Gritz ran as a Populist again in 1992, this time as a candidate for president. He got 0.1 percent of the vote.

That same year, Gritz had made national headlines as the man who ended the Ruby Ridge standoff by negotiating a peaceful surrender for the hapless Randy Weaver. The Ruby Ridge incident was a watershed event in the simmering conflict between well-armed and paranoid antigovernment groups and an increasingly bold and militarized federal law enforcement establishment. Weaver was an army vet and Identity follower who, with his wife and three children, lived in a remote cabin in the Selkirk Mountains of northern Idaho, where they had moved to get away from what they saw as government interference in their life. They socked away a supply of food and weapons and waited for the End Times to commence. When a fellow Identity believer asked if he could buy some sawed-off shotguns, Weaver sold him two modified weapons. The man was an undercover ATF agent, and the gullible Weaver was busted. When Weaver refused to work for the government as an informant, which appeared to be the object of the exercise, he was indicted for gunrunning.

Since he didn't recognize the authority of the federal government, Weaver ignored his trial date. Once he was officially a fugitive, the U.S. Marshals Service set up surveillance on his home and waited for the right time to take him into custody. The Weavers stayed holed up on their property on Ruby Ridge for seventeen months, relying on friends in the militia movement to bring in supplies. The standoff turned into a siege on August 21, 1992, when a group of armed marshals dressed in camouflage crept through the woods, casing the area around the Weaver cabin. Striker, the family dog, started barking at the strangers, and Randy Weaver; his fourteen-year-old son, Sam; and an adult friend named Kevin Harris grabbed their rifles and ran out to investigate. When one of the marshals shot Striker to stop his barking, the enraged fourteen-year-old fired in his direction. The deputies returned fire, and in the ensuing gun battle Sammy Weaver and U.S. Deputy Marshal William Degan were killed. The Weavers retreated to the cabin and the marshals called for reinforcements. The next day an FBI sharpshooter killed Weaver's wife, Vicki, in their doorway while she held a baby in her arms. Weaver and Harris were also wounded. At this point the government tried to open negotiations.

Meanwhile a crowd of neo-Nazis and militia members had gathered at the roadblock beneath the Weaver property to jeer at the federal agents in their armored vehicles. Television crews took up position as well. Sensing an opportunity for publicity, Bo Gritz arrived and started handing out "arrest warrants" for various government officials, charging them with murder on Ruby Ridge. Gritz also approached the FBI special agent in charge of the scene and offered to help negotiate with Weaver. The SAC was dubious. But when the standoff continued into its second week, the FBI allowed Gritz to visit Weaver in his cabin. First Harris came out with Gritz. After more talks, Weaver surrendered with his two surviving children.

Ruby Ridge was an object lesson in how quickly an operation can blow up into a tragedy when government agents confront armed fanatics who are expecting Armageddon. It also illustrated how even the most seemingly intractable situations might be resolved through patient negotiation. Sadly, the lesson was not applied to the handling of the Branch Davidian sect in Waco, Texas, only eight months after the Weaver siege. But when a militant antitax group called the Montana Freemen instigated a protracted standoff in the winter of 1996, the FBI showed much greater restraint, and the Freemen were eventually talked into their jail cells. Bo Gritz showed up at the Freemen compound as well, but this time he was rebuffed by their belligerent leader, LeRoy Schweitzer. Gritz left in a huff, commenting that the Freemen all belonged in prison. A local politician and rancher eventually negotiated the settlement.

After Weaver was acquitted of the federal murder charges against him, he settled a lawsuit against the FBI for the wrongful death of his wife and son. He also ended up becoming Gritz's friend and sidekick, and the cherub-faced, barrel-chested Gritz and skinny, pompadoured Weaver often made public appearances together, a sort of white separatist Lone Ranger and Tonto. Gritz has often been accused of secretly working for the CIA, and Weaver gave Gritz instant credibility among the Patriot masses. So it seemed natural to Gritz that Weaver should accompany him to North Carolina to help with the colonel's latest operation, Task Force CROSS, an acronym for Convey Rudolph Obligingly and Safely into the System.

The plan, as announced on Gritz's talk show, required 100 volunteers to converge on the town of Andrews, North Carolina, between August 14 and 21, 1998, to comb the mountains to find Eric Rudolph, convince him to surrender, and provide him safe passage into custody. The alternative for Rudolph, Gritz warned, was a "bullet in the neck." Gritz would collect the $1 million reward for bringing in Rudolph and turn the money over to Rudolph's mother to pay for his defense.

Patricia Rudolph, however, refused to endorse the scheme and stayed conspicuously quiet and out of sight all summer.

Gritz later told me that his aim was to turn Rudolph into a Christian Patriot icon, a galvanizing figure whose trial would serve as a forum on the evils of homosexuality and abortion. He said he understood where Rudolph was coming from. Gritz himself was so "vehemently against" abortion that "if the guy who lived next door to me was a day to day abortionist ... I very frankly would consider some way or other putting him out of business, whether it was intimidation or whether it was with more prejudice." With somewhat convoluted logic, he explained: "That's why I wanted Eric Rudolph to come in. Because I'm also for the law. You cannot keep the law by breaking the law. Eric Rudolph had already killed somebody and maimed somebody so he could be the champion."

Gritz wanted him alive to let a jury decide the case, and hopefully acquit him. "It's called jury nullification. I saw it work with Gerry Spence as Randy Weaver's lawyer. The jury threw away the judge's instructions and found Weaver not guilty." Gritz said he wanted to buy Rudolph some "O. J. Simpson justice" and get his point across. "I thought, boy, what an impact if a jury was to turn Eric Rudolph loose. Every abortion doctor in this country would have to grab his anus and head for wherever he could hide."

But in order to set this scene in motion, Gritz knew, Rudolph had to surrender, and in order to do that he'd have to be convinced that he wouldn't be shot down by the feds in the act. Rudolph had told friends and family members that he believed that government agents were likely to kill anybody who opposed them, just like the Weavers and Branch Davidians. Gritz had to be sure that Rudolph would recognize his volunteers as friendlies. So before he left Idaho, Gritz had special red, white, and blue ball caps printed with an approximation of the Cross of St. Andrew—the Confederate battle flag—for his team to wear as they combed the woods.

Gritz was already familiar with the Andrews area. He had known Nord Davis and had once conducted several SPIKE training courses on his thirty-acre property. (SPIKE, which stands for Specially Prepared Individuals for Key Events, was a survival school for the doomsday set. As the millennium approached, those who subscribed to apocalyptic Y2K prophecies were willing to pay to learn basic weapons skills, field medicine, and living-off-the-land lessons from Gritz's old Green Beret buddies. Despite the fabulous name, SPIKE was not a particularly rigorous program. George Nordmann, for instance, took one of the courses when he was in his sixties.) As a result, Gritz had quite a few contacts in the area, and he called on them to gather "intelligence" for him, and to locate facilities for his volunteer army.

The facilities included the Andrews Senior Center recreation hall, for registration of the troops, and an FOB, or forward operating base, at the Bob Allison campground, near where Nordmann's truck was found. Until the troops arrived, they set up their command post in a motor home parked in a friend's driveway.

*	*	*

Terry Turchie had known for weeks that Charles Stone had been talking to Bo Gritz, but he never paid much attention. It was part of his work with the Southeast Bomb Task Force investigation, and not the fugitive search.

One day Stone came up to him in camp and said, "Listen, Bo Gritz is coming here, and he's bringing some team players and they're gonna find Rudolph. They say they have some leads."

"You've got to be kidding me."

"No. In fact he's already on his way."

Turchie had to digest this information for a few moments.

"Well," he said finally. "I guess that leaves it for you and me to go meet this guy when he gets here."

When the tactical experts found out that Randy Weaver was with Gritz, they wanted to give Turchie a security escort to the meeting. The inspector wouldn't hear of it. He brought only Stone.

"It was kind of surreal," Turchie recalled. "We walk into the trailer, and there's all these guys milling around. They're very cordial, they're putting out their hands." Stone introduced Turchie to Gritz and they sat down at a table to talk. "Then in walks Randy Weaver. I don't know how to tell you how I felt. It was a very weird feeling."

Like the others, Weaver introduced himself and held out his hand. Turchie shook it.

"Terry Turchie," he said. "Obviously we come in peace."

Everyone laughed, breaking the tension. Then Gritz pulled out a map and they got down to business. Gritz circled the areas where he wanted to deploy his teams, which, to Turchie's relief, were in a zone that his patrols had already searched thoroughly. Then he heard Gritz say, "And what we need from your guys is a task force member to go out with each group …"

"Listen," Turchie said. "The bottom line is this: For obvious reasons, we're not sending anybody from the task force with any of your guys. It's just not gonna happen. And secondly, you perhaps could be a lot of help here, but we have to have an understanding. I need to know that you're not getting in my way, and we need to do everything we can here to avoid some sort of major tragedy."

Gritz quickly agreed to abide by the rules. It was an unsettling evening, but Turchie left the meeting feeling better than he did going in. Later, he and Don Bell briefed the task force teams and explained to them why Gritz, Weaver, and their ragtag militia of antigovernment "patriots" had suddenly arrived in their operational area. They didn't want any confrontations, and they didn't get any. "Not even one minor incident," said Turchie. "I was proud of their discipline."

On Friday, August 14, Gritz's volunteer army started arriving in RVs and pickups, bikes and rental cars. A few of them were off-duty marines, but most were middle-aged veterans who looked as if they hadn't walked farther than the length of a Wal-Mart parking lot in decades. One Vietnam vet arrived with his colostomy bag; Gritz assigned him to radio duty at base camp. Others brought their kids along. Gritz greeted them all with delight. More than forty volunteers were issued their caps and scarves and dispatched to the Bob Allison campsite, a lovely rustic clearing in the Tusquitee Mountains, a dozen miles south of Andrews. The media, which had reappeared in full force to cover this bizarre story, followed them to their bivouac but were evicted from the site by burly sentries.

Gritz's operation was a strange mirror image of the task force manhunt. The colonel divided the group into manageable units that were deployed each morning to walk through five-mile search grids. The idea was to let Rudolph find the searchers, who would then provide him a safe passage to the local sheriff. To attract his attention, the troops shouted things like "Eric, we're here to help!" None was allowed to be armed—except one sniper code named "Hammerhead" who stayed close to Gritz, just in case Rudolph took a shot at them. Meanwhile, Gritz put a Green Beret buddy on intelligence-gathering duty with Weaver. Gritz had boasted at a news conference in Andrews that his team had already been collecting information from people in the community who wouldn't cooperate with the feds. This may have been true, but the quality of the information was somewhat dubious. These sources told him that Rudolph had been meeting with people in the forest on a fairly regular basis. Supposedly Rudolph had met his mother at the Bob Allison campground (she arrived in a black Cadillac) and, in early August, had drunk some wine with teenage supporters. (This would have been quite a feat considering the electronic and human surveillance in the area.) In addition, he had information that Rudolph was regularly raiding cabins for food and supplies in the Bob Allison area.

One night three volunteers, including a young marine, armed only with flashlights, radios, and infrared goggles, staked out a cabin belonging to Lee Howard, a fishing guide who was often away from home. They suspected Rudolph had been using it. Two other groups were deployed nearby.

About 9:30 P.M. Bo Gritz and his team were monitoring radio chatter when they heard the thrilling words: "Johnny has sprained his ankle." It was the radio code meaning "Rudolph is in sight." According to Gritz, "Our hearts were pounding in anticipation." What followed, unfortunately, was confusion. Someone thought he saw a man in the woods, who was spooked by the other teams as they approached. Much later that night, in a summer downpour, the marine reported seeing the silhouette of a man with a ponytail creep out of the woods and peer into Lee Howard's cabin. When the marine shouted, "Eric! I'm part of the Bo Gritz team! Please let me help you!" the phantom intruder pitched off the deck in fright and scrambled into the woods. Or didn't. A random bounty hunter later claimed he was the man that Gritz's boys encountered in the woods. In any case, Bo Gritz called a press conference the next day to report the possible contact with Rudolph. "This could have been a test, and the fact is if it was, we passed it perfectly," he said. "He saw we had no weapons and we were not there to apprehend him."

For a full week, the CROSS volunteers tramped through the thick underbrush, shouting into the woods and sometimes tumbling comically off the trails in front of TV cameras. One man had to be evacuated after an attack by yellow jackets. Later a local informant led Gritz on a wild-goose chase up into the mountains for an urgent "meeting" with Rudolph that never materialized. The two got lost near the summit of Tusquitee Bald, and Gritz spent a full night out in the open dressed in only a T-shirt and jeans.

After a week in the field, Gritz and his teams packed it in. The CROSS volunteers lined up for their leader to pin memorial medals on their T-shirts. Some vowed to return to the same spot every summer for a reunion search.

"Our mission was complete," Gritz later wrote in a book about his life called *My Brother's Keeper*. "Eric had missed an excellent opportunity to gain a million dollars, safe conduct, and free court representation. It was his choice."

The task force leadership was convinced that one good way to separate Rudolph from his outlaw-hero image was to officially charge him with the Atlanta bombings. While there was still doubt in people's minds that he had bombed the Olympics, it was easier for them to sympathize with Rudolph as some sort of militant anti-abortion crusader. But many people living in western North Carolina had attended Olympic events or knew somebody who did. Any of them could have been victims, too. On October 14, 1998, the Justice Department made it official: Eric Robert Rudolph was finally charged with three bomb attacks in Atlanta, including the Centennial Olympic Park bombing.

12

END GAME

By mid-October the oaks, hickories, and dogwoods of the Nantahala forest blaze up in extravagant layers of yellow and red, attracting pilgrims from Atlanta and Charlotte and the faceless exurbs of the eastern corridor to watch the show. Cars and RVs filled with foliage watchers crawl reverently along the narrow, winding roads and congregate at scenic overlooks. Mountain bikers navigate the red clay trails, and hikers climb through green and gold tunnels, savoring the sharp mountain air and the musky dirt smell of the woods. Eventually the leaves drop and the tourists depart, clearing the way for an enthusiastic invasion of hunters. As the days get shorter the seasons open up for deer, possum, pheasant, bobcat, squirrel, and the most prized game animal of all, the North American black bear. Hunting for bear—properly pronounced "b'arr"—is a sacred tradition in these mountains. In the fall, ravenous bears, which can weigh anywhere from 125 to 500 pounds or more, roam the forests gorging on acorns, hickory nuts, rotting carcasses, and anything else they can find to bulk up their bodies before hibernation. Serious bear hunters prepare all year for the chance to wake up before dawn and chase through the woods behind their redticks and Plott hounds.

When the Southeast Bomb Task Force first launched its massive manhunt for Eric Rudolph, rumors rippled through local communities that the feds were going to cancel hunting season. Terry Turchie went out of his way to quash those stories. Nothing would alienate the locals faster than interfering with their gun sports. The hunt takes them into some of the most remote and inaccessible reaches of the mountains; if the task force leaders could turn the hunters into allies, they would have hundreds of extra sets of eyes engaged in the search for Rudolph. Turchie enlisted local agents to reach out to hunting groups. The task force organized a news conference to display the vitamin bottles, Emer'gen-C packets and food containers that Rudolph had taken from Nordmann in July, asking hikers and hunters to report back if they found anything like them buried in the woods.

The search teams were always looking for caves, since Rudolph often talked about exploring them and had once been photographed rappelling into a deep hole somewhere in the Nantahala. The mountains were shot through with natural caverns and abandoned gold and ruby mines. The temperatures in these caves were a steady 55 to 58 degrees Fahrenheit all year round. But they were also damp, and sometimes dangerous because of the possibilities of cave-ins and poison gas leaks. But many searchers believed Rudolph would use them to hide his supplies or find temporary shelter.

Once the leaves started dropping, the government team stepped up its aerial surveillance of the mountains. With bare trees and colder ground temperatures it would be easier for the infrared sensors to isolate heat sources such as campfires and human bodies in sleeping bags. The cool weather also coaxed the copperheads and rattlers into hibernation. It was finally safe to search the snake-infested rock faces and cliffs of the Nantahala Gorge, where Rudolph had frequently camped out in the winter. Later in the season, after the snows set in, Danny Sindall was leading a SWAT team from Chicago on a search of some rock cliffs when one of the city agents called him on the radio.

"Hey, Danny, I see a cave."

"Any sign around the cave?"

"No, just some animal stuff."

"That's what I mean by sign," said Sindall, with as much patience as he could muster. "Get a little closer and have a look."

There was a brief pause.

"Danny, you've got to come up here!"

Sindall scrambled up the drainage and joined the SWAT guy, who was standing below a deep fissure in the rock wall. He peered inside and into the eyes of one of the biggest black bears he'd ever seen. The bear was dazed with sleep, looking around to check out the commotion. "Let's not bother this guy," Sindall suggested, as he slowly backed away. The bear settled back into its den. Sindall would later report with satisfaction that not one bear was shot in the course of the manhunt.

Despite the increased visibility in the winter months, the southern mountains remained notoriously difficult to search. This was made painfully clear in early November. Walter Barker, seventy-one, was piloting his own Cessna to deliver a homemade birthday cake for his son, an FBI agent on temporary duty with the fugitive task force. The plane took off from a small airport in Ohio and ran into bad weather in western North Carolina before it went missing. Despite an intensive search by the FBI, the Civil Air Patrol, and local law enforcement, the wreckage wasn't discovered for another six years, when a bear hunter found it in the Slickrock Wilderness, fifteen miles north of Andrews.

When the weather turned, the task force folded up the Appletree command post and moved the whole operation into an empty sewing factory the government had rented at the edge of downtown Andrews. Most of the commercial action in Andrews, a quaint town of 1,700, was south of the shallow Valley River. Among the cluster of shops around the intersection of Main Street and Highway 19/74 were a grocery store, a drugstore, a McDonald's, and a small movie theater. The command post was behind the theater in a large, one-story building with a sizable parking lot and a grassy lawn that was perfect for a helicopter landing pad. Just as they did at Appletree campground, armed prison guards served as sentries to keep out unexpected visitors.

Despite the precautions, on Veterans' Day, November 11, somebody sprayed eight rounds from a high-powered rifle right through the walls of the command post. It happened when the building wasn't very full, so luckily nobody was hit, although a bullet literally singed the hair of one FBI agent who had the good fortune to be leaning over his desk. If he had been sitting upright he would have been killed. The case went unsolved for months, and the FBI assigned extra investigators to the task. Although Rudolph could have been a suspect, the agents ruled him out because the drive-by shooting didn't seem like his style, and it would have required a stolen vehicle. Investigators focused in on a pair of local lowlifes who eventually confessed to taking the shots with an SKS assault rifle. The men said the prolonged manhunt was interfering with their backwoods drug operations, so they got drunk one night and decided to mount their own rebel raid against the invading Yankees. In any case, feds threw the book at them. One was sentenced to eighteen years in prison; the other got thirteen years.

While Terry Turchie stayed in the background, concentrating on the mechanics of the manhunt, Woody Enderson became the public voice of the search. He held frequent news conferences, alternately cajoling Rudolph to give himself up and goading him as a coward. He was sure Rudolph was listening to his radio, and he wanted to make him mad, try to draw him out of hiding. It didn't work.

Enderson regularly commuted from Andrews to Atlanta by helicopter. He eventually rented a house in another county, and preferred to dine outside Andrews and Murphy because all the media exposure made him too recognizable to eat a meal in peace. His favorite place was the Nantahala Lodge, a rustic resort and restaurant perched high above the Nantahala Gorge near Bryson City. There was an outdoor dining area, and in warm weather he liked to eat outside on the porch, looking west over the rolling blue ridges of the Snowbird Mountains. On clear days he had a panoramic view of the entire search zone. Enderson would enjoy his meal and imagine Rudolph hunkered in a hole somewhere below, chewing on game meat and oatmeal, getting skinnier and more desperate. "I'm here, and he's out there," the inspector would think. "Which one of us is in a better position?"

The intensive hunt for Rudolph continued through the winter of 1998–99. Although there were no reliable sightings reported after Rudolph's encounter with George Nordmann, a number of vacation homeowners reported break-ins at their residences, and at least a dozen of them seemed to fit Rudolph's modus operandi. In one case a property owner near Nantahala Lake came up from Florida to check on his trailer and felt that something was wrong as soon as he got inside: Someone had been smoking in there. He called the sheriff, who notified the task force. Evidence technicians never found Rudolph's fingerprints, but they were able to determine that someone had come in through a window, used the shower, shaved, and smoked cigarettes. To disguise his break-in he had replaced the window in its frame and turned off the water pipe under the trailer, just as he had found it. Other unoccupied cabins in the county showed unexplained spikes in electric usage. Some vacation homeowners reported unusual burglaries, in which the thief took only small items such as blankets, boots, ammunition, maps, and antifreeze. The antifreeze was significant: It is sweet-tasting and highly toxic to animals, particularly scavengers like dogs and bears. There had been numerous reports of poisoned watchdogs in the area, starting with George Nordmann's chow-mix, Bobo.

The reports of break-ins continued at a steady pace all winter. Then they abruptly stopped. Once again, agents on the task force had to consider the possibility that Rudolph had finally left the area, or more likely had fallen off a cliff or died of hypothermia. This was always a possibility, but until they found the body, Terry Turchie and Woody Enderson weren't going to believe it.

For a brief moment the task force thought Rudolph had resurfaced when a crude bomb exploded outside the Femcare women's clinic in Asheville in March 1999. The improvised device, however, had nothing in common with Rudolph's known handiwork: It consisted of two PVC pipes filled with an ammonium nitrate mixture, designed to detonate with a lit fuse. Only one of the pipes exploded, causing minimal damage to the facility. The bomber has never been caught, but investigators speculated that he might have been a Rudolph copycat.

In the spring of 1999 the FBI was obliged to reevaluate the size of the fugitive task force. Congressman Charles Taylor, a right-wing Republican who represented western North Carolina in Congress, was also on the appropriations subcommittee that funded the Justice Department. During a routine appearance before the panel, Louis Freeh was grilled by Taylor, who complained that his constituents were growing weary of the federal presence in the area. "My office gets complaints about helicopters being flown over churches and about being stopped by uniformed officers all the time. They wonder how long the FBI is going to be in there."

Freeh assured the congressman that the agents were trying to be as sensitive as possible, and were already looking to downsize the operation. In March he reduced the fugitive task force to about 100 searchers and support staff. Terry Turchie and Joel Moss returned to San Francisco and their grateful families. Turchie would not be there long: Louis Freeh called him to Washington and promoted him to deputy assistant director of the counterterrorism division of the FBI. Woody Enderson retired in July; Charles Stone had already retired from the GBI at the end of 1998, Jack Killorin would stay on in Atlanta until 2002 and then retire. Joe Kennedy transferred to Washington, D.C., to manage the ATF's explosives training program. Agent Jim Eckel was put in charge of special projects, and Danny Sindall took over the forest patrols, which gradually dwindled from daily sorties to one or two a week.

News media interest in the case died down to spurts of coverage during the anniversaries of the Olympic Park bombing and the Birmingham attack. By the year 2000, the task force ceased its flights over the forest and closed up the command center in Andrews. A skeleton operation moved into an office in the National Guard Armory, a squat brick building the size of a small high school, just off the main highway east of Murphy.

In November 2000 a new administration was voted into office, which meant that almost all U.S. attorneys, who are political appointees, would soon be replaced. Before they left office, the U.S. attorneys in Atlanta and Birmingham wanted to finish up the grand jury investigations of Eric Rudolph, which had remained open during his fugitive years. On November 15, 2000, Atlanta issued a twenty-one-count indictment, officially charging Rudolph with bombing the Otherside Lounge, the Sandy Springs clinic, and Centennial Olympic Park. The Northern District of Alabama in Birmingham indicted Eric Rudolph on two federal charges: that he "did maliciously damage by means of an explosive, a building and property used in an activity affecting interstate and foreign commerce ... which prohibited commerce [and] resulted in the death of Robert D. Sanderson and personal injury to Emily Lyons …" and another, similar count, for causing the death of Sanderson while using a "firearm, that is a destructive device" in the course of damaging property that affected interstate commerce.

Doug Jones's term ended in 2001, but he still had unfinished business in the U.S. attorney's office. After the Rudolph investigation, Jones's top priority had been the long overdue prosecution of the Klansmen who bombed the Sixteenth Street Baptist Church in 1963, killing four young girls. The only living plotters were Thomas Blanton Jr. and Bobby Frank Cherry, who for years had escaped murder charges, partly because previous FBI administrations hadn't shared information with state investigations. In the early 1990s the FBI office in Birmingham started looking into the case again, and Jones pushed for their arrest. In May 2000 Jones used his office to file state murder charges against the two bombers. In an unusual arrangement, Jones was designated as special prosecutor to try them in state court. When the Bush appointee, Alice Martin, took over as U.S. attorney, she arranged for Jones to stay on to finish the civil rights case.

He won convictions against Blanton in 2001 and Cherry in 2002, closing the books on a hideous crime that had haunted Alabama for almost forty years. Doug Jones returned to private practice that year, but he could never forget the other Birmingham bombing that remained unpunished.

Danny Sindall was the last of the original investigative team to leave the Nantahala. He kept an apartment in Andrews well into 2001, commuting back to Atlanta on weekends to see his wife and three kids. His colleagues were starting to think he was nuts, but Sindall still believed Rudolph was alive. He kept up his contacts in the community, and periodically reinterviewed his sources to find out if they had heard anything new, or remembered something that might provide a lead.

During one of these conversations, a former friend of Rudolph's remembered that Eric and his brothers had buried a cache of rifles behind the house on Partridge Creek Road. It had happened sometime after 1994, when the Brady Bill regulating handgun sales had passed Congress, and the Rudolphs were convinced it was only a matter of time before the government was going to break down their doors and confiscate their guns. So Joel and Eric gathered up a bunch of guns, including an AR-15 assault rifle, wrapped them in garbage bags, and disappeared into the woods behind the house to bury them.

Sindall decided that this was worth checking out. But he needed Joel Rudolph to take him to the cache. Over the years Joel had maintained a cautious relationship with the task force investigators. From what the agents could gather, Joel was far less political than Dan, Eric, or their mother, Pat. As a young man he was much more of a partyer than a radical. Kenny Cope, the Macon County deputy, had busted him once for DUI, and remembered he seemed like a nice, decent guy. He even shook hands with Cope in the courthouse.

But at first Joel was reluctant to help Sindall find the cache of guns, clearly torn between his loyalty to his brother and his desire to see him brought in alive. Then Jim Eckel posed it as a public safety issue: What if the guns were still out there and some kids found them by accident? Joel said he'd think about it. He called back and said he'd take the agents to the spot—if he could remember how to find it. It had been five or six years since they'd buried the weapons.

Sindall wanted to keep the search party as small and discreet as possible, so it was just him and Joel and Eckel. The group started walking around the woods behind the old family home, but Joel was having trouble remembering the site. They wandered for what seemed like hours until they came up to a large granite outcrop, near where they started. It seemed to Sindall like a perfect landmark for a burial site, but Joel still wasn't sure. On a hunch, Eckel started jumping up and down in the leaf litter at the base of the rock, and sure enough, he found a spot that sounded hollow. He dug down six inches and hit a layer of polyethylene. And then a wooden box.

The agents secured the site and came back with some technicians from the explosives unit to check the box for booby traps. One agent waved a metal detector that squealed a warning when it passed over the site. Sindall's stomach was in his throat; he felt like they were exhuming a grave. He figured that if Rudolph was alive he would have come back to get the rifles by now. He would need them to survive. If the box was full, then Eric was dead. He watched intently as the bomb techs unearthed a four-by-six-foot timber box covered with nineteen layers of plastic. The package was so airtight that the heavy oak boards had dehydrated and the wood was as light as balsa as they lifted it from the ground. The lid was nailed shut; it was likely the nails had set off the metal detector. When they pried open the lid Danny Sindall let out his breath. The box was empty.

The victims: Emergency workers rush nurse Emily Lyons *(above)* to the hospital after Eric Rudolph bombed a woman's clinic in Birmingham, Alabama; she was riddled with shrapnel and lost an eye *(left)*. Police Officer Robert "Sande" Sanderson *(right)* was killed in the same blast. John Hawthorne *(below right)* and Fallon Stubbs *(center)* remember Alice Hawthorne, killed by Eric Rudolph's bomb at the Atlanta Olympics.

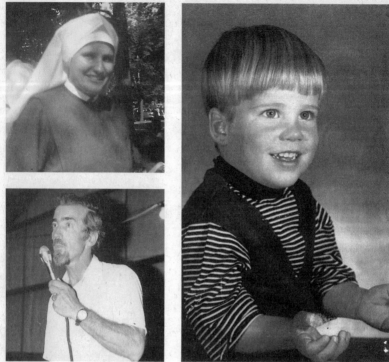

"We were always looking for the perfect rainbow religion," said Patricia Rudolph, Eric's mother, shown above left as a nun novitiate in 1956. *Counterclockwise:* Robert Rudolph preaching in Florida; Pat with three of their six children, Maura, Jamie, and Eric, in North Carolina in the 1970s; Eric at age three. "The others were always in trouble, but not Eric."

Tom Branham *(top left, with beard)* with the Rudolph children and other friends in the Florida Keys; Joel and Eric are in the bottom row. *Left:* Eric Rudolph's first love, Joy Keller (who later killed herself), Eric, and Pat at Dan Gayman's Identity Christian Compound in Missouri, 1984. *Below:* The Rudolph family home on Partridge Creek Road in Topton, North Carolina. *Above:* Eric joined the army hoping to belong to an elite cadre. "I was naïve," he wrote the author.

THE BOMBING IN BIRMINGHAM WAS CARRIED OUT BY **THE** ARMY OF GOD. LET THOSE WHO WORK IN THE MURDER MILLS AROUND THE NATION BE WARNED ONCE MORE — YOU WILL BE TARGETED WITHOUT QUARTER — YOU ARE NOT IMMUNE FROM RETALIATION — YOUR COMMISSAR'S IN WASHINGTON CAN'T PROTECT YOU!

WITH THE DISTRIBUTION OF THE GENOCIDAL PILL

Clockwise from above: Eric Rudolph's rented trailer on Caney Creek Road in Murphy, North Carolina. His bedroom as federal agents found it; there were traces of explosives on the rocking chair, a shotgun in a drawer, and $1,600 hidden in a framed photo by the window. A scene along the main road between Andrews and Topton, North Carolina. One of the letters Rudolph mailed to the media claiming to be part of the Army of God.

The biggest fugitive hunt in FBI history. *Counterclockwise from left:* George Nordmann in his shop in Andrews, North Carolina. Rudolph in an FBI sketch, as described by Nordmann. Two hundred task force agents descended on the Nantahala forest to search for Rudolph. FBI Inspector Terry Turchie *(center),* seen here in San Francisco with Special Agents Joel Moss and Kathleen Puckett, had led the capture of the Unabomber before he set his sights on Rudolph.

"I told myself not to go out that night," Rudolph wrote. *Clockwise from upper left:* Rudolph's handmade calendar. His "summer camp" on a hill above Murphy, North Carolina. Orderliness reveals he took pride in a neat camp. The view of the National Guard Armory from Rudolph's perch across the highway; he didn't kill the agents because he identified with them. Supplies discovered at his "winter camp" on Fires Creek.

Clockwise from upper left: The ritual "perp walk": Rudolph is led from the Cherokee County Jail by ATF Agent C. J. Hyman. Jeff Postell, the rookie Murphy police officer who captured Eric Rudolph. Sean "Turtle" Matthews, the Cherokee County deputy who recognized him. Rudolph's former lead counsel Richard Jaffe *(left)* and attorney Bill Bowen *(right).*

Rudolph told agents where to find 270 pounds of dynamite. *Top left:* The radio control that may have been used in the Birmingham bombing. Joe Hanlin and Joe Kennedy of the ATF with FBI Inspector Todd Letcher, in a hole blown by one cache of hidden dynamite *(left).* Eric Rudolph made a deal to serve life without parole; in his cell on Bomber's Row in the federal supermax prison in Florence, Colorado.

13

THE WATCHER

Eric Rudolph didn't need a timepiece anymore. He could tell the hour by the positions of the sun and the moon and through changes in his environment. He knew dawn was coming when the first birds started to sing; one hour after the Mayfield milk truck rolled down the highway toward Andrews, he knew the road would be filling with morning commuters and it was time to get out of sight. After the first year of the manhunt, which he would later describe as "the starving time," he had found a way to live, unnoticed, just beyond the city limits and the boundaries of society. He had haunted the towns of Andrews and Murphy for years, eating what others discarded, wearing what they'd cast off. Sometimes, when he needed batteries or something else he couldn't scavenge, he'd disguise himself and walk into Wal-Mart and make a purchase. He'd had close calls with hunters and hobos and local cops, but never the federal patrols that were sent out to hunt him. The closest the feds ever came to catching him, he figured, was his first night on the lam.

"On the lam" was, in fact, how he later described it to me in a letter. It made sense that he would use a vocabulary that exists only in Hollywood; during his years as a serial bomber, Eric Rudolph's only regular contact with other humans seemed to be through the fictional characters he watched, alone, on a thirteen-inch screen. He was an avid movie fan, but not a discriminating one. His tastes ran to action and adventure, and the overwrought soundtrack of the last movie he rented, *Kull the Conqueror*, provided a fitting backdrop to his frantic dash for the woods.

The movie was playing in the bedroom when he went into the kitchen to cook a pot of oatmeal and listen to the 6 o'clock news. That was how he learned that the Birmingham police had his tag number and the feds had issued a material witness warrant for his arrest. He knew he didn't have much time. Rudolph tore apart his drawers, packing too quickly and forgetting some things he shouldn't have left behind. He threw what he could into the back of his truck, then took off to get more supplies at the BI-LO in Murphy. But first he stopped at Burger King, knowing he would need some protein and carbs for the long night ahead of him. He packed the groceries into a blue plastic barrel in the truck bed, then drove about a dozen miles east of Murphy to a remote region of the Nantahala forest called Fires Creek. He hid the barrel in some bushes below a campsite he had already chosen for this kind of emergency. Then he drove the truck to Martins Creek, near Murphy, and hid it as far back in the woods as it would go. He walked to his camp along paved and graveled roads, hoping that his scent would fade before the bloodhounds got onto him.

He picked Fires Creek because nobody who knew him would expect him to camp there. It was a secret spot, miles away from the trails he'd hiked as a boy, or anyplace his friends or old girlfriends had helped him tend his marijuana plants. As a pot grower he had hiked the entire Nantahala to find its most remote sites. He bought topographical maps for all of western North Carolina and, as he wrote to me, spent many hours in the woods "looking for southern exposure, camouflage, hidden springs, the kind of places people haven't been through in decades. I became adept at finding these pockets of virgin territory and figuring out how exactly people utilize the woods so as to move when and where I would be unnoticed. Add to this experience a great deal of hunting and camping and I had the ingredients needed to function in the woods for extended periods." The rock outcrop near Fires Creek was far away from any of the popular hiking trails.

He remained there for the rest of the winter, monitoring the search on his radio. He kept warm in a sleeping bag further insulated with layers of dried leaves. His main problem was finding food, which consumed most of his time and energy. During the intense manhunt he couldn't forage or fish in the low country, so he shot the occasional wild turkey and deer to supplement his ever-dwindling food supply. After a while he was catching salamanders in the creek, gutting them and frying them up with pancakes he'd make from the last of his oatmeal and stashed grain. Finally, when he thought he was about to starve, he gathered up his rifle and bedroll and hiked over to Long Branch Road to George Nordmann's house.

He thought his old friend had agreed to buy him supplies and lend him the car, and he was angry when Nordmann reneged on his promise. But Rudolph always had a backup plan and had already hot-wired one of Nordmann's dilapidated old trucks to transport his supplies back to Fires Creek. The pickup sputtered and misfired all the way into the Tusquitee Mountains; Rudolph's late-night getaway was so loud that he woke up a drunk who was sleeping it off on the side of the road. He finally had to ditch the vehicle on the way back from Fires Creek when it broke down about halfway to the spot along the Nantahala River where he'd planned to leave it. Again, he took a circuitous route back to Fires Creek, walking along the roads whenever he could to confound the bloodhounds. He deliberately left clues—trash with his fingerprints on it—at a decoy campsite on Old River Road to throw off the FBI and point them in the wrong direction if the Nordmann operation went bad.

He apparently stayed close to Fires Creek throughout the summer, listening on the radio to Woody Enderson's appeals for his surrender as well as to the antics of Bo Gritz. He assured me that none of Gritz's men had ever been near enough for him to hear them calling his name, that they never saw him, and that he'd never considered turning himself in to them or anyone else.

He seemed to have developed a fixation on Enderson, who reminded him of Tommy Lee Jones in the movie *The Fugitive*. Rudolph enjoyed outmaneuvering him. Every weekend he would listen for the sound of a special helicopter that he assumed was flying Enderson from Andrews back to Atlanta; the flight pattern took it right over Fires Creek. He knew that the nighttime helicopter flights were trying to find him using infrared radar, so when he heard them coming he would burrow under a rock until they passed by.

He had a few close calls in the mountains. One winter he fell into a creek and nearly died of hypothermia, but he managed to build a fire to dry out. In the coldest days of winter he piled leaves three feet deep over him to keep warm and stayed in his sleeping bag to conserve energy. He twisted his knee once and walked with a limp for weeks. Another time he cracked a molar and considered cutting the tooth out with his knife, but it never got infected. In fact he never caught a cold, he said, because he had no exposure to human germs. Bears and bear hunters were his greatest concern. During one of his food-gathering sorties in the Nantahala a group of bear hunters passed so close to his hideout that he could smell their aftershave. The black bears would raid his camp and he had to shoot them or poison them with antifreeze to keep them out. After the Nordmann operation, a bear broke into his staple supply of buried food at Fires Creek. Rudolph had to find a way to replace it or face starvation the next winter.

In the late spring of 1999 Rudolph set up a temporary camp on a "nasty scrubby, sun-drenched spur overlooking the town of Andrews," less than a mile away. From that vantage he had a clear view of the task force command center. The pickings were good in Andrews. At night he would sneak down a path to the valley below and help himself to vegetables from a large garden at the edge of the forest. Then he would tie garbage bags over his legs to wade across the Valley River for a night of foraging in the bins behind McDonald's and the movie theater. It made him laugh that he was eating the same food as the FBI agents who hunted him.

Rudolph still smoked cigarettes whenever he could scrounge them, and he often found half-smoked butts behind the Gibson Furniture store in Andrews, along with discarded magazines and newspapers. Rudolph was afraid that his vocal cords would atrophy after so many months of silence, so he exercised his voice by talking to himself in his camp, and reading aloud from books and newspapers. He would debate the issues, taking both sides and acting them out in different voices. One night he read an article in *USA Today* that caught his imagination: It was a grim story about a sweatshop in Vietnam where the women were treated so badly that their supervisor would make them lick the floor as punishment for misbehaving. Rudolph began acting it out as a comedy, mimicking each of the characters. "You lick the floor!" he said in the stern voice of the boss. "Oh no! Don't make me lick floor!" he wailed in the falsetto voice of an Asian woman. He got so caught up in his own dialogue that he kept it up as he rummaged around in some trash behind a store in Andrews. Rudolph was lifting a large piece of plastic sheeting that he planned to use in his camp when a head popped up from the cardboard box it was covering. "Who's making you lick the floor, buddy?" said the homeless man who was using the box as a shelter.

"Nobody," Rudolph muttered, "nobody is making me lick the floor."

He scrambled back to the river and watched to see whether the man would turn him in. The transient stood up and lit a cigarette, then went back to his cardboard bed.

Rudolph had hoped to attack the task force command center in Andrews that summer. But, as he wrote, he abandoned the idea because his survival took priority and he spent his time stockpiling food. Later that fall he devised an elaborate scheme to steal dried corn and soybeans from a cluster of grain silos in a sparsely populated area a couple of miles west of Andrews, just past the airport. He later wrote about this operation in a lengthy composition he titled "Lil."

"Preparation is the key to success in most human endeavors," he wrote, "but this is especially true when attempting to move two tons of grains twenty miles with no transportation or equipment, and doing this right under the noses of the two hundred FBI agents who were looking for me."

In precise and vivid detail, Rudolph described the dimensions of the thirty-foot-tall silos, the lay of the landscape, and the arduous work required to pilfer the grain. His plan involved stealing several large wheeled trash cans from an auto parts store in Andrews, climbing atop the silos to load his rucksack with grain, filling up the wheelie cans, then "boosting" a truck to transport the goods to his Fires Creek sanctuary. He worked in the early hours of the morning, but as he wrote, he was rarely alone.

The silos were lighted with a mercury-vapor street lamp which bathed the area in a pale white light; bats were diving in and out of the light, scarfing the last of the summer's insects. The weather was cool and clear with the smell of corn stalks rotting in the field. The drought had not been quenched as of yet, and as I walked back and forth through the fields a cloud of dust rose in my wake. The place was crawling with mice in pursuit of the grain accidentally spilled in the process of loading the silos. And with the mice came the owls who hunted them. These sat in the trees overlooking the area, waiting for their prey to move through the bare fields towards the silos. Occasionally as I sat atop a silo between loads trying to catch my breath, an owl would swoop down and nail an unlucky mouse crossing the field, a small dust cloud enveloping them as he struggled to secure his meal. Once the mouse was sufficiently dead, the owl would fly back to the wood line and celebrate his catch by hooting a little tune. Every so often a car would come by, the headlights piercing the blackness. First a steady trickle, then after midnight maybe one car an hour.

Sometime after midnight I was coming down from the silo with a load of beans when a car approached in the distance and as it neared the silos it slowed dramatically and pulled in behind the silos. In this location a car cannot be seen from the road; I quickly learned that this was one of those locations used to engage in the kind of activities teenagers are wont to try to hide, like smoking pot, sex and drinking beer. This couple, male and female, were interested in sex, for they had no time for anything else. I crouched down between the silos and flattened out on my belly, as they started to go to town on each other ten feet away. "God, I hope they don't decide to take a leak after they're done," I thought, as I lay in the perfect place for them to do so. After fifteen minutes of this, they quietly started the car, wiped the heavily fogged windshield and pulled away. The things I saw in out of the way places late at night never ceased to amaze me.

Rudolph removed the pine-branch camouflage from the garbage cans while he loaded them with grain; anyone walking around the fields could see them. One night, while he was on top of a silo, he heard the sound of a small pickup with a bad muffler heading toward him. Rudolph flattened himself against the tin roof and listened while two coon hunters turned their dog loose in the parking lot below. They shined their spotlight around the field and into the trees, hoping to catch the glint of a raccoon's eyes.

"Go get 'em, Lil!" one of them shouted to the hound.

Rudolph strained to see what was happening. "The dog was still roaming about the parking lot as they started to move toward the back of the church and the field where the garbage cans sat uncovered," he wrote.

> Off to the left I could see the headlights of a car coming down the road at a high rate of speed, when just as it disappeared behind the silos to my front a loud bang accompanied by the yelp of a dog broke through the night air. The car momentarily slowed, but then picked up speed and continued on its way.
>
> A very few moments of silence passed as they moved toward the road out of my view, and then one of the coon hunters spoke: "Is he dead?"
>
> "Yep," said the other voice. "He's dead alright. And the som-bitch never even stopped. A $500 dog and he ain't never had a chance to tree a coon. How do ya like that som-bitch never even stopping?"

Rudolph heard a metallic *thunk* as the hunters tossed Lil into the bed of the truck. Then they drove away.

Rudolph tried to finish loading the grain as quickly as possible, and not only because the weather was starting to change. "I didn't like this place," he wrote. "There are some places that just give me the creeps, and this was one of them. A bad vibe, a sense of dread, I don't know what it is, but this place had it all." By the fourth day of moving grain, the wind changed direction and a front moved in, bringing rain. Rudolph broke one of his own rules and decided to cook a meal of porridge in the daytime alongside a tangled creek bed near his camp. Just as he was putting a pot of soybeans on the fire, he saw a man with a rifle walking through the rhododendrons. Rudolph scrambled up the ridge and hid. The hunter stood over his campfire and began poking around his things.

Then he took off, like he'd been spooked. Rudolph panicked. He was sure the hunter was going to report this to the FBI. He figured he had about an hour before the helicopter with infrared sensors was airborne.

> I ran down the hill, grabbed the pot, dumped the gruel into the creek, and quickly tore the fire apart, putting the coals in the creek and camouflaging the area as best I could with some leaves. I bounded up the other side of the ridge to the camp where I expeditiously packed and started to consult my maps and compass. "Think, damn you!" I demanded of myself as I tried to beat down the monster of fear. As anyone who has been in this type of situation knows, the sooner you can get your mind involved in the action the better. The best [antidote] for fear and anxiety is action—one begins to think about the task at hand and therefore loses most of the fear because you don't have time to dwell on it. Your mind becomes consumed by the action.

Rudolph decided to hike to the top of the Snowbird Mountains that rose 1,500 feet above the north side of the valley. From there he could see if the feds were mobilizing a search party. If so, he could drop down into the network of gravel roads on the far side of the mountains and lose their trackers. He climbed through briar patches and old clear-cut thickets as he made his way to the high ground. He sat up all night in the cold, soaked to the skin and "shaking like a dog crapping peach seeds," waiting for the federal posse that never came. He figured that either the hunter didn't turn him in or the feds didn't believe him. "Whatever it was, I prefer to think of it as a piece of kind providence," he wrote.

By the end of October Rudolph finished filling the garbage bins with grains. He had cased a used-car lot on the main road to Andrews and learned that the owner kept the keys to the vehicles inside the office. All he had to do was pry the back door, take the keys, and fix a dealer's plate to the four-wheel-drive Chevy Silverado he picked from the lot.

Rudolph ended his story "Lil" with the successful transfer of grain to his winter camp at Fires Creek. But there was another close encounter in that operation, one that he had mentioned to Turtle Matthews, the deputy sheriff who helped arrest him in 2003. He'd told Matthews that he had almost been caught when he ran out of gas outside Murphy, and two deputies stopped to help him. When I asked Rudolph about it, he supplied the details:

> The truck in the short story [1996 Chevrolet Silverado] used to haul the grain back to my Fires Creek camp was the one that ran out of gas. Unfortunately, when I boosted the truck on Halloween night in 1999 the gas tank was empty. Instead of going into Andrews to fill it up, I decided that if I took it to Murphy there would be less chance of someone I knew seeing me at the gas station. So I left off the grain loading until I could get some gas in Murphy.
>
> A couple of miles short of the station, the truck ran out of gas. I pulled it into the Heilig-Meyers furniture store, which is about a 1/8 mile east of Wal-Mart on highway [19]. This threw a wrench into all of my plans, as time was crucial in moving the grains. I would have to walk to the station. After struggling out of my homemade camouflage clothing—white jeans stained brown and green with walnut husks—behind the store, I put on some street clothes. Grabbing a water jug out of the back of the truck, I started off down the road toward the intersection.
>
> The first car coming in the opposite direction was a Cherokee County sheriff's department cruiser. There were two deputies. They pulled up slowly and asked, "Did you run out of gas?" With my heart in my throat, I nodded yes. They said to get in the back—they would take me to the station.
>
> They took me to the Citgo, waited for me to pump the gas, and finally drove me back to the "borrowed" truck. The deputies were even so kind as to shine their door light for me as I carefully but nervously poured the gas into the tank. Truth is often stranger than fiction.

Rudolph maintained a watch on the command post in Andrews as the search force dwindled to a few dozen agents. When they closed their headquarters and relocated to Murphy with only a handful of men, Rudolph followed them there. He set up a camp on a steep ridge directly across the four-lane highway from the armory, where he carefully noted the schedules and habits of the men who would capture him if they could only find him. Then they, too, were gone.

14

LAZARUS

It was the rainiest spring anyone could remember in Cherokee County. The storms started in April and kept up into May. There were gully washers followed by deluges, and it seemed sometimes that the mountains themselves would turn to mud and slide down into the sodden valleys. It was during one of these storms that a woman who lived in a neighborhood across from the Murphy high school came running in from the car with a bag of groceries in her arms and almost bumped into a stranger hunkered down on her back porch. She couldn't really see his face, since he had his sweatshirt hood pulled up over his head. Before she could say anything, he muttered something about getting caught in the rain. By the time she'd put the groceries in the kitchen and gone back out to check on him, he was gone.

Later, when the neighbors compared notes, certain things started adding up, things they'd chalked up to mischievous kids. Somebody had been stealing vegetables from a garden belonging to Jack Thompson, the former sheriff who lived in the neighborhood. And one morning when he walked down to check on his stocked trout pond, his fishing pole was in the water where he'd left it, but someone had cut the fish off the line. Meanwhile, a neighbor's dogs kept dragging animal hides out of the woods; one was a neatly skinned beaver pelt. A man who was riding his ATV along the muddy trails behind his house found some wet quilts and a soggy sleeping bag hanging in the bushes. Most folks thought it had to be a homeless person camping in the woods. But nobody suspected Eric Rudolph. Even if he was still alive, he wouldn't be so close to town.

"I told myself not to go out that night," Rudolph later wrote, when he was trying to make sense of the string of events that ended his years on the run. He had plenty of food in his summer camp: "enough Taco Bell burritos to cure an anorexic" and an abundance of onions, bananas, and tomatoes drying on a piece of wire mesh he'd set out in the sun. The voice—not a voice, really, but an instinct; "we're not talking schizophrenia here"—the voice told him something was wrong. This time he didn't pay attention to the warning. He wanted to finish his food-drying routine early that year, so he shook off his unease and headed down the hill to scavenge for more.

He would later admit he was getting careless, that his mind was wrapped up in his plans to haul 200 pounds of supplies to his permanent camp deep in the mountains, and the patrol car that whipped into the alley with its lights off caught him by surprise. He'd had just enough time to leap behind some milk crates before the car was on him. He thought about running, and what that would mean: more months and years of hiding, soaked with rain, huddling in a freezing tent through the winter storms, living off garbage. He decided he didn't care anymore. It was fate. He stepped out into the light with his hands in the air.

As soon as they caught him, the news flew like a schoolyard rumor. Mark Thigpen, Murphy's chief of police, called his friend Mark Buchanan, an ASAC with the North Carolina State Bureau of Investigation, who then called his boss to tell him Eric Rudolph was in the Cherokee County Jail. Sheriff Keith Lovin began the official "notification process," phoning Andy Romagnuolo, one of two FBI agents in Asheville who were nominally in charge of the dormant fugitive search.

"I'm 99.9 percent sure it's Rudolph," Lovin told the agent. "If it was Easter, I'd have your prize egg."

Romagnuolo called Jim Russell, who was still with the resident agency, and woke him up on a Saturday morning to tell him they had Rudolph in the Cherokee County Jail.

"That's crazy," said Russell, who was sure Rudolph was dead.

"They say it's him."

Russell had been through false Rudolph sightings many times before. So he took a shower and ate breakfast before he headed out for the ninety-minute drive to Murphy, well behind the two young agents who were racing to the jail.

Somebody in the information chain must have had Charles Stone's home number in his Rolodex, because before the FBI director learned about Rudolph's capture, the news had already leaked to CNN. Retired GBI agent Stone had kept up his contacts in Cherokee County, along with a CNN producer in Atlanta named Henry Schuster. Stone called Schuster, who managed to get a call through to Keith Lovin, who confirmed that he had a man in jail who said he was Eric Rudolph. CNN then broke the story, which was how most of the people involved in the case, not to mention the rest of the world, found out that the biggest domestic manhunt in FBI history was finally over.

Stone kept calling his old buddies from the task force. He called John Behnke and Tracey North. He called Terry Turchie in California. And he called Patricia Rudolph, whom he once had promised to notify if he had any word of her son. He later wrote that when he told her Eric was alive and in custody, she paused for a moment before she said, "I bet you folks are just dancing a jig up there." Then she hung up on him.

Joe McLean, who was now head of the terrorism division at the U.S. attorney's office in Birmingham, was still lying in bed around 7 o'clock that morning. His wife, who was watching TV in the other room, suddenly yelled out, "They've found Rudolph!"

"Is he alive or dead?" said McLean.

"He's alive! They arrested him."

"Oh, shit!" he said. Then he thought about it for a second and said it again, in a different tone of voice. "Oh, *shit*."

McLean was in his late fifties, nearing retirement age, and he had planned on a graceful exit from public service in the not-too-distant future. Now he knew that the next few years of his life were going to be consumed with the prosecution of Eric Rudolph. Assuming Birmingham got to try him first, ahead of Atlanta. That would be the next battle.

He called the FBI office, and they confirmed it was probably Rudolph. Then he rang up Mike Whisonant, who was now chief prosecutor in the criminal division.

"Guess what, Mike?" he said. "You're not gonna believe this ..."

Danny Sindall was still working as a street agent in Atlanta. When he got the news he'd been waiting to hear for five years, he jumped in his truck and made it to Murphy before noon. James Cross, the FBI agent who had interviewed Dan Gayman at his Identity compound, was now the case agent in charge of the Olympic Park bombing investigation. It hadn't been much of a job until this morning. As Cross sped north on U.S. 575 he got on his cell phone to start booking every hotel room he could get in Murphy before the media crews grabbed them up. C. J. Hyman, who was now working as an ATF supervisor in Greenville, South Carolina, was hammering nails into a Habitat for Humanity house with his church group when his cell phone rang with the news. He got up to Murphy as fast as he could. Larry Long, the FBI case agent from Birmingham, drove in from the other direction.

By midday a meeting hall in the old brick firehouse across from the jail had been turned into a temporary command center. It was feeling like old home week for the FBI, ATF, and state agents on the Southeast Bomb Task Force, many of whom hadn't seen one another for years. There were a lot of high-fives all around, as well as expressions of disbelief that the show had ended this way. "I think everybody was flabbergasted," Larry Long remembers. "But I was glad that he was caught in Murphy by a beat cop doing his job. And we were all relieved for the victims. It was a feeling of, 'Okay, now we can get on with it and try this guy.'"

They were all anxious for news from the tiny, makeshift cell across the way, but most of them could only wait. The federal agents who did have business in the jail could peer into the "Intoxilizer" room—named for the machine that tests for alcohol on the breath—through the one-way mirror in the booking area, but they tried to stay out of Rudolph's line of sight when his door was open. He froze up whenever he saw one of them. They agreed not to interview Rudolph. While the prisoner was still in Cherokee County this would be Sheriff Lovin's show.

Lovin wanted a trained police officer in the room with Rudolph at all times—to make sure he didn't accidentally "choke on a biscuit" while he was in custody. The guards were instructed not to question the prisoner, but to talk to him if he started a conversation. A pair of federal agents were posted in the jail, out of sight, to take statements from the deputies when they left the room.

Rudolph did a lot of sleeping and eating. He asked for fresh vegetables and fruits, and Mama Liz, the jailhouse cook, who made better meals than anyone had a right to expect, went out of her way to accommodate him. She made fluffy biscuits with homemade grape jelly, and even served him fresh fish from the trout farm in Andrews because she knew he liked that. Rudolph was so impressed, he asked his jailers if the cook was married.

Several times over the course of the weekend Rudolph asked when he would be getting a lawyer. Sheriff Lovin explained to him that one would be provided when he appeared in federal court in Asheville on Monday. The only time Rudolph was read his Miranda rights was on the first morning of his captivity when Lovin and Mark Buchanan went into the Intoxilizer room to ask Rudolph where he'd been camping. At first Rudolph invoked his right to remain silent. They told him they respected that, but they were worried that somebody might accidentally wander into his camps and get hurt. Rudolph was swayed and started drawing them a map to his Murphy bivouac, on a ridge outside town, and to his "winter camp" on Fires Creek in the mountains east of town. There were no explosives in either site, he said, although he had a hunting rifle at the winter camp. He offered to take them up there, if they wanted. That wasn't going to happen, Lovin said. Instead he called in Edwin Grant, an experienced woodsman from the North Carolina Resources Commission, and had Rudolph mark the locations of his hideouts on a topographic map.

Danny Sindall and Jim Russell, along with a couple of other trackers, were chosen to accompany Grant. The men had all patrolled together during the fugitive hunt in 1998 and 1999. They quickly fell back into

a familiar pattern of fanning out and searching, like a single organism
with a well-trained muscle memory. The first campsite was easy to find.
It was just where Rudolph said it was, a hundred yards up a wooded hill
right across the four-lane highway from the Murphy High School. He
could have sat up there and watched the Bulldogs football team practice,
or monitored the parking lot of the Ingles grocery store and Taco Bell,
down just below his camp. After Russell checked the area for booby
traps, the agents had a look at some of Rudolph's belongings. They found
the homemade calendar, in which Rudolph had scrupulously X-ed out
each passing day. There were some books, magazines, and newspapers—
including a two-day-old copy of *USA Today*—next to his sleeping pallet
under a camouflaged tarp. They found a kit with scissors, nail clippers,
and a plastic razor that helped explain his relatively neat appearance.
Rudolph had stashed a couple of plastic barrels of supplies and odds
and ends, including a stolen Taco Bell uniform. Sindall searched around
for his water supply and found a spring nearby. There was a white paint
bucket buried in the spring up to its lid. When Danny pried it open
he found four scavenged tacos, still reasonably edible in the makeshift
cooler.

Grant's topo map indicated that the "winter camp" was about a dozen
miles east of Murphy on a ridge in the Tusquitee range, roughly halfway
between the town and the Bob Allison campground where Rudolph had
left George Nordmann's truck. They could find the site in a stand of
hemlock and mountain laurel on a ridge above a gravel forest service
road.

They found the spot where a rushing spring marked the beginning
of the trail. Sindall and the others spread out to climb the ridge. They
followed the trace of a very old logging road that wound up through
tangles of laurel and pine, climbing 400 feet in a third of a mile. It was so
steep in places that the men had to pull themselves up hand over hand,
clinging to rocks and small trees. Before long Grant let out a whistle,
signaling that he'd found something. The trackers met him on a ledge
near the top of the rise, where he was staring up at two green city trash
cans and a blue plastic barrel suspended by ropes fifteen feet in the trees.
Russell and Sindall checked the area for booby traps, then lowered the

containers down to the ground. The big wheeled bins were filled with grain and other dried foods. The blue barrel contained an FNC Belgian assault rifle and four rounds of .223 ammunition. It also had an Eagle Creek wallet with Rudolph's North Carolina driver's license, the key to his Nissan truck, a photograph of his mother, a map, and a newspaper clipping announcing that Eric Robert Rudolph was one of the FBI's Most Wanted fugitives.

The camp was laid out on several terraces created by lichen-painted rock outcrops. The main site was a flat spot covered by black duff and pine needles. There was a prominent granite overhang under which Rudolph appeared to have slept and kept a campfire. In the sparse ashes were hundreds of tiny bone fragments, like the remains from a crematory. Rudolph had told one deputy he crushed turkey bones to add calcium to his diet. The agents found a set of deer antlers nailed to a tree, along with the scraggly beards of nine wild turkeys. Rudolph had cached other supplies in barrels buried all around the main camp. There was evidence that a bear had gotten into one of the grain containers and mauled it to pieces. Rudolph had reused the plastic, melting it over the top of the blue barrel to improve its water seal. Then he had apparently hoisted the rest of his food out of reach in case another bear showed up in camp.

The agents found clothes, cooking oil, pots and pans, cooking utensils, and books in the caches, along with an AM-FM cassette-radio. There were a few newspapers dating from the summer of 1999. One of the barrels contained a sleeping bag in almost new condition. Danny Sindall finally located the spring he had been looking for all those years, a hundred yards east of the camp. There was a spent tube of Crest toothpaste hidden under a rock where Rudolph had dug a little basin to wash and draw water. What the agents did not find was any trace of explosives or bomb-making materials, and neither did the evidence techs who scoured the campsite for days to come. The ERTs even cut down whole oak and hemlock trees to recover the nails Rudolph had hammered into them, but nothing matched the bomb shrapnel.

The campsite was in a "bear management area," where hunting was technically forbidden, which the agents thought might have made it attractive to Rudolph. It was also covered with an evergreen canopy that would defeat direct aerial observation as well as the FLIR sensors. But Sindall was puzzled that the site was miles from any of Rudolph's known haunts. It also was relatively close to a road, the backwoods equivalent of hiding from the cops in an abandoned building on a side street. But what truly perplexed the FBI agent was how Rudolph had survived the winters up here. The camp was on a north-facing slope, exposed to freezing winds, rain, and snow. He couldn't figure how a man could keep warm, even with a lean-to shelter and a campfire. He was convinced Rudolph had another hideout, but he doubted they would ever find it.

The sun was starting to go down when Edwin Grant returned to the jail to thank Rudolph for his straightforward directions.

"Glad to help," said Rudolph. He was quietly reading his Bible.

The "lone wolf," supposedly suicidal, homicidal, and alienated to the point of total withdrawal from society, turned out to be entertaining company. It took him a while to warm up, but soon Rudolph was regaling the guards with his adventures in the forest, telling them how he nearly starved to death during the first five months and ended up surviving on salamanders and snails. He laughed at the deputies' jokes and told a few of his own. Grant asked him how he managed to survive without female companionship. He joked that after years without a woman, even the bears were starting to look good to him.

Sheriff Lovin is a devout Baptist with a missionary zeal. He wanted to engage Rudolph, to see what was in his head. They talked about everything from military strategy to the Civil War to their interpretations of the Bible. Lovin's favorite book of the Bible was James. Rudolph, unsurprisingly, was "more of an Old Testament fan." He told Lovin his favorite book was Exodus.

The sheriff also joined in some lighthearted banter with his prisoner. Lovin had recently been elected to his position, and he wanted to know if Rudolph had voted for him.

"That would have been dangerous," said Rudolph with a slight smile.

"You could have voted absentee," said Lovin.

"What's your party?"

"Democrat."

Rudolph laughed. "Sorry, I probably couldn't have helped you, then."

Sheriff Lovin had drafted Jerry Crisp, one of his investigators, to take as many shifts as he could babysitting Rudolph. Crisp came from a big family with a long history in western North Carolina. His father and grandfather had both been sheriffs of Graham County, north of Topton, and Jerry had spent twenty years in various areas of law enforcement. He was also a veteran in the navy reserves who'd had a good deal of survival training. Perhaps most important, he was a good listener.

Crisp walked into the makeshift holding cell and introduced himself to Rudolph, keeping it light. "I'm one of the lucky ones who got picked to sit in here with you and keep you company." Just like the other minders, Crisp found Rudolph to be polite and friendly, as long as they were talking about the weather or other chitchat, as Crisp put it.

Rudolph spent a lot of time dozing or reading. But once he started talking he would keep on going, like a thirsty man gulping water, never getting enough. He talked about his father, and how he was a "good dad" who was strict but disciplined his children with love. Rudolph said he was spanked and whipped as a boy, but not abused. He felt like today's society wasn't strict enough. "Spare the rod and spoil the child," said Rudolph. He used old-fashioned sayings like that. "Preparation is the key" was another; he repeated it over and over.

Rudolph had strong opinions on most things, and characterized himself as a "right wing conservative." The problem with the world today was liberalism, he said. A man should be in charge of the household, and the woman's role was to follow him. He made it clear to Crisp that he didn't like Jews, whom he thought controlled the liberal news media. He said he didn't have a problem with black people, but he didn't think whites and blacks ought to mix. He disapproved of gays and didn't think they should be allowed to adopt children. He said that liberals, environmentalists, homosexuals, and federal agents were "all in one category." It was not a good category.

The only time he talked about his current predicament was when he told Crisp, "The government doesn't have anything on me. It's all just circumstantial evidence" and it would all come out in a trial. But the government was corrupt, he said, and they would set up the evidence any way they wanted.

Jerry Crisp noticed that Rudolph could talk about most things in a philosophical way without getting too worked up about them. But at the mention of a few sensitive subjects, a black look would cover his face like a cloud coming down a mountain.

"He would be talking just like me and you are talking," remembered Crisp. "He'd be smiling, looking like any other person. But when he would get on to something like abortion, that's when he'd get this cold-blooded look about him." He told Crisp that abortion was murder, and that anyone who would kill innocent babies got what they deserved. The more he talked, the colder he got. Crisp said that Rudolph's blue eyes would actually turn dark right in front of him. He had never seen anything quite like it before. Crisp watched him, fascinated, and thought, "Oh, yeah. So *you're* the guy they were looking for …"

Crisp saw that look again on Sunday morning, a full day after Rudolph's capture. "It just came out of the blue," said Crisp. "We were sitting there, chitchatting, and I wasn't even half paying attention because I'd been in there awhile. And he just sits up and starts off badmouthing the media. He says, 'They paint *me*"—Crisp made a frame with his thumbs and forefingers and looked through it, imitating Rudolph—"they paint *me* like a *terrorist*! But that *other* bomber …"

Rudolph started snapping his fingers, trying to remember the name, and Crisp sat up straight in his chair, at full attention now.

"Tim McVeigh?" he suggested.

"No, no the other one, the one that mailed his bombs …"

"You mean Kaczynski?"

"Yeah that's the one!" said Rudolph. "He was just a misunderstood intellectual environmentalist according to the media. But they labeled McVeigh a terrorist."

Crisp waited.

"Of course, the FBI and the media will put their spin on things," said Rudolph. "The world is only going to hear one side of the story."

Crisp considered this as good an opening as he was going to get.

"Maybe this would be a good chance for you to tell your side of things," he offered.

"I think I'll want a lawyer before I do that," said Rudolph. "In fact, I'd like an attorney now if it's possible."

That was it. Jerry Crisp got up and called in the sheriff.

As soon as Sean Devereaux arrived in Murphy his first order of business was to advise Eric Rudolph to stop making statements of any kind to the authorities. Devereaux, a bespectacled defense attorney from Asheville with combed-back gray hair, had been summoned to the Cherokee County Jail as soon as Rudolph asserted his Sixth Amendment right to counsel. This was temporary duty for Devereaux, who would stay only long enough to guide Rudolph through his brief appearance in federal court on Monday, June 2. It was merely a formality to establish that Rudolph was, indeed, the man wanted by the government. He would also waive his right to challenge extradition during his stay in Asheville. The question of where he would go next had been the subject of a heated debate among government officials all weekend.

As soon as word spread that Rudolph had been captured, the old fight over jurisdiction between Atlanta and Birmingham flared up again. Alice Martin, the current U.S. attorney in Birmingham, spent most of the weekend on the phone with her office and with Justice Department officials in Washington, trying to maintain first dibs on Rudolph. Martin didn't shy from a fight. A petite, tough lawyer from Sledge, Mississippi, she had worked her way through law school as a nurse to become one of the few female U.S. attorneys in the system. Before the change of administrations, Janet Reno had decided that when Rudolph was caught, Birmingham would try him first. But lawyers in the U.S. attorney's office for the Northern District of Georgia were now challenging that decision, and they had some powerful allies in the Bush Administration. No fewer than ten lawyers from the Atlanta area had taken significant positions in the Justice Department, including John Ashcroft's right-hand man, deputy attorney general Larry Thompson. David Nahmias, a brilliant and ambitious young prosecutor, had been an assistant U.S. attorney throughout the original Atlanta bombing investigations. Now Nahmias was counsel to Michael Chertoff, head of the criminal division. His colleague, AUSA Sally Yates, had stayed on in the Atlanta office and was once again lobbying to combine all the cases and try them in Atlanta. Yates and her boss, Bill Duffey, argued, with straight faces, that they had jurisdiction in the Birmingham bombing because Rudolph most likely drove through a few miles of northern Georgia on his escape route from Alabama to North Carolina.

In the end, the stronger case prevailed. Despite Atlanta's political juice, it came down to the fact that Birmingham had a witness and Atlanta didn't. Ashcroft decided that the cases would be tried separately, and Birmingham would go first.

Soon after his brief court appearance in Asheville, Eric Rudolph was whisked away for another helicopter ride to Birmingham. There was no federal prison near the city, so the government had a contract with the Jefferson County Jail to house prisoners awaiting trial in the U.S. district court. This was not the notorious Birmingham Jail, where Martin Luther King wrote his famous letter during the civil rights movement. The Jefferson County Jail was a more modern structure occupying a city block at the north end of Richard Arrington Jr. Boulevard, a main artery that connects the university area with the historic, somewhat shabby downtown district. Leroy Moody, Thomas Blanton Jr., and Bobby Frank Cherry had all awaited their trials in the high-security protective-custody area of the jail—which could be any block in the six-story building where the jailers had cleared out the other prisoners.

When Rudolph arrived in Birmingham on Monday afternoon, he was still polite to his captors, but he was also agitated and disoriented. Randy Christian, spokesman for the Jefferson County Sheriff's Department, told reporters, "He seemed a little frustrated. He had not read any news or seen anything and didn't know what was going on." The jailers gave Rudolph a local newspaper to help him get settled. He was placed in an empty block of five eight-foot by ten-foot cells that opened onto a narrow "day room" equipped with a couple of round tables and stools—bolted to the floor—a pay phone, and a black-and-white TV that didn't work. The first thing Rudolph asked was that the jailers fix the television—which they did.

Rudolph was issued a uniform that looked like surgical scrubs, colored a solid red to show he was a high-risk prisoner. He was given slippers, socks, underwear, a bedroll, a towel, and toiletries—although his razor was taken away after he shaved. He was offered a Bible, which he accepted. His quarters consisted of a metal bunk and thin mattress attached to the far wall of his cell. Above it was a slit of a window that looked out on a parking garage. There was a steel sink and toilet near the door, next to a small attached desk and cabinet. Rudolph was fed three hot meals a day, which he was allowed to eat in the day room. As long as he behaved, his cell was left unlocked, although video cameras recorded every move he made, 24/7.

Jay Reeves, a writer for the Associated Press in Birmingham, noted an exquisite irony in Rudolph's circumstances: "Eric Rudolph has been portrayed for years as a rabid hater of Jews, the media and the government," he wrote. "If so, the alleged serial bomber may feel like he's in the lion's den."

It would seem that way: Every time he appeared in court, Rudolph was handed over to federal agents, strip-searched, and shackled. He was paraded before the media. When he returned to jail, his regular guard was a six-foot-eight African-American deputy named Cedric Cole. And the freshly appointed leader of his legal team was not only a liberal anti–death penalty advocate, he was Jewish.

15

THE CHILDREN OF ATTICUS FINCH

The reflective glass facade of the federal courthouse rises nine tiered stories above downtown Birmingham, high enough to throw a shadow over nearby Kelly Ingram Park, scene of some memorably violent civil rights confrontations during the sixties. The new courthouse was completed in 1987 and named after the most renowned jurist Alabama has yet produced, Hugo L. Black, who sat on the U.S. Supreme Court from 1937 to 1971. Black was a son of the South and, as such, embodied many of its contradictions and mysteries. As a young and ambitious lawyer in the 1920s, Black had briefly joined the Ku Klux Klan; thirty years later he was burned in effigy by a furious mob in his home state after he joined the unanimous ruling in *Brown v. Board of Education* that ended the doctrine of "separate but equal" public facilities. He also wrote the majority opinion for another of the Supreme Court's most significant cases, *Gideon v. Wainwright*, which extended the reach of the Sixth Amendment to require that all defendants have access to a lawyer, regardless of their ability to pay for one.

On June 2, 2003, forty years after that landmark ruling, U.S. District Judge C. Lynwood Smith sat in his chambers in Black's namesake courthouse and prepared to apply the fundamental right to counsel in the case he had just been assigned: *United States of America v. Eric Robert Rudolph*. The case name itself underlined an inherent imbalance in the situation—the resources of the entire government leveled against one man who was, by law, innocent until proven guilty—that Judge Smith was required to mitigate. Rudolph was indigent and his family was not wealthy. There was no federal public defender program in northern Alabama, so the judge needed to appoint some highly qualified lawyers to ensure Rudolph a fair trial and to lessen the possibility that a guilty verdict would be overturned on appeal.

Even though the Northern District of Alabama, which includes Birmingham, the college town of Tuscaloosa, and the space center at Huntsville, is home to more than 2.6 million people, it functions like a small town with porous borders. At its center is a core group of business leaders, doctors, politicians, lawyers, and judges, many of whom have known one another, gone to the same schools, and worked in the same arenas for years.

Judge Smith was well placed to make the selection. By 2003 he was at the top of Alabama's judicial food chain. He had the steel-haired, hearty look of a man who would rather be outside working his bird dogs than trapped behind a bench, but any lawyer would underestimate him at his or her peril. Smith was known as an interactive judge, the kind who dominates his courtroom and often interrupts testimony to ask his own questions. He attended law school at the University of Alabama in Tuscaloosa and practiced law in Huntsville until he was elected to his first judgeship in 1981. President Bill Clinton appointed him to the federal bench in 1995. Smith divided his time between courtrooms in Huntsville and Birmingham, and by now was familiar with every prominent criminal attorney in his district. Bill Bowen, a former state appellate judge with a reputation as a legal scholar, had already been appointed to represent Rudolph. But since the charges against Rudolph qualified him for the death penalty, Rudolph's lead counsel had to be, according to federal statute, "learned in the law of capital cases." As it turned out, Smith didn't need to look any further than his own courtroom.

Richard Jaffe, the fifty-three-year-old owner and senior partner in the Birmingham firm of Jaffe, Strickland and Drennan, had earned a reputation as the most successful death penalty trial lawyer in the state, and one of the best in the nation. By coincidence, Jaffe was in Smith's courtroom the day Eric Rudolph arrived in Birmingham, defending another lawyer accused of witness tampering. Smith called Jaffe to his chambers that afternoon to talk to him about the possibility of taking on a new client.

Judge Smith knew that Jaffe was Jewish, and he was careful in his choice of words when he broached the subject of Rudolph's reputed views. Jaffe took this to mean that the judge was referring to Rudolph's anti-Semitism. "He wanted to know if there was anything about Eric's views that would impact or influence me in my representation of him," Jaffe told me. "I made clear to the judge that I believed in the system. I told him that if I always had to agree with my clients I probably couldn't represent anybody." Jaffe was more concerned that Rudolph would accept and trust him as his lawyer. "My real question was, 'Will he have a problem with me, and my views and my religious preference?' I told Judge Smith that, even before meeting Eric, I didn't expect that it would be an issue between us. And that my record spoke for itself in federal and state court, especially in death penalty cases." Smith instructed Jaffe that if any "problems of any nature" arose between them he should notify the judge immediately. Jaffe willingly agreed. But first he had to have a discussion with his partners.

The prospect of the death penalty in any prosecution instantly escalates it from a straightforward criminal case to an all-out war. Particularly when the charges have resulted from a long, complicated federal investigation, the strain on a defense lawyer's time and resources can be overwhelming. Jaffe and his partners operated their small, boutique law firm out of a rambling turn-of-the-century house in Southside Birmingham, just a few blocks from the clinic where the bombing took place. Everyone in the office understood that taking on a case of this magnitude meant that the rest of their criminal practice would fall by the wayside until it was over. Luckily the firm had a civil practice to keep it going, but Jaffe would have to farm out his lucrative white-collar criminal work to other lawyers. One of Jaffe's partners, Derek Drennan, predicted that Rudolph's case would be the hardest they'd ever fought, and it would totally consume the firm. Still, everyone was on board. They knew there was no way Richard Jaffe could turn this case down. In a way he had been preparing for it his entire career.

* * *

Ask a group of criminal litigators born after WWII to name the role model who first inspired them to pursue a career in law, and odds are that most of them will mention the same name: Atticus Finch, the fictional hero of *To Kill a Mockingbird*. This is especially true if the lawyers questioned are defense attorneys in the Deep South, particularly Alabama, where the author of the book, Harper Lee, set her tale of moral courage against the backdrop of segregation and racism. Of course it was the actor Gregory Peck who brought Atticus to life and spawned a generation of understated, folksy trial lawyers with the will to defend the underdog against all odds, or in the case of Doug Jones and other young Southern prosecutors, to seek justice in the resolution of unfinished civil rights cases.

While the sons and daughters of Atticus Finch pop up everywhere in the country and in every field of law, they are most prevalent in the rarefied world of death penalty defenders. These are the high-wire acrobats of the legal system, who defend the poorest and most detested clients with the most to lose. An affinity for Atticus is one reason Richard Jaffe chose his path in criminal law. Another, more visceral motivation arose in 1969, when Jaffe was a student at the University of Alabama at Tuscaloosa and the campus was about to go on strike to protest the war in Vietnam. Jaffe and some fellow antiwar activists were having a late-night hamburger at the Krystal diner when a phalanx of state troopers marched through the restaurant, picked the kid with the longest hair, dragged him out on the sidewalk, and beat him to a pulp with their batons. Jaffe and his friends watched through the window, horrified. "That created a pretty huge impression on me," said Jaffe. The incident drove home what he had always known in his heart about the abuse of power. Even though he'd grown up white and privileged in a wealthy Birmingham suburb, he had seen how black people were humiliated with daily indignities like separate drinking fountains, and that they could be arrested, beaten, even killed for minor infractions against whites. "I knew people were being mistreated in a system that was very unfair," he said. "I realized that the people who keep authority in check are those who defend people accused of crimes. There really is no one else standing between the people and the excesses of government except criminal lawyers."

Jaffe graduated from U. of A. law school in 1976 and spent a year as an assistant attorney general under Bill Baxley, a liberal reformer who appointed Alabama's first black prosecutors. It was an uneasy but, for some, hopeful time in the state's history. On the legal front there was a short-lived suspension of capital punishment during the 1970s while the U.S. Supreme Court wrestled with the legality of the practice. In 1972 the Court essentially threw out all state and federal death penalty statutes, ruling that they were so arbitrary and capricious as to be unconstitutional. But many states, including Alabama, rewrote their laws to address the Court's objections, and capital punishment quickly returned with a vengeance. Alabama's death row was again filling up with inmates.

Jaffe briefly worked as an assistant district attorney in Tuscaloosa County, but in 1978 decided to switch sides and open a criminal defense practice. Most of those charged with capital murder were poor and black and couldn't afford private attorneys. Even though *Gideon v. Wainwright* had mandated free counsel for defendants charged with crimes that could send them to jail, it was still up to the states to decide who would be appointed and how much they would be paid. There was only one public defender in the whole state of Alabama. Sometimes judges would appoint local real estate lawyers to capital murder cases. These court-appointed attorneys were paid only $10 per hour, with a cap on fees and expenses at $500 per case. A death penalty case often requires hundreds of hours of preparation, not to mention the costs of private investigators, expert witnesses, forensic analysis—all things the prosecutor usually has in unlimited, free supply. The decks were hopelessly stacked against the accused, and a lot of people were getting death sentences who were either improperly charged or outright innocent.

Richard Jaffe became obsessed with slowing the deluge of executions in Alabama. Over the years he has been involved with fifty capital cases, tried nineteen of them to completion, and has never yet lost a client to the death chamber. He became something of a legend in legal circles for retrying three seemingly hopeless capital cases and winning releases for his clients. Doug Jones, one of Jaffe's close friends, compared the feat to "climbing Mt. Everest."

Bo Cochran had spent nineteen years on death row after twice being convicted of killing a grocery worker during a robbery; Jaffe tried his case a third time and won an acquittal. A handyman named Gary Drinkard spent five years on death row for the shooting death of a junkyard dealer. He wrote to Richard Jaffe for more than a year, asking him to take up his case. In his retrial, the jury took only forty-five minutes to find Drinkard not guilty. Then there was Randall Padgett, a chicken farmer from northern Alabama who was convicted of murder after his estranged wife was found dead with forty-six stab wounds on her body—and Padgett's semen inside her. In a 1997 retrial Jaffe won an acquittal by convincing the jury that Padgett's spiteful lover had killed his wife and framed him by planting his semen on the victim. Jaffe still keeps in touch with the clients he's helped rescue from death row; Cochran, Padgett, and Drinkard have become anti–death penalty advocates and often appear with Jaffe at capital punishment seminars and conferences.

During the 1990s, when Jaffe wasn't in court, he was often teaching courses in criminal law and evidence at the historically black Miles Law School in Birmingham. The relentless pace took a toll on his personal life, as did the pressure of his self-imposed mission. But by the spring of 2003 Richard Jaffe was finally in high cotton. He was sharing custody of his teenage daughter with his ex-wife, whom he still considers his best friend. He had financial security in his practice, which he had expanded to include well-paying white-collar work to support his defense of indigent clients. He'd made some investments, including part ownership of a popular Southside restaurant. Jaffe could often be seen tooling around Birmingham in his seafrost green Jaguar, talking into his cell phone and missing turns; a satisfied, if distracted, pillar in the legal community.

Since Birmingham is such a small town at heart, it is inevitable that professional relationships will intersect with personal ones. Jaffe, who was the son of a successful local businessman, had gone to the same college and law school as many of his colleagues, including Doug Jones, also a Birmingham native. Jaffe had friendly relations with his adversaries in the U.S. attorney's office, particularly Joe McLean and Mike Whisonant.

He had also known and liked the police officer Sande Sanderson, who was killed in the bombing. He had often met him while trying cases, and he remembered Sanderson as an easy-going, jovial guy. He didn't know Emily Lyons, but Jaffe knew the man who had hired her: Dr. Bruce Lucero, former owner of the New Woman All Women clinic. Jaffe had successfully defended Lucero when he was charged with assaulting some anti-abortion protesters. In all, Jaffe felt terrible and heartsick about the whole violent tragedy of the clinic bombing. But by training and necessity and inclination, Jaffe would set aside all that history and all those feelings to focus on the tasks he had been given: making sure his client's rights were protected, and trying to save his life.

Richard Jaffe met Eric Rudolph for the first time on the morning of his arraignment. Jaffe is short and athletic, with trim brown hair and empathetic eyes. He keeps his face as composed as a Buddhist's, but he wears the worry of every case he's tried in a deep crease that traverses the length of his forehead. He had prepared for this meeting by conferring with Bill Bowen, who had already met Rudolph. Bill Bowen was Jaffe's physical opposite, a heavyset man with large, round eyeglasses and white hair that made him look older than his fifty-five years. Bowen was also a Birmingham native, married with three children, and a religious man. He kept a quote from St. Ignatius Loyola posted by his desk: "Work as if everything depended on you. Pray as if everything depended on God." Bowen was the consummate behind-the-scenes player. His job on the team would be to concentrate on the legal aspects of the case, including drafting and filing motions; Jaffe would handle the courtroom drama.

After talking to Bowen, Jaffe read through a thick stack of newspaper clippings about Rudolph's arrest, and some older material dating back to the Olympic Park bombing in 1996. The media's impression of Rudolph was already set in stone, with almost nothing out there to challenge the perception that this man was an alienated white-supremacist, anti-abortion fanatic. Jaffe knew better than to believe most of what he read about his clients. He always kept his mind open to see them as full, complex human beings, not to pigeonhole them according to the crimes they were accused of committing. He had no agenda in mind that day except to introduce himself to Eric Rudolph and try to get to know him a little.

When Jaffe first saw Rudolph he was sitting at a table outside his cell in Jefferson County Jail looking gaunt and exhausted, and still shell-shocked by the weekend's events. The jailers let Jaffe into the room and locked the door behind him. The lawyer shook Rudolph's hand and took a seat next to him. He noticed that Rudolph's posture seemed taut, almost rigid. Eric Rudolph clearly hadn't trusted anyone in a long time. It was going to be a challenge to get this man to open up to him. Jaffe told him that he believed in complete candor between a lawyer and a client, and he started off his end of the conversation by informing Rudolph that he was Jewish.

"Why are you telling me that?" said Rudolph, to Jaffe's mild surprise. "Why would it matter?"

"Well, I thought you needed to know my beliefs," said Jaffe. "And if you have any reservations about me, it's plenty early enough for another competent lawyer to take over."

Rudolph said he had no problem with Jaffe's faith. What he wanted to talk about was his record and his strengths as a trial lawyer. Jaffe told him about Cochran, Padgett, and Drinkard as well as some of the other cases he had tried and won. Rudolph wanted to probe deeper into Jaffe's motivations. As it turned out, he would ask a variation of the same question of every attorney assigned to his case: "Why do you do this kind of work?"

A long and intricate conversation ensued. Jaffe told him that he was not a "cause" lawyer who chose his cases solely to chip away at capital punishment statutes. "Although I may work to get the death penalty off the books, my interest is in you as a person and in saving your life. Period. My cause is each of my clients, one at a time."

They talked about the issue of abortion, and Rudolph's intense opposition to it. Rudolph volunteered, in hypothetical terms, the possible motivation of someone who would bomb an abortion clinic. "Eric said that whoever did this obviously believed that nothing was more important than the defense of an unborn child," Jaffe recalled. "His opinion was that whoever did this was so concerned about unborn children that it was their obligation to protect them." Jaffe told Rudolph that his own views on abortion were not anywhere close to Rudolph's. Although from a personal standpoint Jaffe might have had mixed feelings about it, he certainly wouldn't consider himself part of the pro-life movement. "If anything I would be on the other side," he'd said. Rudolph had no problem with this, either.

Then Rudolph asked, "If you knew someone was guilty, how could you defend them?"

It was a good question, of course, and one Jaffe had been asked many times, though rarely by a client. "I think there are multiple answers," he told Rudolph. It began with his belief that only God can create life and that only God should be able to take it away. He believed that the state didn't have the right to sanction murder, in effect saying, "Do what I say, not what I do." And Jaffe believed that, with few exceptions, every human being can be redeemed. And no matter what someone was accused of doing or might have done, "as long as there was a beating heart, I was going to defend that person."

As they talked, Jaffe sensed a gradual thawing in Rudolph. "He looked me right in the eye," the lawyer recalled. "I felt no paranoia about me being there. There was no fear of human connection. A warmness had already started to develop between us."

Whatever warmth enveloped Eric Rudolph that morning had chilled completely by the time he appeared in U.S. magistrates court for his arraignment later that afternoon. The U.S. marshals had picked him up in his cell, had him stripped and cavity-searched, chained him at the wrists and ankles, and hustled him off in a black Suburban for the high-speed convoy ride to the courthouse, ten blocks away.

This was Rudolph's first public appearance in Birmingham, and the wooden pews of the wide, modern courtroom were packed with reporters, prosecutors, past and present federal agents, and law enforcement officers, all of whom wanted to see this phantom with their own eyes. No one made a sound as the marshals led Rudolph in from a side door. He was still dressed in red togs with "Jefferson County Jail" stenciled across the back. His grown-out crew cut formed a spiky black halo around his large head. Although the handcuffs were off now, his leg shackles clinked a few faint notes as he shuffled to the defense table to take his place between Bill Bowen and Richard Jaffe. The prosecutors were lined up behind their long desk on the other side of the aisle: Alice Martin, Joe McLean, Michael Whisonant, and Will Chambers, the men all dressed in somber suits, like bankers at a funeral.

Simple pleadings did not require the district judge, so the appearance could be handled by a magistrate. When Chief U.S. Magistrate Michael T. Putnam entered the room, all rose. Rudolph looked straight ahead, chin high, hands behind him like a soldier at ease, while a hundred sets of eyes stared at the back of his head. Jaffe, who wore a dark double-breasted suit and a red tie, rocked almost imperceptibly on the balls of his feet to dispel excess energy as he waited for Putnam to be seated and the procedure to begin.

After a few words to preface the event, Putnam read the charges to Rudolph and asked him a few questions. Rudolph was polite and attentive, consistently addressing the judge as "your honor." When Putnam asked if he wished to enter a plea, Rudolph replied in his low Southern drawl, "Yes. I enter a plea of not guilty."

The judge set an initial trial date of August 4, which would last about as long as a Popsicle in the sun. The defense needed at least a year to prepare its case and would quickly ask for a continuance. Rudolph was then removed from the courtroom before the spectators could leave. The pleading had taken only a few minutes.

Doug Jones had postponed a vacation at the beach to attend the hearing. "I'll meet you there," he told his wife, "I've got to see this son of a bitch first." When he finally laid eyes on Rudolph, all he felt was relief to see the man in chains. Jones had a front-row seat in the jury box during the proceedings, so he had a good view of the defendant. "He looked about like I thought he would look, maybe skinnier," Jones told me later. "But even though he was polite to the judge, there was no soul behind his eyes. I just saw someone who liked to play God."

At the end of the hearing, Rudolph's new defense team stood on the steps of the Hugo L. Black courthouse to take a few brief questions from the media. Flanked by Bowen, his partner Derek Drennan, and their associate Hube Dodd, Richard Jaffe took his first stab at challenging the preconception that Rudolph was guilty. "It is only fair, I think, to suspend judgment and allow the courtroom to test whether the proof is really proof or speculation and hearsay." Jaffe was wary of the media, but he felt that he had to try to counteract the avalanche of negative news reports he'd been seeing all week. Rudolph's arrest had filled the front pages of every paper in the region and had led every local TV news broadcast. CNN's coverage was practically wall-to-wall Rudolph, with each show in turn trotting out a chorus of interviewees with the same message: Rudolph was guilty. Charles Stone, the retired GBI agent, had become a constant fixture on the news shows, rehashing the government's case. Deborah Givens, Joel Rudolph's ex-wife, was on CNN again, repeating her claims that Eric Rudolph was a dope-smoking, Hitler-loving, Jew-hating fanatic. Jaffe decided to make himself available to the national media for a short time to appeal for a fair trial and to warn against a rush to judgment. He agreed to appear on the *Today Show*, where he told Katie Couric that his client had no problem with being represented by a Jewish lawyer, and that he had seen no evidence that Eric Rudolph hated Jews, gays, or anyone else. Jaffe later held a brief news conference at his law firm, to tell the same story to the print media and other TV stations: "There's no evidence of anger or extremism that I've seen in any form or fashion," he said. Jaffe characterized Rudolph as "very calm, very concerned, very reflective, very thoughtful." He urged the media to hold off convicting anyone until they had heard the evidence. "We are really not Salem, Massachusetts, in the 1600s. We are in Birmingham, Alabama, where people get fair trials," he said, without a hint of irony in his voice.

Ten minutes after it began, Jaffe left the news conference to return to his upstairs office. The U.S. government had just released more than 17,000 documents to him, the first installment in the long, arduous process called, optimistically, the "discovery" of evidence. Before the case was over, there would be 700,000 such documents and exhibits, along with 20,000 photos to sort through. The government had spent many millions of dollars and employed hundreds of investigators to prepare its case against Eric Rudolph. And they had a five-year head start. Jaffe and his team had a lot of catching up to do.

Luckily there was an agency designed to help out with cases like this one, the Federal Defender Program, and attorneys at its Atlanta office had been closely monitoring the case from the first word of Rudolph's arrest. The program was started by an act of Congress back in 1964, soon after the *Gideon v. Wainwright* decision, so that federal judicial districts with big enough caseloads could have a ready pool of well-trained attorneys dedicated to providing free services to indigent defendants. They are the federally funded counterparts of the U.S. prosecutors. When there are no federal defenders available locally, as in the case of northern Alabama, a private "learned counsel" with experience in capital cases can be appointed, but only after consulting a federal defender. Stephanie Kearns, who ran the federal public defenders office in Atlanta, endorsed Jaffe's appointment. She then put together a group of trial lawyers to work in concert with the Birmingham defense. Paul Kish, a compact, bearded man with lively blue eyes, who'd had nearly twenty years experience with the Atlanta federal defenders, would lead the Atlanta defense and would eventually become a consulting member of the Birmingham team. He was joined by his colleagues W. Carl Lietz III and Brian Mendelsohn.

Soon after Jaffe was appointed, Kearns set up a conference call to discuss the needs and priorities of the two teams. One of the first things Jaffe needed was help accessing the discovery documents.

The documents dated back to 1996, when the U.S. government, in particular Louis Freeh's FBI, was barely computer literate. Since then, a new electronic case filing system had been inaugurated in federal courts, and most documents, lab reports, photos, and other exhibits had to be converted to digital formats. And since the Justice Department had been suing Bill Gates for antitrust violations during the 1990s, the government did not use Microsoft software for any of its work products, so they were unreadable on most private computers.

Kearns immediately freed up half a dozen laptops loaded with the appropriate software to read some of this discovery material. Five minutes after the conference call ended, Paul Kish jumped in his old Camry station wagon and drove to Birmingham, the first of many four-hour round trips he and his teammates would make down Interstate 20 in the next two years. Sometimes the discovery came in the form of thousands of paper documents, which had to be copied for each attorney, but the court would reimburse Jaffe's team for only one photocopy of each page. When that happened Kish got in his wagon again and picked up the boxes of discovery materials to have multiple copies made in Atlanta. The federal defender services volunteered to index everything as well, since like the U.S. attorney's office it had sufficient man-hours to devote to its cases. Kearns was willing to assign all available resources to the project.

The Atlanta lawyers deferred to Jaffe's decisions about how to put together his defense strategy and how to handle his client. Jaffe wanted to build his relationship with Eric Rudolph slowly and gently. Rudolph had been alone in the woods for a long time, and Jaffe didn't want to overwhelm him by introducing too many new people at once. Jaffe and Bowen visited the jail at least once or twice a week, as did several other investigators and associates from Birmingham, including Derek Drennan and Hube Dodd, a young lawyer in the firm who hit it off immediately with Rudolph. The two spent hours and hours talking about everything from hunting and fishing to house remodeling.

Within a few weeks, Jaffe decided it was time to introduce the new set of attorneys from Atlanta. Brian Mendelsohn accompanied Paul Kish to the first meeting. Once again, Eric Rudolph asked the lawyers why they did what they did. Mendelsohn, who is a head taller than Kish, with long, thin features and a mop of curly black hair, made no bones about his position as a "cause" lawyer. "I'm an ideologue," he told Rudolph. "I am anti–death penalty, no matter what the circumstances." Kish had never had a client ask him that question before. He told Rudolph he became a defense attorney because he doesn't like an unfair fight. "I hate bullies," he said. "Whenever there's a criminal case, where it's everybody against one person—it almost doesn't matter to me what that person did or didn't do, or what he's accused of, it's not fair." Richard Jaffe left them together in the day room, where they spent the rest of the afternoon talking. And Rudolph's small circle grew larger by two.

* * *

Throughout his months guarding Rudolph in the Jefferson County Jail, Cedric Cole watched his prisoner closely from the console of video monitors at the center of the floor. His job, said Cole, was to "house him and feed him and make sure he didn't kill himself." But his relationship with Rudolph grew to something more than that over time. "He had a good sense of humor," Cole told me. "We'd joke about certain things. We set up a kind of rapport." Cole was taking night courses at Miles Law School, going for his degree while he supported his family as a bailiff and a county deputy. He is by nature a warm and friendly man who controls his prisoners by the strength of his personality and his enormous, towering presence.

"Rudolph was the ideal inmate," said Cole. "He was never disrespectful, always proper. You'd never know he was from the hills of North Carolina." Cole knew what all the newspapers said, that Rudolph was a racist and a Nazi, but he never acted that way. "You never know what's on another person's mind. But racist? I never saw it, and believe me I've seen racists. When he got here my twins were a year old. And he overheard me talking about them, and he wanted to see pictures of the babies. Now I'm a big black man, and me and Rudolph would sit back there and we'd talk about the twins. He's always ask how they were doing, knew their names. Rudolph and me, we're the same age. And just talking, we found we had a lot of things in common."

Cole liked to needle Rudolph about his food preferences in the jail. The prisoners could buy snacks from the commissary, and most of them ordered soda pop and candy bars. But not Rudolph. He wanted water or juice or trail mix, four or five bags of it a week.

"Why are you eating that rabbit food?" Cole joked with him. "I thought you'd have enough of that stuff when you was out there in the woods all that time."

"Hey, this is good stuff!" Rudolph told him. "The best."

Rudolph put on about twenty pounds in jail, even though he constantly exercised in his cell. He wasn't too fond of the school cafeteria–type food they served, but he told Cole it was good compared to what he had been eating. Cole couldn't resist ragging him about it. "I asked,

'What were you eating in them hills?' He said he ate acorns, even some kind of lizard. Salamanders! That kind of knocked me over my shoulders. I *had* to tease him. I said, 'You've got to be kidding me! Then this is like the Waldorf Astoria to you!'"

Rudolph had his good days and his bad days. He was always low when he came back from court, particularly if he had been transferred to Huntsville for an appearance in Judge Smith's courtroom there. Cole watched how it took a while for Rudolph to readjust. He passed his time meeting with lawyers, reading, watching television, and writing letters on the table out in the day room. His mother and two of his brothers eventually came to visit him, although Cole never met them. Visitors sat on the other side of a glass partition and talked to the inmate on a telephone. (Toward the end of his stay, Rudolph was finally allowed to sit with his mother in a conference room.)

Rudolph was curious about everything going on in the jail. But Cole could tell he didn't want many people to know he was there, and he would disappear into his cell when one of the jail officials gave a tour of the facility to a class of schoolchildren or special visitors. The other prisoners didn't mix with him, but they were aware of his celebrity. Cole had to ban a jailhouse barber from cutting Rudolph's hair when he learned that the man was going to sell the clippings on eBay.

"Rudolph told me, 'You got rid of the only guy who could cut my hair!'" said Cole. "He cared about his appearance, he was mindful of what people thought about him, what people said about him. He was in tune with what was going on in the media about him. He was always watching those newscasts, especially when he came back from court."

One afternoon Rudolph returned from a hearing and asked Cole, "Did you see me on TV?"

"Yeah, sure did," said Cole. "You looked kinda fat."

"Ahh, Cole," said Rudolph, laughing. "You're something else."

"Just be sure when they make the movie about all this, you get Denzel Washington to play me."

While the mountains of discovery material piled up, Jaffe started mapping out his defense strategy. He quickly decided he needed more help.

He asked Judge Smith to let him hire Michael Burt, a specialist in forensic evidence and a federal death penalty expert from San Francisco. Jaffe wanted another trial lawyer at the table with him, someone skilled at cross-examination, since the eyewitness accounts of Rudolph in Birmingham were the most damaging element of the prosecution. Jaffe called on Emory Anthony, a Birmingham attorney who had worked on several death penalty cases with him. There was nobody better at cross, and few who could relate better to a local jury. As the newspapers also pointed out, it didn't hurt to have an African American on the defense team. Jaffe also needed another attorney with experience in organizing a huge federal case and a large legal team. The best in the business, he'd heard, was Judy Clarke. He had met her in passing and knew her by reputation from two famous cases: She served as second chair to the legendary David Bruck in the 1995 trial of Susan Smith, the young mother who drowned her two infant sons in a South Carolina lake. The jury gave Smith life in prison, and Bruck later called Clarke "a one-woman Dream Team." Then, three years later, as a federal defender, she joined Ted Kaczynski's defense and engineered the plea bargain that spared him the death penalty (a deal he later tried to rescind). She was currently working as the federal defender in San Diego, and when Jaffe interviewed her she seemed eager to join the defense. Not everyone he spoke to agreed she would fit in with his team. But to Jaffe, always confident in his instincts about people, she seemed charming, talented, and perfect for the administrative job.

As soon as it was announced that Clarke had joined Rudolph's defense, the phone rang in Joe McLean's office. It was a fellow attorney, someone McLean would rather not name.

"Richard's gone," said McLean's friend.

"What are you talking about?" said McLean.

"I know Judy. Richard Jaffe will be gone before this case is over."

"That can't happen. Richard's the lead attorney!"

"You just wait," said the lawyer. "It's only a matter of time."

16

ONE ON ONE

A trial is a contest of competing narratives; the side that tells the best story wins. The assistant U.S. attorneys in Birmingham who were preparing the case against Eric Rudolph decided to keep theirs short and simple. They wouldn't bring in the web of circumstantial evidence connecting him to the Atlanta bombings, nor would they overwhelm the jury with months of forensic testimony. There was no need to over-try this case, they believed; the basic evidence was strong enough to convict. What they needed to do was to weave a collection of simple facts and observations into a believable plotline, one in which causes produce effects, and a persuasive logic is imposed on the most inexplicable of human actions.

The story, as Mike Whisonant would tell it, began on Christmas Eve, 1997. While most Christians were doing their last-minute shopping for gifts, Eric Rudolph was in the Wal-Mart in Murphy, North Carolina, buying bomb components and planning mass murder. Just over a month later, Rudolph drove his bomb to Birmingham, Alabama, disguised it with plastic foliage, and buried it under some low shrubbery along the walkway leading to the New Woman All Women Health Care Clinic, a place where legal abortions are performed. Crime scene and autopsy photos of Sanderson would show how he was killed by the devastating shock wave and heat flash generated by the blast, so intense that parts of his body looked more like charred firewood than human flesh. The nurse, Emily Lyons, would be put on the stand to describe how she was permanently maimed and nearly blinded by the dozens of nails and bomb fragments that tore into her body. Whisonant would show how the bomb had been positioned to kill not just Sanderson and Lyons, but the dozen or more people who would soon have been in the waiting room. Eric Rudolph, he would tell the jury, was nothing less than a domestic terrorist trying to play God. And he was nothing more than a coward who killed from a safe distance, then ran away to hide.

Eyewitnesses and emergency personnel who attended the victims that morning would paint a picture of the horror and violence of the event. The prosecution would produce a detailed replica of the device, recreated by the ATF based on fragments that survived the blast, demonstrating the makeup of the bomb: approximately ten sticks of nitroglycerin dynamite removed from their wrappers and packed into a tube made of aluminum flashing, placed in a Popular Mechanics plastic toolbox and packed with another five and a half pounds of nails for shrapnel. Other components included a hose clamp sold only at Wal-Mart, a Rubbermaid plastic container, gray duct tape, batteries, an egg timer, the remnants of a homemade detonator, and a JR-brand servo and receiver, the kind that is used to fly model airplanes using radio controls. A crystal from the circuit board, which was surgically removed from the tissue just above Emily Lyons's liver, would be produced as evidence. The prosecution would tie all these objects to Rudolph, or show that he had ready access to them.

But the centerpiece of the government's case was the eyewitness account of Jermaine Hughes, the UAB student who could identify Rudolph as the man he had followed from the clinic to his truck on the other side of Red Mountain. Larry Long, the FBI case agent who was now in charge of rounding up witnesses and keeping track of the evidence, had been in touch with Hughes over the years. He had graduated with honors from UAB and decided to change his career from medicine to law. Now, as the Rudolph case was moving toward trial, Hughes was preparing to graduate from Harvard Law School.

To bolster Hughes's testimony, the prosecution intended to trot out more fancy visual aids. FBI artists built an elaborate scale model of the clinic and the Southside neighborhood, showing the layout of the streets and nearby buildings, including Rast Hall, where Hughes had been doing his laundry when the bomb went off. The agency also devised a computerized 360-degree virtual tour of Hughes's route as he followed the suspicious stranger through the winding streets above the university, showing where Rudolph ducked into an apartment complex to shed his disguise, and where Hughes saw him again across from the McDonald's while he was on the phone with a 911 operator. They would play that 911 tape, and introduce the testimony of Jeffrey Tickal, the attorney who joined the chase and saw Rudolph get into his truck. They would introduce the McDonald's coffee cup on which Tickal had written the North Carolina tag number: KND1117. There were other unpublicized witnesses who saw Rudolph's truck in the vicinity of the clinic the night before and the morning of the bombing. And there was a middle-aged businesswoman who had withdrawn money from her bank at 9:18 A.M., then bought a cup of coffee at a fast-food restaurant just before she drove to the Trussville on-ramp of I-59, the main north-south artery running through Birmingham. As she tried to merge into northbound traffic a gray Nissan pickup with a cream-colored camper top and North Carolina plates hugged the right-hand lane and refused to let her in. She was so angry that she raced up beside the truck and gave the driver the finger. He turned his head and looked at her blankly, without anger or any sign that he'd seen her, then continued on in the slow lane. He was going only about 55 mph, so she raced ahead and quickly forgot about the incident. That weekend, when Eric Rudolph's picture was all over the news, she realized she had flipped off the clinic bomber.

The prosecution would show how the tag number on the Nissan was traced to Eric Rudolph, an unemployed construction laborer who lived in a trailer in Murphy, North Carolina, five hours by road from Birmingham. They would detail his movements that day and the next and show how, when his truck was recovered in the woods ten days later, there were traces of the chemical EGDN on the steering wheel, indicating that the driver had handled nitroglycerin dynamite—and that Rudolph's were the only fingerprints found in the cab.

The government's attorneys would show the jury the condition of Rudolph's trailer when the agents arrived there on Friday night, shortly after local media outlets carried the story that he was wanted as a material witness. They would contend that the pulled-out drawers, the open front door, the oatmeal next to the stove all suggested that Rudolph fled in a hurry to avoid arrest. They would argue that receipts in the truck showed he had bought food and supplies with an intent to evade the law.

Searches of the trailer uncovered a wig, sunglasses, ball cap, and plaid jacket, items described by Hughes and Tickal. There were also traces of EGDN all over Rudolph's bedroom: on his chair, bed, socks, NASCAR cap, and the video of *Kull the Conqueror*. Agents had tested videos he had rented earlier in the week and found explosive residues on one of them as well. In a spare room agents found a blue plastic Wal-Mart bag, like the one he was seen carrying in Birmingham, and in it a receipt dated 4:41 P.M. on December 24, 1997. It showed that Rudolph had paid cash to buy two deadbolt locks, a pair of gloves, a pack of light bulbs, and a set of hose clamps of precisely the same brand as the one removed from Officer Sanderson's body.

To show that Rudolph knew how to handle explosives, the prosecution would bring in witnesses from his days in the U.S. Army, where he was taught how to build and detonate improvised explosive devices. After he was discharged from the service in 1989, Rudolph not only kept his military manuals about explosives and tactics, he added to his collection. In early 1996, using the alias "Z. Randolp," Rudolph purchased a postal money order to buy a paperback titled *Ragnar's Homemade Detonators*, which was shipped to his box in Topton, North Carolina. The book contained specific instructions on how to make the very detonator that was used in the bomb that exploded outside the New Woman All Women clinic.

They planned to call the witness from Tennessee who had discussed flying model airplanes with Rudolph, and had told him where to buy JR radio-control devices. They also planned to produce "Dana," the woman from Nashville with whom Rudolph had discussed bomb-making techniques.

They weren't so sure what to do about George Nordmann. The government felt that Rudolph's flight from the law was compelling proof of his guilt. Nordmann was the only one who had talked to him after he disappeared in the woods. He could establish that Rudolph knew the authorities were after him, and was determined not to be captured. But Rudolph had also told Nordmann he was innocent, and that he'd run only because he was sure the feds would frame him. And, like a gallant outlaw, Rudolph had left behind money for the food he'd taken and the trouble he'd caused. The unpredictable Nordmann's testimony might just add to Rudolph's mystique, and play into the hands of the defense. But it was a risk they were willing to take, because everything Rudolph had said to the sheriff and deputies in Cherokee County about his years on the run, and the fact that he knew he was wanted, was probably inadmissible in court.

Even though Rudolph may not have insisted on a lawyer until his second day in custody, he had talked repeatedly all weekend about getting one, so his attorneys would certainly challenge any of the statements he'd made after he was arrested. The same problem applied to the evidence found at his campsites, which Rudolph revealed without the presence of counsel. Although nothing found in the woods was crucial to the case, the driver's license and truck key found at Rudolph's winter camp would have provided the prosecution with a little more ammunition, as would the clipping he'd saved about being posted on the FBI's Most Wanted fugitive list. The article showed that Rudolph was fully aware he was wanted by the law, and it would have advanced Whisonant's theory that Rudolph had a need to be seen as an important person in history.

Although the government team didn't feel they needed to establish a motive to convict Rudolph, jurors typically want to explore *why* something happened, even when the answer remains a mystery. Joe McLean felt that Rudolph was expressing a generalized hatred and rage, something so deep-seated that even Rudolph didn't understand why he needed to kill. "This guy hated everything and everybody," said McLean. Most of the FBI investigators believed that law enforcement personnel were Rudolph's real target, and that his hatred of the government was his motivation. Whisonant believed Rudolph was driven by a complicated pathology, and that many overlapping motives came to play in Rudolph's decision to set off his bomb in Birmingham. None of the cops and prosecutors in this case thought Rudolph was motivated solely by his anti-abortion views. While Whisonant felt that they had to somehow explain why Rudolph targeted an abortion clinic, they didn't want to turn the trial into a referendum on the morality of abortion. Even with the careful vetting of jurors, there was always the chance that a "stealth" anti-abortion juror would get on the panel and hang up the verdict. The prosecutors wanted to keep the trial focused on the murder of a police officer and the maiming of a nurse.

While Whisonant planned to skip lightly around Rudolph's views on abortion, he was ready to confront the jury directly with testimony from witnesses who would characterize Rudolph as a racist and antigovernment fanatic. He planned to call the army buddy who kept the letter that Eric had signed "Adolph Rudolph." And there was his ex-sister-in-law Deborah Rudolph, aka Debbie Givens, who could testify on any number of topics, such as Rudolph's marijuana business, his obsessive anti-Semitism, and even statements he'd made about opposing abortion because it killed white babies and threatened the survival of the white race. Along with witness statements, the government was prepared to expose Rudolph's murderous impulses by introducing the spooky notations about bombs and Christian soldiers scribbled in the margins of the Thompson Chain-Reference Bible that was found in Rudolph's bedroom. That is, if they could use it in court.

Joe McLean didn't expect to find anything unusual when he began to review the search warrants in North Carolina. But since they had originated in Asheville, and the Birmingham U.S. attorney's office hadn't reviewed them before they were issued, he wanted to familiarize himself with the documents. As McLean started reading through the first five warrants to search Rudolph's storage unit and rented trailer, he began to shake his head. Then he started to groan. "Oh, Lord," he said to himself as he flipped through the pages to see if something had fallen off or was missing. "Houston, we have a problem ..." Then he called Mike Whisonant and Will Chambers with the bad news.

Critics of trial lawyers tend to refer to such legal obstacles as "technicalities," but the safeguards against unlimited searches can be found in the Bill of Rights, shortly after the freedoms of speech, religion, and the right to own guns. This is the entire text of the Fourth Amendment: "The right of the people to be secure in their persons, houses, papers, and effects, against unreasonable searches and seizures, shall not be violated, and no Warrants shall issue, but upon probable cause, supported by Oath or affirmation, and particularly describing the place to be searched, and the persons or things to be seized." There is a raft of case law that has appended and interpreted this amendment (and a rogues' gallery of elected officials and spy agencies that have ignored it), but the basic rule of "particularity" has remained intact: A search warrant does not give you license to go rummaging through a person's property indiscriminately; it has to spell out what you are looking for.

Unfortunately, three of the first five warrants to search Rudolph's property were completely lacking in particularity. In the space where the government is supposed to specify the person or items to be seized, somebody typed: "Property that constitutes the fruits, evidence, and instrumentalities of crimes against the United States." That was it. No statute cited, no list of items to be taken. The three warrants were essentially worthless.

Although he wasn't as concerned about the first two warrants, McLean could see that there might be challenges to them as well. The first warrant to search Cal's Mini Storage unit 91 was issued for a misdemeanor federal offense—illegally storing explosives—and it did not list any specific items to be taken. In a subsequent affidavit, the agents admitted they found "no visible high explosives" yet, in the course of the search, seized a cigarette butt, a piece of green plastic, a paper bag of nails, and some shell casings where Garrett, the trained canine, had indicated the presence of explosive residue. They also noted some other things they saw in the shed that they wanted to seize in a future search.

This was a potential problem, since the defense was bound to argue that the search had exceeded the scope of the warrant. If they were successful, the problem would be compounded because the probable cause to search Rudolph's Caney Creek trailer was contained in an affidavit that included evidence from the first, possibly unconstitutional search of

Cal's Mini Storage. If one warrant is bad, subsequent ones can be tainted by it—this is called the "fruit of the poisonous tree" doctrine.

The defense was bound to challenge these searches. If they won, the government wouldn't be able to use any of the evidence from the trailer or the storage unit—not the explosive residues, not the arsenal of weapons and the hidden money, not the wig and sunglasses, the Bible, the Wal-Mart receipt, the military manuals, or the book on disguises. And, of particular concern to Atlanta, not the flooring nails that apparently matched the Sandy Springs bombing or the drywall sander that matched the wooden dowel used in the Olympic Park bombing. The government had to come up with a remedy or risk forfeiting half of its case.

To prepare the best possible defense, a legal team wants as much information as possible about both the case and the client. They want to learn everything about his life, from his family's history, through his childhood, and up to the moment he stands before the jury. An effective defense has to be a collaboration on every level, and that requires faith on both sides.

Richard Jaffe felt there was a covenant between himself and his clients in death penalty cases. His client had to trust him with his life. In return, Jaffe had to be willing to go the distance with his client, and if the worst should happen, to be there with him at the moment of his execution. "You know that if you fail, you are going to be there watching your client die, and wondering what you could have done differently to save him," said Jaffe. "In a sense you're fighting for your own life, as well." He felt that, with so much at stake, there should be no holding back in this relationship. That trust was as essential to the defense as evidence and witnesses and motions.

Jaffe sensed his bond with Eric Rudolph growing stronger with the passing months. Jaffe visited him in jail at least once or twice a week, and felt his client's wariness melting away as they got to know each other better. Then the two got the chance to become acquainted in a different arena.

There is a small, makeshift basketball court on the second floor of the Jefferson County Jail where prisoners can shoot hoops during their exercise hour. Rudolph kept asking for time on the court, but because he had to have special supervision, his jailers rarely found time to let him play. One day Jaffe was meeting with Rudolph in a private interview room when he saw Cedric Cole walk by the glass wall. Cole had been one of his students at Miles Law School, so they knew each other well. Jaffe banged on the glass to get Cole's attention.

"Hey, Cedric! Maybe today's the day that you could let him on the court?"

Cole poked his head in the room and grinned. "I'm gonna let you both on," he said. "You can have your meeting in there." He led them to the empty court and shut the door behind them. Then he locked them in together.

Jaffe suddenly wished he'd planned for this. He was wearing a white dress shirt, blue jeans, and hard-soled shoes. Rudolph was in his loose uniform and sneakers. The air was humid and the afternoon sun streamed into the room from the high windows, firing it up like a kiln. They began tossing shots into a basketless hoop bolted to the wall above the concrete floor. Jaffe was a runner who could shrug off ten-kilometer races in the Birmingham weather, but he had never been this hot in his life. Plus, he hadn't played ball in years, and it took a while before he started hitting the mark. Rudolph, a natural athlete, had kept himself in shape by doing calisthenics and wind sprints in the day room. By the time they started playing one-on-one, Jaffe's clothes had already soaked through, but Rudolph was barely breaking a sweat. He dodged and weaved as he nailed shot after shot. Jaffe did his best to block him, scored a few points here and there, but it was no real contest. As Cole, who was watching through the door, later told me, "Mr. Jaffe got his ass beat."

Jaffe couldn't agree more. He thought he was going to have a stroke in there, but he didn't want to give up. "Eric was starting to feel sorry for me, saying 'Are you okay?'" Jaffe recalled. "I'd say, 'I think so,' and keep going." He kept on because he felt that "something shifted" between them during the game, the last barriers had come down. "I'd never felt closer to him, before or after," said Jaffe. "It was really an epiphany, almost a communion between souls."

When Jaffe finally called it quits they sat together against the wall, the older man trying to catch his breath while Rudolph talked. He told Jaffe how great this was, two people having fun together on the same level, not just a lawyer and client. "You know I didn't really speak to a human being for four years," he said. He told Jaffe that he liked being around people and cared about them, but after so many years of silence it had been hard to communicate with anyone. The extent of his social interaction had been an occasional trip into town to buy something he needed, never saying more than "yes" and "thank you." When he was alone in jail, it kicked him back to that feeling of isolation in the woods. Every time someone visited, it took a while to transition back to the world of human connections. But once it happened, he had a need to keep going. Now he was talking about how much sports had meant to him as a boy, that when he lived in Florida his coach told him he had potential as a baseball player. He had trophies to prove it. But when his father was dying he shuttled back and forth between Homestead and Topton, finally enrolling in the Nantahala School after his father died. The school wasn't big enough to have a baseball team, and he was forced to give up the sport.

"I felt the sadness as he talked about it on the basketball court," said Jaffe. "He never got to challenge himself to see how good he could have been if he'd had the opportunity. The loss of baseball and his family at the same time wounded him. And it affected his ability to make friendships, because he was moving all the time."

Jaffe's notes from his visits with Rudolph are filled with long conversations like this one. They talked about the case, but also about Rudolph's beliefs and about his life before and during his fugitive years. Ordinarily, attorneys do not speak to outsiders like me about conversations with their clients. But Eric Rudolph released certain members of his legal team, including Jaffe, from the constraints of lawyer-client privilege so that they could talk to me. It was a calculated risk on his part, and an astonishing act of faith from a man who had rarely, if ever, shown much trust before in his life.

As lead defense attorney, Jaffe had to plan his strategy on several parallel tracks. The trial itself would be divided into two parts: the "guilt phase," which would determine the verdict, and then, if Rudolph were convicted, the "penalty phase" or "mitigation phase," in which the jury would have to choose between a life sentence without the possibility of parole and death. There was also the appeal process. The team was preparing for a fight over the searches, and if they weren't able to exclude the evidence, at least it would be one of the issues they could take up on appeal. But they had to lay the foundations for appeals before trial.

As might be expected, Rudolph wanted to be as involved as possible in every aspect of his defense. His lawyers say he proved to be smart and intuitive, with impressive tactical abilities, and his writings on the subject bear this out. Rudolph started from the position that he was not guilty of the charges against him. Further discussions took place as hypotheticals: If this bomber of the New Woman All Women clinic truly believed that he was required to save innocent babies from execution, then couldn't his actions be presented as justifiable homicide?

This argument is technically known as the "necessity defense," in which a defendant admits to committing a lesser crime in order to prevent a more serious crime, such as murder. It is a rare and tricky strategy, because the client has to admit to a level of responsibility. The team researched it and considered it, but everyone, including Rudolph, felt it was unrealistic, as he wrote to me after his case was resolved:

No court in the country would allow a justifiable homicide defense in a case like mine. For that to have happened, I would have had to argue that my killing of Sanderson was a legal action in defense of others who were under direct threat of bodily harm. Paul Hill [who killed a doctor and his escort in Florida] attempted this and was quickly shut down, as it would have indeed put abortion on trial and allowed the jury to decide whether abortion is murder and whether killing an abortionist is justified in defense of those being aborted. Since the court can under no circumstance recognize that the unborn child is a person, they would never allow a defense of other argument.

Since he realized the judge would never let him use this defense, he decided it wasn't worth submitting the request. He thought he had a good enough chance by trying the case on the facts. As he put it, "The evidence was not so overwhelming as to attempt such an agreement that involved the admission of my involvement."

Rudolph's lawyers held open the possibility that Rudolph could bring up justifiable homicide in the penalty phase, if he were later convicted and trying to convince the jury to spare his life. This was one of dozens of variables the defense team had to consider, as each decision touched off a cascade of possible consequences. If they planned to raise justifiable homicide in the penalty phase, they risked losing credibility with a jury that had been told he was not guilty for several months. And such a strategy would influence their choices during jury selection.

While the team mulled over all the possible strategies, the defense investigators and lawyers dove into the discovery evidence to look for ways to refute it. They hoped to turn the government's greatest strength—the eyewitnesses—into a weakness. As the prosecutors had, Jaffe and his team revisited the crime scene dozens of times. They went over Jermaine Hughes's accounts of that morning, in the 911 tapes and the police and FBI interviews, matching them up with their own observations as they walked the route over Red Mountain. "We found huge gaps and inconsistencies," said Jaffe. They felt the timing didn't add up. And the description of the suspect Hughes followed was constantly changing, perhaps indicating that he had trailed more than one person. The defense would suggest that the man who popped out of the woods across from McDonald's was not the same one that Hughes saw walking away from the clinic. They were even preparing to produce an expert witness who had studied the flaws in eyewitness identifications, who would testify that people of different races had difficulty distinguishing each other's features. There would, of course, be challenges to the physical evidence and the forensic analyses of it, as well as to any other witness testimony that placed Rudolph in Birmingham. They even hoped to explain Rudolph's flight to the woods by introducing expert testimony from a historian who could explain why residents of Appalachia are distrustful of authority.

While the prosecution's job is to present a linear, rational argument that leads to the inevitable conclusion of guilt, the role of the defense is to challenge that logic and to create confusion in the minds of the jurors. Confusion translates into reasonable doubt, and doubt is all a defense attorney needs for acquittal.

Sometimes the best thing a defense team can do is to let the government do the work for them. Think of it as a jujitsu defense—turning the weight and momentum of the enemy to your advantage. In the case of *U.S.A. v. Rudolph*, the government did such a thorough job of investigating the bombing, creating thousands of pages of interview summaries and producing so many red herrings and false leads, the defense could simply choose a few and ask, "What if?" One of the several possible scenarios revolved around the strange case of Jeffrey Dykes, an anti-abortion protester in Birmingham.

The police and the FBI interviewed dozens, perhaps hundreds of people who were in the area around the New Woman All Women clinic on the morning of the bombing. The prosecution was interested only in the witnesses who supported the theory that Rudolph was the bomber; the defense discovered that there were just as many who didn't. Dykes, a white man in his thirties, was a regular and particularly fanatical sidewalk protester at the New Woman All Women clinic. He was on the scene immediately after the bombing, and he made himself conspicuous outside the yellow police tape, snapping pictures of the victims and offering some memorable quotes to reporters. "I don't like to see anybody die, but they're in the business of death," he told the *Birmingham News*. "You live by the sword, you die by the sword." He added, "We've told them that they're in a grisly business, the flesh trade. You never know what's going to happen to you." All of this amounted to enough probable cause for the SANDBOMB Task Force to get a warrant to search his apartment. Inside they found bomb-making instructions, anti-abortion literature, including an Army of God manual; a can of smokeless powder and photographs of the crime scene. The FBI and Birmingham police turned Dykes's life inside out looking for a connection to Rudolph or the bombings, but they found nothing. Dykes eventually left Birmingham and settled in another state and got married. Yet, if the FBI hadn't already established Rudolph as their prime suspect, Dykes could easily have suffered the same fate as Richard Jewell. This was something the defense hoped to exploit.

In fact, if Jaffe could manage it, he wanted to put Jewell himself on the stand to demonstrate how the government had a track record of blaming the wrong man. (Jewell's ordeal would explain why Rudolph feared being framed and why he ran from the law for five years.) Without going so far as to call for the head of the real killer, Jaffe and his team intended to bring up as many other suspects as he could to suggest that someone else could have carried out the attack, or that there might have been others involved in the crime.

While the government wanted to keep out the Army of God letter, with its language suggesting a group of bombers—"We will target anyone . . ."—the defense was considering bringing it in to demonstrate that there was an organization out there with a history of attacking abortion clinics, and that it had claimed responsibility for the bombing. Since the government was never able to connect the letter to Rudolph through forensics, it might be a reasonably safe way to open up the abortion issue and to divert suspicion to other actors in the anti-abortion movement. And it helped that Eric Rudolph had never been seen at an anti-abortion demonstration in Birmingham or anywhere else in the country. He had no history with the movement at all.

Of course, if the defense admitted the AOG letter, the government would likely bring in the other letters that tied its author to the Atlanta bombings. Although the defense fought for, and got, access to all the evidence in the Atlanta bombings, they weren't sure whether they wanted to use it in the defense. It was a regular source of debate. Everyone in the Alabama jury pool with half a brain would have to know that Rudolph was accused of being the Olympic Park bomber. Do you acknowledge the Atlanta bombings, or do you pretend to ignore them?

Despite the confident posturing of the U.S. attorney's office in Atlanta, the defense felt that their case was weak as stone soup, particularly when separated from Birmingham. "Setting aside the seriousness of the crimes, it was a defense attorney's dream," said Paul Kish.

The prosecutors in Atlanta were depending on a web—not a chain— of circumstantial evidence to attach Eric Rudolph to all five bombings in Atlanta and to the one in Birmingham. While the Army of God letters linked the Birmingham bombing to the Otherside Lounge and Sandy Springs attacks, none mentioned the Centennial Olympic Park bombing. And in terms of components, target, and modus operandi, the Olympic Park bombing was an anomaly. Kish was prepared to use a child's game to point this out, should he get to present the case to a jury: "I was going to say which one of these things doesn't match: Apple, pear, banana, elephant?" said Kish. Centennial Park was the elephant. And it was the only crime in Atlanta that carried the potential for the death penalty. In the end, Kish's strategy would have depended on the outcome in Birmingham. But he and his team felt that the Centennial Park case had reasonable doubt all over it. As in Birmingham, they planned to try to exclude evidence from the searches of Rudolph's trailer and storage unit. If the nails recovered from the storage unit were allowed into the trial, they had experts who would testify that there is no scientific way to prove they matched the shrapnel in the Sandy Springs bomb. They would also attack the 911 tape, which might or might not have sounded like Rudolph's voice. While at least fifteen people who knew Rudolph said they recognized him as the croaky 911 caller who warned there was a bomb in Centennial park, defense investigators found an equal number who said it did not sound like Rudolph. And some of the positive witnesses had changed their statements in the course of the investigation.

But Paul Kish's principal defense theory was again based on a child's game: "Where's Waldo?" Like players looking for the cartoon character whose face seems to disappear in the intricate human landscapes that surround him, a virtual army of federal agents searched for Eric Rudolph's image at the 1996 Atlanta Olympics and never found him.

"It was one of the most photographed and videotaped events in the country," said Kish. "There were 50,000 people in Centennial Park that night. The government collected 20,000 or more images, and how many thousands of people they interviewed within that very small, discrete space. How many dozens of security cameras were taking pictures. And where's Rudolph? That was going to be our defense. Not one eyewitness identified him. And there was not a single piece of physical evidence that

Eric Rudolph was ever in Atlanta. Of all the places on earth you could not place him, that was it."

The government would, of course, disagree, pointing to some very high-tech evidence, including a long-distance video image super-enhanced by NASA that showed the blurry figure of a human sitting on the bench above the backpack bomb in Centennial Park, minutes before it detonated. The NASA experts estimated that the seated person was a male, about 180 pounds, between five-ten and six-two, dressed in shorts, light-colored socks, and a size 9 to 9½ hiking boot. Amazingly, those are Rudolph's measurements, and he had even been photographed wearing the same outfit. But the defense team was not too concerned about this, since once the enhanced image was projected onto a screen, it was easy to guess why even the task force investigators nicknamed the suspect "Blob Man."

There was just one other picture that might have been of Rudolph, taken by a security camera outside the Days Inn in downtown Atlanta, near where the 911 call was made. It was taken in daylight, and shows a young man with a dark beard and long brown hair wearing a large pair of dark sunglasses, much like the disguise described by Jermaine Hughes in Birmingham. Again, the picture is fuzzy. An observer might say it looked liked Rudolph wearing a disguise, or that it was a lost roadie from a heavy metal band wandering the streets of Atlanta.

Both the Birmingham and Atlanta defense teams had to prepare to deal with the government's theory of motive, and be ready to counter witnesses such as Deborah Rudolph, Claire Forrester, Randy Cochran, and others who had heard Rudolph make racist, antigovernment, anti-gay, and anti-abortion statements. They would point out that most of these people hadn't seen or spoken to Rudolph in at least a decade, and that they presented a skewed view of his actual beliefs.

As the Birmingham case moved toward its new trial date of August 2, 2004, defense investigators and mitigation specialists fanned out across western North Carolina and Tennessee to try to reinterview the witnesses the government might use against Rudolph. A different set of questioners with a different agenda—to mitigate instead of prove guilt—often come up with new information from the same witnesses.

Rudolph also provided the names of some other friends and acquaintances from his past who could show a different side of him. The defense team spent countless hours with Rudolph and his family, particularly his mother, going over every detail of his past and his family dynamics. The idea was to explain how he came to be where he was today.

"People don't become death penalty candidates overnight," said Jaffe. "We have to get inside our clients' hearts and souls. We have to imagine their life as they lived it, and their losses as they suffered them, in order to understand who they are. Very few people are as bad as their worst deed or as good as their best."

Their purpose of mitigation was not only to refute the government's portrait of Rudolph as a cold, heartless monster. It was to find an alternative narrative to tell, a story that might touch the jury and save his life.

17

A HISTORY OF THE OTHERWORLD

He was a famous prisoner, and every day more cards, books, and letters flowed into the Jefferson County Jail addressed to Eric Robert Rudolph. Some were from lonely women who habitually wrote to inmates for romance; most were from Christians offering help to save his soul. Others were from journalists looking for interviews. I am still not sure why he chose to write to me after refusing all media requests. It may have been as simple as my German-sounding last name. More likely it is because one of his lawyers told him I was working on a book about his case, and that I had written *Ghosts of Mississippi*, about the murder of a civil rights leader, Medgar Evers, and the trial of his assassin, Byron De La Beckwith. He was a movie fan, and there had been a film made with the same name, although it was not technically based on my book. I wrote him a letter asking some questions, and this was his reply:

Dear Maryanne,

I have never read your book, Ghosts of Mississippi, but I have seen the movie, starring James Woods, based upon it. Based upon your previous choice of subject matter, I fear that you may have been influenced to write a book about my case based upon news reports which characterize me as a racist Identity believer on a rampage—a sort of 90's version of Beckwith. If the racist maddog threat to progress is the character basis of your villain, you are factually mistaken. If you wish to flesh out your villain with more accurate information, I will do my best to give you the facts …

Sincerely,
Eric R. Rudolph

And so we began a correspondence. His letters generally came back on lined paper, in a slightly childish, slanted cursive. Unlike Beckwith, who wrote me convoluted, frenetic, vaguely frightening letters from his jail cell, Rudolph was always polite and businesslike. Some answers would run on for pages, some would be terse, but almost all were thoughtful.

You've been labeled a loner. How would you describe yourself?

I would describe myself as an idealist with average intelligence. I associate with people and enjoy social situations, especially if there is stimulating conversation. I like serious conversation. This has narrowed my social circle considerably. Most of the people I have associated with don't enjoy serious subject matter, so I have tended to keep to myself. This is probably where they get the loner label. I don't mind. If the "normal" man is expected to sit around all weekend drinking beer and watching greased men beat each other with folding chairs on television, then please put me down as a loner.

How would you characterize your childhood, growing up in Florida?

We were a typical lower middle class family. We had six children altogether, so the budget was tight. Despite the lack of material wealth, my parents were able to meet our basic needs. I played football and baseball for many years and for my age I was pretty good. I enjoyed outdoor activity.

What do you remember best about your father?

My father was a St. Louis German who loved fine carpentry, mu-

sic and day dreaming. He made his own acoustic guitars and most of
our furniture. He was a quiet, gentle, unassuming person.

What was your mother's family background?

My mother came from Philadelphia Irish. After a brief flirtation
with the nunnery, she moved to New York City, where she met my
father. They quickly married after a short courtship and moved to St.
Louis, MO.

*How did you come to love books and philosophy? Was philosophy discussed
at home?*

My family kept a small library. I recall the Old West Time-Life
series ... I loved sitting for hours looking at the pictures and reading the captions. There was also a book on the Civil War put out
by National Geographic. I imagined myself to be an Arapaho or
Sioux warrior. I sewed my own buckskin moccasins and rode my
Ft. Lauderdale neighborhood with my bows and arrows hunting
sand doves. There was something otherworldly and addictive about
history. However, I didn't read complete books until I went to live
with Tom [Branham]. He had an extensive library. Tom never read
his books he just collected them. After watching Fahrenheit 451
which is a 1960s movie that depicts a tyrannical government that
will not allow its citizens to possess books, Tom decided to stock up
on books. He was never the same since. Every time he went to the
swap market he would return with a box or two full of books. Stuck
in the mountains without a television, I started to read—history and
biography mainly.

My parents were religiously oriented when I was growing up, so
there was a great deal of serious talk about salvation and related issues, but we didn't discuss philosophy per se. I suppose living in an
environment where serious ideas were present may have led me to
pursue a little philosophy; however, we never sat around pontificat-
ing on Plato or Kant.

It's been reported that you belonged to a family of "seekers," people who frequently tried new ideas and means of worship. Is this true?

I expose myself to new ideas every day in the hope of expanding my horizons, but my core beliefs do not swerve too radically. My beliefs have remained fairly constant since I was in my teens. My mother, on the other hand, has dabbled in everything from Catholicism to New Age religion. Perhaps this latter is where they get the "seeker" label.

If you could only have ten books, which ones would they be?

Bible, Will Durand's History of Civilization, Shelby Foote's The Civil War, John Keegan's The Face of Battle, Oswald Spengler's The Decline of the West, Ortega Y Gasset's The Revolt of the Masses, Montaigne's Essays, Dostoyevsky's Crime and Punishment and the Brothers Karamazov, Norton's World Masterpieces.

If you could create your own Utopia, what would it be like?

I don't believe a Utopia is possible in this world, so I simply endeavor to do the best with what I've been given.

"They always blame the mother, you know," said Pat Rudolph as she spread out a stack of family photographs on her kitchen table. "People have come right up to me and told me that what happened is my fault. I suppose they're always ready to burn women as witches."

Her voice is at once high-pitched and husky, and oddly soothing. She is a handsome woman in her late seventies with white hair, a thin face, a sharp nose, and intense hazel-blue eyes. This morning she wore pale salmon-colored pants and a matching patterned tunic. Her tidy apartment is bathed with light and filled with mementos and house plants. "I'm still an Irish gardener," she had told me on the phone as she gave me directions to her place in a development south of Tampa Bay. "Look for the tomato plants outside." There was a neat row of them, staked in front of the two-story building, distinguishing her unit from the others in this standard Floridian mid- to lower-income "adult community." She moved here for the privacy and security she couldn't find in her mo-bile home in nearby Bradenton. This apartment is five minutes from the beach and looks out on a small grove of pines and palms that she calls "my forest."

Pat Rudolph has been in poor health since she suffered a fall around the time Eric was captured. She lost thirty-five pounds while trying to heal her broken ribs and torn ligaments with natural remedies and the ministrations of a chiropractor and acupuncturist. Her shelves are stocked with books and pamphlets with titles such as "Patient Heal Thy-self." An enormous glass jug of spring water sits on the kitchen counter, next to framed watercolors of vegetables painted by her old friend Rich-ard Baxter.

Her son Dan, who is divorced and now in his mid-forties, drove down to help her recover after her accident and ended up moving into the second bedroom. He was still living with Pat when I came to visit, although every time I showed up he was nowhere to be seen. His loath-ing for the media hasn't subsided much since the incident Pat refers to as "that craziness with Dan cutting off his hand." Recently he has "gone natural," she said, wearing his hair long and growing his beard. The foyer of the apartment is decorated with a hollow drum that Dan carved out of a solid block of wood. He has a crane tattooed on his chest, she said, his "spirit guide" that came to him in a dream. Every day a pair of cranes visit the bird feeder in the grove behind the apartment. Most evenings, after Dan finishes his carpentry jobs, he and his mother go fishing to-gether in the bay.

Pat has been able to visit Eric in jail only a handful of times, but she writes to him at least once a week, and keeps thick folders of the many letters he has sent to her since his arrest. Eric, she believes, is the intel-lectual of the family, someone who would have been more comfortable living in an earlier era as part of a small group of scholars or as an Oxford don in the time of Chesterton. "I think Eric was a monk in another life," she told me.

Pat worked with her son's lawyers and mitigation experts to prepare a

profile that would counter the prosecution's view of Eric as an irredeem-
able racist killer. Along with her family albums, she saved the pages of
photographs that were to have been used in a PowerPoint presentation
for the jury. Her favorite is a large color picture of Eric at age two, a
sunny, chubby toddler with bright blue eyes.

"He was such a cute baby," she said. "And so easy. The others were
always in trouble, but not Eric."

The defense experts had clipped together a montage of the Rudolphs'
family history, with pictures of the children playing together in the sand,
of the family gathered for the holidays, of Eric in his baseball uniform and
dressed for the prom he attended even though he had already dropped
out of high school. There were pictures of Pat as a young nun and of Bob
Rudolph working as a lay preacher with a prison ministry. There was a
photo of an interracial couple who were part of the Rudolphs' close circle
of friends in Florida. One of them was expected to testify for Eric during
the penalty phase, if it came to that.

"This is the last picture I have of Eric before he went to the woods,"
said Pat, using the family euphemism for Rudolph's years as a fugitive.
She plucked it out of a stack of photos from their road trip up the East
Coast in November 1997 to show me. "I took it on the boat coming back
from Cape May." It shows a rigid young man with wind-tossed hair and
a strange, tight smile on his face, leaning against the railing in front of a
green and unsettled sea. Two months later, he had the whole U.S. government hunting for him.

When Eric was on the run, Pat Rudolph told a documentary producer for Court TV that she believed that her son was being framed
by the government, which "pinpoints certain people, and he was one
of them." When I asked her about this she smiled and rolled her eyes.
"Who knows? I tend to believe in conspiracies. I just look at all the
things that happen and there has to be something more behind it than
what meets the eye."

Pat Rudolph has been searching for that "something more" her entire
adulthood, looking for the answer to explain away the sudden losses and
terrifying uncertainties of living. Some people find it in religion, others
in history or in nature or in a web of sinister and coordinated forces that

manipulate the workings of the world. It is, for many, much more comforting to believe in a controlling power than to acknowledge that life's random cruelties might have no meaning at all.

Yet Pat Rudolph is one of the few people I have met who, when she insists the government has had her on their "list" for many years, may actually be right.

This is her story as she tells it:

She was born Patricia Murphy in 1928 to a well-to-do family of Irish stonemasons in Philadelphia. When she was a year old, the stock market crashed and her grandfather lost the business and his real estate investments. Her father had to find work building roads with the WPA and she didn't see him for years. Her mother took a job in a department store and sent Patty to live with her grandmother and five aunts in a big stone house. Despite the separation, she remembers her childhood fondly. It was a musical family, everyone sang and played the piano, and there were summer visits to Cape May, New Jersey, to swim in the ocean. Eventually she was reunited with her parents and the family began to prosper again. They opened Murphy's Tavern near the University of Pennsylvania, and her mother got involved in city politics. Pat's two brothers, Jimmy and Joe, eventually took over the business.

Pat was raised in a strict Catholic household, but she was "pretty wild as a teenager." After graduating from high school she entered St. Joseph's College, while working part-time at a hospital. Before the end of her first year she was engaged to marry a handsome baseball player. But before the wedding she had "a religious conversion, my first encounter with the other world, or realm." She didn't know what to do about it. She broke off the engagement and entered a convent. At first her mother was appalled. "I felt like the prodigal daughter," said Pat.

She joined the order of Medical Mission Sisters and stayed two years as a novitiate, but dropped out before taking her vows. "I just wasn't made for it," she explained. But she still wanted to lead a spiritual life, and she made a pilgrimage to New York City to join the Catholic Workers. The movement—it was too anarchistic to call itself an "organization"—was cofounded in 1933 by Peter Maurin, a Christian communalist, and Dorothy Day, a colorful and charismatic writer who had renounced a glamorous career to devote her life to serving the poor and agitating for world peace. Maurin died in 1949. Day presided over the Catholic Workers from an old farmhouse and cluster of bungalows on New York's Staten Island.

One afternoon in 1956 Pat Murphy walked into Dorothy Day's office and said, "Do you have work for me?"

"Oh, there is always work to do," said Day.

"For instance?"

Day pointed to a room with a huge old washtub. "Well, you can help me wash these sheets."

Pat's next job was to nurse an old prostitute who was dying of cancer. She stayed on and became one of Day's trusted aides. She thought of Day as her "spiritual mother."

"I lived a very graced life," she recalled. "Day by day we never knew whether we'd have any money or what would go on. We had thirty or thirty-five people living out there in Staten Island for a while, and I learned to bake and cook for a lot of people."

She was sent to live in another communal home on the Lower East Side of Manhattan, and it was there that she met Robert Rudolph, who had come from Missouri on his own spiritual pilgrimage. He was a veteran of World War II and the Korean War, although he had spent the latter in Germany as an army translator. He was fluent in German, which was spoken in his house. After returning to St. Louis, Bob studied to become a Catholic priest.

"He had applied to join an order, but they turned him down," said Pat. "They claimed he had a nervous breakdown or something in his teen years. Bob never discussed it. He was a private type of person, compared to me. He was not much of a talker."

Bob, a talented carpenter and mechanic, joined the Workers as a laborer. Photographs from the time show a thin, good-looking man with a long, narrow face; dark hair; and sharp features. Pat was impressed that he made his own guitars and wrote songs. He quickly decided he wanted to marry her, but she wasn't so sure. She had work to do. There were hospices to run and meals to prepare and serve to the poor from the Workers' kitchens.

"Those were exciting days," said Pat. "We had meetings every week where different anarchists and pacifists would come and talk." Day sent Pat as her representative to the earliest meetings of the movement to ban the H-bomb. "People from all different walks of life were there," she recalled. "Bayard Rustin, Dave Dellinger, a few Quakers. We decided to go down to Washington as a group. We rented a house and I was down there at least three months. We would have prayer vigils outside the White House and carry signs. Then in my spare time I'd sell the Catholic Worker newspaper on the corner."

These antiwar activities took place during the darkest years of the Cold War, when J. Edgar Hoover's FBI was routing out suspected Communist enemies everywhere, from the NAACP to the Almanac Singers. The ACLU later discovered through the Freedom of Information Act that the FBI considered the Catholic Workers a subversive group and kept a thick file on the movement. (Pat has never checked to see if she was investigated.) Dorothy Day was often arrested at nonviolent protests, as were her followers.

"Bob was afraid I'd get arrested at a peace rally and we wouldn't be able to marry," said Pat. "I told him, 'If you want to marry me, then come with me.' And he did."

Peter Maurin's dream, shared by Day, was to establish a network of progressive agrarian communities around the country, where city people would relocate to practice a primitive form of Christianity. In 1958 Day asked Pat Murphy to start a new community on a blackberry farm in Massachusetts with four volunteers from New York City. Bob followed her there, and again asked her to marry him. "I was almost thirty years old," said Pat. "I thought, 'If I'm going to have children, I guess this is it.'" They decided to wed at the farm.

Both Pat and Bob had grown distant from their relatives during their years with the Catholic Workers. The first time Pat's family met Bob was the night before the wedding. "They accepted it," said Pat. "They knew it wouldn't make any difference to me if they didn't."

Soon after they were married, Bob and Pat Rudolph left the Workers community and moved back to his mother's house in St. Louis. Bob took a job as a mechanic for TWA, and the couple began to have children.

Damian arrived in 1959, with five more following in the next ten years.

"I had too many kids," said Pat, showing me pictures of herself during the sixties, looking worn-out and stressed, surrounded by children. "Not that I would turn any of them back. But it's a problem to have so many you just can't give them the attention they need."

Pat and Bob were still very involved in the Catholic Church in St. Louis. They applauded the reforms initiated in the Vatican II council and joined a progressive group within the church called the Christian Family Movement. Pat was happy with her life in Missouri, but she and Bob had a restless streak. So when TWA got a maintenance contract at the Cape Kennedy space center, Bob transferred to Florida. Pat wanted to live by the ocean; she was tired of putting her kids in snowsuits during the winter. She was already pregnant with Eric, her fifth child, when the family moved to Merritt Island in 1966.

The Rudolphs were strict naturopaths. None of the children was vaccinated against childhood diseases. Pat practiced natural childbirth and taught the Lamaze method to other couples. She found a Seventh-Day Adventist doctor in Florida who allowed her to give birth to Eric at home, the only one of her children born outside of a hospital. Pat had been hoping for a girl to keep Maura company. After Eric she tried again, but instead had another boy, Jamie, who was born in 1969. She was forty-one years old.

Because Bob worked for TWA the family was able to fly everywhere on free tickets. Once, when Eric was a small boy, Pat and Bob took all the children to England, where they stayed on the estate of wealthy friends they had met through the international Ban the Bomb movement. Another time they traveled to Germany to visit a priest who was a family friend.

Although the weather was better in Florida than in Missouri, Pat was disappointed in their new, conservative Catholic diocese.

"We tried over and over to penetrate these thick-headed Irish priests to get more innovation going in the church," she said. "It was so discouraging. I just went into a terrible depression."

Pat attended Mass in the evening, while Bob watched the children after work. Sometimes she would make it through the Benediction, but she often left early, in disgust. Then one warm night she passed a Nazarene church on the drive home. "I heard this beautiful music coming through my rolled down window," she remembered, "so I stopped the car and went in. Me, a Catholic, going into this unfamiliar church. It had to be the Holy Spirit leading me in there. I sat in the back and listened to a man singing this hymn called 'The Love of God.' And I never stopped crying until I left. I went back there every other week to hear this man sing." At first she was afraid to tell Bob about her revelation. But a woman from the Nazarene congregation lived in their neighborhood and invited them to a prayer meeting at her home. Bob came along. The Nazarenes believe, like other Pentecostals, that the spirit shows itself in the form of faith healing and speaking in tongues. The Rudolphs were mesmerized by the experience. It was the beginning of their break with the Catholic faith, and the start of a quest for the perfect church, what Pat calls "chasing the religious rainbow."

While the youth counterculture was getting most of the media attention in the late 1960s, another, equally momentous revolution was taking place in traditional Christian churches. A charismatic movement was sweeping up believers from all denominations, including Roman Catholics, who sought a more personal, direct, and ecstatic relationship with God. It was at one of the home meetings with the Nazarene woman that Pat Rudolph was born again. "I don't know what you call salvation, but to me, I just got awakened," she said. "From a lot of things. My whole life changed."

Eventually the Rudolphs became completely absorbed in the Pentecostal movement, and left Catholicism behind. "We would take the children to various churches to expose them to religions, but we never forced them," said Pat. "We felt they had their own lives, and they would either grow into it, or they wouldn't." She said Eric resisted all of them. "I don't think he liked the emotionalism of the Pentecostals. We wouldn't force him. He went on retreats with the kids, and Maura said he would sit there by himself and wouldn't get involved. Of course those preachers try to push them. He wouldn't be pushed. Whatever he decided he wanted to do was fine with us."

While the Rudolphs didn't force the dogma on their children, they did insist on discipline. They adopted a Bible-based method of raising children that, according to Pat, finally brought some peace and order to the large, chaotic household. The basic philosophy was simple. "They taught you that children are like animals, they have to be trained to learn the commands of their elders," said Pat. "They were right. They shaped right up." Bob and Pat set up a list of requirements for the kids: Be home from play in time to eat. Don't wander off. Go to bed at a certain time. Do chores every day. Their lives were suddenly very structured and infused with Scripture. The children were required to memorize biblical proverbs such as, "Foolishness is bound up in the heart of a child; But the rod of correction shall drive it far from him." If they broke the rules, they were punished.

"They were told they would be warned once if there was an infraction. And the second time they would be paddled, pants down. Not severely, but enough to know it hurt. Bob dealt with it, not me."

The older kids had a harder time adjusting to the new discipline, particularly Damian, a surfer who ended up moving away from home as a teenager. As the younger children grew more independent, they chafed against the rules as well. Except for one. "Eric never broke the rules," said Pat. "He was a smart cookie, and he avoided getting paddled because he knew what he was gonna get."

By the late 1970s the Rudolphs were again restless. Bob wanted to join a congregation in northern California, so he transferred to San Jose and started to look for housing. By the time the couple realized it would be too expensive to relocate the family, Bob had lost his option to return to work in Florida. TWA laid him off after nineteen years with the company, taking away his pension and his health benefits. He was forty-eight years old and had to start over. In 1978 the family moved from the beach to the stifling inland city of Homestead, where Bob took a job with a contractor building animal cages at the Miami Zoo. Then he got sick.

"I don't think cancer comes out of the blue," said Pat. "I think it was stress. He was in such good health until that happened."

The melanoma began as a spot on his upper chest. The lesion was removed, but the cancer quickly spread through his body. "Bob didn't want chemo and all that stuff," Pat said. Despite their commitment to alternative therapies, Bob died in a matter of months, and the loss was devastating to Pat. She was angry with God. "Why would he take such a kind, good man, just like that?" she said. "Poof. Gone. I didn't want anything to do with God for a long time."

She concentrated on making a home for her youngest children, and trying to find a way to get through each day. The last years of Bob's life had been particularly hectic for Eric. He had started school in Nantahala while he was living with Branham, then returned to stay with his sister and her husband in Homestead. He reentered ninth grade at the huge, mostly black and Hispanic Homestead High School, where he quickly ran into trouble.

"Eric was beaten up by black kids, and that leaves a real imprint," said Pat. "He was walking down the hall one day and this big black kid pushed him down. After that it was kind of like 'You're gonna be the tough black guy, then I'm gonna be the tough white guy.' I had to pull him out of that school."

I asked her if there was any truth to the stories that Eric was a racist when he was younger.

"I think so," she said. "And I think lots of teenagers go through that. Because they've seen so much at school."

I asked if she talked to him about it, tried to push back against these ideas.

"I told him it's just a matter of maturity," she said. "When you grow up, you're gonna see it differently. I taught my kids to think for themselves. I didn't intervene. Okay, some of the things they were doing are bad in the eyes of everybody else, but that's part of their learning process. And maybe some of the things they're doing are good. But I don't live in that realm of good or bad, if I'm a spiritual being …"

There were other things Eric was picking up during that time, things that were bad in the eyes of almost everyone else. It was a time Pat refers to as Eric's "Nazi kick." She blames it on her neighbor, Tom Branham. "Tom had these books about the Holocaust. Eric was reading them over there at his house. Then he wrote that school paper [denying the Holocaust]. I didn't know anything about it until it came out in the papers. I never heard from anybody up there at the school."

At first she considered Tom a good friend, but she says she wasn't aware of his "militancy" when she moved up from Florida. "Eric looked to Tom for guidance. That's one of the reasons I took the kids up there," Pat told me. "Tom seemed to me very sincere, especially about community life. I thought Tom would supply good Christian values." She paused and shook her head. "Holy Moses. It sort of backfired on me. Tom was really involved with all that Patriot stuff and with the Christian Identity thing. He was involved with Nord Davis, and I didn't even know Nord Davis. I knew him as I knew other people in the town. I saw him in the health food store and stuff like that. But there was no intimate tie-up with Nord."

Eric Rudolph later called Davis "a petty con man with a little Ponzi scheme ... I never spoke two words to Nord Davis, let alone joined his little group." Eric also wrote that he had never adopted the Identity faith. "I was born a Catholic, and with forgiveness hope to die one."

Pat describes the family's brush with the Identity sect as just another attempt at chasing the religious rainbow. "I guess we sort of investigated it [Identity]. It was all very strange and new and nothing we had ever heard of before." She said that Dan Gayman was very helpful with the homeschooling she had sought for her sons. "Of course he wanted disciples, but we weren't about to do that," she added. "We listened and went to his services. But Eric wasn't into it. And neither was I. Especially when they got into the anti-Semitism and they got into the racial stuff. And then their business with the Old Testament with Yahweh. So we left. But they were not nasty or anything. They were very nice."

Eric Rudolph has explained the reason he remained at Gayman's compound in one of his later writings: "The purpose for my prolonged stay at this church was because I met a wonderful young lady whose father attended the church. We became engaged for a short time, but when the relationship ended, I left the church ..."

His mother keeps a photograph of Eric and Joy in the family album. "I guess you could say she was the first love of his life," said Pat. She was petite and pretty, with long blond hair—something his later girlfriends had in common. In the picture, taken outside at the Gayman farm, Eric looks proud and happy, with one arm around Joy's waist, and the other around his mother.

A few years after they broke up, Gayman's daughter-in-law called Eric at the house in Topton. She told him Joy had killed herself and her two children. "I found out about it from Eric," said Pat. "He was very upset. It was right before he went into the army."

Like Pat, Eric wanted to clear up what he felt were misrepresentations in the media. When I asked what had possessed him to join the army, his answer was long and detailed and designed to refute the story that he had been kicked out for smoking dope. He had, in fact, smoked dope in order to be offered an early discharge from an organization he'd come to loathe.

"Like many young men I joined the military looking for a challenge," he wrote.

> I wanted to find some last remaining pocket of unselfishness and inward mobility, some nook and cranny of meritocracy sheltered from the stench of egalitarianism. I was naïve. What I found was mediocrity of the lowest common denominator—floor-moppers, toilet jockeys in camouflage.
>
> My early army experience was tolerable. The training was moving at an adequate pace. I went through basic infantry school and then Airborne School at Ft. Benning. At that point, so I was told by my recruiter, I would be given an opportunity to volunteer for the Ranger Indoctrination Program (RIP). After successfully completing this school I would have been posted with a Ranger battalion and been on the fast track to the elite infantry outfits. Unfortunately for naïve little Eric the recruiter lied. There were no slots open for RIP when I completed Airborne school, so I was posted to a basic "leg" infantry unit at Ft. Campbell, KY (101st). I later learned that I needed to get RIP written into my military entry contract. (This contract contains what the military is required to give you in exchange for your four-year enlistment.) To get RIP in one's contract requires more time and effort on the part of the recruiter, so in order to get a quick enlistment and increase his monthly bonus, he lied and

said the only thing available in my contract was a slot in Airborne School, which is a less exclusive school and consequently easy to get into an enlistment contract.

As a result I was posted to Campbell and was looking at three years of moving up through the ranks before I would have come up for reenlistment. Then in order to get me to sign for another 4 or 5 years the army would have again offered me a choice of assignments and schools including Ranger battalion and Special Forces Schools. But to get this I would have had to do at least 10 years altogether, which was out of the question. If I'd have been moved into the elite units early on, and liked it, I might have stayed in, who knows. But I was not about to do 10 years just to get an opportunity to join a better unit. One injury during training would put you back in a leg unit where you would have to complete the same period of enlistment ...

While at Campbell I was able to get one more school—Air Assault School. That was it. Frustration set in. I was dead-ended with a pack of underachieving lifers going over the same techniques in a mindless routine. The experience was like standing in a long, long line. The routine was broken with a few enjoyable moments: Field exercises including rappelling from choppers, firing machine guns and grenade launchers and some basic land navigation. But those were brief moments sandwiched between long periods of weapons maintenance, guard duty, painting parking lot lines, cleaning toilets and picking up trash.

When I was informed that I would be transferred to Germany, things started to slip. Not only was I stuck in a basic leg line infantry outfit, now I was to be sent to a mechanized unit in Germany. Instead of working with small tact teams, I was to spend two years riding around in tracks (Bradley Fighting Vehicles). This was work for bus drivers and REMF's (Rear Echelon Mother F____s).

I was immature and impatient 20 years ago and my drinking and frustration led to clashes with my "superiors." Nothing physical just the kind of verbal spats that let them know I was not a happy camper. After a couple of incidents, that were more or less deliberate, and after a failed urinalysis (marijuana) I was given a battalion Article 15 and asked if I wanted to leave the military. I said yes, and received a discharge under honorable conditions with no questions asked. I was given a choice. If I had wanted to stay and ride tracks all over Germany I could have. At that time the army would remove a soldier only after two failed urinalyses.

Pat Rudolph dug out a color photograph of Eric in his camouflage fatigues taken after basic training. She laid it on the kitchen table, on top of his baby pictures. In it he looks like the perfect soldier, a clear-eyed, serious young man with a future ahead of him.

"I think something happened to Eric when he was in the army," said Pat. "He was at Fort Benning, and they teach them to be assassins there." She points out that Tim McVeigh and Terry Nichols were there at about the same time (although their tours did not overlap). She wonders if some kind of mind control took place there, if Eric was "being groomed" to be a patsy. "He was a different person when he came back," she said.

Pat Rudolph saw much less of her son after he left the army. She was living near Maura and Keith, who had moved to Hendersonville. Eric was spending a lot of time in Nashville. They visited during the holidays. And Joel and Eric once came along with her on a trip to Germany. The brothers had a fine time drinking beer while she visited Father Ludwig, a priest the family knew. Eric got so drunk on the flight back home that he threw up on the customs agent after landing in Charlotte.

By 1995 only Eric was living at the Topton house, and he was talking about moving out West. Nobody else in the family wanted to live there full-time, so they decided to put it on the market. It took eighteen months to sell. Pat came back to stay from time to time. She loved to sit on the back porch and look out over the rolling hills. It was particularly beautiful in the spring, when the redbuds and dogwood trees were in bloom and the forest floor was carpeted with wild violets and trilliums. She was visiting in the spring of 1996, helping Eric get the house ready to show to potential buyers, when a bobcat raided their chicken coop and killed all the hens.

"I'm going to get that goddamn bobcat," Eric told her. He took his rifle and disappeared into the forest for two days and nights. He returned carrying a bobcat pelt, and he nailed it to the garage wall.

After they sold the Topton house, a vital connection seemed to have been lost between Pat and Eric. He would call, but he would never tell her how to reach him. During one of his rare visits to Hendersonville in the summer of 1997, Eric noticed Pat sorting through a box of religious articles that had belonged to her aunt Mary, a nun who had recently died. "He wanted to know where they came from," she recalled. "I said, 'I don't really want to keep these, do you want them?'" She was a bit surprised when Eric took the nun's rosaries and one of her scapulars—two small rectangles of cloth attached by a string that are worn as emblems of a Catholic's most private and passionate devotion to Christ. "I don't know why he wanted them," said Pat. "Maybe George Nordmann had gotten to him. We didn't discuss it." Maura saw Eric wearing the scapular around his neck later that summer, removing it when he went swimming.

Nordmann had, in fact, invited Eric Rudolph to attend a traditional Catholic service with him at a chapel in Benton, a small town just over the Tennessee line. The chapel was owned by Dr. John Grady, a fundamentalist Catholic and former anti-abortion leader in Florida, who once ran an NRA-like organization. Nordmann kept an album of photographs that included a picture of Eric attending one of his daughter's weddings at Grady's chapel. Grady told me in a brief phone conversation that he had been interviewed by the FBI about the photograph. "I simply said he (Rudolph) was not a member of the congregation, I was not a witness to him being here." Grady went on to say that he wrote a booklet condemning abortion in 1966, before *Roe v. Wade*. While he hasn't been active in the anti-abortion movement for years, Grady says he is still against the "culture of death" that abortion represents. "Abortion supports the immoral lifestyle," he said. "It is the biggest violence in the world today." Grady also claims to belong to a chivalrous order call the Knights of St. John. When I asked him to explain its purpose he simply said "they defend women and children." And then he ended the conversation.

When I wrote to Eric Rudolph asking him why he returned to the Catholic church, he answered in two sentences: "In the 90's I started attending a traditional Latin Mass. I like my religion straight, with deep roots."

The trip Pat and Eric took together in the fall of 1997 to visit Jamie was the last time Eric saw his younger brother. Jamie had come out to her the year before, and, as Pat put it, she'd learned to "cope" with his gay lifestyle. She believes that homosexuality is caused by chemistry, not choice. "I think Eric feels like I do," Pat told me. "Homosexuality has been around forever. It's just so in your face now ..." The trip to New York was pleasant and uneventful. Jamie, who has spoken to only one reporter, the New York writer Jeff Stein, said his brother "seemed comfortable, I could talk to him openly." The disengaged language is telling. Even though Eric and Jamie spent so much time together as children, he and Jamie were never close. "I don't know why," said Pat. "They were very different. Jamie was good at music, and not a good writer. It was the opposite for Eric." Still, she believes that Eric loves his brother. That's why it made no sense to her when he was accused of bombing a gay nightclub. The abortion clinic attacks were just as incomprehensible. Throughout his fugitive years Pat Rudolph believed her son was innocent, and when he was arrested she hoped he would be able to prove it. "An anti-abortion crusader? He never spoke to me about abortion. Never, ever," she told a reporter for *USA Today* after he was captured.

She said that a mother would know if her son was guilty.

"Eric was never a good liar."

18

THE END OF SOMETHING

Eric Rudolph was the second most famous prisoner to appear in federal court in Huntsville, Alabama. The most famous was Frank James, brother of the notorious Jesse James, who was tried on April 25, 1884, for robbing the government payroll outside Muscle Shoals. In a makeshift courtroom packed with reporters from all parts of the United States and Europe, James's high-profile defense lawyers tried to win sympathy for their client by pointing out that he had fought alongside the rebel William Quantrill. The jury, reportedly packed with Confederate veterans, acquitted him.

The present federal courthouse in Huntsville was built in the early twentieth century, and compared to the starkly appointed Vance Building in Birmingham, it seems folksy and intimate. The main courtroom is decorated with an enormous New Deal mural depicting muscular workers and the copious green bounty of the local Tennessee Valley dam projects. Judge Lynwood Smith lives in Huntsville and maintains his office in this outpost of the northern judicial district. The Eric Rudolph road show commuted between the two cities according to Smith's schedule and, in June 2004, he convened a hearing to decide whether Rudolph's trial would be moved out of Birmingham entirely. Richard Jaffe and the defense team had filed a motion to change the location of the trial, which was scheduled to begin in six weeks. Judge Smith was prepared to hear arguments from expert witnesses who would testify that there had been so much "sensationalistic and biased" pretrial publicity that it would be impossible to find an impartial jury there. A defense consultant had polled potential jurors in the area, and found that 97 percent of them had heard about the case and 65 percent believed Rudolph was either definitely or probably guilty. Among those who supported the death penalty, 78 percent believed Rudolph deserved it. The U.S. attorneys wanted to keep the trial in Birmingham, and disputed the methods used by the pollster.

Eric Rudolph hadn't been seen in public for almost a year. He shuffled into the courtroom wearing a blue blazer and gray pants, his dark brown hair cut short but still defying all efforts to tame it. After so many months in a sunless cell, his face and hands seemed luminous, like the skin of a deepwater sea creature. Rudolph was greeted warmly by his defense attorneys. Richard Jaffe and Emory Anthony shook his hand and clapped his back. Judy Clarke put her hand on his shoulder and kept it there for a long moment as she murmured something into his ear.

Clarke is a tall woman in her early fifties, with crinkly blue eyes and no-nonsense light brown hair. Her courtroom uniform never varies: gray suit, low heels, and a floppy foulard tie. She stands an inch or two taller than Rudolph, so when she is around him she tends to hunch over and lean in close. Despite her reputation as a top attorney in death penalty cases, very little has been written about her—most likely because of her aversion to the media. One brief profile appeared in the *Sacramento Bee* in 1996, just before she was brought into Ted Kaczynski's defense team. She told the writer that, as a child growing up in Asheville, North Carolina, "I wanted to become either the chief justice of the Supreme Court or Perry Mason." Since starting her career as a federal public defender in San Diego, Clarke had won just about every accolade a defense attorney can win, and had served as the first woman president of the National Association of Criminal Defense Lawyers. But at the time she joined the Rudolph defense team, she had never been the lead attorney in a major death penalty trial.

When the lawyers took their seats at the defense table, I noticed that Clarke was positioned between Rudolph and Jaffe. Bill Bowen sat on his other flank. Paul Kish was in the first row behind the bar, next to the paralegals and private investigators for the defense.

As it turned out, the hearing was merely a formality. The defense and prosecution had already arrived at a compromise the day before: Both sides agreed that the trial would be held in Birmingham, but that the jury pool would be chosen from across the entire Northern District of Alabama. The rest of the session that morning was given over to the mechanics of jury selection and the wording of the questionnaire that would be used to screen potential jurors. There was also a discussion about a recent defense motion to postpone the trial until next year. Several hundred thousand pages of discovery material from the Atlanta bombings had only been released to the defense in February, and not all of it had yet been delivered. Jaffe argued that the defense needed more time to process it in preparation for trial.

Two days later Judge Smith said he was rescheduling the trial for May 2005.

Even though the defense team expected to be granted some sort of continuance of the trial date, they had already been gearing up for jury selection. Most lawyers believe that picking the right jury is the single most crucial element of a trial. Richard Jaffe had already retained one of the best jury psychologists in the country to help with the process. But it turned out that his most valuable asset was his own client.

"Eric wrote this brilliant, detailed twenty-three-page analysis of the type of juror that we wanted or didn't want," said Jaffe. "I was blown away."

It was a nuanced document, according to Jaffe, but in essence Rudolph's ideal juror was a single white female in her thirties, a little heavy, a little lonely. She would be someone with a maternal attraction to him. She would read a lot of books, mainly romance novels. She would be conservative and probably religious and not particularly comfortable in modern society. On the negative side, he felt the defense probably didn't want a happily married female in a stable relationship, who was college-educated and pro-choice. For male jurors he liked "bubbas" and rural grandfathers with flags on their pickups. "And maybe we'll get lucky and get some libertarian bubbas," he said.

The defense team spent weeks honing the questions they would submit for the questionnaire, which is sent out to the 500 or so initial jury candidates. Both sides have to agree on the list, which can run to dozens of pages. Jaffe asked Rudolph to offer his suggestions; among pages of serious, thoughtful queries, Rudolph slipped in this question: *"Does the juror like Neil Diamond music? And if so, explain."*

Paul Kish was astonished that someone who was facing a death sentence could have such a sense of humor. When he was in a good mood, Rudolph often goaded Richard Jaffe to "lighten up," and start telling jokes.

"I guess I am too serious," allowed Jaffe. "I'm not good at jokes. But I thought Eric could be hilarious."

Rudolph regularly entertained his lawyers with expert imitations of celebrities, politicians, and even members of both legal teams. "I never really knew what I looked like until I saw Eric's impression of me," said Kish. "He was so funny that you had to think that under different circumstances he could have been a professional satirist."

His skills as a mimic seemed tied to his acute powers of observation. Rudolph was intensely sensitive to his environment, something Jaffe credits to his time on the run. "He was hypervigilant in the woods, and therefore he was hypervigilant in the jail and the courtroom," said Jaffe. "Nothing escaped him. He was able to feel all kinds of things that most people can't feel. I wouldn't describe it in an animal sense; it was intensely human."

The lawyers have described the relationship that developed between them and their client in terms of family: Jaffe was like a father figure to Rudolph; Kish was more of an uncle. Their younger associates, such as Hube Dodd and Carl Lietz, filled the roles of his brothers. The women who joined the inner circle, Judy Clarke and a mitigation expert named Scharlette Holdman, took the parts of mother and sister. Jaffe had brought Holdman into the team for her long experience working on high-pressure cases. Her clients had included Ted Bundy, Tim McVeigh, and Ted Kaczynski, among many others. She was a pioneer in the field, but she was also a feminist and a pacifist with offices on Castro Street in the gayest section of San Francisco. Jaffe felt he had to pave the way for Eric to accept Scharlette on the team. It wasn't necessary. Once they met, they bonded instantly.

Kish believes that the public perception of Eric Rudolph is completely off the mark. "Frankly, Eric has been miscast as a human being," said Paul Kish. "He's one of the most genuinely considerate and kind people, in terms of one-on-one relations, that I've known."

Jaffe maintains that while Rudolph genuinely likes people and wants to be around them, the "loner" label is not entirely misplaced. "He could be really outgoing and the center of attention if he wanted to be. And he could also be reclusive. You don't read like he reads unless you enjoy your own company. Or live in the woods for four or five years unless you can survive with yourself."

Rudolph's renowned arrogance may have come from a self-protective detachment. "Generally people who drift from home to home during developmental years tend to be loners," said Jaffe. "Eric can have an aloofness to him, and people who are aloof are often perceived to be arrogant. Eric was self-educated and he prided himself on his intelligence. And he was highly opinionated. He was not afraid to express himself and he could be very candid. He didn't suffer fools lightly."

Jaffe admits that not all discussions with Rudolph were calm. "I thought it was important for him to have a safe place to say what he wanted, with the emotion he felt needed to be expressed."

For months, Rudolph thrived in this attentive circle of surrogate parents and siblings. Unfortunately, like so many real families, Rudolph's legal family was becoming increasingly dysfunctional as the case moved to trial. An internal struggle developed over who was running the show. Jaffe tried to shield Eric from the arguments going on between him and Judy Clarke and Bill Bowen. But after Judge Smith postponed the trial, the rifts in the team turned into open warfare.

The court record of what happened among the defense attorneys over the next six weeks has been sealed by Judge Smith. And for this reason, Richard Jaffe would not discuss the causes of the conflict or its outcome. Judy Clarke and Bill Bowen have declined to be interviewed about any aspect of the case. But Eric Rudolph felt no such constraint, and many months later he explained to me in great detail what went on behind closed doors:

I had never been arrested before I came to Jefferson County in the summer of 2003. It was all a slow learning experience. I had no idea what to expect or how to effectively offer my input into the case. The discovery was massive; the investigation produced tens of thousands of documents. All of these had to be read and assessed. Obviously it was too much for me to handle, so I relied heavily on Jaffe to put the thing together. He was the professional.

For the first year Jaffe was the lead attorney and primary contact with me. He or Hube Dodd would come in once or twice a week and stay for about one or two hours each visit. I had no serious qualms with Jaffe's handling of the case. But as this was all new to me, I really didn't know how a case was run or how I could or should influence the case. Also, I was not in a position to see how the case was being organized outside of the jail. According to Judy Clarke, it was not being organized.

Little did I know a cold war had been going on for some time between two factions in the team. Eventually an irreconcilable split developed: Judy, Bill, Scharlette, and Mike [Burt] on one side and Jaffe and his crew on the other. Judy accused Jaffe of dropping the ball and of not possessing the leadership and organization skills necessary to tackle a case of that magnitude: briefs were not being filed on time, and nobody seemed to know what their assigned roles were. She insisted that the judge dismiss him and put her in charge of the case.

Before a hearing could be scheduled, I was appointed a third-party lawyer, Bobby Segal. I was being asked to choose which of the two sides I preferred, and Bobby was to help me do this and then present this to the judge.

Finally, the issue was brought before Judge Smith in a late night closed hearing. Smith was not a happy camper. He chastised the lawyers, all of them. He told them he would "fire all of your asses if something ever happened like this again." It was not a pretty scene. When asked my opinion, I told the judge that I resented being placed in that position. But because I was forced to choose, I had to stick with what I knew best—Jaffe. At that time the others were an unknown quantity. Judy or Bill came to visit maybe once or twice a month. Furthermore, Judy was an out-of-town lawyer, whereas Richard had had an extensive record with Alabama juries and was quite successful. I thought that an Alabama jury would probably respond better to a local attorney than one from California. However, the judge did not see it my way and after an extensive ass chewing dismissed Richard.

Whether there was any real merit to Judy and Bill's contention, I don't know. I was not in a position to observe how Richard was handling the case. As far as I knew, he was doing an adequate job. Perhaps it was a personality clash; maybe they just didn't get along. With Richard's tremendous record, it's hard to see how he could have completely lost control ...

The personality difference between the faction leaders was apparent. Judy is a highly organized type A person who needs things to be very structured. Bill's personality is very similar. He probably organizes his sock drawers with a ruler. On the other hand, Jaffe has an artist's personality and has probably been known to wear different colored socks every once in a while. Perhaps it was this "Odd Couple" type difference that was the underlying cause of their rift.

Paul Kish was dismayed. "I was on vacation when I got a call on my cell phone from a lawyer I'd never heard of named Bobby Segal," he recalled. "He explained to me that he had been appointed by Judge Smith to try to help Eric work his way through some problems with the defense team in Birmingham." Segal asked Kish whom he would recommend to represent Rudolph. "My first recommendation was they should all stay in it together," said Kish. "I told him they were a tremendous team with a lot of skills. But eventually after conferring with people in our office we did make a recommendation that, if there had to be one, we would recommend Richard. There were a number of considerations. Jaffe had a fabulous record of trying and winning death penalty cases in Alabama. And if I was trying to save my life, I would have put my eggs in that basket. Beyond that, I can only tell you that we had an excellent working relationship with Richard."

All Richard Jaffe will say is this: "There did come a point where it became clear that the two teams were not able to work together. And we felt that Eric had a right to a team that was harmonious, that it would be detrimental to engage in infighting. Our decisions were always made in the best interest of the client, from the very beginning."

On August 9, 2004, Richard Jaffe, Emory Anthony, Derek Drennan, and Hube Dodd submitted a motion to withdraw from the case. (Rudolph was mistaken that Jaffe was "dismissed" from the case—he was allowed to withdraw.) On the same day, Judge Smith accepted the motion and appointed Judy Clarke as lead counsel. He also authorized that two attorneys from Michael Burt's law firm be added to the team.

After this decision was recorded, Richard Jaffe was not able to see or communicate with Eric Rudolph again. There were no good-byes.

A couple of weeks later, Jaffe got an e-mail from Rudolph's mother.

> *I have waited for U to contact me but I am told it is not permitted. Well, I say hooey on that. I still consider U a great guy and would like to continue knowing U as a person if that is possible.*
>
> *A big hug*
> *Patty*

Jaffe had spent a great deal of time on the phone with Pat Rudolph to keep her informed about the case, and he had visited her at home in Florida to discuss mitigation issues. He'd enjoyed their conversations, and had grown fond of her. Jaffe sent her a polite reply, saying that he appreciated her kind words, but rather than have it misconstrued as an indirect communication with Eric, he thought it best that they not write or see each other until the case was over. And with that his contact with the family ended.

Although Rudolph was perplexed by Jaffe's sudden departure, he quickly warmed up to the new team, which lavished him with attention. Instead of getting visits twice a week, Rudolph now spent one or two hours a day, six days a week with his lawyers. And he felt he was getting much more influence over the direction of the case. "After Judy's regime was in place things changed dramatically," he wrote. "I felt included." For him, the best new development was that his lawyers successfully argued a motion to allow him access to a laptop computer in the jail. The mountains of discovery documents would have filled the entire cell block, and for Rudolph to effectively help in his defense, he needed to view the evidence in digital form. "The laptop helped tremendously," he wrote.

> Now I was able to read dozens of 302s a day and develop leads and offer investigative advice ... There were virtually hundreds of potential witnesses. With my input, we were able to winnow this list down considerably. I was able to point out the lies told, how to defeat these lies, and which witnesses to look out for at trial. There was full disclosure among us ... I was an integral part of the team and this gave me a sense of <u>control</u> over my destiny. I was very happy with their work.

As the new trial date approached, the defense team stepped up its attack on the government's evidence, papering the court with briefs and keeping the U.S. attorneys busy responding to their challenges. As expected, the defense filed a motion, written by Carl Lietz, to suppress all evidence that resulted from the searches. For good measure, they also filed a motion challenging the legality of Rudolph's detention and arrest in May 2003. A hearing was scheduled to be held before the U.S. magistrate on Election Day, 2004.

There was also some staff turnover in the U.S. attorney's office after Judge Smith postponed the trial date until 2005. Joe McLean was due to turn sixty in July 2005, and in August 2004 he had been offered a generous early retirement package by the Justice Department. But before he left the U.S. attorney's office, he had devised a strategy to overcome the problems with the faulty searches of Rudolph's rented trailer and storage unit: The government would maintain that the agents didn't actually need search warrants because Eric Rudolph had abandoned his property—along with his expectations of privacy—when he fled to the woods.

John Horn, a talented lawyer from the U.S. attorney's office in Atlanta, refined this theory and presented it at the suppression hearing. He called as a witness Jim Russell, the FBI agent from Asheville, who described his initial search for Rudolph, and how he found Rudolph's trailer open and empty, looking as if it had been abandoned in a hurry. Horn also called Joel Moss, the FBI supervisor from San Francisco, to describe his interviews with George Nordmann. He related Rudolph's disclosure that he knew he was wanted by the law, and that he had planned ahead for his flight. In fact, Moss said, he'd bragged to Nordmann that he had deliberately given his friend Randy Cochran misleading information about where he might hide, guessing correctly that Cochran would betray him once he was pressured by law enforcement. One of the requirements of abandonment is forethought, and the magistrate felt the government had made its case. A month later, he recommended that even though the three nonspecific warrants were unconstitutional, the evidence would not be suppressed because they were carried out on abandoned property.

With four months left before the start of jury selection, the defense team tried another tactic, called "Daubert" challenges, to block the government's evidence. The term arose from a 1993 Supreme Court ruling in the case of *Daubert v. Dow Pharmaceuticals*, which established the obligation of the judge to decide whether the methods of processing and testing scientific evidence meet empirical standards. Rudolph's defense team filed a flurry of motions challenging the validity of the techniques used by the FBI's fingerprint experts, forensic linguists, and the document handler who authenticated Rudolph's signature and handwriting samples. And they called into question the methods used to identify and physically reconstruct bombs—something that had never been done before. The judge decided to rule on several of these issues following a Daubert hearing that was scheduled for late March 2005. In effect, Michael Burt planned to put the ATF lab and its most basic procedures on trial.

Felecia Sanderson, the widow of the murdered policeman, had kept a low profile as the case against Eric Rudolph slowly moved to trial. She had publicly thanked Jeff Postell for his fine police work shortly after Rudolph was captured, but refused all interviews and television appearances. Those who knew her said her grief had not lightened with time, and she did not expect Rudolph's trial to provide her with an artificial sense of "closure." She only hoped it would provide justice. She kept in constant contact with Mike Whisonant and the other AUSAs prosecuting the case, but, after watching the arraignment, she did not attend any of the hearings in Alabama. She preferred to leave Rudolph's fate in the hands of the courts.

Emily Lyons and her husband, Jeff, by contrast, almost never missed a court appearance and frequently made themselves available to the news media. When I called to ask for a meeting, Jeff answered the phone and gave me directions to their house.

The Lyonses live in a suburb south of Birmingham in a wood frame house in a tranquil, older development planted with crepe myrtles and pines. Three boisterous dogs barked in the back yard as I climbed the stairs to the front door. Jeff, a clean-cut man with a round, fleshy face, led me inside. He obviously screens Emily's visitors as well as her calls. The Lyons home was overflowing with knickknacks, family pictures on the walls, candy dishes, stacks of paper and copies of *Better Homes* magazine on the coffee table. Two full-sized PCs shared space on the dining room table. Jeff is a software designer.

Emily Lyons, barefoot and wearing shorts on a warm fall afternoon, walked into the living room and curled up on the couch to talk. A one-eyed cat named Popeye followed her in and rubbed and coiled around the furniture legs as she spoke. Like the dogs in the back yard, Popeye was rescued from the animal shelter. Jeff and Emily like to take in strays.

Emily is taller than her pictures suggest, stronger than her subdued appearances on television let on. The bomb that exploded in January 1998 blew wires, rocks, chunks of metal, and three-inch nails into Emily Lyons's body. The X-rays of her injuries look like pictures of debris from a construction site. She had, at this point, endured seventeen operations to restore her legs and her eyesight; many more were planned. Her skin was pocked with dozens of pale white scars, and the grafts on her shins looked waxy and stiff. One eye is synthetic, the other barely functional. She has been trying to piece together the remnants of her life, but her nursing career is over, and she's been having a hard time contemplating the future.

Right now her mind was focused on the trial of Eric Rudolph. She had felt a tremendous relief when he was finally captured. While he was still a fugitive Emily always watched her back, always wondered if he would return to Birmingham to try to finish her off. The Lyonses first laid eyes on Rudolph a month after his arrest, when he appeared in court for a hearing that updated his indictment to qualify him for the death penalty. They had missed "Eric's" initial arraignment because they were in New York, "doing the morning shows." Both Emily and Jeff refer to Rudolph by his first name, and talk about him with a familiar contempt.

"Eric looked like a punk in court," Emily said. "He was cocky." She saw a lack of remorse in him, an arrogance that didn't come through in the courtroom drawings. Jeff noticed his military bearing. He said it reminded him of Tim McVeigh, the Oklahoma City bomber.

Jeff and Emily were happy to talk about rescued pets and barbecue restaurants and Birmingham traffic. They were, however, reluctant to discuss the bombing in any detail or talk about the upcoming trial. They had decided to write their own book about Emily's experiences, and they'd already settled on a title: *Life's Been a Blast*.

By early 2005, months before Rudolph's scheduled trial, there were a number of media projects in the works, including my own. Two hour-long television documentaries about the case had already aired and at least one full-length feature documentary was in the works; the USA network was supposedly planning a TV movie about Rudolph's time on the run, and three books about the case had already been published— not including *Life's Been a Blast*, which would appear several months later. Two of these books were obscure self-published efforts, but were nonetheless available to an international readership through the magic of Amazon.com. One of these was a paperback account of Rudolph's life written by a woman who lived near Murphy; the other was a bizarre offering, entitled *Eric Rudolph and Me*, by a Southern preacher who had never met Rudolph, but had been inspired to write a song about him and felt their lives were somehow connected. A few more were in the works. Deborah Rudolph later told me she was putting together a book about her "spiritual journey" from the hold of Identity Christianity to "you know, being saved and baptized."

Patricia Rudolph had been toiling on a manuscript for years that she had tentatively titled *Man Most Wanted: The Eric Rudolph Story: A Mother's Perspective.* And those without manuscripts were considering writing one. When I called Tom Branham for an interview he complained that everybody wanted information from him but nobody would pay him for it. He was thinking of writing a book.

One of the books about the Rudolph case, however, was published by a major house and was getting immense coverage on CNN, and for good reason. *Hunting Eric Rudolph* was written by Henry Schuster, the senior CNN producer who had covered the case from the beginning, and an unlikely coauthor: the retired GBI agent Charles Stone. When Stone and Schuster's book arrived in stores in March 2005, the U.S. attorneys were not pleased. Although the authors were careful to say that Rudolph had not yet been convicted of any crime, the book exposed much of the unpublished evidence against Rudolph and made a relentless argument for his guilt. Its release just before the trial was timed to maximize sales, but because it was so highly publicized in Alabama, it could have complicated the process of finding an impartial jury. But as Stone and Schuster began their book promotion tour, they were unaware of the series of urgent backroom meetings taking place in Atlanta, Birmingham, and Huntsville. For once a crucial development in the Rudolph case remained a deeply guarded secret.

19

LIFE OR DEATH

The prosecutors were certain they could convict Eric Rudolph; they were not so sure that they could get the death penalty. The U.S. attorneys in Birmingham and Atlanta felt that if anyone deserved to be executed it was Rudolph, a domestic terrorist and a cop killer. But juries had proven reluctant to impose capital punishment in federal cases. The statistics said it all: According to a study by the Death Penalty Resource Council, 382 federal defendants have qualified for the death penalty since 1988. Of these only three have been executed, including Timothy McVeigh; forty-four are currently on death row, and sixty-two are still awaiting trial.

Of course, if a federal jury doesn't vote for death, local district attorneys can try the same defendant under state law. But this doesn't always work: After a federal jury failed to impose a death sentence on Terry Nichols, the Oklahoma City bombing conspirator, he was tried in district court on 160 counts of first-degree murder. That jury deadlocked on his sentence, and he was again given life without parole. By 2003, when Eric Rudolph was formally certified as a death penalty candidate by the attorney general's office, execution was becoming an increasingly rare and vastly expensive outcome in federal court.

The government first signaled its willingness to discuss a plea bargain as early as January 2004. Richard Jaffe, after finishing a routine meeting with Mike Whisonant, Joe McLean, and Will Chambers, was standing up to leave when Whisonant said to him, "Richard, I want you to know that if this case is going to be resolved by plea, do not wait till the last minute, because we're not going to play that game."

Jaffe sat back down. "What are you saying, Mike?"

"Just that if you would like to explore a plea, and if you wait until the last minute, it's not going to work."

Jaffe was slightly stunned by this development, but he was interested in "beginning the exploration process," as the lawyers put it, to take the death penalty off the table. Joe McLean remembered that the discussions began informally. "In death penalty cases there's always the chance of a plea," he said. "And the government doesn't want to prepare everything and then have the guy come in and enter a plea. And if the guy is ready to give up his accomplices or lead us to a ticking bomb or a plot on the Capitol, we want to hear about it sooner than later."

They all agreed that if there were to be a plea, an awful lot of people would have to sign off on it, from the district attorney in Georgia to the U.S. attorney general. "We knew we were going to have a difficult time convincing John Ashcroft that he should go along with life without parole," said McLean. Ashcroft was an evangelist of capital punishment. He had been aggressively pressuring U.S. attorneys around the country to ask for the death penalty more often. And in nearly a third of the cases that passed his desk, Ashcroft overruled the recommendations of his own prosecutors, almost always to increase the defendants' charges to make them eligible for execution. But 2004 was going to be a presidential election year. And whichever way it went, the controversial attorney general was not likely to be there for a second term.

Jaffe wanted to be sure there was a real potential for a settlement before he raised the hopes of his client. "I asked these three prosecutors not to put me in the position of going to Eric and talking about a plea if they weren't going to be in a position to offer one," he said. And he wanted assurances that Atlanta wouldn't derail the talks. The prosecutors, he recalled, felt that Atlanta would go along.

Everyone knew it was going to be a long and arduous negotiation, involving months of meetings. Jaffe held discussions with the government lawyers two more times before he gently began to feel Rudolph out on the subject of a plea.

"I didn't walk in there and say, 'Hey, you want to plead guilty?'" said Jaffe. First they discussed Rudolph's views of life imprisonment versus death. And then Jaffe asked what he would do if he knew, hypothetically, that he could resolve all the cases at once, including the potential state cases. They were acutely aware of what happened to Terry Nichols. Rudolph realized he would probably be tried and tried again until some jury finally sentenced him to death. Even if he managed to avoid the death penalty in Jefferson County, state law allows a judge to override a jury to impose capital punishment. A plea was most probably the only way to avoid execution.

Jaffe finally broached the question. "How important is it that you live?" he asked. "Do you want to risk trials in two places, or do you want to live?"

"I want to live," Rudolph said. He told Jaffe that he wasn't afraid to die, but that he felt he could still have a meaningful life in prison.

"He just felt that he could accomplish more by living than by dying," said Jaffe.

Unlike his lawyers, Rudolph was not morally opposed to the death penalty. He said that the Green River killer, who had murdered nearly fifty women (and who had plea-bargained for life without parole) deserved execution. So did Scott Peterson, who killed his pregnant wife, Laci. After all, Rudolph was a Christian fundamentalist who believed in an eye for an eye. But in his own case, Rudolph didn't think he deserved the death penalty. He told Jaffe to pursue the plea discussions and to keep him informed. He would consider the possibilities.

The cautious "explorations" continued under strict secrecy through the spring of 2004. Just before the trial was postponed, Jaffe told Paul Kish that he felt confident that he could plead out the Birmingham case, although no deal had yet been offered. Then, in August, Jaffe left the defense team, and Kish heard nothing more about a plea until that December.

In the middle of a routine phone call with Kish, one of the Atlanta prosecutors casually mentioned that "she was wondering why they hadn't heard a plea proposal yet." Kish and his team were "blown away" by the overture. When he called Judy Clarke in Birmingham, he learned that the prosecutors there had given her a similar signal. After a few more phone calls, the legal teams in both Atlanta and Birmingham decided to meet after the holidays to discuss a joint plea agreement that would resolve all the cases against Eric Rudolph.

Several things had changed between Birmingham's first, tentative overture to Jaffe and this coordinated effort by the government to work out a deal. First, John Ashcroft announced he was stepping down as attorney general after the November elections. He was to be replaced by the White House counsel, Alberto Gonzales, a former chief justice of the Texas Supreme Court and close adviser to President Bush. Gonzales was known to be far more pragmatic about capital punishment than Ashcroft, and his appointment signaled to both sides of the Rudolph case that the plea was a real possibility.

Then, as the second Bush Administration took shape, David Nahmias was appointed U.S. attorney for the Northern District of Georgia. Nahmias, who was an AUSA in Atlanta in the early days of the bombing investigations, had spent most of the first term of the Bush Administration as a major player in the Justice Department. He held blue-chip conservative credentials, having clerked for both U.S. Circuit Judge Laurence Silberman and Supreme Court Justice Antonin Scalia. After serving in Justice under Michael Chertoff, he had been promoted to deputy assistant attorney general. Nahmias was essentially in charge of the legal end of the war on terror. He prosecuted al-Qaeda. He was an architect of the Patriot Act. As long as conservative Republicans held power, Nahmias's future seemed unlimited. The last thing he needed was to preside over a high-profile gamble like the Rudolph prosecution.

Of course Dave Nahmias would not agree with this assessment. He has always maintained that Atlanta had a strong circumstantial case against Rudolph, and that a jury would be swayed by the "web" of evidence that tied Rudolph to all the bombings. Still, he acknowledged, "there's always doubt in capital case situations." He told me he was not "crystal clear" about who opened the plea discussions, but that "the issue was raised, both in Birmingham and here, and went fairly quickly."

While Atlanta had the weaker case, and a greater incentive to get Rudolph to confess to all the bombings, Birmingham was having its problems as well. The prosecutors there had held at least two mock trials—a common practice in high-stakes cases—and the results were apparently discouraging. The U.S. attorney's office won't discuss the outcome of these dry runs, but according to Jeff and Emily Lyons, who wrote about it in the book they eventually published, the prosecution had difficulty getting a guilty verdict, let alone a death sentence.

Kish recalled that the two defense teams and two prosecution teams—about thirty people in all—sat down around a huge horseshoe-shaped table in a conference room at the U.S. attorney's office in Birmingham. Based on the discussions there, Kish felt that Atlanta was driving the negotiations. The defense came prepared to make its case for a deal, but it seemed to Kish that the government wanted one as much as Rudolph's team, if not more.

Certain issues were kicked back and forth over the next few weeks. Federal agents wanted to interview Rudolph, and the defense insisted that wasn't going to happen. Rudolph might be willing to plead to the Birmingham, Otherside Lounge, and Sandy Springs bombings, but he didn't want to confess to the Centennial Olympic Park attack. The government insisted that the plea had to cover all the bombings. And for offering Rudolph his life, they needed something in return. So Sally Yates, the first U.S. attorney in Atlanta, called Paul Kish to ask for it: Would Rudolph be willing to divulge any hidden explosives?

Ten minutes later, Kish and Brian Mendelsohn were on their way to the Birmingham jail.

"The dynamite became an issue during the discussions," said Dave Nahmias. "It had always been of concern to us in Atlanta." The task force forensic team, led by ATF agent Joe Kennedy, had investigated every sizable purchase, theft, and loss of nitroglycerin dynamite in the Southeast around the time of the bombings. They had narrowed their search down to a robbery of more than 340 pounds of nitroglycerin dynamite at the Austin Powder Company in Asheville, North Carolina, in December 1996, and though they could never conclusively tie that batch of dynamite to the Atlanta and Birmingham bombs, they were almost certain Rudolph was behind the burglary. Lloyd Erwin estimated that about thirty pounds of high explosives had been consumed in Rudolph's five dynamite bombs. That meant that a lot of dynamite was still out there somewhere, growing more unstable with each passing month. If Rudolph mentioned his cache to a prison buddy or someone else with a grudge against the government, the feds might have another bombing spree to investigate—one they could have prevented. Plus there was the danger of boxes of deteriorating dynamite lying around in the woods where an unsuspecting Boy Scout could be digging a latrine one day and blow his troop to smithereens. If Rudolph could be persuaded to give up the location of the explosives, the public safety benefit might be enough to sell a sentence of life without parole to Washington, and to the public.

Paul Kish realized he had to tread very carefully. While he needed to be able to tell the government whether Rudolph had hidden any dynamite, he didn't want to know too many details. If the deal fell through, it would put him in the difficult legal and moral position of knowing the location of damaging evidence that also endangered public safety. "We had never flat-out talked with Eric about this," Kish recalled. "We didn't want to. We were all concerned about the ethics of it. Finally we got up the nerve to ask him, and being the straight-shooter that he is, he told us what was out there." Kish called Yates and gave her a rough idea where there was dynamite hidden in four or five sites. "When I told Sally that, she almost dropped the phone," said Kish. "They were definitely interested, but they wanted more specifics."

As the negotiations continued, the government prosecutors were cautiously contacting Eric Rudolph's victims to raise the possibility of a plea. Felecia Sanderson had never sought the death penalty. She knew that executing Rudolph would not bring Sande back, and it would not heal her wounds. She just wanted the ordeal of the trial to be over and the killer locked away forever, where he could never hurt anyone again. John Hawthorne, the widower of Alice and stepfather of Fallon Stubbs, was also willing to show mercy to the man who had destroyed his family. And if offering Rudolph life in prison without parole would yield hundreds of pounds of stolen dynamite, then he was willing to forgo a trial.

The only notable victim who objected to the deal was Emily Lyons. She and Jeff had obsessively prepared for Rudolph's trial, and Jeff regularly lobbied the prosecutors for a larger role in the proceedings. They had already written her testimony, and they'd felt ignored and marginalized when the prosecutors were less than enthusiastic about their input. When Mike Whisonant asked for their views about a possible plea, they, in Jeff's words, "gave it to him with both barrels." The Lyonses insisted that they would never be satisfied with anything less than death for Eric Rudolph, even though the maximum penalty for injuring Lyons—life in prison—was exactly what Rudolph was being offered. But when they were told about the dangers of the buried dynamite, Jeff and Emily Lyons reluctantly agreed to support the deal.

When Rudolph finally began revealing the details he had been withholding—there were at least 200 pounds of dynamite hidden in the woods, and a partially constructed bomb buried 200 yards from a residential neighborhood—it was enough for the government to start drafting the papers. But negotiations continued back and forth for several weeks as the spring trial date drew nearer. Both teams had to move forward with the case. The defense plastered the court with last-minute motions. Mike Burt, the forensic specialist, prepared for his showdown over the government's scientific evidence at the Daubert hearings, scheduled to begin March 29. It wasn't until March 28 that the U.S. attorneys and subcabinet officials at the Justice Department finally agreed on the language of the deal. All they had to do was to convince Attorney General Gonzales to approve the plea bargain, and he was about to take off for a round of talks on cross-border issues in Mexico.

Paul Kish remembers the week of the Daubert hearings as one of the strangest and most stressful of his life. On the first morning in Huntsville, Kish stood in an open parking lot across the street from the courthouse, talking to Sally Yates on his cell phone as she told him that Gonzales was reading the document on the flight to Mexico. He was making some minor changes, and she would get back to him.

Inside the old courtroom, with its heroic mural and polished marble floor, the hearings proceeded. The reporters sat in their assigned rows, utterly oblivious to the nervous scrums of lawyers who gathered at every break, whispering furiously in the corners. Eric Rudolph was again wearing his too-tight navy blazer, sitting next to Judy Clarke, who patted his back and rubbed his shoulder as she spoke to him. Every once in a while he cut his eyes in the direction of Emily and Jeff Lyons, who sat on the aisle, clutching each other's hands. This morning Michael Burt was grilling Richard Strobel, the chief of arson and explosives at the ATF lab in Virginia. He was asking Strobel to explain every aspect of the collection of explosive residues. He wanted to know why all the agents taking samples of explosive residues in Rudolph's trailer were wearing Tyvek suits but the bomb-sniffing dog, Garrett, was allowed to walk around uncovered. Could the dog have contaminated the scene with residues from another site? Do these canines ever wear Tyvek to prevent cross-contamination? Of course Burt was able to produce a photograph of an explosives-detecting dog dressed up in Tyvek. Will Chambers, who handled the hearing for the government, pointed out that the snapshot had been set up as a joke for the handler.

Later in the hearings, Lloyd Erwin took the stand to describe the portable EGIS machine he brought to North Carolina from Atlanta and how he collected and analyzed swabs for explosive residues. The San Francisco lawyer was putting on a masterful performance trying to find flaws in his methods, but the ATF chemist was so relaxed and convincing on the stand that attacking him was like beating on everyone's favorite uncle. Erwin had been testifying in courtrooms since Burt was in grade school. It was impossible to shake him. Joe Kennedy, Jim Cavanaugh, and a contingent of ATF agents sat in the back rows, arms crossed over their chests, watching the fundamentals of their profession dissected in open court.

Rudolph, who took detailed notes on a yellow legal pad, was enjoying the hearings so much that he had started to wonder if the plea was such a good idea.

Late that afternoon Kish got a call from David Nahmias telling him the attorney general had signed off on the deal. The defense team met with Eric late into the night at the Huntsville jail. The government wanted to end the Daubert hearings as soon as possible and have Rudolph direct them to his buried dynamite. Rudolph wanted to wait until after the hearings. The prosecution put on the pressure for him to sign right away but Rudolph balked. "Eric doesn't make decisions that way," Carl Lietz recalled. "He makes them on his own terms."

It was a wrenching time for everyone. Kish and Lietz had grown particularly close to their client after months of intense negotiations. Now they had to face two awful choices with him. If he turned down this deal, there was a strong possibility that he would go through ten more years of trials and eventually be executed. If he took it, he would be buried alive in a supermax prison, with no chance to change his mind.

"The decision was rough on us. It was rough on Eric," said Kish.

The discussions went on for days. Danny Sindall, the FBI agent, was standing by in Huntsville, waiting for instructions to find the buried dynamite. Sindall was hoping to finally talk to Rudolph, but Rudolph refused to meet with the FBI agent or any other member of law enforcement. Instead Sindall gave Kish a list of thirty-five questions the government needed answered if the search was to go ahead: What kind of landmarks are around the caches? How deep are they buried? Are there any booby traps?

Rudolph still hesitated to give his answer, despite warnings from the government that the delay might endanger the deal. But in the middle of the week Judge Smith's old friend and mentor, the former Alabama senator Howell Heflin, died, and Smith cut the Daubert hearings short so that he could attend the funeral. Rudolph returned to Birmingham on Friday afternoon. On Saturday, with all his remaining attorneys around him, he decided to accept the deal.

"Eric chose to live," said Kish. "He is one of the most strong-willed people I know. If he had taken a different point of view and turned down the deal, obviously my job would have been to try to talk him out of it. But this is where I'm slightly different from a lot of death penalty opponents. It's still his life."

Brian Mendelsohn, the self-described ideologue, considered the deal a clear victory. It saddened Kish, knowing what was ahead for Rudolph. But he understood Rudolph's reasoning. "Eric felt that he still had abilities to make a difference in the world. That he still had a voice, that he wanted to be heard," said Kish. "Setting aside what he has done, I have an awful lot of respect for him and his willingness to live his life according to his code. I might not agree with it, but I have a heck of a lot of respect for it."

Rudolph spent the weekend going over topo maps of western North Carolina and working out the details of the deal with his legal team. One of the remaining obstacles was the language of the plea agreement, which detailed each bombing. Rudolph had insisted that the nails that were found in his storage shed had nothing to do with those used in the Sandy Springs bomb—despite the government's forensic work. But he had capitulated to the government's version of events early in the negotiation process. When it came time to sign the paper, however, Rudolph decided he couldn't do it. This time the other side balked. But in the end, the government dropped all mention of the nails from the final agreement.

Rudolph also spent long hours with his lawyers and private investigators trying to pinpoint the locations of five buried stashes of dynamite. Carl Lietz, a fellow hunter and hiker, had a special rapport with Rudolph. Paul Kish sat nearby, slack jawed with wonder, listening as the two of them pored over the maps, parsing each green line of altitude, while Rudolph described every rock and stream from memory. Four caches were hidden in the northwestern corner of Cherokee County: Two were deep in the national forest near the Tennessee state line, and two closer to the hamlet of Unaka and the house of his late friend Richard Baxter. The other site, containing a completed bomb with the detonator detached, was located just outside Murphy on the ridge directly across the road from the National Guard Armory.

Alan Hawkins had just finished rotating the tires on a customer's van when he noticed something going on down on the four-lane highway. There were six or seven state patrol vehicles crawling along Highway 19, slowing down traffic in both directions from Murphy, eventually blocking off cars for several hundred yards on either side of his business. Hawkins is an observant man, and he suspected right away this must have had something to do with Eric Rudolph. His Tirezans (pronounced "Tarzans" in these parts) tire shop was perched on a hill directly above and east of the National Guard Armory, and he had a clear view of its entrance and parking lot. Hawkins had noticed a big increase in activity down there in the past couple of days, a steady accumulation of American sedans with government plates and big black Suburbans with darkened windows. Agents were buzzing in and out of there like bees on a hive. The last time he'd seen activity on that scale was when Rudolph was on the run and the armory was used as a base of operations for the manhunt. Hawkins had been following the papers and he knew Rudolph's trial was coming up. This had to be connected. He wiped the grease off his hands with a rag and walked over to get a better view.

Suddenly—KABOOOM! Hawkins was rocked by a concussion that lifted the hair on his head and shook his shop walls. He saw a cloud of smoke spout up over the hill directly across the highway, not more than a football field's length away. Hawkins guessed that they'd finally found Rudolph's hidden dynamite. And, man, it was close enough to feel personal. In a week's time, Hawkins would learn that the location of Rudolph's stash was more personal than he could have imagined.

That was the first blast. For the next couple of days, citizens reported hearing explosions in different parts of Cherokee County, some of them loud enough to rattle their windows. The sheriff's office fielded some worried calls. Earthquake? Illegal demolition? Only the sheriff, Keith Lovin, knew what was going on, and he was sworn to secrecy. All he could do was assure people that they weren't in any danger.

It was another reunion for task force alumni up in Murphy, only they couldn't tell anyone the reason for this mission, not even their wives and partners. Danny Sindall had driven from Birmingham with the topo maps and met with Todd Letcher, the last task force leader; FBI case agents Larry Long and James Cross; Joe Kennedy from the ATF; Will Chambers from Birmingham; and John Horn from Atlanta, along with an assorted group of trackers and bomb techs. They kept as low a profile as they could while they searched for the caches. If news of the deal leaked to the media before the team could find all the dynamite, there was no telling what kind of press riot and general panic might develop.

The most troubling site, across from the armory, was the easiest to find. Bill Preston, one of Judy Clarke's investigators, simply led the agents to it. For Joe Kennedy, opening the five-gallon plastic bucket buried in the orange clay soil was like a hundred Christmases. It was waterlogged and rusted after so many years in the ground, but inside it was a fully assembled bomb with twenty-five pounds of dynamite and most of the components the ATF had spent so long trying to identify. There was the duct tape, the red and black Radio Shack wires, the Energizer batteries and the JR servo device with two arms cut off, attached to the switch with orange twine. Best of all, there was a JR F400 radio-control unit, possibly the same one used to set off the bomb that killed Sande Sanderson. The dynamite in the container had all but liquefied, and the bomb technicians were afraid to move it far, and for good reason. When they set it off on the far side of the ridge, away from the highway, it blew a four-foot-deep chunk out of the hillside.

The next four sites were harder to find. When agents couldn't find the two caches that were hidden deep in the forest, Lietz acted as the intermediary between Rudolph and the feds to help keep the deal from falling apart. Finally the agents were able to retrace Rudolph's steps through the woods, starting at the more remote location and working backward. Once all the caches were found, Joe Kennedy was able to answer a lot of the questions that had plagued him for most of a decade: The agents found tools and supplies for Rudolph's bomb-making factory, including wire cutters and a soldering iron, Rubbermaid containers with almond-colored lids, unused Estes rocket igniters—long suspected to be part of Rudolph's detonation system—and tubes of hexamine tablets, a solid fuel used in camping stoves and a key ingredient in homemade chemical detonators. One of the sites yielded another partial bomb housed in a Lil' Playmate cooler. The cache also offered a solution to the mystery of the missing hose clamp. There had been two in the package Rudolph purchased at Wal-Mart. One of them was removed from Sande Sanderson's body. The other was found in a partially assembled detonation switch attached to the cooler. In total, the agents recovered 270 pounds of dynamite, all of it in deteriorated condition, but most of it still wrapped in paper signifying its source: the Austin Powder Company of Asheville, North Carolina.

* * *

On Friday, April 8, Sally Yates called Paul Kish to tell him that Eric Rudolph "had complied" with the plea agreement. All the explosives had been found; the deal was sealed. About the same time, a local reporter had figured out what was blowing up in the forests of Cherokee County, and the AP was about to go with the story. So the Justice Department issued a statement to stay ahead of the news cycle. The headline read: "Eric Robert Rudolph to Plead Guilty to Serial Bombing Attack in Atlanta and Birmingham; Will Receive Life Sentences. As Part of Plea Agreement, Rudolph Disclosed Locations of Hidden Bomb and Dynamite." It hit the news that afternoon.

James Cross, the FBI case agent, was driving back from the last site when he heard the news was going to break. The feds cleared out of the command center before the media could descend; on the highway leading back to Atlanta, Cross passed the CNN live truck heading north toward Murphy. It was a great day for Cross. He felt elated that the long investigation was finally over, and that the operation had stayed secret until they'd found the dynamite. He hadn't been allowed to tell his family what was going on, and so the first call he made was to his son's cell phone. Mark Cross was an officer with the Atlanta Police Department's elite antidrug "Red Dog" unit. Since Rudolph was captured, the FBI supervisor hadn't been able to spend much time with his thirty-one-year-old son, his daughter-in-law, or his two grandchildren. When he got his son on the phone, James Cross was bursting with news. "Mark, I can tell you now, Eric Rudolph is going to plead guilty," he said. "I wanted you to know first."

They lived on opposite sides of the city, and a couple of days later Cross met his son at their prearranged "rendezvous spot," a BP station midway between their houses. As a police officer, Mark had lived the case with his father. Now, finally hearing all about the hidden explosives and the successful operation to render them safe, Mark got emotional. He was crying when he told his father, "Dad, you don't know how proud I am of you."

It was the last time James Cross saw his son. Two weeks later Mark Anthony Cross was killed in the line of duty, shot dead as he approached a suspicious car. More than 1,800 mourners attended his funeral, including Atlanta's mayor and the heads of all the area's law enforcement agencies, including the FBI, the ATF, and the U.S. attorney, David Nahmias. Looking back on it, James Cross still wonders about how life can abound with such highs and lows, and in such close proximity. Since that time, Cross has prepared a PowerPoint presentation that he gives to young police officers in honor of his son. He shows slides from the Rudolph investigation and talks about the long manhunt and its surprising resolution. He talks about Sande Sanderson and of the last time he saw Mark, and reminds his audience how suddenly one's life can change. The presentation includes a passage from the eulogy delivered at Mark's funeral. "The minister talked about police officers being sheepdogs and the general public being sheep," said Cross. "And of course, then there's always the wolves out there ..."

Judge Smith sat behind a massive, dark wood bench flanked by huge wooden pillars, set in a field of somber green walls and carpeting. Despite the oversized decor, the seating in the eighth-floor courtroom in the Vance Building was limited to about 120 spectators. There was a closed-circuit video feed, so they could watch the action live or turn to one of two large television monitors fixed on the side walls of the courtroom.

The press was ushered in well before the hearing began, so there was time to contemplate the scenery. The prosecution area, located to the judge's right, was neatly arrayed with white plastic legal binders, lined up like soldiers awaiting their orders. The defense position, to the left, was piled with overflowing boxes that looked as if they had just been dumped out of a delivery van.

Shortly before 8:30 A.M., the lawyers filed into court. The U.S. attorney's team all wore their blackest suits; Alice Martin livened up her outfit with an orchid pink silk shirt. The defense team favored, of course, shades of gray.

Seats in the spectator gallery were filling quickly with law enforcement agents and lawyers who wanted to witness the outcome of the case. The jury box turned into a VIP section, with past and present players in the hunt for Eric Robert Rudolph stacked up like a Greek chorus in the wings. Jim Cavanaugh and Doug Jones had front-row seats.

The victims sat in the first row behind the government's table. Jeff Lyons kept his arm wrapped around Emily throughout the proceedings. A former owner of the Otherside Lounge had come in from Atlanta to hear Rudolph's plea, as had John Hawthorne, widower of Alice Hawthorne, and Fallon Stubbs, the daughter who was injured in the Olympic Park bombing that had killed her mother nine years ago. Fallon was a lovely young woman now, who arranged her hair in neat cornrows and wore a dark business suit. Last to enter was Felecia Sanderson. She, too, was dressed for the office, in hose and heels and a skirt that revealed legs so thin, a breeze might blow her over. Her strawberry blond hair hung straight over her shoulders, partially concealing a drawn, worried face that she struggled to keep composed. Jermaine Hughes, the witness who was most responsible for this outcome, was in town, but not in court. He had never given an interview, and had hoped to remain anonymous. He sat out the hearing in Mike Whisonant's office.

The rustling and murmuring gave way to an abrupt stillness when a side door opened and Eric Rudolph entered the room, flanked by U.S. marshals. As a final statement from his hosts in Birmingham, he was again dressed like a common prisoner in red jail togs and slippers. His ankles were shackled in irons. But his mood seemed light, almost ebullient as he greeted his lawyers with smiles and handshakes. He twisted around in his seat to acknowledge the second tier of defense attorneys and investigators on his legal team. Then he looked over at the row of prosecutors and flashed them an impudent wink.

It was an astonishing departure from the sober defendant who had sat through weeks of pretrial hearings with all the animation of an Easter Island stone head. Still, he didn't venture to glance in the direction of the victims who stared at him from their seats in the gallery, or the lawmen who glared from the jury box.

Judge Smith entered the room and the clerk called the proceedings to order. No one outside the defense team had heard Rudolph speak more than a few, perfunctory words at his previous court appearances. Now they would get an earful.

Eric Rudolph rose and shuffled to the podium, Judy Clarke at his side. He assumed an at-ease posture, legs parted, hands clasped behind his back as Judge Smith began to ask a perfunctory list of questions about his name, aliases, and understanding of the proceedings.

Michael Whisonant stood to read the charges against Rudolph. When he said Sande Sanderson's name, Felecia raised her chin slightly. Emily clasped Jeff's hand as Whisonant described her injuries.

"How do you plead?" asked the judge.

"Guilty, your honor."

Was he satisfied with his legal counsel?

"More than satisfied," Rudolph said. "They are very, very good, superlative lawyers."

Was his motion to withdraw his plea influenced by the withdrawal of his previous attorneys?

"No, it had nothing to do with it."

Now Rudolph had released himself from his military stance. He leaned on the podium with one arm, a perfect facsimile of a lawyer at the bar, always keeping one hand clenched behind his back, as if he were holding something in reserve.

He turned to face Whisonant, who began to read a summary review of the evidence against Rudolph. Whisonant looked even paler than usual, and like the rest of the prosecutors, he seemed subdued, even deflated. They had psyched themselves up for battle, and now suddenly there was nobody to fight. Rudolph, in contrast, seemed pumped and eager. He shook his head in agreement when the prosecutor said he was motivated by his hatred of abortion. And he rolled his eyes when Whisonant described items of evidence that Rudolph clearly found lacking.

When Judge Smith asked him if the prosecution had enough evidence to prove his guilt at trial, Rudolph smirked.

"Just barely, your honor."

Smith seemed stunned by the defendant's sudden cockiness. He snapped back, "Let me just cut to the chase. Did you plant the bomb that exploded at the New Woman All Women clinic?"

"I did, your honor."

Rudolph pulled himself back to attention and raised his chin, glancing sideways at Felecia Sanderson, who sat motionless below him.

"And did you cause that bomb to detonate?"

"I *certainly* did, your honor."

There was no mistaking the note of pride in his voice.

John Hawthorne had never pushed for the death penalty in this case, and he'd agreed to the plea bargain that withdrew the threat of execution. Now he stared up at this unrepentant man and wondered if he'd made a mistake. Hawthorne believed in redemption, and he was hoping to see at least a flicker of remorse in the killer's eyes, an acknowledgment of the suffering he'd caused. But Eric Rudolph gave him nothing. Fallon Stubbs leaned into her stepfather's shoulder and wept. After it was over, she gave a brief statement. "I came looking for a man today," she said. "I found a monster."

Rudolph was transported to Atlanta, where he entered his plea in those cases as well. Among the spectators in court was Richard Jewell, who now worked as a deputy sheriff in rural Georgia. Rudolph's confession had finally dispelled the last whiffs of suspicion that lingered around him. "Now everybody, the whole world, knows (Rudolph) did this," Jewell told a reporter. None of the victims spoke at these brief hearings. They would be given a chance to address the confessed bomber when he was formally sentenced later that summer. But Eric Rudolph was just beginning to have his say.

20

MANIFESTO

As the reporters and television producers filed out of the Atlanta courtroom, some members of the defense team handed them an eleven-page document titled "Statement of Eric Robert Rudolph April 13, 2005." It began:

"After much thought and consideration, I entered into an agreement with the government. After potentially facing 4 trials in 4 separate jurisdictions on circumstantial evidence that would likely lead to a conviction in at least one of these jurisdictions, I have deprived the government of its goal of sentencing me to death ..."

Most media commentators mentioned that quote and dismissed the rest of the statement as the incoherent ravings of a mad bomber. It was hardly that. In fact, this was the carefully reasoned manifesto that Eric Rudolph had been holding back for so many years while he waited for the right moment to be heard. What was most chilling about it was the cold logic of Rudolph's arguments as he explained his reasons for killing. It was a first glimpse into a remarkable and frightening mind, one that was now expressing itself as a legal tactician as well as a defender of Western civilization.

"Washington had two major facts that were difficult for us to overcome in this case," he continued.

First, was the fact that my truck was in Birmingham that morning, over a mile away from the scene. Even though the first, and chief witness's explanation as to what led him to my truck was highly vulnerable to our attack, there was another witness to contend with who helped him confirm the identity of the truck. Second, and most importantly was the fact that after I was identified I fled into the woods for five years and engaged the FBI in one of the most intensive and well publicized manhunts in history. Absent any corroborative fact or witness to explain why I was in Birmingham that day, a city I have never visited before, and a good reason for fleeing to the woods for five years, I was fighting an uphill battle. Add to these two paramount facts Washington's junk science about explosive residues, a media obsessed with the specter of right wing extremist violence, we had an extremely difficult case to win. But Washington had a problem and this is why they entered into this deal.

The problem that they had was that a significant minority of the population, especially here in Northern Alabama, regarded what happened there at the abortion facility on that day of January 29, 1998, as morally justified ... [The prosecutors] were afraid that in at least one jurisdiction they were going to run into [a] recalcitrant pro-life juror who would hang the jury and deliver a political defeat and embarrassment to Washington's efforts to make an example out of the person who assaulted their specially protected policy of child murder.... The fact that I have entered an agreement with the government is purely a tactical choice on my part and in no way legitimizes the moral authority of Washington's government to judge this matter or to impute guilt.

Here, at last, was Rudolph's stated motive: It was all about the unborn.

Abortion is murder. And when the regime in Washington legalized, sanctioned and legitimized this practice, they forfeited their legitimacy and moral authority to govern. At various times in history men and women of good conscience have had to decide when the lawfully constituted authorities have overstepped their moral bounds and forfeited their right to rule. This took place in July of 1776 when our

Forefathers decided that the British Crown had violated the essential rights of Englishmen, and therefore lost its authority to govern. And, in January of 1973 the government in Washington decided to descend into barbarism by sanctioning the ancient practice of infanticide and by that act consigned 50 million unborn children to their graves. There is no more legitimate reason to my knowledge, for renouncing allegiance to and if necessary using force to drag this monstrosity of a government down to the dust where it belongs.

Because I believe that abortion is murder, I also believe that force is justified … in an attempt to stop it. Because this government is committed to maintaining the policy of abortion, the agents of this government are the agents of mass murder, whether knowingly or unknowingly. And whether these agents of the government are armed or otherwise they are legitimate targets in the war to end this holocaust, especially those agents who carry arms in defense of this regime and the enforcement of its laws. This is the reason and the only reason for the targeting of so-called law enforcement personnel.

He continued to build his argument against abortion in passionate but familiar terms. But when he described the hypocrisy of his pro-life critics, his tone changed from argumentative to furious, and another persona emerged in his writing: Eric the Avenger.

You so-called "Pro-Life," "good Christian people" who point your plastic fingers at me saying that I am a "murderer," that "two wrongs don't make a right," that even though "abortion is murder, those who would use force to stop the murder are morally the same," I say to you that your lies are transparent. Tell me plastic people, are you not the ones waving the flag in support of the coward Bush's operation in Iraq? Do you not say that Washington's cause justifies the bombing and shooting of thousands of people? Answer me, is the *causus belli* of promoting democracy in the Middle East more weighty for waging war than the systematic murder of millions of your own citizens?

As the manifesto ground on, Rudolph turned to the other object of his ire, the "homosexual agenda." His feelings on the subject are an odd mixture of compassion and rage.

Along with abortion, another assault upon the integrity of American society is the concerted effort to legitimize the practice of homosexuality. Homosexuality is an aberrant sexual behavior, and as such I have complete sympathy and understanding for those who are suffering from this condition. Practiced by consenting adults within the confines of their own private lives, homosexuality is not a threat to society…. But when the attempt is made to drag this practice out of the closet and into the public square in an "in your face" attempt to force society to accept and recognize this behavior as being just as legitimate and normal as the natural man/woman relationship, every effort should be made, including force if necessary, to halt this effort.

…Whether it is gay marriage, homosexual adoption, hate crimes laws including gays, or the attempt to introduce a homosexual normalizing curriculum into our schools, all of these efforts should be ruthlessly opposed. The existence of our culture depends upon it.

At this point in his statement, Eric Rudolph offered the government what they could not extract from him in the plea deal. He decided to tell the world why he chose each of his targets and how he carried out his bombings. His descriptions are so detailed and revealing that they ought to be read unedited, in their entirety:

For many years I thought long and hard on these issues and then in 1996 I decided to act. In the summer of 1996, the world converged upon Atlanta for the Olympic Games. Under the protection and auspices of the regime in Washington millions of people came to celebrate the ideals of global socialism. Multinational corporations spent billions of dollars, and Washington organized an army of security to protect these best of all games. Even though the conception and purpose of the so-called Olympic movement is to promote the values of global socialism, as perfectly expressed in the song "Imagine" by John Lennon, which was the theme of the 1996 Games—even though the purpose of the Olympics is to promote these despicable ideals, the purpose of the attack on July 27th was to confound, anger and embarrass the Washington government in the eyes of the world for its abominable sanctioning of abortion on demand.

The plan was to force the cancellation of the Games, or at least create a state of insecurity to empty the streets around the venues and there by eat into the vast amounts of money invested. The plan was conceived in haste and carried out with limited resources, planning and preparation—it was a monster that kept getting out of control the more I got into it. Because I could not acquire the necessary high explosives, I had to dismiss the unrealistic notion of knocking down the power grid surrounding Atlanta and consequently pulling the plug on the Olympics for their duration.

The plan that I finally settled upon was to use five low-tech timed explosives to be placed one at a time on successive days throughout the Olympic schedule, each preceded by a forty to fifty minute warning given to 911. The location and time of detonation was to be given, and the intent was to thereby clear each of the areas, leaving only uniformed arms-carrying government personnel exposed to potential injury.

The attacks were to have commenced with the start of the Olympics, but due to a lack of planning this was postponed a week. I had sincerely hoped to achieve these objections without harming innocent civilians. However, I knew that the weapons used (highly uncontrollable timed explosives) and the choice of tactics (placing them in areas frequented by large numbers of civilians) could potentially lead to a disaster wherein many civilians could be killed or wounded. There is no excuse for this, and I accept full responsibility for the consequences of using this dangerous tactic.

The first and largest device was placed in Centennial Park. There was a 55 minute delay on the device. After placing the device it took approximately 10 minutes to walk to the telephone booth where a call was placed immediately. The 911 operator answered the call, and after acknowledging that she could understand my voice (I was using a little plastic contraption to disguise my voice), I proceeded to deliver my message and much to my chagrin the operator terminated the call.

I had to assume that the call had been traced and that in less than a few minutes a responder would be headed to that particular booth. So I walked approximately one block and frantically sought out a booth to make another call. I was not paying attention to the time as the minutes ticked off. Thinking perhaps the operator was put off by the sound of my distorted voice coming through the plastic device, I ditched the contraption and sought out a booth by the Days Inn where I then tried to deliver a clear message while holding my nose. The crowd was pushing in and after the first couple sentences, I was eyeballed closely by at least two individuals. This caused me to leave off the last sentence which indicated the exact location of the device. The result of all this was to produce a disaster—a disaster of my making and for which I do apologize to the victims and their families.

This second call that was made is the only one that has been made public. Unfortunately, Washington's government has not released all of the recordings of the 911 calls made within the hours before the blast. If they had, the public would discover that a call was made from the immediate area approximately 40 to 45 minutes before the blast. The call began with the words, "Do you understand me?" After an acknowledgment by the operator the message began: "We defy your ..." and at this point the call was terminated.

After the blast and the consequent chaos, I decided to discontinue the operation. I hurried back to the vacant lot I had used as a staging area which was east of Atlanta on I-20. Off to the right side of the interstate is what appeared to be a huge vacant lot with woods and bulldozing excavations, perhaps the place where a mall would be erected. Amid the piles of illegal garbage dumpings, I primed and detonated the other four devices and left Atlanta with much remorse.

After the disaster at Centennial Park, I resolved to improve my devices and focus the blasts upon a very narrow target. Towards this end I acquired a quantity of high explosives (dynamite). I shaped the charges in order to minimize the potential range of their destruction. However, I was still using clock timers which put the detonation outside of my control, thus leaving room for the same kind of disaster that occurred at the Park. Fortunately this did not happen and my intended targets were the only ones placed in jeopardy from that point on.

Two attacks were carried out in the winter of 1997. The first in January was an abortion mill (Northside Family Planning). The second was a homosexual establishment (The Otherside Lounge). The abortion mill was closed that day but occasionally there was staff on hand to clean their blood-stained equipment, and these minions and the facility itself were the targets of the first device. The second device placed at the scene was designed to target agents of the Washington government.

The next attack in February was at The Otherside Lounge. Like the assault at the abortion mill, two devices used. The first device was designed not necessarily to target the patrons of this homosexual bar, but rather to set the stage for the next device, which was again targeted at Washington's agents. The attack itself was meant to send a powerful message in protest of Washington's continued tolerance and support for the homosexual political agenda.

Despite the inherent dangers involved in timed devices, all of these devices used in both of these assaults functioned within the parameters of the plan, and I make no apologies.

After laying low for a year, I succeeded in making operational a command-detonated focused device that would greatly reduce the risk for harming innocent civilians when carrying out these operations. Over a million human beings had died in the past year, and as the anniversary of Roe v. Wade approached, the idea was to send yet another message to the killers and those who protected them.

Birmingham and that particular abortion mill were chosen purely for tactical reasons. The city was a sufficient distance away from any location I was known to have frequented. Three abortion mills were looked at in Birmingham, none of which I truly liked for a target. New Woman All Women was tactically the least objectionable.

This facility routinely kills and mutilates an average of 50 human beings every week. Every employee is a knowing participant in this gruesome trade. The security guard is instrumental in protecting these murderers and their facility from those who would intervene to stop this bloody practice, and therefore he is on the front lines of this fight. The object was to target the doctor-killer, but because the device was prematurely discovered by the security guard, it had to be detonated with only the assistant-killers in the target area. A protester was across the street, and customers waiting to have their child killed were in the parking lot just yards away, but because of the focused nature of the device and being command-detonated, only the killers were caught in the blast zone ...

Rudolph went on to say that he has "nothing personal against Lyons and Sanderson. They were targeted for what they did, not who they were as individuals."

This was news to Emily Lyons, whose suffering was extremely personal. She declared herself "nauseated" by the plea bargain and Rudolph's statement. Felecia Sanderson reserved her comments for the sentencing hearing, scheduled in July.

Although Rudolph was clearly behind the Birmingham bombing and the two similar attacks in Atlanta, until this detailed confession, even some of his defense lawyers doubted he had bombed the Olympics. The only direct evidence tying him to the crime was the ambiguous 911 tape. The type of device used in the bombing and the target itself were so different from the subsequent attacks that it was possible to believe that a different, or at least another, bomber was involved. And so Rudolph's revelation that he had made another call to 911 that night was a shock to everyone involved in the case. If the call was taped, nobody had noticed it in the discovery materials.

As soon as Rudolph released his statement, FBI agents went back to the 911 center in Atlanta, where all the raw tapes are stored, and listened to the earlier calls. It was there. At 12:46 A.M., thirty-four minutes before the bomb exploded in Centennial Olympic Park, a tinny male voice asked the operator, "Can you understand me?" When she said yes, he continued, "You defy the order of the militia ..." Before he could finish the sentence, the operator hung up.

Nobody in the government has been able to explain how this vital piece of evidence was overlooked. The FBI spent more than $20 million on the manhunt and tens of millions more on the investigation. Agents were able to identify and trace the movements of thousands of spectators in Centennial Park, almost to the minute, cross referencing them with photographs and audiotapes, in one of the most detailed, expensive, and impressive feats of police work in the history of law enforcement. But for some unfathomable reason, nobody had bothered to transcribe all the 911 calls that evening, so nobody noticed that the bomber called 911 twice.

When I asked U.S. attorney Dave Nahmias about it, he said, "We had all the 911 calls, and they were in discovery. We were not aware of the call, but once we learned about it we went and found it. And it was there as he had said. I don't know why they missed that. You never know."

Rudolph's attorneys and investigators in Atlanta also missed the call. Paul Kish told me that the first time he'd heard about it was also in Rudolph's statement. The Atlanta team might have discovered it if their case had moved to trial, or maybe not.

Along with the revelation about the 911 call, Rudolph's April manifesto contained a number of other surprises for federal investigators. Key agents such as the FBI's Danny Sindall and the ATF's C. J. Hyman, who led the ground searches, operated under the assumption that Rudolph would not, as Sindall put it, "go on the offensive." But according to Rudolph, he had considered attacking the command post in Andrews, and came within inches of blowing up the National Guard Armory at Murphy. Again, Eric Rudolph tells the story in his own words.

Washington was lucky that day in Birmingham, they had a witness who happened into a fortuitous position, and my truck was identi-

fied. I knew something was amiss based upon the early reports coming out of Birmingham so I prepared to make a move as I debated
within myself whether or not to run or fight them in court. I chose
the woods.

The next year was a starving time. Hunted and haggard, I struggled to survive. But I am a quick study, and so I learned to adapt to
my situation. I adapted so well, I decided to take the fight to my
enemies.

I then planned to strike the FBI headquarters in Andrews in the
summer of 1999. But after a summer devoting most of my time to
gathering food, I was never able to put together the necessary equipment to accomplish my plan. It had to be put off. In the meantime
the FBI presence shrunk from a large headquarters with helicopters
and hundreds of agents, down to a tiny office in the national guard
armory in Murphy.

The new plan called for an attack in the fall of 2000. I had stockpiled a large supply of food that would sustain me for many years
in the mountains, and I was now ready to concentrate my energies
exclusively on the plan. The equipment was located many miles away
on the border of Tennessee. After some effort I had managed to cob-
ble together an effective device and move it to the ridge overlooking
the FBI headquarters in Murphy.

The initial plan was to steal a truck, transport the device to Asheville, and attack an abortion mill before the presidential election. This
plan fell through when the truck used was not capable of driving two
miles let alone 200. The election slipped away and I fell back upon
my original target—the agents at the armory.

A circuitous getaway was then laid out. Two secondary booby
traps were placed on the trail to discourage and delay any possible
pursuers. The agents were pigeon-holed, their schedules noted to the
minute. Finally, the device was moved into place and as the agents
approached the door that morning, the final decision had to be made.
The agents didn't die that day. Perhaps after watching them for so
many months their individual humanity [had] shown through the
hated uniform. It was not that I had lost my resolve to fight in the

defense of the unborn, but rather an individual decision about these individual agents. I had worn the uniform of their legions, served in their ranks, I had no hatred for them as individuals. Even though they served a morally bankrupt government, underneath their FBI rags, they were essentially fellow countrymen.

The device was removed the next day and buried upon the ridge across the interstate where it has recently been unearthed by these same agents. The booby traps were highly sensitive, and a render safe line was built into the system when they were put into place. Not wanting to approach them again, I detonated them and removed the remaining debris.

The next three years were spent living a fairly comfortable routine, which involved mostly hunting and camp life. After so many years ducking and hiding and eating crappy foods you tend to let your guard down, and this is what led to my capture in Murphy in 2003. It has been a long journey up to this point, but I still have a ways to go.

When I was in the woods I used a small dugout underneath a rock to avoid helicopters and their heat sensitive equipment. One cold day in December of 1998 I huddled underneath the rock for half an hour as the chopper slowly hovered overhead scanning the ridge. The whir of his blades became less audible and finally he was over the ridge, and then there was silence. I climbed out of my hide brushing off the icy dirt and remembered thinking about the words of the Psalmist who wrote about seeing his enemies in "great power, spreading his branches and roots like a large tree," but after a little while he looked and beheld his enemies were "nowhere to be found." In defiance I looked toward the ridge over which the chopper had just gone and said, "I am still here."

And now after the agreement has been signed the talking heads on the news opine that I am "finished," that I will "languish broken and unloved in the bowels of some supermax," but I say to you people that by the grace of God I am still here—a little bloodied, but emphatically unbowed.

* * *

Danny Sindall told me there were only two agents regularly working out of the Murphy armory in the fall of 2000, and he was one of them. And so it is likely that Eric Rudolph watched him for weeks, maybe months, and somehow grew to know him. Maybe Rudolph was only involved with the agents in the way a boy might become attached to his plastic army men. Or maybe it had become personal, after all.

Sindall and his fellow agents still wanted to talk to Rudolph. They had an overwhelming curiosity about him, not to mention a professional interest in his techniques. The profilers at Quantico wanted a crack at him, too. But Rudolph wasn't interested in talking to federal agents. He was sitting in his cell in the Jefferson County Jail furiously unloading all the stories he had held inside for so long onto sheets of lined paper and sending them to his lawyers, to his mother, and to me.

21

THE TIPPING POINT OF VIOLENCE

Patricia Rudolph maintained her faith in her son's innocence right up to the moment that a junior member of the defense team arrived at her apartment on a Friday afternoon. "I'm afraid I have some really hard news for you to swallow," she told her.

"I felt my whole life stop, right then," said Pat.

Nobody had told her a thing about the plea deal until it was over. Eric had never given her a clue, except perhaps unconsciously. When she'd finally had a chance to hug him during her last jail visit, she felt him tense up, as if he were holding something back. But he never discouraged her from believing he was being framed for the bombings. Now she was angry and bewildered and immersed with regret. "I don't know why he did it. I can see and understand some of it. But that never justifies taking someone's life," she said. "I felt just terrible about all the people who were hurt."

She had to take a critical look at herself, to see what she did wrong. "It is hard to forgive, particularly oneself," she said. "All of this shows you can never truly know another person's heart. Even your own."

Pat Rudolph continues to search for her perfect "rainbow" church. These days she describes her faith as more spiritual than religious. But she still believes in the Holy Ghost, and the gift of grace.

The rest of his family cut Eric off, but Pat continued to write. A few weeks after his confession, Rudolph sent her a sentimental card with a preprinted message that read: "I'm thankful, for countless reasons, that

God brought you into my life. Happy Mother's Day with all my love …"
He signed it: "Your wayward son, Eric R. Rudolph."

The letters Rudolph sent to his mother offered the first public glimpse of
his hidden life. (To his great irritation she shared them with a reporter
from *USA Today*, which published excerpts before Rudolph's final sentencing.) His lawyer Bill Bowen later sent around e-mails containing
polished versions of his writings to people on his correspondence list.

In my letters I asked Rudolph whether he was living in the woods the whole
time he was on the run, and if he had sometimes used seasonal cabins for
shelter in the winter months. It was one of many questions he declined to
answer. But he did solve a mystery for me and for Alan Hawkins, the
owner and operator of the Tirezans tire shop next to the Murphy armory.

I drove up to western North Carolina a few days after Rudolph's
dynamite caches were blown up *in situ* around Cherokee County. Although the TV crews had moved on, the town of Murphy was still buzzing with the news of Rudolph's plea bargain. I parked my car at the stone
quarry on Tomotla Road, just east of town, and walked up an orange
dirt track to the crest of a narrow ridge. There was a campfire ring near
the top where the track split off into a footpath through thick trees. A
two-minute walk off the trail led to a large, raw gash in the dirt where
the explosives experts had set off Rudolph's dynamite. It was easy to find
the spot where Rudolph sat with his binoculars and watched the federal
agents come and go from the armory, where he planned their murders
and then decided to let them live. The ridge offered a perfect yet concealed view of the parking lot across the highway, and an equally good
view of the tire shop next to it. I climbed down the hill and drove over
there to ask if anybody had witnessed the demolition.

Alan Hawkins is a sociable man in his late thirties with a full head
of light brown hair combed back from his forehead. He wiped the axle
grease from his hands with a shop rag as he described the highway patrol
roadblock and the blast that rattled the walls of his business. Hawkins
is slightly older than Rudolph and had met him in passing years back.
He followed the case closely. In fact he had read the text of Rudolph's

manifesto in the local newspaper, and it made him wonder: Rudolph mentioned stealing a truck to drive a bomb to the abortion clinic in Asheville, but the plan fell through when the truck couldn't get him there. Hawkins thought maybe this explained the mysterious events of Halloween weekend, 2000.

That fall Hawkins had a red 1970 Chevy pickup in good condition for sale in the front of his lot, displayed behind the chain-link fence that surrounded his property. The shop is closed on Sundays, and the metal gate locked. It was still locked on that Monday morning the red Chevy was parked outside the fence. When he looked closely, he could see that somebody had meticulously cut through the steel mesh, removed the truck, and replaced the fence panel, bending the wires back in place so that nobody would notice anything unusual. There was no obvious damage to the body, but the ignition had been torn up as if to hotwire the truck. And when Hawkins got it started again the engine seized up: he suspected that somebody had put diesel fuel in the tank that was designed to take gasoline.

Hawkins reported the theft to the police, but he says they didn't do anything more than take a statement. But when he read Rudolph's manifesto, Hawkins put two and two together. There was only about a gallon of gas in the tank, and he figured that if Rudolph stole the truck he might have filled it up with a fuel can he'd found at a construction site—which would likely be diesel. When it was taken, the gas gauge had been a hair above empty. Now it was a quarter full. It took Hawkins days to clean out the engine and get the truck back on the road.

"If you ever talk to Rudolph, ask him if he was the one who took the truck," Hawkins asked me. "And if it was him, I'll bet you he won't admit he put in the wrong fuel. He doesn't seem like the type who wants to admit a mistake."

So I wrote to Rudolph and asked him if he had "borrowed" the truck from the tire shop next to the armory.

"The tire store fellow is correct," he replied.

The truck I refer to in the statement is one and the same. As I remember it, the truck was an orange 67 Chevy with mag wheels and a serious timing problem. The plan was to use it to transport me and my device to Asheville (Oct 2000) and hit an abortion mill before the presidential election.

I hotwired the truck, cut an opening in the fencing that surrounds the place and drove it out onto the highway. The truck was a piece of crap. It was loud and severely out of time, backfiring and wheezing down the road. The lights wouldn't work until I pounded on the dashboard, creating a connection. I barely made it to the staging area where there was a stockpile of siphoned gas, food and, of course, the device. After a great deal of hushed cursing I concluded that the thing wouldn't make it out to Asheville. The truck was driven back to the tire shop and I parked it outside of the gate.

I took this as a bad omen and decided that the Asheville operation was too complicated. This left option number two—the agents at the armory.

If you talk to the tire store fellow again, tell him I'm sorry for damaging the wiring in order to hot wire it.

I corresponded with Eric Rudolph for the rest of the spring and summer. What was most striking about his letters was his mild, polite, generally formal tone—and the fact that he never asked me a single question about myself or the book project. He wanted me to send lists of specific questions about his background and his beliefs, although he cautioned me he wouldn't go into any detail about the bombings. He held out the possibility of a phone call or in-person visit, but said that he was more "comfortable" writing his answers. This format kept our dialogue orderly and professional. I learned a few things about his childhood, his techniques for cultivating marijuana, and his taste in music: Although he preferred Bach, he was raised on classic rock, and found himself "tapping my feet if I hear 'Hotel California' or 'Honky Tonk Woman.'" But I was most interested in hearing what turned him into a bomber. It was hard to find the right way to phrase this without aggravating him, so I asked:

Was there a moment of revelation or an event—in the popular phrase, a "tipping point"—that transformed belief into action?

There was no one experience, incident or "tipping point" that caused me to act in the way I did. Most people, it is true, make their life choices based upon emotional reactions to their experiences. And, of course, I'm influenced by momentary experiences, and sometimes I act upon them. But most of the time I thoroughly consider any major decisions that will affect my life. This goes doubly so for the decisions that have led me to here. The decision to act was the result of many years of my being confronted with the decline of Western Civilization and the realization that only radical action would slow or halt this decline. Abortion is the most glaring example of this decline. And like most people, I have been personally confronted with the horror of abortion; however, this particular experience was just another brick in an extensive wall, not a tipping point.

You mentioned in your letter to me that you've been "personally confronted with the horror of abortion." Would you be willing to explain what you mean? Was it a girlfriend of yours?

My ex-girlfriend [he never told me which one] had a close acquaintance who had an abortion. I can still remember the sense of hollowness, the atmosphere of indifference that surrounded her "choice." It was the kind of rotten, superficial, amoral feeling that MTV specializes in promoting. I felt dirty and wanted to wash the "cool," "hip" indifference off me with a Brillo pad.

Many people feel passionately about injustice and see the horrors of this world; few go beyond writing checks or carrying placards. I suppose what I am most interested in learning is how you reached that point where you could no longer stand by as an observer. What makes you different from the rest of us who do not act?

First, I will try to answer your overriding question: why did I act in the way that I did, and why don't others act in a similar manner. I acted because I actually believe in the ideas contained in my statement and allocution. I operate my life based upon my ideals. The ideas I believe in are not unique to me; they are indeed professed by millions. The difference between me and them is merely a matter of consistency, method and means. They believe that my methods are not warranted or justified by the circumstances. On the other hand, I believe that legal remedies have been exhausted and that if armed struggle is ever justified, it is certainly justified to end abortion.

The real question is not why I acted the way I did, but rather why the majority of so-called pro-lifers <u>don't</u> act in a similar manner ... My actions were wholly consistent with my beliefs. After being imprisoned for abolitionist activities, Thoreau was visited in prison by his friend, Emerson. Emerson asked him why he was in prison, and Thoreau said, "For anti-slavery actions, of course. The real question, Emerson, is why aren't you in here with me?" This sums up my position.

You've written that abortion is the most glaring example of the decline of Western Civilization. What are some of the others?

The problems threatening Western Civilization are too numerous to list here, but here are a few. Generally all that now parades under the leftist banner is pathological, especially where it touches upon domestic cultural social issues: The homosexual agenda, multiculturalism, diversity, the counter-culture, gun-control, Feminism, anti-Christianity, affirmative action and racial quotas, socialism, liberalism, Marxism, Pacifism, the destruction of the family, dissolution of the small family farm.

However, economically I share many things in common with the Left: Job protection, protectionism for industry, universal health care and college education, and most things that would fall under the populist banner ...

Oswald Spengler wrote, "Every act alters the soul of the doer." With that in mind, how are you different now from the person you were ten years ago?

Before I acted I had choices, options, retreats to explore in my life. After I crossed that line, my life has become unequivocal, my choices limited. This has focused my energies on a limited range of choices. Consequently, I approach my decisions more seriously, as if they are fate-laden. It is kind of like a cancer patient with a limited time to live: he doesn't have time to deal with things casually.

Rudolph was just getting warmed up. Between May and August of 2005 he was busy writing two lengthy academic essays. The first, titled "Pacifism," expanded some of the themes he touched on his manifesto and his letters to me. It is essentially a 135-page justification of the use of force to achieve righteous ends. In it, Rudolph derides the practice of nonviolent resistance as naïve and hypocritical.

"Eric denounced everything Bob and I stood for," said his mother, Pat, who has always considered herself a pacifist. "But then he always was contrary."

Later that summer I opened my e-mail inbox and found another of his essays, again forwarded by his lawyer, Bill Bowen. This one was titled "Pyrrhic Victories: The Problems with American Policy in Iraq." It was eighty-six pages long, including the table of contents and a three-color map of Iraq that included strategic features such as airfields and rail lines. The essay was surprising in a number of ways. By now I expected Rudolph's writings to be cogent and well-argued. But this essay's contents and references were so mainstream that I would never have guessed its author without a title page. It could easily be the product of a Ph.D. candidate at Pepperdine University, or maybe an undergraduate at George Mason. Rudolph does not appear to view world history as a sinister conspiracy orchestrated by powerful, hidden forces, which is the hallmark of the paranoid right. Instead he sees it as a round-robin of endless aggression, a Nietzschean struggle between the weak and the powerful.

So what is Rudolph's advice for George W. Bush? Pay attention to history. Avoid pulling out of Iraq and exhibiting weakness, although that scenario is probably inevitable, given the treacherous nature of the liberal elite who are determined to undermine the war effort.

The story of the war will be told by the victor. And the victor in this war, as in Vietnam, is the little leftist agitator, the college professor, news reporter and congressman who sabotaged the war effort.

This may sound harsh, but it's really standard fare for someone like Rush Limbaugh, who, incidentally is regularly broadcast to the troops on American Forces Radio. Rudolph makes his own appeal to those same troops, warning them that the liberal elite is not worth defending:

If I would tell you anything, it is that this leftist subversive is not worth dying for. To fight for those who will ultimately spit on your grave and build you a long, black, somber monument symbolizing the futility of your sacrifices is not worth it. Your true enemies are right here at home: in the universities, in the newsrooms, in the Hollywood studios, and in the halls of Congress.

One of the often-repeated stories about Rudolph's brief school career was that he shocked his ninth grade teacher by turning in a history paper denying the Holocaust. So I asked him about it, and added:

Was there a time when you admired Hitler and agreed with his beliefs? Do you now? Have your views of Judaism evolved over time?

All of my views evolve over time, including my views of Judaism. But even with this evolution, at no point have I ever hated Jews as has been reported in the press. Because they refused to assimilate Jews were persecuted in the West for centuries. After the Second World War and the establishment of the state of Israel, much of this hostility has disappeared. Even so one still sees the same hatred. The recent attacks by such hate groups at the ADL [Anti-Defamation League] on Mel Gibson's The Passion of the Christ are evidence that the old hatreds have not completely died. That said, the Jews and the West now have shared interests which tend to push them together rather than push them apart …

Most of the news reports that pegged me as a Nazi are based

upon information provided by people—Debbie Givens, Claire For-
rester, military people—who are not capable of understanding my
beliefs. It's as simple as that. I will readily admit that my views on
WWII are not orthodox but that are far from being pro-Nazi.... No
one person is more responsible for the lamentable conditions that
now prevail throughout the world than Adolf Hitler ... The Nazi
ideology of race, its Weltanschauung, was a pile of wrong-headed
crap. Applied to Europe during Hitler's brief reign, it was a mon-
strous disaster....

These questions touched on some of Rudolph's most passionate beliefs, and his answer went on for seventeen pages. Essentially, he blames
Hitler for dragging Germany into a war that destroyed Europe and
pushed Western civilization toward ruin. As to denying the Holocaust:
He acknowledges the horrors of the Nazi slave labor camps, and he says
he does not agree with the opinions of David Irving, the British academic who was recently arrested in Austria for challenging the histori-
cal fact that the Nazis planned the extermination of Jews and carried it
out in gas chambers. But he is infuriated that Irving is being silenced
because he "threatens the established world view and the political struc-
tures built around that view." Again, it is the hypocrisy of "liberals" that
angers Rudolph.

He has a theory about why he has been so often misunderstood:

My reading over the years has probably caused many people to
get the wrong idea about me and what it is exactly that I believe. I
read topics until I exhaust my interest in them and then I move on.
At times I will read only Civil War material, at others only colonial
period stuff. Now I am reading about feminism—Betty Freidan and
Kate Millett. Twenty years ago, when I was in the military, I spent a
great deal of time reading about the Second World War, especially
the European theatre. While other soldiers would pound beer and
watch television in their spare time, I would lay in my barracks bunk
reading something like the war memoirs of Erich von Monstein,
Lost Victory. Add to this my taste for out of the ordinary WWII lit-

erature, my foolish attempts to discuss my interests with whomever would listen and I quickly got a reputation as a Nazi lover. But simply because I spent an inordinate amount of time reading a particular topic didn't mean I shared the opinions of those I was reading about. I was no more a Nazi then than I am a feminist today.

There were a few other questions I wanted to clear up. There had been some speculation about his continuing relationship and possible collaboration with Tom Branham. He tried to put this to rest:

> Tom and our family were among a small group of non-locals living in Nantahala in the early 80's. The majority of the people were long-time natives whose families go back hundreds of years. Because we lived right next door to each other, and because I had once lived in Tom's house, the locals had always considered us to be family members. To the locals, we were "Florida people," "foreigners." When the case broke in '98 the locals kept telling the feds that Tom must be a co-conspirator helping me hide. The feds finally exhausted this line of inquiry after a few months, but it still persists in public perception. Actually, once we moved next door, Tom and our family kept our own space.
>
> He was a friend for many years and I look back fondly on those times we spent together. But ideologically we share very little in common. Tom cares very little about anything beyond his six acres. The fate of our civilization is something completely alien to his sensibilities.

Have you been influenced by the writing of Francis Parker Yockey?

> I've read his book, but I wouldn't say that he is a significant influence on me.

You've said that you are not a racist. How would you define "racist"? Do your beliefs prohibit mixing the races?

My definition of a racist is Lance Armstrong. He still dominates after seven tours. There is no such thing as race in a concrete sense; race is a subjective generalization based upon continually changing population shifts. The "races" have been mixing since the beginnings of time and it would be foolish to assume that a "race" can remain static and pure.

Is there truly such a thing as the Army of God or the Phineas Priesthood?

I have never heard of the Phineas Priesthood. The Army of God is an idea not an organization. Anybody who believes that force is justified to end abortion is a member of the AOG.

It is hard to believe that someone as well read in so many areas would never have heard about the Phineas Priesthood, a loose affiliation of violent extremists who have made headlines for the past two decades. Byron De La Beckwith, the assassin of Medgar Evers, belonged to this fraternity. So did Buford Furrow, the skinhead who shot up a group of preschoolers at a Jewish community center. And Paul Hill, the anti-abortion assassin whose case Rudolph studied closely, had written about his affinity for the Phineas Priesthood.

Rudolph's definition of the Army of God is less ingenuous. It is as much a state of mind as an association, and if its adherents were to organize themselves in a meaningful way they would be indicted for conspiracy. There are, however, a number of agitators who claim to speak for the Army of God. And one of them, the Reverend Donald Spitz, had been corresponding with Eric Rudolph in jail. In fact he was included on Bill Bowen's e-mail list, and all of Rudolph's public writings were being posted on his own homepage, among the bloody pictures of dismembered fetuses, on Spitz's website: www.armyofgod.com.

22

TRUE BELIEVERS

The New Woman All Women clinic reopened one week after it was bombed in 1998. The disrupted appointments were all rescheduled. The clinic has been back in business ever since, providing reproductive health care services that include birth control support, adoption referrals, counseling, and, on three mornings each week, legal abortions. On the days when there are abortions, there are also protesters.

Minzor Chadwick is a constant fixture on the sidewalk across from the clinic. He was at his usual spot when Rudolph detonated the bomb, although, since he is legally blind, he didn't see anything of use to the FBI. When I met him he was sixty-three years old, with thin, straw-colored hair and a strangely young face. He has never been married and he had not held a job in many years. He wore comfortable shoes and carried a small backpack stuffed with packets of yellowing anti-abortion literature held together with rubber bands. By law, Chadwick can't force these pamphlets into the hands of a patient or do anything to block her way. Instead he positions himself as close as he can get to the entrance so that the women can see his pièce de résistance: a large, laminated color photograph of a bloody seven-month-old fetus with his head ripped off. As they approach he unfurls his picture while screaming: "Don't kill me, Mama!" Then he carefully refolds it again. Chadwick has been doing this for almost twenty years. Although he is aggressive, he has never crossed the line into violence. He knew Sande Sanderson and says Sanderson was a nice man who always treated him with respect. Chadwick thinks that what Eric Rudolph did has hurt the cause of saving babies. So does David Lackey, Chadwick's mentor and the local representative of Operation Save America, formerly known as Operation Rescue.

I met Lackey for the first time one busy morning of protests outside the New Woman All Women clinic. Lackey is a tall man in his forties with bright yellow hair and a trim beard. That morning he was dressed in a black motorcycle jumpsuit and dark aviator shades. He stood on Seventeenth Street next to his enormous Honda Valkyrie freeway cruiser and spoke loudly into his flip phone, working out details of an impending trip to Amsterdam. When a teenage girl and her mother walked up to the door of the clinic, Lackey interrupted his conversation to shout, "Don't kill your baby! Don't let her do it, Grandma!" The mother glared at Lackey as she ushered the frightened girl inside. When the door closed, Lackey resumed his call where he had left off. I eventually caught his attention and asked a few questions.

"I was out here about an hour after the bombing, doing media," Lackey told me. He wanted people to know that he and his organization did not condone murder. Lackey was called to testify before the federal grand jury that indicted Rudolph. He has always denied any knowledge of the attack and says he has never met Eric Rudolph. His message has been consistent over the years. "We certainly deplore the violence that goes on in this clinic, we certainly don't think these babies ought to be killed," said Lackey. "But killing someone else to stop it doesn't accomplish anything."

Saturday is the biggest day for anti-abortion actions in Birmingham. Often several dozen people show up to protest, including a regular contingent of Catholics led by Franciscan Missionaries of the Eternal Word. This morning two dozen of the Catholics arrived in a prayerful procession, following a large rustic cross draped with an agonized carving of Jesus. For the next hour they stood or knelt passively in front of the clinic, praying for the souls within. The other protesters were more belligerent, but none of them tried to stop anyone from entering. Only a handful I spoke to would even consider the use of force to end abortion. In other words, they were precisely the kind of pro-lifers that Eric Rudolph claims to despise.

* * *

Eric Rudolph's Army of God web page lists a phone number for its host, the Reverend Donald Spitz, so I called and left a message. He called back a few weeks later. He had just returned, he said, from a trip to Israel. According to Spitz, a Pentecostal minister from Virginia, the Army of God is a "belief system" more than a true organization. Some members want to be identified and others don't. He told me he had reached out to Rudolph in jail, "because of what he did. He is on the same page as me." They sent some letters back and forth, and Spitz started posting Rudolph's writings on the website. He objected when I asked him if he supports the use of violence to end abortion. "There's a difference between violence and force," he told me. Violence is random while force is directed to a goal. "The use of force is justified to save a born baby," he said, "so it's also justified to save unborn babies." And that is all you need to believe to be a member of the Army of God.

Spitz himself has never used lethal force to stop abortions. "God calls people to do different things," he has said. Apparently God called Reverend Spitz to serve as a cheerleader and coat holder for some of the most violent anti-abortion extremists to emerge in the past decades. He maintains websites for them while they are in prison or, in the cases of Paul Hill and John Salvi III, dead. Among them are Shelly Shannon, a founding member of the Army of God who is serving time in Kansas for shooting a doctor in the arms, and the sniper-assassin James Kopp, a Catholic extremist who murdered Dr. Barnett Slepian in front of his family in suburban Buffalo, New York, in 1998. There is Clayton Waagner, a Christian terrorist in prison for sending 550 hoax letters containing phony anthrax powder to women's clinics and pro-choice leaders around the country. Spitz even has a page dedicated to Stephen Jordi, who is in prison for plotting to bomb abortion clinics, although he never got the chance to carry out his plans. He had told an FBI informant that he wanted to emulate Eric Rudolph.

Rudolph's web page, like the others at armyofgod.com, is adorned with a link inviting visitors to "click here" to "view helpless babies murdered by BABYKILLING ABORTIONISTS." The viewer is then transported to a gallery of gruesome color photos of dismembered fetuses, some of which appear to be stillborn infants—one with a hospital band still on its wrist. Their little limbs, guts, torsos, and faces are shown scattered in grotesque tableaux. Some of them are famous images, repeatedly enlarged to make huge posters like the ones protesters like to wave in front of clinics. The pictures are a kind of fetus porn, in which the dead are deprived of their dignity and humanity to become fetishes for adults with ugly and dark urges.

Psychologists and sociologists have made much of the anti-abortion extremists' obsessive focus on dismembered fetuses. Carol Mason, in *Killing for Life: The Apocalyptic Narrative of Pro-life Politics*, advances the theory that fear and hatred of women motivates anti-abortion fanaticism. She cites the writings of a convicted clinic bomber, John Brockhoeft, who visualized himself as an aborted fetus to prepare himself for violent action: "My skull will be crushed until fragments of my skull cave inward and cut into my brain," he wrote. "It would hurt so bad!" He fantasized about his right arm being torn from his torso, and the pain and terror of seeing it gone, with blood gushing out of the empty socket. It doesn't take a Ph.D. to guess which appendage the bomber was unconsciously afraid of losing. "The fantasy of being aborted can be said to be derived from deeply rooted psychological fears," she writes. Mason also makes much of the fact that Eric Rudolph's brother, Daniel, cut off his hand on videotape to protest his family's persecution by the FBI and the media in a grisly enactment of the mutilation fantasy.

There are as many perspectives on the roots of clinic violence as there are social theorists who study it, but they all seem to agree that anti-abortion extremism is not entirely about abortion. Dallas Blanchard, an expert on the religious right, ascribes it to a kind of toxic moralism. He writes that, among other things, "the desire to control the behavior of others underlies the anti-abortion movement." Frustration fuels the violence.

Former FBI special agent Kathleen Puckett agrees that Eric Rudolph was not motivated to kill by his hatred of abortion. His pathology, she says, is much more complicated. But at its heart is a gnawing loneliness to belong.

Puckett spent twenty-three years with the FBI studying the behavior of spies, serial killers, and terrorists. She was never a part of what she calls the "profiling unit" at Quantico, although she often worked side by side with its members. She operated "on the other side of the house, the quiet side of the bureau," as a behavioral expert in the counterintelligence and counterterrorism divisions in San Francisco and Washington. In 1994 Puckett, who is tall, blond, and ebullient, joined the UNABOM Task Force and began working closely with Terry Turchie and Joel Moss. After Kaczynski was captured, she read and analyzed everything he'd ever written. This included the thousands of pages of diaries, some written in code, that were found in his cabin. He kept meticulous records of every thought that ran through his head, and every move he made. ("More than you want to know ..." Puckett said with a chuckle.) Turchie later brought her into the Rudolph case on temporary duty to help advise him in the fugitive hunt. For years she had put herself through graduate school at night, eventually earning a Ph.D. in clinical psychology. When Turchie was sent to Washington in 2000 to head the counterterrorism division, he assigned Puckett to produce a study on the phenomenon of "lone offenders." Eric Rudolph was still at large, and Turchie wanted a comparative psychological analysis of the types of individuals like Rudolph, Kaczynski, Tim McVeigh, and others who were capable of causing the American public and the FBI so much grief. He gave her ninety days to do it. She got it done in six months. It was printed up and delivered to FBI headquarters in September 2001.

I had been hearing about the existence of a lone offender study since I began researching the Rudolph case, but I could never find a copy of it. It had been classified as "law enforcement sensitive" and shelved somewhere in the back offices of the FBI. Both Turchie and Puckett retired from the FBI at the end of 2001; Terry Turchie landed a job as the director of security and counterterrorism at the Lawrence Livermore Laboratory in Berkeley, and Kathy Puckett came along as his deputy. By the end of 2001 the bureau not only had a new director, it had become fixated with fighting international terrorism in the aftermath of 9–11. Studies of domestic terrorists were considered low priority.

Puckett, though, was able to talk about some aspects of her orphaned study, which was commissioned within the FBI as an aid to local law enforcement agencies. As far as she knows, not many have seen it. Puck-ett assures me that it is only a matter of time before another Rudolph or McVeigh emerges on domestic soil. In fact the "Anthrax Killer" who surfaced after the September 11 attacks most likely belongs in this fra-ternity. And though he has gone dormant, he is still probably at large. Certainly other lone offenders are out there. Luckily they are extremely rare.

"Thank God there were only ten people in my study," said Puckett. "Not many people can live five years in the woods, or twenty-five years in a cabin, building bombs. This is a very hard thing to be. It requires a lot of dedication."

Puckett reviewed all cases the FBI had investigated as domestic ter-rorism or hate crimes and narrowed her subjects down by certain criteria. "The group sorted itself out by psychological and behavioral factors," said Puckett. Other than the fact that they were all white males, they appeared to have little in common except their crimes. Until you looked into their histories. "They all were very different on the surface, but they all shared very similar psychological characteristics. Social isolation or rejection was a constant in the developmental history of all of them. They all desperately wanted to be a part of a group, but because of some personality deficit, none of them was able to fit in. This was the crucial hallmark."

There are a few famous names in Puckett's list; others might ring a bell, but for some reason never captured the imagination of the Ameri-can media. Besides Eric Rudolph there were Paul Hill, Michael Griffin, Buford Furrow, Tim McVeigh, Terry Nichols. Puckett also included Ben Smith, the acolyte of Matt Hale who went on a shooting spree through Illinois in 1999, targeting Jews and people of color and killing two be-fore he committed suicide; John Salvi III, who in 1994 shot his way into a Boston abortion clinic and murdered two staff members—and killed himself in prison two years later; and Joseph Paul Franklin, a serial sniper who may have killed more than twenty people during the 1970s and 1980s. Among his surviving victims are Vernon Jordan, the lawyer and civil rights leader, and *Hustler* publisher Larry Flynt. "I was on a holy war against evil doers," Franklin told the *Indianapolis Star*. "Evildoers were interracial couples, blacks and Jews. I was the executioner, the judge and the jury." He is on death row in Missouri.

Like all profiles, the lone offender model is never a perfect fit. Several of these killers were married and had families; some had an accomplice or two, which set them apart. But what they had in common psychologically was more compelling. The similarities began in their childhoods.

"Almost all of them were quiet and withdrawn when they were kids. They were described as having few friends," said Puckett. The exceptions are McVeigh, who was gregarious as a very young child, and Paul Hill, who was, as Puckett describes him, "a very cheerful psychopath." But as he got older, McVeigh was more of a loner. And Paul Hill started spending more time in his attic, writing sermons and speeches and obsessing about abortion.

Except for Hill, who had an agreeable marriage, these subjects had unsatisfactory relationships with women. In the cases of Kaczynski and McVeigh, according to Puckett, there were apparently no sexual relationships with women at all. "Kaczynski wrote long passages about being a social cripple," she said. "He was desperate to find a woman to share his life with, he was anguished about it. Rudolph had physical relationships with some women. But that's primarily what they were. I remember one woman who said he was kind of hard to talk to. She dropped him because he was boring."

Puckett was interested in what she calls Rudolph's "encapsulated pathology," and the curious stability in his personality. "He's very resilient compared to some of these guys. Paul Hill was resilient in a kind of a weird, jolly psychopathic way. But Rudolph has a kind of impervious composure about himself that Kaczynski and McVeigh didn't have. His defenses are so strong." Puckett attributes Rudolph's self-possession to the approval he felt within his family, and his mother's unconditional support for him and his beliefs. "His family accepted him the way he was. I think that has a lot to do with his stability," said Puckett. "The interesting thing about it is that he didn't have close relationships with his family. He'd meet with them and be around them, but he wasn't really a part of them. He was self-isolated."

In the fall of 1998 Puckett accompanied the forensic psychiatrist

Park Dietz to North Carolina to help the task force anticipate Rudolph's possible moves. "It's impossible to predict human behavior, but you can make educated guesses about it," said Puckett. Along with where he was hiding, Turchie wanted to know whether Rudolph would continue his bombing campaign, and if so, where he was likely to strike.

"All we knew to say was that he'd successfully isolated himself, so he was unattached. He's careful. He's under pursuit so he'll probably lie low. He's probably going to monitor the pursuit, and he's probably going to stay in the woods. It was his comfort zone, and he knew that other people were not as comfortable there." Based on her knowledge of the Unabomber, Puckett also predicted that Rudolph would be preoccupied with keeping himself safe.

"Ted was like him. Rather fastidious, concerned about his health. McVeigh was the same way. Rudolph had a strain of that exaggerated self-protectiveness that helped him survive. Not many people would take a case of Emer'gen-C to the woods with them."

Care is another trademark of bombers, because careless bombers select themselves out of the species. "None of these guys was missing fingers," Puckett observed. "Bombers are so covert. They have some things in common with pyromaniacs who are so drawn to fire and destruction. Their exploits thrill them. But they would never get into close combat situations. McVeigh was famous for having blown the heads off Iraqi soldiers from a huge distance and a protected vantage point. And then blisters put him out of commission."

Puckett is referring to the turning point in Tim McVeigh's life, when he dropped out of the competition to qualify for the Special Forces because he was out of shape and his feet hurt. Eric Rudolph, who was only a year ahead of McVeigh in basic training, also wanted desperately to join the elite army unit but ended up bitterly disappointed. Paul Hill was thrown out of a fundamentalist sect because they thought he was too radical for them. Joseph Paul Franklin tried joining the American Nazi Party and the Ku Klux Klan but dropped out. Like Rudolph, he said the Klan was a joke. "Franklin felt they weren't walking the walk," said Puckett. "So he was the one who decided to go out on these sniping missions to start the race war."

Another common trait among the study group is their intelligence. Kaczynski is a genius. McVeigh's IQ was high. Rudolph is extremely bright and knowledgeable about what he thinks is important.

"In psychological terms, the more intelligent you are, the more likely it is that your 'locus of control' is internal rather than external," said Puckett. "That means that you look to your own ideas for authority for your actions rather than to the direction of others, like a government or a terrorist group. It's not just a matter of narcissism, it's a matter of intellect. You're able to look to yourself as an authority." This is an important trait when you can't fit into society. And you're smart enough to compensate for this by coming up with your own ideological agenda.

According to Puckett, each of these supposedly "lone" offenders wanted to affiliate with a known terrorist or extremist group—or a fictitious one "like this Army of God formulation that Eric Rudolph came up with. Even in somebody who's socially immune enough to exist five years in the woods, he found it necessary to represent himself as a member of a group." She explains it as a basic fact of human nature. "Except for the most schizoid personalities, humans are socialized in groups. They are engineered to be attached to other human beings. But the loner is excluded. And you can't really be excluded and be important. So you have to present yourself as a group." Ted Kaczynski pretended to be a member of "FC"—the Freedom Club. Tim McVeigh traveled the country looking for people to recruit to his cause before he blew up the federal building in Oklahoma City.

The lone offenders in Puckett's study are "totally unlike the stereotypical, Hannibal Lecter–type serial killer," a fictional concoction that doesn't exist in the real world. The killers she studied were not cool and unemotional; they were passionate in the extreme. "They all have tremendous amounts of feeling," she said. "But they have a failure of empathy, an inability to put themselves in other people's positions. This is a hallmark of psychopathy."

Puckett was fascinated by Rudolph's statement after his plea deal in which he described his decision not to kill the FBI agents he had been watching at the National Guard Armory. "He spared them because he identified with them," she said. "I honestly think it had to do with his wanting to belong to a special cadre of people. That was his image of himself. They were doing what he would have done if he were an elite FBI agent."

But while Rudolph could identify with them, he could never "affiliate" with them, or be one of them. "This is a key difference," said Puckett. "Everything happens in his head. Nothing really happens in real life. Lone offenders like Rudolph can idealize and identify until the cows come home. What they can't do is engage with real people. That's why their true affiliation is with ideas instead of with people. They trust ideas, they don't trust people."

In 1951, the philosopher Eric Hoffer wrote a classic book on the nature of mass movements and the people who are attracted to them, called *The True Believer*. Among many other wise observations, Hoffer wrote: "We cannot hate those we despise ... The undercurrent of admiration in hatred manifests itself in the inclination to imitate those we hate."

According to Kathleen Puckett, people like Eric Rudolph and Tim McVeigh make up the ranks of the true believers. They are the pure idealists of whatever cause they espouse. "They always wanted to be members of the group that held the ideology they found attractive," said Puckett. "But since they couldn't, and they still had to attach to something, they attached to the ideology in a very pure, passionate, clear, savage kind of sense." These men are so dangerous because they are willing to act on behalf of their beliefs "at a societal level"—on the biggest possible stage—which makes the magnitude of their crimes so extreme. "Their violence is not retaliatory," said Puckett. "The lone offender says 'I am doing this for a higher purpose.'"

If this is true, then perhaps men like Eric Rudolph are simply writing roles for themselves to fill up the blank and meaningless lives they lead. Perhaps they tell themselves stories in order to survive. The love of the unborn is a story Rudolph tells himself so that he doesn't have to confront his own anger and hatred. His desperate war to prevent the decline of "Western Civilization" may just be a strategy for keeping himself from flying apart.

*   *   *

July 18, 2005, was Emily Lyons's forty-ninth birthday. It was also the day when Eric Rudolph was to be sentenced for the Birmingham bombing. When Judge Smith found out about the coincidence he offered to change the date of the hearing. But Lyons later wrote that her life was so tangled with Rudolph's that it didn't matter. From now on each birthday would mark another year Rudolph had spent in prison, and another one that he had tried but failed to take away from her.

Again it was standing room only in the eighth-floor courtroom. And again, Eric Rudolph was wearing his red jail uniform. The chains around his ankles jingled as he took a seat at the defense table next to Judy Clarke and his defense team. An enormous framed photograph of Officer Robert Sanderson had been placed by the witness stand in front of them.

First Judge Smith handled some judicial housekeeping. Rudolph's crimes had maxed out the federal guideline system, where each offense accrues a number of points. He received forty-three points, the highest offense level. He was given two consecutive life sentences with no possibility of parole, and he was expected to pay over a million dollars in restitution. He also owed $200 for court fees, now. It would be taken out of the $1,600 seized from his trailer. He had no other assets.

Mike Whisonant recounted Rudolph's crimes in an eloquent summary of the closing arguments he never got to use. Then it was time for the victims to speak.

Because it was hard for her to stand for long periods, Emily Lyons sat at the prosecution table with her chair turned toward Rudolph. Years of surgery and careful makeup had hidden most of the scars on her face, but she still had difficulty reading with her remaining eye. The pages of text stacked on the table were printed in twenty-point type. Rudolph watched Lyons intently as she began to recount the events surrounding the bombing of the New Woman All Women clinic. She described his trip to Wal-Mart on Christmas Eve, 1997, where he purchased some bomb components.

"Eric's life is full of blunders and failures," she said. "Not only did he provide proof of his guilt with the sales receipt, he wrote the word 'bomb' in the margin of his Bible and left EGDN residue throughout his trailer. Thank you, Eric, for leaving such wonderful evidence behind for us."

Lyons looked over at him as she said this. He smiled and mouthed, "You're welcome."

She went on with a speech that was both sarcastic and defiant. She again thanked Rudolph for making her a stronger person. "I found a voice inside me I did not know existed, and you are the one who brought it out. My legs were shattered, but I was able to walk in a march on Washington, D.C., for freedom of choice. A hole the size of a fist was torn in my abdomen and large sections of my intestines were removed, but I have more guts in my broken little finger than you have in your entire body. The joint in my middle finger had to be fused—an injury I have longed to show you."

And then she did. The crowd chuckled but Rudolph was impassive. When her speech was finished, she winked at him dramatically as she stood up and walked to her seat.

Felecia Sanderson was dressed in a black cotton pantsuit as she stood at the podium facing the judge. She did not look at Rudolph and said that she did not care to address him: "I have nothing to say to that piece of garbage that murdered my husband." Her remarks were for the court. She talked about her husband and her family and what they'd all lost. "Eric Rudolph is responsible for all the tears my boys have shed, and I despise him for it," she said. Even though she'd never demanded the death penalty for Rudolph, she said, "I've got no forgiveness for him."

When she was finished she walked out of the courtroom. She had no interest in hearing what Eric Rudolph was about to say.

He, too, stood at the podium with his back to the gallery. Rudolph's time in jail seemed to have diminished him. He looked shorter, thinner, and paler than before; his shoulders were hunched, his head slightly bowed. But anyone expecting an act of contrition from Rudolph was mistaken. When he opened his mouth the sound that came out was deep and sonorous and angry. "I'm here today to be sentenced for my actions on January 29, 1998," he said. "On that date I detonated a bomb at an abortion mill here in Birmingham, killing the abortion mill's security guard and injuring one of the abortion mill's employees. I had nothing personal against either of these individuals, Sanderson and Lyons. I did not target them for who they were but for what they did …" Rudolph's voice grew louder as he continued. He turned his allocution into a history lesson about the dashed promise of America in the wake of *Roe v. Wade*, and he used it as a sermon to denounce abortion as a symptom of moral and cultural decay of his beloved Western civilization. "Thousands of years of moral progress were sacrificed upon the altar of selfishness and materialism!... Every variety of filth is tolerated and aggressively pushed with the complete support of the state—abortion, homosexuality, pornography—but this country does not tolerate the values of life, family, and human dignity!" He went on for thirteen minutes, thrusting and jabbing his hands in the air like a jackleg preacher at a tent revival. "God is not fooled, posterity will certainly judge differently," he concluded. "Even if it should take ten years, fifty years, or five hundred years before this black night of barbarism is swept into the dustbin of history, I will be vindicated, my actions in Birmingham that overcast day in January of 1998 will be vindicated! And as I go to a prison cell for a lifetime, I know that 'I have fought a good fight, I have finished my course. I have kept the faith.'"

Everyone sat in stunned silence. The prisoner was led out of the courtroom. I stared at the empty space where Eric Rudolph had just been and tried to imagine the somber but rational man who wrote me letters, or the funny, thoughtful person his lawyers had come to love, or the wayward son his mother had forgiven, but all I could see was a self-righteous bastard in sunglasses and a cheap wig, his blue eyes darkening as he clutched his remote control and flipped the switch.

I remembered what Jerry Crisp, the detective in Murphy, said when he finally met the other Eric Rudolph.

"So you're the guy they were looking for."

Centennial Olympic Park looked different nine years after the blast. On a hot weekday morning, the park was sparsely occupied by a handful of tourists, some local office workers on coffee break, a few parents with strollers. It was hard to find the spot where the bomb exploded, and I had to ask a bicycle cop for directions. The site is now sheltered behind an assertive landscaping scheme of connecting water gardens, beds of holly and verbena, and arrangements of tall shrubs and trees that create quiet little cul-de-sacs where the homeless can rest unobserved. The fan-shaped sculpture that absorbed much of the blast is a constant curiosity. When I found it several couples were using it as a backdrop for snapshots, standing in the same spot that Alice Hawthorne posed for her daughter moments before she was killed. The sculpture, which a plaque says was inspired by ancient Hellenic art, is seventeen feet tall and twenty-four feet wide and embedded with three larger-than-life runners, representing phases of the Olympic movement. The first is a naked, bearded male who runs barefoot. The middle figure is a Victorian gentleman, and the frontrunner is a ponytailed woman who signifies the 1996 Atlanta Olympics.

The sculpture of the woman seems to have absorbed most of the shrapnel from the bomb. The surface of the bronze figure is pocked with nicks and divots; just below her knee there is the perfect inch-long impression of a nail, rubbed black by fingers touching it like a talisman. Another nail nicked her lower thigh, and appears to have exposed a patch of raw metal that weeps brown rust, like a trickle of blood. None of it has been retouched; it stands as a monument to the night when, according to a quote from the *Atlanta Journal-Constitution*, "In the spur of a heartbeat, the crowd's joy turned to horror ..." This is inscribed in the margins of a stone "Quilt of Remembrance" that is part of a tasteful monument to the victims of the bombing. There is a small memorial to Alice Hawthorne near the blast site, but it, too, is difficult to find.

Eric Rudolph's final public appearance took place in an overly air-conditioned courtroom in the huge federal building on the edge of downtown Atlanta, less than a mile from Centennial Park. This sentencing hearing would take much longer than the one last month in Birmingham, because there were so many more victims of the five bombs that went off around this city in 1996 and 1997. Richard Jewell, who had attended the April plea hearing, did not show up at this one, although many would argue that he, too, was a victim of the Centennial Olympic Park bombing.

Security was tighter than ever in the federal courtroom. Only a few weeks earlier in the nearby county courthouse, a crazed prisoner had grabbed a deputy's gun and killed several people, including the judge.

While waiting for this hearing to begin, two huge U.S. marshals—one black, one white—stood behind Rudolph and hovered over him, ready to jump if he decided to cause any trouble. He did not, of course. They sat down after the judge entered the room.

The morning was devoted to a litany of wrenching stories from the disparate group of victims who chose to attend the hearing. It was shocking to be reminded how much agonizing and permanent damage can be caused by a powerful explosion. Mary Agnes Lee, forty-six, a Centennial Park groundskeeper working on her college degree, suffered brain damage from the concussion and now can barely function. She told Rudolph that she hated him for what he did to her. Ron Smith, forty-five, was a spectator whose sciatic nerve was severed by shrapnel and who lost a finger in the blast. Even worse, he said, was his lost sense of security. Now he never felt safe. Rudolph paid reverent attention to the testimony of those injured from the Centennial Park blast. But he turned away and looked bored when victims from the Otherside Lounge and the Sandy Springs building described their experiences.

Rudolph's Atlanta allocution was a shortened version of the written statement he'd issued in April. Unlike his Birmingham sermon, he delivered this testimony in a subdued, almost regretful manner. And unlike Birmingham, where he emphatically did not apologize, he acknowledged the pain of his victims at Centennial Park—he did not mention the other targets—and ended his final public statement with these words: "The responsibility for what took place that night in the park belongs to me and me alone. Despite my belief in the justice of my cause, despite the mishandling of the 911 call, the choice to use that particular tactic was mine, and I accept full responsibility for the consequences. I fully realize that all of this may be no consolation to the victims who suffered as a result of my actions, but I would do anything to take back that night."

The centerpiece of this hearing had been a short video presentation about the life of Alice Hawthorne, whose husband, John, also addressed the court. Like Felecia Sanderson, he had no forgiveness in him for Eric Rudolph, and he vowed never to speak his name again after this day. But when Fallon Stubbs took the podium, an amazing thing happened. She looked directly at Eric Rudolph and said, "My message is not of hate; my message is of forgiveness and acceptance." Rudolph returned her gaze, head to the side, listening like a deer waiting for the shot that never came. Instead she continued with a calm that can only be described as grace.

"Not for you, but for me, I forgive you," she said. "I look at you. I love you. And if I cry it's not for me. It's not for my mother. It's not for my father. It's for you."

EPILOGUE: BOMBER'S ROW

Highway 50 runs straight as a pool cue from Pueblo, Colorado, through twenty-three miles of greasewood flats before offering an exit to the scruffy town of Florence. Like Flint, Michigan, or Bethlehem, Pennsylvania, or Orlando, Florida, Florence is a company town. The single industry here is prisoners, and the company is the U.S. Bureau of Prisons. It's a growth industry. Twenty years ago the people of surrounding Fremont County ponied up the money to buy 600 acres in the foothills of the Wet Mountains and then offered them to the U.S. government. The plan was to entice the BOP to build a prison complex that would provide more jobs and revenue to the faltering oil town. Today Florence is a virtual theme park of penal experiences, ranging from a minimum security camp for insider traders and small-time meth cookers to the place the Bureau of Prisons has billed as the most secure prison in America: the Administrative Maximum U.S. Penitentiary, or ADX for short. It has other nicknames: "ADMAX," "Supermax," and the colorful "Alcatraz of the Rockies." The two-story, delta-shaped facility houses about 400 of America's most violent and high-risk inmates, including drug lords, gang leaders, hit men, snipers, white supremacists, and Islamist terrorists, including Richard Reid, the al-Qaeda–connected "shoe bomber"; Ramzi Yousef, mastermind of the first World Trade Center bombing; and most recently, the crazed September 11 wannabe terrorist, Zacharias Moussaoui. In fact, there are so many bombers at ADX that one wing of the highest security "control unit" is known as

Bomber's Row. Since late August 2005, it has also been home to Eric Robert Rudolph.

The administrators of ADX do not like media attention. They would, in fact, seem to prefer that their facility remain all but invisible to the public. My requests to visit Eric Rudolph in prison were flatly denied on the grounds that my presence might "disrupt the good order and security of this institution." A tour of the facility, an interview with the warden, and even a face-to-face briefing with the public information officer were denied for the same reasons. I was politely referred to the Bureau of Prisons website for any information I might need. The ADX Florence page contains visitor regulations and photos of some buildings, but omits directions to the facility.

Rudolph continued to write to me from ADX, and he received most of my letters. But for a long time his replies were repeatedly returned to him for objectionable content of some sort or another. After a few months he was finally able to send me a package with some answers to my latest questions. (When our town postmaster noticed the name and the return address, he gave me a strange look and handed me the envelope with the tips of his fingers.) The prison censors seemed far more relaxed about Rudolph's correspondence with his mother, Pat. When I visited her in Florida she shared some of his letters with me. Like Rudolph's other writings, his prison letters are minutely observed and vividly written. Together they offer a unique window into his life among the damned.

Rudolph describes his "new home" as an eight-by-twelve-foot box with two doors. "One enters the cell through the first, which is a solid steel door that has a slit window and locking mail slot. Controlled from a central 'bubble' (control center). The door slides side to side, Star-Trek style, closing with a loud clank. Once through there is a small vestibule (3′ by 6′) and another barrier, this one is a traditional set of bars with another sliding door and open mail slot. The floor of the cell is a baby blue, the walls off-white, and the steel trim and bars a baby shit green." He describes the furnishings as "city park-esque—all of it is reinforced concrete." There is a small table attached to the wall, and a concrete stool "that looks like a five gallon bucket turned topside down." His bed runs almost the length of one wall, and under it is a built-in storage space for clothing and books. In one corner there is a stainless steel shower and in the other is a combination toilet and sink. The inmates are fed three times as day through the door slot. They eat alone. Rudolph reports that the food is much better than the cafeteria-style fare at the Jefferson County Jail, "and probably is the most amenable aspect about our conditions."

The cells are bathed day and night with artificial light. There is a four-inch by four-foot window over Rudolph's bed that looks out on the prison yard. "Through the slit window one can see the sky, but other than this and the few small birds that roost on the prison roof, there are no signs of the natural world," he writes. "It is a very Spartan, monk-like existence."

To keep his mind occupied, there are two libraries from which he can borrow books. Some of his pen pals, particularly women, send him other reading materials. There is a small black-and-white TV—encased in Plexiglas to prevent tampering—on a concrete shelf above the desk. Recently published reports about the prison describe the programming as limited to educational and religious shows, local news, and courses on topics such as anger management.

Rudolph is housed in a section of the prison called "the tube." There are eight cells in his "range," and another eight on the level above him. The inmates here spend at least twenty-three hours a day in their cells. "It is where they house the political offenders, what they call 'terrorists,'" Rudolph writes. For security reasons, he is not allowed to name his fellow prisoners, but he says there is one American at the end of the range; the rest are Muslims from places like Egypt, Sudan, and Palestine.

Many of the victims who testified at Rudolph's sentencing hearings voiced their expectation that he would be "buried" in prison, locked in a soundproof room until he dies, with no sight of the sun and no human interaction. In reality, while the amount of sunlight is highly limited, the opportunities for communication abound. As the psychologist Kathy Puckett has observed, humans are social creatures, and they will overcome great obstacles to somehow connect with one another. This is true even in a cell block populated by socially inept bombers with language barriers and cultural barriers, who are kept apart by tons of steel and glass.

And so Eric Rudolph's "monk-like" existence is actually very noisy. There is the constant "can-opener-like sound of the doors opening and closing," the echoing of steel hitting concrete in the vast prison corridors. And then there is the shouting. Even if the cells are meant to be sound-proof, they are no match for a good pair of lungs yelling in Arabic. The Muslim prisoners shout to one another constantly. Rudolph is getting them to teach him Arabic so that he can understand them. He picks it up one phrase at a time. He tells his mother that *"Kyfa ta Kool,"* which he spells out phonetically, means "How do you say …?"

Rudolph seems fascinated by his neighbors, like an anthropologist dropped into an exotic village. "It is Ramadan now and the Muslims are fasting," he writes in one letter from the fall of 2005. "The call to prayer echoes through the halls five times a day giving this place a decidedly otherworldly feel."

To try to keep the prisoners from going completely insane, the guards offer interactive games of bingo, crossword puzzles, and trivia competi-tions. "The Muslims are obsessed with the games…. they chatter end-lessly about the possible answers," Rudolph writes. The winners, he says, are rewarded with a candy bar or a picture of themselves.

Being a Westerner puts Rudolph at a distinct advantage when playing trivia games, and the Middle Easterners have come to depend on him to help them with the answers. "Moments after they post the questions on Monday morning the yelling begins. 'Areek, what the answers? Who is president in the War of 1812?'" After winning a couple of Jeopardy games for them, Rudolph has become very popular with the Muslims. But he says they get upset with him when he doesn't match their enthu-siasm for games. He only gets involved, he tells his mother, for the sake of their mental health, and to maintain his rapport with them.

The inmates are allowed out of their cells four or five days a week for one hour of "rec." Most days the prisoners in his range stay indoors and take their exercise in one of two fifteen-foot by twenty-five-foot rooms across the hall from the row of cells. People in the rec rooms can watch one another through a double-paned, barred window in the wall that divides them. "There is no view of an outside world," he writes. "The ceiling is high, shooting up past the second floor of cells," but the window at the top of the room only lets in a diffused light. In one of the rooms there is an exercise machine that "looks like a guillotine minus the blade and bench." And that is it.

Rudolph complains that his group rarely gets to exercise in the open prison yard, and when they do, it is a major production.

"Whenever we leave the cells we are taken out one at a time," he writes. "First the outer door is opened, two guards enter the vestibule, I strip, place my clothes on the bars and do the little strip search dance—lift arms, open mouth, run fingers through hair, and finally turn and bend for the hemorrhoid exam. After they search the clothes, I dress, place my hands behind my back and thrust them thumbs up through the mail slot where they are cuffed. With a sharp command from the guard the door slides open and one guard grabs hold of the chain on the cuffs pulling me out of the cell and then leads me like a dog while the other paces behind with a steel tipped club in hand." The guards repeat the procedure with each prisoner in turn until the entire range is empty and the prisoners are ready to be brought to the yard.

Rudolph describes the yard as "a large concrete enclosure that looks like a giant kidney-shaped pool with 25-foot walls." Often they are taken out just at dawn. It is their only chance to breathe some fresh air, and if they look straight up they can see a patch of the blue Colorado sky through the chain mesh that encloses the top of the yard. Inside the enclosure, Rudolph writes, there are about fifteen chain-link cages, which he compares to dog kennels. The prisoners are placed in the cages, one per cage, and their cuffs are removed through the door slot. "The yard is quickly filled up," he writes, "the awkward greetings made and the exercise begins—the exercise of voices. It is awkward adjusting my voice from the necessary yell of the cell block to the face-to-face conversation in the yard. Unlike me the Muslims don't adjust the volume of the voice and the yard reverberates with very loud Arabic yelling. 'Hiawa, Haiwa,' they yell back and forth." (*Aiwa* means "yes" in Arabic.)

Rudolph describes how the Muslim inmates pair up in their separate cages and then "walk the length of the cage in unison, back and forth, yelling as they go. If you've ever seen big cats at a zoo, this is what they do as well. They pace back and forth for hours, rhythmically, like a pendulum. Across the yard, this is what one sees: seven pairs of inmates pacing together, all the while yelling in Arabic."

Once in a while, Rudolph writes, the guards mix his range with others and he gets to observe the "common criminals" at ADX. "Some of the cons are tattooed head to foot; others attempt to wear their prison-issued clothes in a distinctive gangland fashion. One even has a large tattoo on his cleanly-shaven head. While the Arabs yell at each other, the common criminals strut around posing their toughness. When the hour is up, the slow process of moving us back to the cells begins in reverse. And there we sit in our darkened cells for the rest of the week, staring out at the empty sun-drenched yard."

Rudolph has spent enough time with his neighbors to form an impression of their psychological makeup. He wants to understand them better, and he seems to have sympathy for the ones who are depressed, the ones who sit in their cells and wail. "Some days the Arabs are a pain in the ass, other days they're friendly," he writes. "They're an extremely fatalistic people. This time must be very rough on them for they have very little interest in anything other than the Middle East, President Bush and Islam.… But at least they have each other and rattle on endlessly in Arabic. Whereas besides the other American at the other end of the range, I'm by myself here. And this guy has not emerged from his cell since I've been here."

The American at the end of the range is Theodore Kaczynski.

ACKNOWLEDGMENTS

One cold December day in 1990, David Hirshey, who was then deputy editor of *Esquire* magazine, called me up to tell me he had found the perfect story for me: Byron de la Beckwith, the deranged Klansman who had gone unpunished for twenty-seven years after shooting the civil rights leader Medgar Evers, had just been rearrested for the old murder. Hirshey's hunch led to an article in *Esquire* called "The Haunting of the New South," and, in 1995, my first book, *Ghosts of Mississippi*. In 2003 the phone rang again. Hirshey was now an editor at HarperCollins and this time he had the perfect *book* for me: Eric Robert Rudolph, the accused Olympic Park Bomber, had just been captured after five years on the run in the mountains of North Carolina. I was slightly skeptical of the prospect of another book about a fanatical right-wing killer, but how could I refuse? As it turned out, the story of Eric Rudolph's life and crimes was far more complex and rich than I could have expected, and Hirshey was, again, right on the mark. For this, and for nearly thirty years of support and friendship: my deepest thanks.

Thanks, too, to Kris Dahl, my agent and friend, who was there at the beginning and saddled up for the long ride. Also Jud Laghi and Montana Wojczuk from ICM.

I also want to thank Nick Trautwein for his skills as an editor and for his wide-open heart; Jonathan Burnham, Clare McMahon, Tom Ward, and the team at HarperCollins also have my gratitude.

For their extraordinary help with this project, special thanks to Jim Cavanaugh, Will Chambers, Lloyd Erwin, Richard Jaffe, Paul Kish, Joe Kennedy, Carl Lietz, Larry Long, Joe McLean, Tom Mohnal, Tom Neer, Kathleen Puckett, Danny Sindall, Patricia Rudolph, Terry Turchie, and Mike Whisonant. Thanks also to Glenn Anderson, John Behnke, Angela Bell, Don Bell, Dallas Blanchard, Bill Bowen, David Brose, Michael Burt, Dave Campbell, Minzor Chadwick, Cedric Cole, Kenny Cope, Paul Costa, Jerry Crisp, Patrick Crosby, Pat Curry, Diane Derzis, Jim Eckel, Stephen Emmett, Woody Enderson, Bill Fleming, Gus Gary, Jack Glaser, John Glenn, James Bo Gritz, Ken Gross, David Hale, Bill Harris, Alan Hawkins, Lee Howard, Bill Hughes, C.J. Hyman, "Irish," Doug Jones, Larry Kasperek, Jack Killorin, David Lackey, Todd Letcher, Emily and Jeff Lyons, Richard Marianos, Alice Martin, Sean Matthews, Charlie and Janet McCowan, Don McLamrock, Scott Morro, Joel Moss, David Nahmias, Tracey North, Jeff Postell, Mark Potok, Krista Rear, Jay Reeves, Jerome Rogoff, Joe Ronsisvalle, Joel Rudolph, Jim Russell, Steve Siegel, Dorothy Smith, Mark Thigpen, Jack Thompson, Ron Tunkel, Harrietta Turner, Chuck Watson, Jake Watson, and Tony Woody.

I would also like to acknowledge Eric Rudolph for answering my questions and allowing me to speak to his attorneys in order to present all sides of this complex story.

Thanks to Ned Mudd and Joyce Hudson, compadres and tour guides in Birmingham, and to Bob Lawrence and Paul Mahon in Washington. In North Carolina, special thanks to Aurelia Stone, Doyle Smith, Karen Michaels, and Robin Barton.

To my friends and family, who keep me sane and put up with the long stretches of absence: Josephine Vollers; Judy and Mert Martin; Jim, Cynthia, Donovan, and Cassandra Kohler; Jessie Kohler; Glenn and Liz Fay; my brothers Joseph Vollers and Chuck Vollers, and their families; and my father, Joseph E. Vollers, who didn't get to see these last two books but is my continuing source of pride and inspiration.

To my friends and colleagues who make Livingston, Montana, one of the best places to live and work as a writer: Charlotte Freeman,

Margot Kidder, Jim Liska and Geri Lester, Scott and Jennifer McMillion, Tim and Linnea Cahill, and so many others.

Most of all to Bill Campbell, my husband, partner, and best friend.

In Memory of:
Hunter S. Thompson, 1937–2005
Patrick McGuinn, 1965–2003
Jeff Pollard, 1954–2005

A NOTE ON SOURCES

My goal was to tell the story of Eric Robert Rudolph from as many points of view as possible. To this end, I asked for and was granted cooperation from an extraordinary variety of sources, including Rudolph himself. I was able to conduct written interviews with him in the Jefferson County Jail and, later, in federal prison. I spoke to acquaintances and family members, including his mother, Patricia, and his brother, Joel. Rudolph released members of his defense team from the restraints of attorney-client privilege so that they could discuss details of his case with me, as well as their impressions of him. At the same time, I interviewed the U.S. attorneys in Birmingham and Atlanta about their roles in the investigation and prosecution. I also interviewed both retired and active agents and supervisors from both the FBI and ATF—many of whom were speaking to a reporter for the first time—about their search for Eric Rudolph and the evidence they gathered to convict him. I also had access to hundreds of pages of transcripts from two lengthy evidentiary hearings, as well as more than four hundred unsealed motions filed in the U.S. District Court in the Northern District of Alabama. I was also shown certain source material from the investigation and crime scenes. Any conversations recounted within this book either come from these investigative resources or from interviews with the actual participants who re-created them for me.

As I have said, this book is an extended act of journalism, and I have chosen to forego the extensive use of source notes. Instead, the source of information within each chapter is generally self-evident or culled from multiple, redundant sources. Wherever unique, previously published material was used, I have cited it below:

Chapter 2: Information about the Walter Leroy Moody investigation can be found in *Blind Vengeance: The Roy Moody Mail Bomb Murders* by Ray Jenkins (University of Georgia Press, 1997). For Louis Freeh's role in these and other cases I also consulted *My FBI: Bringing Down the Mafia, Investigating Bill Clinton, and Fighting the War on Terror*, by Louis J. Freeh with Howard Means (St. Martin's Press, 2005). This book also contained details of the Richard Jewell episode. More information about the improper handling of the Jewell investigation can be found in a report issued by the Justice Department's Office of Professional Responsibility in December 1996, and in testimony before Congress by Freeh and FBI Special Agent in Charge Woody Johnson. Another excellent source is "American Nightmare—The Ballad of Richard Jewell" by Marie Brenner (*Vanity Fair*, February 1997).

Chapter 4: I re-created the bombing scene and aftermath through interviews with witnesses, as well as viewing transcripts of the 911 tape along with statements Jermaine Hughes and Jeff Tickal made to FBI and police investigators. I relied on Chief Sorrell's memory of his conversation with Janet Reno, as phone logs from the Clinton administration have not yet been made public. The interview with Susan Roper appeared in the *Birmingham News* on February 15, 1998.

Chapter 6: Quotes from pro-choice and anti-abortion activists and members of the City Council were reported in the *Birmingham News* on January 30, 1998, and February 2, 1998. The tape of Dan Rudolph amputating his hand has never been made public; several federal agents who have seen the video described it for me.

Chapter 7: The narrative of Rudolph's friends and family in this chapter comes from reports by federal agents who interviewed them, and mainly reflects the government's point of view. Additional information about Tom Branham came from my written interviews with Eric Rudolph, and from Pat and Joel Rudolph. I interviewed several of Nord Davis's friends and followers, who gave me copies of his pamphlets. Information on William Dudley Pelley and the Protocols of the Elders of Zion can be found in James Ridgeway's seminal work on right-wing racism and violence titled *Blood in the Face* (Thunder's Mouth Press, 1990). Mark Barrett of the *Asheville Citizen-Times* wrote the exposé of right-wing fanatics in western North Carolina (April 18, 1996), which Nord Davis denounced. *Intelligence Report*, a publication of the Southern Poverty Law Center, ran an article about western North Carolina ("Hills of Rebellion", issue 95, Summer 1999), about Davis's group and other radicals. The article presumes that Eric Rudolph was a Davis follower, although federal investigators could never establish that link and Rudolph has denied it. There are various corroborating sources about Dan Gayman's group in Missouri. My information comes from discussion with Pat Rudolph and FBI agent James Cross, as well as several articles in the *Intelligence Report*, including a long and detailed interview with Deborah (Givens) Rudolph (Issue 104, winter 2001) and Gayman's son Tim and daughter-in-law Sarah (Issue 102, summer 2001). Roy Decker, one of Rudolph's army buddies, allowed the FBI to process his letters from Rudolph for fingerprints. Federal prosecutors expected to use them, along with Decker's testimony, at Rudolph's trial. He also shared some of them with the *Newark Star-Ledger*.

Chapter 8: Popular books by former FBI profilers abound, but the seminal work on serial killers and the history of the Behavioral Science Unit is *Sexual Homicide: Patterns and Motives*, by Robert K. Ressler, Ann W. Burgess, and John E. Douglas (The Free Press, 1992).

Chapter 9: There are many versions of the story of Tsali, who refused to join the Trail of Tears. This one relies on an article by Duane King and E. Raymond Evans in the *Journal of Cherokee Studies* (volume IV, number 4, Fall 1999). Other information about the history of the Eastern Band of the Cherokee can be found at www.cherokee-nc.com. The story of Goldman Bryson and other renegades can be found in *Bushwhackers!: The Civil War in the North Carolina Mountains*, by William R. Trotter (John F. Blair Publisher, 1988).

Chapter 11: Some information about the Claude Dallas case came from an excellent package of articles in the *Idaho Statesman* on February 5, 2005. I also referred to the book *Outlaw: The True Story of Claude Dallas*, by Jeff Long (William Morrow, 1985). A great deal has been written about Bo Gritz and Randy Weaver, including *Gathering Storm: America's Militia Threat*, by Morris Dees with James Corcoran (HarperCollins, 1996). I interviewed James Bo Gritz about his role in the Rudolph search; he has also written about it in his self-published book *My Brother's Keeper* (Lazarus Publishing Company, 2002).

Chapters 13 and 14: This account of Rudolph's life on the run and his capture is based on letters he wrote to me and to his mother, excerpts of writings he sent to me through his lawyer, which were also posted on the Web, and reprinted here, and statements he made to his jailers and attorneys. The brief conversation between Pat Rudolph and Charles Stone can be found in *Hunting Eric Rudolph: An Insider's Account of the Five-Year Search for the Olympic Bomber*, by Henry Schuster with Charles Stone (Berkley Publishing Group, 2005). The reactions of John Hawthorne and Fallon Stubbs were recorded in the *Birmingham News* and other papers.

Chapter 17: The Court TV documentary was part of the *Mugshots* series, titled *Eric Rudolph: "Man Most Wanted*,*"* produced by John Parsons, 2000.

Chapter 19: Emily and Jeff Lyons expressed their views about the plea bargain and other issues in the case in their self-published book, *Life's Been a Blast* (I Em Press, 2005).

Chapter 20: I got the content of the missing 911 call from FBI case agent James Cross. I have seen longer versions in other printed sources.

Chapter 22: The quote from Dallas Blanchard, who was very generous with his time in helping me with this project, comes from his book, *The Anti-Abortion Movement and the Rise of the Religious Right: From Polite to Fiery Protest* (Diane Publishing Company, 1994).

Epilogue: The description of the ADX prison in Florence, Colorado, comes from various published sources, including the Bureau of Prisons website and Don Plummer's article in the *Atlanta Journal-Constitution*, April 13, 2005. Patricia Rudolph shared Eric Rudolph's letters from prison with me.

INDEX